Handbook
of Solution-Focused
Brief Therapy
Clinical Applications

The HAWORTH Handbook Series in Psychotherapy
Yvonne M. Dolan
Editor

Handbook of Remotivation Therapy edited by Michael L. Stotts and Jean
A Dyer

*Handbook of Anger Management: Individual, Couple, Family, and Group
Approaches* by Ronald T. Potter-Efron

Handbook of Solution-Focused Brief Therapy: Clinical Applications
edited by Thorana S. Nelson and Frank N. Thomas

Handbook
of Solution-Focused
Brief Therapy
Clinical Applications

Thorana S. Nelson
Frank N. Thomas
Editors

The Haworth Press
New York

For more information on this book or to order, visit
http://www.haworthpress.com/store/product.asp?sku=5135

or call 1-800-HAWORTH (800-429-6784) in the United States and Canada
or (607) 722-5857 outside the United States and Canada
or contact orders@HaworthPress.com

PUBLISHER'S NOTE

The development, preparation, and publication of this work has been undertaken with great care. However, the Publisher, employees, editors, and agents of The Haworth Press are not responsible for any errors contained herein or for consequences that may ensue from use of materials or information contained in this work. The Haworth Press is committed to the dissemination of ideas and information according to the highest standards of intellectual freedom and the free exchange of ideas. Statements made and opinions expressed in this publication do not necessarily reflect the views of the Publisher, Directors, management, or staff of The Haworth Press, Inc., or an endorsement by them.

Identities and circumstances of individuals discussed in this book have been changed to protect confidentiality.

Cover design by Kerry E. Mack.

Library of Congress Cataloging-in-Publication Data

Handbook of solution-focused brief therapy : clinical applications / Thorana S. Nelson, Frank N. Thomas, editors.
    p. ; cm.
Includes bibliographical references.
ISBN: 978-0-7890-2394-0 (hard : alk. paper)
ISBN: 978-0-7890-2395-7 (soft : alk. paper)
    1. Solution-focused brief therapy—Handbooks, manuals, etc. I. Nelson, Thorana Strever. II. Thomas, Frank N.
    [DNLM: 1. Psychotherapy, Brief—methods. 2. Counseling—methods. 3. Problem Solving. WM 420.5.P5 H2363 2007]
RC489.S65.H362 2007
616.89'14—dc22

                2007000474

To Steve de Shazer and Insoo Kim Berg, cofounders of the Solution-Focused Brief Therapy approach. You gave us new sight—thanks for the vision. We dedicate this work to you.

CONTENTS

ABOUT THE EDITORS

Thorana S. Nelson, PhD, is a professor of family therapy in the department of Family, Consumer, and Human Development at Utah State University in Logan, Utah. She co-edited (with Terry Trepper) *101 Interventions in Family Therapy* and *101 More Interventions in Family Therapy*, which have been translated into Chinese, edited (with Frank Thomas) *Tales from Family Therapy*, and edited *Education and Training in Solution-Focused Brief Therapy*, all published by The Haworth Press. With Joel Simon, she has written *Solution-Focused Brief Therapy for Long-term Users of the Mental Health System*, published by The Haworth Press. She has written numerous articles and book chapters on a variety of topics related to family therapy and family therapy training. She is series editor for two Haworth Press book series: *101 Interventions in Psychotherapy* and *Interventions in Psychotherapy: Step-by-Step*. In addition to her graduate teaching, she teaches AAMFT-approved Foundations of Supervision courses and consults and trains on Solution-Focused Brief Therapy. She has a small private practice and consulting business in Logan, UT. She and her husband, Vic, live in northern Utah with their two cats. She can be reached at thorana.nelson@usu.edu.

Frank N. Thomas, PhD, LMFT, is an associate professor in the Counseling Program, School of Education, Texas Christian University in Fort Worth and has practiced therapy for over 30 years. Frank has co-authored and co-edited over 60 articles or book chapters and two books: *Competency-Based Counseling* (with Jack Cockburn, Fortress, 1998) and *Tales from Family Therapy* (with Thorana Nelson, Haworth, 1998). His current writing is focused on well-being, best practices in therapy, and working with children and their families. He is the inaugural humor editor for *The Journal of Systemic Therapies* and the current English editor of *RATKES: The Journal of the Finnish Association for the Advancement of Solution and*

Handbook of Solution-Focused Brief Therapy: Clinical Applications
© 2007 by The Haworth Press, Inc. All rights reserved.
doi:10.1300/5135_a

Resource Oriented Therapy and Methods. In addition, he has taught graduate students in psychotherapy since 1989 and has presented over 150 workshops in ten countries. Frank is best known for his humorous systemic approaches to clinical work, training, and relationships and lives in the Fort Worth/Dallas area with his wife, Lori, where they both enjoy birding and photography. Feel free to contact Frank at f.thomas@tcu.edu.

CONTRIBUTORS

Duane R. Bidwell, PhD, is an assistant professor of Pastoral Theology, Care, and Counseling, and the director of Presbyterian Formation at Phillips Theological Seminary in Tulsa, Oklahoma. In addition, he is the former director of the Pastoral Care and Training Center at Brite Divinity School, Texas Christian University. He is the author of *Short-Term Spiritual Guidance* (Fortress Press, 2004), and is a pastoral theologian, certified pastoral counselor, and licensed spiritual director. He can be reached at duane .bidwell@ptstulsa.edu. His Web site is www.spondizo.net.

Brian Cade is in private practice in Sydney, Australia. A founding member of The Family Institute, Cardiff, Wales, he is registered as a family therapist with the United Kingdom Council for Psychotherapy. For over 35 years, Brian has offered a wide range of conference papers, workshops, and courses in brief family and solution-focused therapy, and in 1989, he gave a plenary address to the First World Family Therapy Congress in Eire. Primary author of *A Brief Guide to Brief Therapy* (with Bill O'Hanlon, Norton, 1993) Brian has published over 80 articles and chapters as well as numerous cartoons. He can be reached at bcade@netspace.net.au.

Yvonne Dolan is president of the Solution-Focused Brief Therapy Association. She conducts training seminars internationally and has authored and co-authored several books on Solution-Focused Brief Therapy, including *More than Miracles: The State of the Art of Solution-Focused Brief Therapy* (The Haworth Press, 2007) with the late Steve de Shazer, the late Insoo Kim Berg, and colleagues.

Heather Fiske, PhD, is a clinical psychologist in Toronto, Canada. She maintains a private practice and teaches programs and courses in various solution-focused applications. Heather received her PhD from York University. She is the author/co-author of numerous articles on solution-focused practice and training, and is currently writing a book on solution-focused applications in suicide prevention. Heather can be reached at heatherfiske@yahoo.ca.

Handbook of Solution-Focused Brief Therapy: Clinical Applications
© 2007 by The Haworth Press, Inc. All rights reserved.
doi:10.1300/5135_b

Cynthia Franklin, PhD, LCSW, LMFT, is professor and Stiernberg/ Spencer Family Professor in Mental Health at The University of Texas at Austin's School of Social Work, where she coordinates the clinical social work concentration. She has authored over 100 publications, with many focused on at-risk youths and dropout prevention, the effectiveness of solution-focused therapy, alternative school programs, and adolescent pregnancy programs and prevention. Cynthia also is the author of *The School Services Sourcebook: A Guide for School-Based Professionals* (Oxford), *Family Treatment: Evidenced-based Practice for Populations At-Risk* (Brooks/ Cole), and *Clinical Assessment for Social Workers: Quantitative and Qualitative Methods* (Lyceum Press).

Daniel Gallagher, MDiv, is a part-time member of the faculty of the Graduate School of Religion and Religious Education at Fordham University, Bronx, New York where he teaches Solution-Focused Brief Therapy for pastoral counseling students. A graduate of the General Theological Seminary in New York City, Dan is an Episcopal priest who has extensive experience doing Solution-Focused Brief Therapy since the early 1980s. He has authored several articles and chapters, including a chapter, "The Listen and Describe Approach to Training in Solution-Focused Brief Therapy" in *Education and Training in Solution-Focused Brief Therapy* (Haworth, 2005). Dan has a private practice near his home in Millbrook, New York, and is an internationally known trainer, consultant, supervisor, and workshop presenter. He can be reached at Be_Brief@msn.com.

Beth Gerlach is a doctoral student at the University of Texas School of Social Work. Prior to entering the doctoral program, she was a school social worker at the high school level. Her research interests are in urban poverty and public education.

Paul Hackett, MA, is a social worker in Brighton, UK. He primarily works with families and their children trying his best to remain solution-focused. The author of numerous articles on solution-focused ideas, he can also be found on occasion nervously training and presenting workshops.

Mo Yee Lee, PhD, is a professor in the College of Social Work, The Ohio State University. She grew up in Hong Kong and graduated from the University of Toronto in Ontario, Canada. She has authored a number of articles, chapters, books in Solution-Focused Brief Therapy and cross-cultural clinical social work practice. She co-authored *Solution-Focused Treatment With Domestic Violence Offenders: Accountability For Change,* published by The Oxford University Press in 2003. Her new books include *Solution-Oriented Social Work: A Practice Approach to Working with Client*

Strengths and *Evidence-Based Integrative Therapy: An Eastern Holistic Approach Toward Harmony and Transformation.* She can be reached at lee.355@osu.edu.

Alasdair J. Macdonald, MB ChB, FRCPsych, DPM, DCH, is a physician and consultant psychiatrist with the National Health Service in the South of England. He graduated from the University of Glasgow and has worked and studied in various parts of the United Kingdom. As a qualified family therapist and supervisor, he works as a freelance trainer and management consultant. He has published on a variety of topics with a special interest in psychotherapy outcome and in solution-focused therapy. He can be reached at www.psychsft.freeserve.co.uk.

Mark Mitchell has been a licensed marriage and family therapist and organizational consultant for the past 25 years in the Los Angeles area. He can be reached at www.markspeaks.com.

Teri Pichot, MSW, CSW, received her master's degree in social work from the University of Denver, additionally achieving certification as an addictions specialist. She is a Delta Society Pet Partner with her canine companions, Rockefeller and Jasper, and has designed and implemented innovative programs that utilize solution-focused therapy (with and without therapy dogs) with both adults and adolescents. Teri is currently the program manager of the Substance Abuse Counseling Program at the Jefferson County Department of Health and Environment and maintains a private practice in the Denver area. With Yvonne Dolan, she has authored *Solution-Focused Brief Therapy: Effective Use in Agencies,* published by The Haworth Press.

John Sebold, LCSW, is the director of Plumas County Mental Health in Quincy, California. He has been a solution-focused practitioner, clinical supervisor, and trainer for over 20 years. He is extensively involved in applying solution-focused approaches in wilderness-based treatment programs for youth. He is the co-author of numerous articles regarding solution-focused treatment of domestic violence offenders and of the book, *Solution-Focused Treatment of Domestic Violence Offenders/Accountability for Change* (Oxford).

Guy Shennan is a solution-focused practitioner and trainer with BRIEF, London, UK. He trained as a social worker and has always been interested in the use of solution-focused ideas with children and families and in a statutory setting. A prolific presenter and author, Guy also has lead responsibility for the diploma in solution-focused practice run by BRIEF.

Sabine Tolksdorf currently works as a primary school teacher near Cologne, Germany. She finished her studies in 2004 with degrees in English and primary school education. In her free time, she enjoys reading, music, and going out.

Andrew Turnell, PhD, is with Resolutions Consultancy, Perth, Australia. An independent social worker, brief family therapist, and cocreator of the Signs of Safety approach and spends most of his professional time exploring the application of brief therapy ideas to child protection casework. Andrew teaches and consults with child protection organizations in Australasia, Europe, and North America and his most recent book, written with Susie Essex from England, describes the Resolutions approach to working with denied child abuse. Andrew has just completed his doctorate but has managed to stay moderately sane by cycling as much and as far as he can. Contact Andrew at www.signsofsafety.net.

Adriana Uken, LCSW, currently works as a consultant and trainer in Solution-Focused Brief Therapy. She is recently retired from Plumas County Mental Health, where she worked for 27 years and developed, in conjunction with John Sebold and Mo-Yee Lee, the "Plumas Project," a solution-focused domestic violence program that has attracted international attention because of very low recidivism rates. She co-authored *Solution-Focused Treatment of Domestic Violence Offenders: Accountability for Change,* Oxford University Press, 2003, as well as numerous journal articles.

John Wheeler, MA, gained his masters degree in systemic practice at the University of Northumbria in the United Kingdom and is registered with United Kingdom Council for Psychotherapy as a Systemic Psychotherapist. John has published a number of articles and chapters, as listed on www.johnwheeler.co.uk. He works part-time in a child mental health service (UK) and part-time as a solution-focused trainer, supervisor, and consultant. John can be contacted at John@johnwheeler.co.uk.

Phillip Ziegler, PhD and **Tobey Hiller, MFT,** are co-authors of *Recreating Partnership: A Solution-Oriented, Collaborative Approach to Couples Therapy* (W.W. Norton, 2001). They have over 50 combined years of clinical and teaching/training experience, have been married to each other for 30 years, and have two grown sons and three granddaughters. They can be reached at ziegler@igc.org and tobey@igc.org.

Foreword

A FRIENDSHIP TRIBUTE TO INSOO KIM BERG

July 25, 1934 to January 10, 2007

My longtime friend and mentor, Insoo Kim Berg, died suddenly on January 10, 2007, just a few days before this book was scheduled to go to print. Our friendship spanned more than 20 years.

Insoo remains to this day the best clinician I have ever seen and one of the wisest. Her impressive intellect was balanced by an abiding compassion for others and a modest, informal demeanor. After watching her work with clients at the Brief Family Therapy Center that first week, I remember thinking *Even if it takes my whole life, I want to learn to do therapy the way she does.* In retrospect, it turns out that perhaps I wasn't so far off with that time frame. Two decades later, when we were working together on *More Than Miracles* (de Shazer, S., Dolan, Y., Korman, H., Trepper, T., Berg, I.K., & McCollum, E., *More Than Miracles: The State of the Art of Solution-Focused Brief Therapy.* Binghamton, NY: The Haworth Press, 2007) during what became the final year of his life, Steve de Shazer confided to me with infinite good humor that he had spent most of his career trying to accurately identify and describe in writing everything Insoo did when she did solution-focused therapy so that other people might have the possibility of replicating it. After 30 years, he felt he was just now really, really close to finally getting it all down on paper! I could readily appreciate what he meant.

Over the years, Insoo and I often stayed at each other's homes and taught at conferences together in many countries. It was nearly impossible to get up earlier than Insoo. An extremely early riser even in midwinter, she had usually taken a walk, made the coffee, and prepared breakfast for everyone around her, and was ready to get started working on some project by 7:30 a.m. As the years passed, Insoo never stopped taking her early morning

Handbook of Solution-Focused Brief Therapy: Clinical Applications
© 2007 by The Haworth Press, Inc. All rights reserved.
doi:10.1300/5135_c

walks, but she added other physical activities as well: daily yoga and stretching exercises, free weights, and whenever possible, long vigorous hikes in the mountains, forests, and other serene places in nature. Once, shortly after her seventieth birthday, when I marveled at the fact that she was in better shape than many people half her age, she explained, "I have to stay in top shape so I can keep up with my schedule."

And what a schedule it was! It seemed that every time we spoke or exchanged an e-mail over the years, Insoo was either just putting the finishing touches on a journal article or working on yet another book, including two on which we collaborated. To my knowledge, she never missed a deadline. She also served on the editorial boards of the *Journal of Marital and Family Therapy, Family Psychology and Counseling Series, Families in Society,* and *Family Process.* In addition to being the executive director of the Brief Family Therapy Center, she was a founder of the Solution-Focused Brief Therapy Association, a clinical member and approved supervisor for the American Association for Marriage and Family Therapy, and was active in the Wisconsin Association for Marriage and Family Therapy. She also was a member of the National Association of Social Workers and the European Brief Therapy Association. She had a schedule that would have wearied most mortals, but Insoo's energy and enthusiasm seemed never to wane. I used to tease her that rather than having simply *joie de vivre,* she had *joie de travail* (joy of work), and she would laugh and say, "That's right. I do!"

And, of course, at the same time that Insoo was doing all this writing, editing, serving on boards, and founding the SFBTA, she was also teaching seminars on solution-focused therapy all around the world, speaking at international conferences, and consulting throughout Europe, Asia and the Pacific Rim, and North America. I felt privileged to have the experience of traveling and teaching with Insoo in many countries over many years. Most of the time, we both donated our full fees to charity organizations. It may not have been the smartest thing for us to do from a financial standpoint, but Insoo and I were following our hearts, and we sure had a lot of fun doing it.

One of the most poignant international travel experiences I had with Insoo was on a SF teaching trip to Asia that culminated in her former homeland, Seoul, Korea. While in Seoul, I was on a mission to complete some unfinished family business. Long ago, as a young American army officer going off to fight in the Korean War, my father had promised to bring home a string of pearls for my mother when he returned. He died in the fighting, and one of my first memories is of my mother crying at his military funeral. Now, 40 years later, I wanted to bring home that promised string of pearls for my mother.

Insoo got some advice from family members who still lived in Seoul, and we set out together for an area of the city where jewelry stores were known to sell good pearls at fair prices. We went into several shops until we found what felt to us to be the right one. The salesman showed us row after row of strings of perfectly matched pearls and my eyes began to blur. It was impossible to choose. The strings of pearls came in various sizes and subtly different shades, but basically, to my untrained eyes, they looked pretty much the same. The salesman stood on one foot and then the other, and finally he said he had something that might make it easier to choose. He opened a drawer and pulled out a silk drawstring pouch. Inside was a carefully knotted string of very unique pearls. He explained that we could hold these "different" pearls up for comparison in order to best evaluate the other strings and thereby choose the ones that we thought were best for us.

Insoo and I were fascinated by this so-called "different" string in which every pearl had some small unique quality that prevented it from being exactly like any of the others. Some had a bit of a curve to their shape, others were larger on one side than the other side, a few had slight indentations, and so on. These differences delighted Insoo. As she explained, "Each one is unique and for that reason has its own integrity and, in fact, they actually are very well matched because they all have that special difference in common." We left the store with two necklaces. For my mother, I chose the most evenly matched string of pearls I could afford, and Insoo talked the shop owner into selling her the string of "different" pearls. She wore them for many years.

I think Insoo would have particularly liked the chapters of this book, because, like the two strings of pearls, each one has its own integrity, individuality, and beauty, and yet they all share a common thread. And I predict that, like all genuine pearls, they will maintain their value for a long time.

Yvonne Dolan
President of the Solution-Focused Brief Therapy Association
Hammond, Indiana
January 15, 2007

Introduction

In the world of Solution-Focused Brief Therapy (SFBT), many books have been written about different applications of the approach. At workshops and trainings, we are asked, "Does SFBT work with _____ (pick your favorite clinical problem)?" or, "SFBT seems like a 'quick fix' or band-aid. How can it work with *real* problems?" Numerous books that explain how to use the approach with different issues (in schools, in agencies, with children, with domestic violence offenders, with trauma victims, etc.) are testimony to the fact that many who use the approach strongly believe that it is more than a quick fix or cover-up that ignores *real* problems. However, if you are one of those who are learning the approach but do not necessarily have the resources or time to read all of those books, this volume is for you.

The aim of this book is to provide some concise writings on various common and not-so-common uses of the SFBT approach. Each contributor was asked first to describe the phenomenon that is the subject of the chapter. Because there is an early chapter on the assumptions, concepts, and common practices of the approach, the contributors did not need to repeat the basics of the model. Therefore, readers are often directed to the first chapter of the book. Contributors were asked to describe how the approach could be used with a particular situation and to provide liberal case material. We believe this book is suitable for those who are new to the approach, those who may understand the basics but would like additional and specific ideas for particular situations, and those who enjoy being reminded of the multiple ways the approach can be used. As a text, the book could be used in graduate training and in advanced training settings. The book also could serve as a handy reference because each chapter includes a reference section, which, when combined with references from other sections, is a rich resource of SFBT writings.

We hope we have brought together useful resources for our readers. Each chapter is contributed by someone we believe to be well versed in the content topic as well as experienced in the application of the approach. Following the Foreword written by Yvonne Dolan honoring the late Insoo Kim

Handbook of Solution-Focused Brief Therapy: Clinical Applications
© 2007 by The Haworth Press, Inc. All rights reserved.
doi:10.1300/5135_d

Berg, we continue with "Foundations," which includes chapters on the assumptions and practices, history, and epistemology behind the approach. The chapters by Cade and Bidwell are especially noteworthy and unique contributions to the field. Next, we include chapters on using the approach with several clinical issues and populations: couples, depression, domestic violence, schools, children, pastoral work, therapist burnout, medicine, and "outside the therapy room" applications. The third section of the book focuses on training and supervision. We end with a "Last Words" section that includes an application and Frank's ideas about potential limitations of the approach. The last chapter of the book, written by Brian Cade, is a tribute to the late Steve de Shazer, who with his wife, Insoo Kim Berg, cofounded the SFBT approach.

Acknowledgments

We would like to acknowledge a few of the wonderful people who have inspired us and been with this throughout this project.

From Thorana

To my good friend and colleague, Frank Thomas. Over the years, we have had fun, worked together, and supported each other through both great and not-so-great times. We started this project because we have mutual interests and enjoy collaborating. We ended with what we hope is a modest contribution to the field of Solution-Focused Brief Therapy.

To Terry Trepper, a friend and mentor who started me on this path of editing.

To my friends in the Solution-Focused Brief Therapy Association, too numerous to name.

To my students and clients who have taught me the art of therapy.

I send kisses and hugs to my children, Travis and Stacy (and Mary), and to my grandchildren, Taylor and Deryk, who do not know how much their love and laughter support me.

Finally, to my husband, Vic, who has been an incredible support and love over the years that I have pounded away at keyboards, torn my hair out, and jumped at the chance to work with wonderful colleagues.

From Frank

To Thorana Nelson, whose creativity and patience has made this project both enjoyable and valuable. Through thick and thin 'Rana has been the quintessential collaborator . . . and friend;

To my daughter, Allison, whose determination inspires me;

To the Boys—Patrick O'Malley, Tom Chancellor, Duane Bidwell, and Peter Kahle—for keeping it real—*esse quam videri*;

Handbook of Solution-Focused Brief Therapy: Clinical Applications
© 2007 by The Haworth Press, Inc. All rights reserved.
doi:10.1300/5135_e

To Brad Keeney, who asked me to join him in my first writing collaboration more than 20 years ago. You lit the fire, brother—thanks for believing in me;

To my students and clients, who teach me lessons in life and humility;

And finally, to my wife, Lori . . . your love sustains me—thanks for suffering and celebrating with me.

From Both of Us

First, we thank the heavens that the two of us are still friends after editing two books together. We also thank Steve and Insoo for developing SFBT and for their ongoing passion for the solution approach. In addition, we are ever grateful for the blood, sweat, and tears that our authors sacrificed to create this book with us—thanks to all of you. And finally, we tip our hats to the practitioners of Solution-Focused Brief Therapy—without your creative work "in the trenches" assisting the change process with thousands upon thousands of clients around the planet, this approach would burn out and quickly be relegated to the Psychotherapy Model Memorial Hall of Fame. The SFBT approach grows because of everyday contributions from the real experts, mental health professionals . . . and the clients who guide us.

SECTION I:
FOUNDATIONS

In which we lay the groundwork for the book, beginning with the assumptions, concepts, and practices of the Solution-Focused Brief Therapy (SFBT) approach; follow with a history and context of SFBT; and end with its underlying epistemology.

doi:10.1300/5135_P1

Chapter 1

Assumptions and Practices Within the Solution-Focused Brief Therapy Tradition

Frank N. Thomas
Thorana S. Nelson

When paradigms change, the world itself changes with them.

Thomas Kuhn, *The Structure of Scientific Revolutions,*
1962, p. 111

Never assume anything except a three percent mortgage.

Bob Branon, *Let Us Prey,* 1994, p. 5

INTRODUCTION

Beginning with de Shazer's (1982) *Patterns of Brief Family Therapy,* authors and trainers within Solution-Focused Brief Therapy (SFBT) have purposefully articulated many assumptions of this approach to therapy. Although any list that one generates is transitory, keeping one's conscious assumptions public has allowed SFBT to track change and openly discuss similarities and differences. As a whole, SFBT seems to value exactness

Handbook of Solution-Focused Brief Therapy: Clinical Applications
© 2007 by The Haworth Press, Inc. All rights reserved.
doi:10.1300/5135_01

and transparency; that is, a clear statement of your guiding ideas ties you to a body of people and a tradition while simultaneously encouraging accountability.

It is not as though everyone coupled to SFBT believes the same things about change, therapy, or human nature. We are a composting of Erickson, Bateson, and Wittgenstein, de Shazer and Berg, fertile humus that has sustained growth for over 30 years. The result is a continually expanding and contracting list of presuppositions, some unique to particular authors, and some durable that continue to withstand the test of time.

We have whittled down a fairly comprehensive list from SFBT publications and attempted to organize these assumptions within two categories: (a) philosophy, posture, or stance (clinical thinking), and (b) conceptual/ practical (what we say we do).

THE "INTERACTIONAL VIEW"

SFBT grew out of the brief therapy tradition, best exemplified by the work of the Mental Research Institute (MRI) in Palo Alto, California. The forewords to de Shazer's first book, *Patterns of Brief Family Therapy* (1982), were written by two men who were firmly aligned with this tradition: John Weakland and Bradford Keeney. Both promoted de Shazer's work as a contribution to brief therapy as conceptualized and practiced by people tied to Erickson and Bateson. Although de Shazer's later work (c.f., *Words Were Originally Magic,* 1994) is philosophically quite different from *Patterns,* the lineage was established: SFBT and MRI are and would be sisters in theory and practice.

> Precisely what is the interactional view? Many have referred to it as a "theory," an "epistemology," a "research and therapy program," a "perspective." Taken as a whole, it is probably none of these. *It is a viewpoint of therapy or research which provides a new way of looking at old problems. . . .* We would find its greatest benefit if we considered the interactional view to be *a state of mind, an attitude or framework* which we can bring to the therapeutic or the research setting. Consequently, we should not expect the interactional view to provide answers or results but, rather, to provide a *framework* within which we can contemplate our old questions. (*Emphasis added;* Fisher, 1982, pp. 197-198)

CLINICAL THINKING:
TAKING A SOLUTION-FOCUSED POSTURE

Curiosity

A stance of curiosity is common to many therapy approaches, but it is indispensable in SFBT. For the solution-focused practitioner, therapy is a context in which old perceptions, ideas, and behaviors are examined without prejudice, and new concepts and actions are practiced within ethical and moral limits of those involved (clients + therapist). Essential to this unpacking process is a persistent questioning driven by the therapist's interest in client experiences and meanings. If the conversation lacks this obvious attention and the therapist is more focused on his or her own views than on the clients', it is not SFBT.

Therapists' optimism plays a part in maintaining curiosity within the SFBT frame. Curiosity is not directed so much toward causes, explanations, and categorization as it is toward positive outcome, partial success, and client/contextual resourcefulness. Tom Lee, a social worker from Fort Worth, Texas, told me that he must maintain his beliefs in order to be effective—his belief in the usefulness of the SFBT approach and his unrelenting faith in clients' abilities to create positive changes in their lives (personal communication, November 22, 2003). Tom's posture epitomizes this stance of curiosity.

SFBT therapists want to learn from clients because clients have so much to offer. While both therapists and clients contribute to the change process, clients are the experts on their lives, and therapy cannot proceed without tapping into both dominant and less prominent aspects of the clients' experiences (Thomas & Cockburn, 1998; Weiner-Davis, 1992). Without curiosity about clients' experiences, meanings, and expectations, therapists have little to offer. A communications cartoon on the Internet sums up this position well: A suited expert sits behind a desk in front of a wall filled with framed certificates. The expert says, "There's so little we know." Although the irony is obvious, SFBT practitioners move beyond it by recognizing what we know can only be a partial contribution to the success of therapy. The primary ingredients must come from the clients.

Respect

Nearly all approaches to therapy promote respectful treatment of clients, but few articulate the specifics as well as SFBT. Although many approaches state a commitment to being nonjudgmental and focusing on unconditional positive regard, SFBT purposefully yields to clients' descriptions of experiences, and what those experiences represent. This respect—a belief that people know themselves better than therapists or other experts ever could—permeates the approach (Måhlberg & Sjöblom, 2004).

Perhaps the most prominent aspect of a respectful posture is the recruitment and endorsement of clients' expectations for therapy. The goals that clients wish to achieve and the focus they choose for therapy take top priority within this approach. Therapists have a responsibility to clearly communicate to clients that the clients' attitudes regarding who is involved in the therapy, the topics of conversation, and the importance of their history will be valued.

Clients' views on the role of the therapist are also carefully considered. Since the expected amount of directiveness varies greatly among clients seeking help (Prochaska, DiClemente, & Norcross, 2003), SFBT therapists are clear that respectful interaction means the therapist has the primary responsibility to adjust in order to form the best fit possible with each client. Although every therapist has limits (because one must consider ethical, legal, moral, and clinical restrictions), SFBT therapists elicit client views on how comfortable they are, what they expect, how they are best motivated, and what they believe are essential ingredients in a successful therapeutic relationship. For example, a male client tells his female therapist that he does not like it when people repeatedly ask him questions. Because of recent litigation, he spent a great deal of time being "badgered on the witness stand" by county prosecutors attempting to convict his employers. His reason for seeking therapy revolves around the humiliation and fear he has experienced as a coerced witness, and he is clear that he does not want to be "interrogated" in his therapy. Although SFBT is question-centered, the therapist adjusts her style of practice to minimize direct questions while explaining the place of curiosity in her orientation. The two of them come to an agreement that whenever he feels overloaded with questions or she feels she is using the interrogatory form too often, both have permission to bring the subject up.

Being Tentative

We—Thorana and I—are unabashed experts (see Cade, 1992). We admit it freely and are eager to discuss our expertise with anyone who will listen. So, if you would like to get an earful, please ask! For example, Rana knows more about Lutheran politics, Utah weather patterns, and running a COAMFTE-approved family therapy master's program than anyone else I know. My own expertise—on living with a lawyer, Jere Lehtinen's value to the Dallas Stars and Finnish Olympic hockey teams, and aikido—pale in comparison, but it is a pretty full bag as well. What we have found in clinical and supervisory practice is this: Most of our expertise has little value to clients. Things we know—how children develop, what makes for good relationships, the most effective ways to conduct therapy—cannot take precedence in the therapy room. This fits with what "every schoolboy knows," according to Gregory Bateson (1979): "The generic we can know, but the specific eludes us" (p. 43).

Harlene Anderson and the late Harry Goolishian (Anderson, 1997, 2005; Anderson & Goolishian, 1992) are the primary contributors to what is known as "the not-knowing position." However, it is important to note that they are committed not to ignorance, but to "not *having* to know" (Anderson, 1997, p. 64, emphasis in original). In one of their earlier manuscripts addressing this idea, they clearly stated their understanding of this stance:

> The not-knowing position entails a general attitude or stance in which the therapist's actions communicate an abundant, genuine curiosity. That is, the therapist's actions and attitudes express a need to know more about what has been said, rather than convey preconceived opinions and expectations about the client, the problem, or what must be changed. The therapist, therefore, positions himself or herself in such a way as always to be in a state of "being informed" by the client. (Anderson & Goolishian, p. 29)

According to Anderson (1997), therapists need to maintain a not-knowing position because they are always in "a state of *being informed* by the other, and always need to learn more about what has been said or may not have been said" (p. 134).

Because the term "not knowing" is linguistically oppositional (know/not know) and stated as an absence (i.e., no knowledge), it has sometimes been promoted as a preferred position of complete ignorance. Paulo Bertrando (2000) wrote:

> It is impossible to adopt a true not-knowing position, because the therapist cannot avoid knowing her own experience. . . . Thus not knowing risks either becoming a form of wishful thinking in which knowing simply sinks into the untold, or of becoming a strategic stance; pretending not to have an idea or a point of view is just a *simulation* of not knowing. (p. 92, emphasis in original)

We believe that talk centered on "not knowing" can be counterproductive. To diminish the confusion created by this inherently dichotomous terminology, we propose that the SFBT therapist take a stance of *being tentative*. In order to maintain this perspective, a therapist should always view his or her conclusions as hypotheses, as temporary rather than complete. (For more on solution-focused not-knowing, see Iveson, 2005.)

For example, a client may state that the cause of distress that led her to seek counseling is a recent diagnosis of cancer. Assume for a moment that this is the only reason she has for coming to see you. You should still be tentative regarding the approach you take, because her distress may (and probably will) change during the time she is in therapy. Traditional counseling approaches may immediately address grief responses and mortality fears, missing the continuous reinterpretations and evolving experiences of a person with cancer. Being tentative means allowing oneself to be continually informed by clients as their current experiences become past understandings. One might also hear several presenting problems that parallel the diagnosis: fear of losing her marital partner, the impact of the treatment regimen on the family finances, the impending physical changes, and so on. Some therapeutic approaches attempt to create a hierarchy of cause or importance of presenting problems, while others work to form a hypothesis that condenses all presenting concerns into a form that can simultaneously address everything that troubles the client. SFBT therapists assume complexity of human experience without assuming complexity in responses to human problems. The result is that SFBT therapists do not marry their ideas or techniques; instead, they hold loosely to assumptions, apply techniques lightly, and are cautious with their language ("I wonder if . . ."; "This might be . . ."; "Is it possible that . . .?" etc.). Maintaining a tentative posture gives the client the freedom to (re)form goals, (trans)form counseling approaches, and in-form you of changes that she is experiencing in her thoughts, perceptions, and actions. Keeney (1983) has called this stance the "chameleon on a mirror" (p. 172). Being tentative allows the therapist continuously to adjust while maintaining goals and agreements. I have found that being slow-to-know is a more realistic stance (Thomas, 2007). First, being slow-to-know encourages the expansion of people's descriptions, allowing diversity to emerge as clients restate positions and overexplain themselves. Because I am driven to be open to correction and I am constantly revising my ideas, this slowness is not an act—the client knows that I am not mentally slow, but they re-act and re-search with me in hopes of re-creating some meaningful differences from their own language and experience.

Nonnormative and Nonpathologizing

SFBT assumes that every client's experience is distinctive, and that therapy should create a space within which clients can expose and discuss their experiences without pejorative conclusions being drawn. To quote Milton

Erickson, "Each person is a unique individual. Hence, psychotherapy should be formulated to meet the uniqueness of the individual's needs rather than tailoring the person to fit the Procrustean bed of a hypothetical theory of human behavior" (Zeig, 1985, p. viii). Because of this firm commitment, SFBT generally places little value on diagnostic categories (e.g., *Diagnostic and Statistical Manual of Mental Disorders* [DSM-IV], American Psychiatric Association [APA], 1994) or generalizations (i.e., normal human development).

SFBT has long assumed a nonjudgmental stance; that is, most SFBT authors and practitioners defend the premise that there is no "right" way to view/experience things (Durrant, 1995; O'Hanlon & Weiner-Davis, 1989). Generally, SFBT does not address lineal explanations of "cause" (which usually ends in conclusions of normal/abnormal). "'Finding' the causes of clients' problems is not necessary to constructing solutions, and the time devoted to the search for causes may actually make the problems worse" (de Shazer & Miller, 1998, p. 370). Instead, practitioners of SFBT focus on other client experiences related to their problems. These include (but are not limited to) concentrating on (a) exceptions, (b) resources for resolving difficulties, (c) developing hope by scaling the range of problem experiences compared to dichotomous (presence/absence of problems) conceptualizations, and (d) strengths clients bring to bear on their problematic situations. It is vital to remember that a problem is what the client experiences as a problem (Durrant, 1995) and that is what matters most.

Defending the nonnormative nature of human experience does not eliminate practices of "normalizing" (De Jong & Berg, 2002). Many clients find comfort and motivation in knowing that they are not the only ones who have gone through such trials, that they are not alone in their experience of troubling thoughts, feelings, and behaviors. It can be quite heartening for clients to hear that their experiences are unique while, at the same time, tied to ordinary human responses to stress, loss, and anxiety. Instead, emphasizing the nonnormative allows room for difference—one can view life/problems/ states as changeable rather than intractable. American culture has placed a great deal of emphasis on permanence of personality, which constantly shows up in both public and professional arenas. In the professional world, the understanding and assignment of personality disorders (i.e., narcissistic, borderline) are part of the diagnostic criteria of a great deal of counseling practice. In the public sphere, books abound that have turned self-diagnosis of traits into a pejorative art form (just look back to the 1980s and the explosion of books on codependency). Within SFBT, people have their experiences and are continually making (new) sense of these experiences . . . period. Michael Durrant has gone so far as to predict that the DSM will either become a 20-volume encyclopedia of dysfunction or (what he would like to see) a one-word document: everyone is "stuck" (Thomas, Durrant, & Metcalf, 1993).

It is important for SFBT practitioners to keep in mind that problems do not indicate pathology—they are just one way of describing things. Labeling is an attempt to make sense of things we experience by classifying or categorizing. When describing others' behavior and emotion, all we can have is description, not actual knowledge or unbiased explanation. Problems exist in language, experience, and context, not "in the wild."

Finally, SFBT is true to nonnormative and nonpathologizing positions by constantly considering *context*. One of the greatest deficits of SFBT is that contextual understanding and application is not promoted because those practicing SFBT often have little training in developing the conceptual, perceptual, and participatory skills necessary to see connections within and outside the therapy room. Our own educational background has entrenched us in always considering the commanding influence of context on one's life since our first years in family therapy, and we still hold to the idea that one must still live in context and that the individual story and experience always is framed by context (Bertrando, 2000).

Client Competence

Along with nonnormative and nonpathologizing stances, SFB therapists assume that clients are competent. Clients may not have all the answers at hand or may be stuck due to attempted solutions that have not worked but are being repeated. We all tend to look around our own areas when we are stuck and sometimes need reminders that there is more outside the room. Clients may have limitations, such as physical or contextual, but SFBT assumes that clients are a lot more competent than most in the mental health field give credit. Utilizing this competence is the hallmark of SFBT.

BASIC ASSUMPTIONS

Change is constant and inevitable; just as one cannot not communicate, one cannot not change.

"Change is so much part of living that (people) cannot prevent themselves from changing" (Berg & Miller, 1992, p. 11). Problem saturation tends to dominate people's perceptions of difference, resulting in an experience of sameness or stuckness. Assuming that life is *both* stable *and* constantly changing allows the SFBT practitioner to see both, an important perspective that is often missing in the problem system.

In therapy, this sometimes is taken to mean that we can effect change in the direction we want. On the contrary, sometimes change occurs in unexpected and unpleasant directions. Rather than become discouraged by these changes, SFBT practitioners see them as opportunities to learn about how the client system is cooperating with us, what the change may mean in positive terms, and, sometimes, directions that we can go for redirecting change. It often is easier to channel change when things are moving than when they are stagnant.

For example, an attempt to be assertive at work might backfire and lead to disappointment and, even, humiliation. The SFB therapist will help the client figure out what the client learned from the situation, what worked even a little bit, how the client coped with the feelings, and what others might see as a good attempt rather than a dismal failure.

***"If it ain't broke, don't fix it! Once you know what works,
do more of it! If it doesn't work, then don't do it again—
do something different!"***

A favorite syllogism (Berg and Miller, 1992, p. 17) with three components, this assumption is derived in part from the MRI manner of looking at problems in which patterns of interaction suggest categories of solutions. This SFBT idea goes a step further and suggests that patterns of solutions suggest solutions: We simply need to focus on them differently, just as we focus differently on the famous optical illusion when we try to see the two faces rather than the vase.

In SFBT, this means a difference in emphasis, in which syllable gets accented, if you will. Instead of doing something differently, SFBT begins with recognizing and preserving what should be left alone and what works for the client. One takes action only when action must be taken, and complexity is assumed only when a perspective of simplicity is shown to be inadequate. Ockam's Razor has perhaps never been so elegantly applied in the social sciences.

***Clients come to us with resources and strengths, both personal
and contextual. Our job is to create a milieu in which these
become important and are identified.***

This assumption is different from assumptions found in other modes of working in which clients are assumed to have deficits. In other approaches, it is the expert-therapist's job to tell clients not only what is wrong, but also what they need to do to correct the problem. SFBT assumes that clients are the experts on their own situations and that the therapists can never have certainty in their knowledge of clients' experiences, and that clients are the only ones who can know which solutions are best for them. Therapists, therefore, are experts on a process of solution-building, on therapeutic conversations, but not on exactly what clients need to do to improve their lots.

Some therapists seem to think that this means clients already have all the answers, and that our job is simply to help them see what is already in them. We believe this means that clients are capable of *using* resources and that part of our job is to help expand the noticeable resources.

Blaise Pascal, the seventeenth-century mathematician and physicist, once said, "We are generally better persuaded by the reasons we discover ourselves than by those given to us by others" (http://www.Quotationspage.com, April 10, 2005). We agree with Pascal's observation—clients often make better use of resources if they are the ones to notice them. They seem to "stick" with them better and make a bigger impression. Our job is to help them notice possible resources that assist as the clients move in a helpful direction.

There is not necessarily a logical relationship between the problem and the solution. The therapist's role is not to diagnose and repair but to identify and amplify potential solutions.

This assumption, which is closely related to the previous assumption, is a fundamentally different way of thinking. It assumes that problems and solutions are not necessarily related. Many so-called "traditional" therapies assume that one must know the source, cause, or construction of problems in order to find solutions to them. This may be important for particular medical conditions, such as accidental poisoning or drug reactions, but is not necessarily true for mental health and relationship difficulties. For example, one may know that the origin of a problem is some trauma in the past. Knowing about this traumatic event may even lead to a recognizable diagnosis upon which many mental health professionals agree. However, that does not tell us much about possible solutions for the client's present distress. We cannot change what happened in the past. We may even be able to change a person's recollection of or affective state around a situation. Neither diagnoses, nor symptom identification, nor altered recollection necessarily alleviates current symptoms. But we may be able to assist clients' efforts to find solutions to their current suffering and accompanying troubles through distinguishing and promoting solutions that are already a part of the clients' lived experiences.

An analogy that works for some people is this: Let us say you find a nail in an automobile tire. We do not really need to know where the nail came from to fix the flat. The solution of removing the nail and patching the hole is not directly related to the presence of nails in the road somewhere or knowing where the nail came from. It might be useful to know that in order to prevent further flat tires ("I think I will avoid that street with all of the construction going on"), but it is not necessary for fixing the current problem.

It is amazing to us how few solutions seem directly related to the problem. As you will see in subsequent sections, following questions logically from client responses often leads to ideas that seem quite unrelated to the original complaint. We believe that this may be due, in part, to our Western way of thinking that automatically leads most clients to try to understand why things are happening rather than simply describing them and to our propensity for solving problems by first dissecting them. SFBT is *not* a problem-solving approach; it is solution- and future-oriented.

In SFBT, this is the direction of potential solutions:

- that have worked in the past for similar problems,
- that sometimes work in the present,
- that may work for similar but not identical situations,
- that may have helped other people with similar situations, and
- that may not be directly related to the problem but that make the situation less problematic.

The therapist's role, based on these assumptions, is to open possibilities by asking more and more questions that identify and amplify possibilities. Clients are then left to decide on their own which ones are best for them.

Paula Underwood, a Native American medicine woman, taught a game that we call "Sixes" (V. Nelson, personal communication, March 23, 2001). In this game, before one may act on a belief about another person's intentions, one must first develop at least six possible reasons for their behavior. It is amazing how difficult this exercise is at first and how easy after the fourth, fifth, and sixth meanings are mentioned. People usually continue with seventh, eighth, and more possibilities.

A focus on the possible and changeable is more helpful
than a focus on the overwhelming and intractable.
(Thomas, Durrant, & Metcalf, 1993)

Some things are situations, not problems (Steve de Shazer, personal communication, November 7, 2004). That is, some things cannot be changed. For example, an adult cannot become taller (although, with age, one may become shorter!). If I have a genetic condition, I have a genetic condition, period. One's past may involve tragic events or even acts of stupidity, but the facts of the past are usually unchangeable.

In general, we cannot change the past—we can only change (parts of) ourselves and the meanings we attach to past events. Sometimes, the best we can hope for is a different way of relating to a situation, not a change in the situation itself. What this means in therapy is that sometimes the best help a therapist can provide is to be with the client as she or he accepts the inevitable and then explore different ways of thinking about, coping with, or interacting with the situation. The possible and changeable may be evident in the present (exceptions) or in the future (presuppositional, future-oriented questions), but focusing on past events can easily promote the feeling of being overwhelmed.

For example, everyone will experience loss, with one of the most difficult losses being the death of a loved one. Grieving loss seems to be a universal human experience; grieving is to be expected and not avoided. What SFBT counselors bring to therapy with clients who have suffered loss is an ear for the reality (a death has occurred), the inevitable (grief is a natural reaction to significant loss), and the possible (how the client's grief may decrease in intensity and be less debilitating over time; see Peller & Walter, 1992/1993).

A Small Change Can Lead to Bigger Change

Bateson (1979) taught us that perturbations can have wide-ranging effects in a system. We do not always need a sledgehammer—sometimes a little tap will have ripple effects that lead to bigger changes (O'Hanlon & Weiner-Davis, 1989). The "ripple effect" idea is more than the concept of the stone dropped in the pond producing ramifications far beyond the splash point; it also assumes that clients will create additional changes once the initial change takes place (see de Shazer, 1985). For example, if a father makes a small change when interacting with his son (say, from speaking more to listening more), the assumption is that the son will also change (e.g., he may move to greater participation in these conversations). What may also happen is that the son's response to the father's change may lead the father to listen more carefully and ask questions about the son's experiences, further prompting the father to make changes in other areas of family communication.

In these situations, the best thing for a therapist to do is keep quiet and get out of the way. We sometimes think we need to "cement" change by overdoing interpretations, giving more homework, or requiring insight. The aim for the therapist is to help make a small difference that will make a difference (Bateson, 1979).

Therapy is Client-Centered—The Client is the Expert on His or Her Experience

In SFBT, we privilege the clients' experience above that of the therapist. Therapy is not focused on concepts from a model or the therapist's expert knowledge. The therapist does not look, for example, for cognitive distortions and then use standard techniques for un-distorting them. Nor do we find it helpful to categorize clients and/or problems (i.e., DSM-IV). Rather, the therapist listens to the way the client describes the difficulty, asks questions about other experiences of the client, and explores possibilities that are relevant to the client rather than to the approach or to the therapist.

This assumption specifically addresses the posture of the therapist toward the client. Referring back to the second assumption, the therapist assumes if what we are doing is not working, we should "do something different." This may take many forms: recruiting additional people, reexamining goals, or even transferring the client or changing therapy approaches. But the major emphasis is on honoring the client's words, descriptions, wishes, and goals. "Sensitivity to the unique client in the room should be the central guiding principle, rather than the need to ask solution-focused questions" (Sharry, Madden, & Darmody, 2003, p. 18). For example, when a client expressed frustration that progress was not being made toward goals that had been decided upon in an earlier session, the therapist explored with the client how reaching the goals might make a difference in the client's life. This discussion led to a discovery that the earlier-stated goals were not precisely what the client wanted, and therefore, new, more relevant goals were established. Clients sometimes want to know how their family-of-origin experiences affect the problem, how it developed, and how it can be resolved. Doing a solution-focused genogram (Kuehl, 1995; Kuehl, Barnard, & Nelson, 1998) might be just enough of a difference to make a difference for such clients.

PRACTICES

Importance of the Client-Therapist Relationship

Wampold (2001) suggested through examination of many studies of factors that influence positive outcomes in therapy, that the single biggest factor is the client-therapist relationship. That is, without rapport, without a connection, without trust on the client's part that therapy will be helpful, therapy is not likely to be helpful to the client. Failure quite often is attributed to client factors, such as motivation. Sometimes, failure is attributed to an incorrect approach or technique. Berg and Miller (1992) have suggested three types of client-therapist relationships: visitor, complainant, and customer. Too often, this idea has been reified into a characterization (often, character flaw) of the client. That is, a *person* is a visitor, a complainant, or a customer rather than the *relationship* is of the visitor, complainant, or customer sort. Putting the emphasis on the relationship also puts accountability on the therapist's shoulders because relationships are (at a minimum) *two*-person responsibilities, not one-person. It takes two people to make a relationship, only one to mess it up, and the therapist as the expert on therapy is largely responsible for recognizing the type of relationship that is being enacted and for moving it, if necessary, to the next level.

Visiting relationships call for good hosting. That is, the therapist helps the person to be comfortable, listens for their needs, sympathizes, and asks what else they can do. People who are visiting often are checking us out. Are we nice? Do we seem to know what we are doing? Can we be trusted with their problems? In this relationship, attempts to begin solution-building are usually fruitless. People who are "just browsing" (visitors) in stores are usually not very open to sales pitches. Rather, giving them room to shop and to ask questions in their own way is often a better strategy.

So, what is the role of the therapist in a complainant relationship? Think about it. What is the best thing to do, the only *effective* thing to do, when someone is complaining? *Listen! Sympathize!* Some clients find a great need to begin therapy by listing their concerns, often about other people (people seldom complain about their own behavior—they have other ways of describing it when they are dissatisfied with themselves). Therapy with the complainant-type relationship is not one of solution-building. Solution-building is effective only when there is a client-or customer-type relationship, when a person is a client for change rather than visiting or complaining. The aim of the therapist in complaining situations must be, at best, to help the person move toward a client-type relationship and, at worst, to help the client feel heard. Attempts to find solutions are usually met with "yes, but" sorts of responses, which are very frustrating for therapists. Rather, sympathetic listening and questions such as, "how have you been coping so far with this difficult situation" are often more effective at helping move into client-type relationships with the therapist.

The therapist in the client-type relationship has been "hired" and can get down to the business of helping to build solutions from the client's story. In this relationship, the client is open to new ideas, suggestions, reframes, and encouragement. Solution-building can begin in earnest.

Well-Formed Goals

Often, clients give us vague directions (if any) for what change would look like. For whatever reason, clients usually begin counseling with a clear set of complaints and little idea of what the future without the problem would look like. "The emphasis in goaling is on describing what will be different, that is, the end, rather than how it may be achieved, that is, the means" (Sharry et al., 2003, p. 37). In SFBT, it is central that the therapist and client work toward goals that show the following characteristics (see De Jong & Berg, 2002):

Important to the client. The goals for therapy cannot be goals that others have set for the client. Clients are more likely to be motivated if change takes a direction that will improve their lives, remove barriers, and increase agency.

Stated in terms that show awareness of context. Situating change in the client's relational context personalizes change and increases the possibility that the client's experience will fit with the changes he or she is seeing. "I want to be happy" is a laudable goal, but "I want to be happy, and my significant others will notice and reinforce my positive changes" has a greater chance of sustaining change.

The presence of something desirable rather than the absence of something undesirable. As the old mathematics maxim states, one cannot prove the negative. If a client says, "I don't want to be angry anymore," it is likely that he will continue to pay attention to anger—both increased and decreased experiences and expressions—and it is unlikely he will reach this goal (nor is the cessation of anger an appropriate goal for anyone, in our opinion). Instead, if the goal is stated in the positive—"I want to be more easygoing," the exceptions move to the foreground, and anger takes a back seat.

Emphasize first steps rather than end points. The "brief" in "Solution-Focused Brief Therapy" has often been misunderstood as "short" or "rapid." de Shazer clarified this years ago (personal communication, September 14, 2002), when he stated that "brief" within this approach to therapy means "not one more session than necessary." In order to keep to this definition, therapy goals focus on the beginning rather than the completion of therapy, and clients decide when to say, "Enough." Since the therapy process is inherently short-term, no matter what model one uses (Asay & Lambert, 1999; Garfield, 1994), client success cannot be tied to an unachievable standard. Instead, SFBT uses scaling questions, mentioned later in the text, to place emphasis on progress toward goals and encourages clients to decide when they have achieved enough to end therapy.

Concrete, achievable, and measurable. This characteristic may be the most difficult for those first learning SFBT, but it also is one of the most important. Use of the miracle question (De Jong & Berg, 2002) is one way SFBT practitioners have approached the important step of visualizing "success" through the eyes of the client. Articulating what one wants when the presenting problem(s) no longer dominate the client's life requires therapists to focus client's dreams into a form that the client, therapist, and others can witness. There is no greater achievement than knowing you have achieved a goal that is not only significant, but also public. The easiest part of this characteristic is making it measurable, and scaling questions that are anchored to the client's experience are quite useful.

Realistic: Given the life of the client. There is one paradox of the miracle question: Goals are to fit with clients' miracles, but they must be realistic. It takes practice for the SFBT therapist to guide clients toward the possible and away from the impossible and/or improbable. For example, many clients who have suffered a catastrophe yearn for the clock to be turned back to a time just before the event hit them. When asking the miracle question (discussed in the next characteristic), the focus must be on what the client will be *doing differently* rather than what would be different than the current problem state.

Magical thinking may also come into play, and children are especially prone to create a future that has few connections to the possible realities they could co-create with therapists. Leading clients toward the possible reduces frustration and failure and promotes goals that can be sensed and experienced.

Include a role for each client. Many complaints involving interpersonal relationships require change on the part of a party not involved in the therapeutic process. Hearing complaints like, "If my _____ (husband, mother, son) would change, things would be just fine" is not uncommon. When developing goals, therapists must ask, "And what do you see yourself changing as a part of this miracle?" In fact, one can avoid sabotaging couples/relationship counseling by avoiding questions that allow one party to demand change from the other. Instead, a therapist can ask, "A: What small change are you willing (and able) to make that you think would make a positive difference in your relationship?" (followed by a question directed to the partner B: "If A began to make changes in this area, would this make a significant positive difference for you?") Since SFBT is a therapy of solution and not a therapy encouraging complaints, this aspect of "goal-ing" (Walter & Peller, 1992) avoids the messiness of demands and criticism by directing clients' views toward appropriate responsibility and meaningful change.

The Miracle Question

We have found that adopting an SFBT approach for one's practice sometimes involves memorizing questions. The reason: The research and clinical experimentation of others who have gone before us should inform us as we adopt their ideas. Like a second-born child, we can learn from the mistakes (and successes) of the pioneers in SFBT.

Here is an example of a well-formed miracle question:

> *Suppose* that while you are sleeping tonight and the entire house is quiet, a *miracle* happens. The miracle is that *the problem which brought you here is solved*. However, because you are sleeping, you don't know that *the miracle has happened*. So, when you wake up tomorrow morning, *what will be different* that will tell you that a miracle has happened and the problem which brought you here is solved? (de Shazer, 1988, p. 5; c.f. De Jong & Berg, 2002, p. 85)

The miracle question has become central in SFBT practice over the past 15 years and is a vital part of the research definition of what constitutes SFBT (Beyebach, 2000). Using this question as an integral part of practice will place practitioners in the stream of the current SFBT approach and situate them in the tradition that is tied to a broad stream of relevant clinical and research data. It is hard for us to imagine an SFBT case without a clearly articulated miracle question that forms the base for goaling, exceptions, and termination.

There is one caveat to the statement in the previous paragraph, however: To be most useful, the miracle question *process* must include questions about what differences the miracle would make. This includes not just the end goals, but what those goals will accomplish, what difference they will make in the clients' lives, what others would notice, how certain changes were accomplished, and what difference those changes might make to others or what meaning others would make of the differences. Novices to SFBT often use the approach as though it were a set of techniques divorced from (a) the clients' context and (b) the meanings associated with changes. These meanings are often more meaningful than the changes themselves.

For example, one client, in response to the miracle question, started with the obvious, "my co-workers would be nice to me." However, as we explored what differences these changes might make, she noticed that she thought she would be less mean to her daughter (taking out her frustration). That change would mean that she and her daughter would be getting along better and her daughter might be using her more as she prepared for life after leaving home. *This* change was something that the client declared was more meaningful than her relationship with her co-workers and also something that she could affect.

Identification of Exceptions

SFBT assumes that exceptions (plural) happen; that is, we assume that there are times in the client's experience when they expect their problems to occur but they do not (or the problem recurs with less intensity, frequency, or regularity; see De Jong & Berg, 2002). The identification of exceptions, as well as the context and behaviors accompanying these irregularities, is fundamental to SFBT practice.

Not all exceptions are created equal. One need not force meaningfulness or importance of particular exceptions on clients (see Nylund & Corsiglia, 1994). Since "nothing happens all the time" (Michael Durrant, personal communication, June 7, 2002), SFBT simply locates and calls attention to useful events and behaviors by asking questions highlighting the possibility of exceptions in the client's lived experience. Examples of such questions include:

- "There are times, I am sure, when you would expect the problem to happen, but it doesn't. How do you get that to happen?"
- "What is different when the problem could have gotten the best of you, but you did something to prevent it? What did you do?"
- "Who else noticed that change? In what way could you tell that she or he noticed?"
- "When is it less frequent (intense, severe)?"
- "When is it different in any way? How did you figure out that doing _____ helps?"

A key ingredient in utilizing exceptions is this: one should always assume that the client had some element of control over the change that has taken place unless there is strong evidence to the contrary. When seeking out exceptions, following up with questions such as,

- "How did you do that?" or,
- "What part did *you* play in this (change, difference)?"

By assuming that clients have some agency in exceptions that are noted, therapy highlights the control clients may have and invests in this part of the change process.

Scaling

Change is easier when it is removed from the all-or-nothing dichotomy. Learning to move away from "10s" (or perfection) and "0s" (or complete failure or catastrophe) allows both the therapist and the client(s) to succeed at something before the problem is completely solved. Progress on any facet of therapy can be anchored and observed/experienced.

Here are some examples of scaling questions:

- "On a scale from one to ten, with one being 'pretty bad' and ten being 'pretty good,' how would you rate how you're doing now?" (Follow with, "And when you're able to say (the client's response plus one or two), what will be happening differently?"
- "I would like for you to rate your depression (client's word) each day. Mom, I would like for you to rate his depression each day, also. Don't tell each other what your rating is, but keep track of it and we'll talk about it next time."
- "On a scale from one to ten, how bad is your anger (client's word) right now? What would it take for it to get better, say, one or two points?"
- "So your laziness (client's word) has improved from a two to a four. What did you do to move up from two to four in such a short time?"
- "What would it take to get the problem from a five to a six?"

Midsession Break

Most SFBT practitioners take a break, using the time to create a review of the session, create compliments for each client, and form tasks for the time between sessions. Breaks can be physical (leaving the room for a few minutes) and/or temporal (simply asking the client[s] to allow the therapist a few minutes of thought) near the end of a session. The key to useful breaks is to distill the session, highlighting exceptions and complimenting client change, so any and all progress toward goals or skills that may help the client are emphasized. Spanish researcher Mark Beyebach and his colleagues with the European Brief Therapy Association (EBTA) feel that the compliments that follow the break are fundamental; without compliments, Beyebach and his colleagues would not apply the SFBT label to the therapy (Beyebach, 2000).

Suggestions, Experiments, and Tasks

The use of tasks within SFBT seems to be dependent upon the practitioner. de Shazer and Molnar's (1984) tasks are classics. These tasks acknowledge ties to the Mental Research Institute (MRI) although placing less emphasis on covert strategies and more on transparent activities such as noticing/"paying attention" and trying on behaviors as "experiments." Others (including Nelson, 1998; Sharry et al., 2003; Thomas, 1998) continue to develop tasks that are collaboratively constructed and have broad applicability, much like the early SFBT tasks that asked people to flip coins, pretend, and pay attention differently.

CONCLUSION

Perhaps the fundamental shift from being problem- to solution-focused is in how we think about and respond to our clients. All our questions and responses are imbued with a belief in client strengths, skills, and resources. This is not to deny that clients have problems or to minimize their impact on their lives, but rather, it is out of a belief that a reorientation is more helpful (Sharry et al., 2003, p. 7).

SFBT is many things: a movement, a mindset, a worldview, a practice. But most authors in the SFBT circle would agree with Sharry and his colleagues: To adopt Solution-Focused Brief Therapy as one's approach requires more than adding techniques to one's bag of interventions. It is, in the best sense of Kuhn's (1962) use of the word, a paradigm shift from traditional psychotherapy's claim to knowledge, therapist expertise, and interventive practices to a solution orientation that is single-minded in its dedication to client knowledge, client expertise, client competence, and client agency. Without such a worldview shift, one is simply putting new wine into old wineskins.

REFERENCES

American Psychiatric Association. (1994). *Quick reference to the diagnostic criteria from DSM-IV.* Washington, DC: Author.

Anderson, H. (1997). *Conversation, language, and possibilities: A postmodern approach to therapy.* New York: Basic.

Anderson, H. (2005). Myths about "not-knowing." *Family Process, 44*(4), 497-504.

Anderson, H., & Goolishian, H. (1992). The client is the expert: A not-knowing approach to therapy. In S. McNamee & K. J. Gergen (Eds.), *Therapy as social construction* (pp. 25-39). London: Sage.

Asay, T. P., & Lambert, M. J. (1999). The empirical case for the common factors in therapy: Quantitative findings. In M. Hubble, B. Duncan, & S. Miller (Eds.), *The heart & soul of change* (pp. 23-55). Washington, DC: APA.

Bateson, G. (1979). *Mind and nature: A necessary unity.* New York: Dutton.

Berg, I. K., & Miller, S. D. (1992). *Working with the problem drinker: A solution-focused approach.* New York: Norton.

Bertrando, P. (2000). Text and context: Narrative, postmodernism, and cybernetics. *Journal of Family Therapy, 22*, 83-103.

Beyebach, M. (2000, May). *European Brief Therapy Association outcome study: Research definition.* Retrieved December 20, 2004, from http://www.ebta.nu/sfbt-researchdefinition.pdf.

Branon, B. (1994). *Let us prey.* New York: HarperCollins.

Cade, B. (1992). I am an unashamed expert. *CONTEXT: A News Magazine of Family Therapy, 11*, 30-31.

De Jong, P., & Berg, I. K. (2002). *Interviewing for solutions* (2nd ed.). Pacific Grove, CA: Brooks/Cole.

de Shazer, S. (1982). *Patterns of brief family therapy: An ecosystemic approach.* New York: Guilford.

de Shazer, S. (1985). *Keys to solution in brief therapy.* New York: Norton.

de Shazer, S. (1988). *Clues: Investigating solutions in brief therapy.* New York: Norton.

de Shazer, S. (1994). *Words were originally magic.* New York: Norton.

de Shazer, S., & Miller, G. (1998). Have you heard the latest rumor about . . .? Solution-focused therapy as a rumor. *Family Process, 37*(3), 363-377.

de Shazer, S., & Molnar, A. (1984). Four useful interventions in brief family therapy. *Journal of Marital and Family Therapy, 10*, 297-304.

Durrant, M. (1995). *Creative strategies for school problems.* New York: Norton.

Fisher, B. A. (1982). Implications of the "interactional view" for communication theory. In C. Wilder & J. H. Weakland (Eds.), *Rigor and imagination: Essays from the legacy of Gregory Bateson* (pp. 195-209). New York: Praeger.

Garfield, S. L. (1994). Research on client variables in psychotherapy. In S. L. Garfield & A. E. Bergin (Eds.), *Handbook of psychotherapy and behavior change* (4th ed.) (pp. 190-228). New York: Wiley.

Iveson, C. (2005). Teaching the difficult craft of not knowing. *Solution News, 1*(3), 3-5.

Keeney, B. P. (1983). *Aesthetics of change.* New York: Guilford.

Kuehl, B. (1995). The solution-oriented genogram: A collaborative approach. *Journal of Marital and Family Therapy, 21,* 239.

Kuehl, B., Barnard, C., & Nelson, T. S. (1998). Making the genogram solution-focused. In T. S. Nelson & T. S. Trepper (Eds.), *101 more interventions in family therapy.* Binghamton, NY: Haworth.

Kuhn, T. S. (1962). *The structure of scientific revolutions.* Chicago: University of Chicago.

Måhlberg, K., & Sjöblom, M. (2004). *Solution-focused education.* Smedjebacken, Sweden: ScandBook AB.

Nelson, V. (1998). Noticing the difference. In T. S. Nelson & T. S. Trepper (Eds.), 101 *more interventions in family therapy* (pp. 467-470). New York: Haworth.

Nylund, D., & Corsiglia, V. (1994). Becoming solution-focused forced in brief therapy: Remembering something important we already knew. *Journal of Systemic Therapies, 13,* 5-12.

O'Hanlon, W., & Weiner-Davis, M. (1989). *In search of solutions: A new direction in psychotherapy.* New York: Norton.

Peller, J., & Walter, J. (1992/1993). Celebrating the living: A solution-focused approach to the normal grieving process. *Family Therapy Case Studies, 7*(2), 3-7.

Prochaska, J. O., DiClemente, C. C., & Norcross, J. C. (2003). In search of how people change: Applications to addictive behaviors. In P. Salovey & A. J. Rothman (Eds.), *Social psychology of health* (pp. 63–77). New York: Psychology Press.

Quotationspage.com (2005). *Blaise Pascal.* Retrieved April 10, 2005 from http://www.quotationspage.com/quotes/Blaise_Pascal/

Sharry, J., Madden, B., & Darmody, M. (2003). *Becoming a solution detective: Identifying your clients' strengths in practical brief therapy.* Binghamton, NY: Haworth.

Thomas, F. N. (1998). I rewrite with a little help from my friends. In T. S. Nelson & T. S. Trepper (Eds.), *101 more interventions in family therapy* (pp. 134-139). Binghamton, NY: Haworth.

Thomas, F. N. (2007). *Simpler may not be better.* Manuscript submitted for publication.

Thomas, F. N., & Cockburn, J. (1998). *Competency-based counseling: Building on client strengths.* Minneapolis: Fortress.

Thomas, F. N., Durrant, M., & Metcalf, L. (1993, October). *Focusing on solutions in schools and residential settings.* Workshop presented at the American Association for Marriage and Family Therapy annual conference, Anaheim, CA.

Walter, J. L., & Peller, J. E. (1992). *Becoming solution-focused in brief therapy.* New York: Brunner/Mazel.

Wampold, B. E. (2001). *The great psychotherapy debate: Models, methods, and findings.* New York: Lawrence Erlbaum.

Weiner-Davis, M. (1992). *Divorce busting: A revolutionary and rapid program for staying together.* New York: Summit.

Zeig, J. K. (Ed.). (1985). *Ericksonian psychotherapy. Volume I: Structures.* New York: Brunner/Mazel.

Chapter 2

Springs, Streams, and Tributaries: A History of the Brief, Solution-Focused Approach

Brian Cade

We believe that it is useful to think about solution-focused therapy as
a rumor.
It is a set of stories that circulate within and through therapist communities.
The stories are versions of the solution-focused therapy rumor.
While the names of the major characters usually remain stable,
the plots and contexts that organize the action may vary
from one story telling episode to the next.

Miller and de Shazer, 1998, p. 364

INTRODUCTION

I have recently been reading an interesting book with the extremely
modest title, *A Short History of Nearly Everything* (Bryson, 2003). I was
fascinated to find out how many of the well-known originators of ideas or
inventions throughout the history of human endeavour were neither the
only person nor often the first to have come up with either the idea or the in-
vention. Some were oblivious to this fact; some acknowledged it, gra-
ciously or otherwise; some were happy to ignore the work of others or
deliberately to claim sole credit.

Handbook of Solution-Focused Brief Therapy: Clinical Applications
© 2007 by The Haworth Press, Inc. All rights reserved.
doi:10.1300/5135_02

For example, a year before Charles Darwin submitted his manuscript for the now famous *On the Origin of Species,* a draft of a paper was sent to England from the Far East by a young naturalist named Alfred Russel Wallace. It was titled, *On the Tendency of Varieties to Depart Indefinitely from the Original Type.* Its proposals about evolution were very much along the same lines as those of Darwin and based on similar observations. Becoming aware of this paper, Darwin apparently offered to stand aside but, in the end, the ideas of both men were unveiled at the same scientific meeting on 1 July 1858, with neither man being actually present and exciting little interest. Wallace then disappeared into obscurity, becoming increasingly concerned with other and somewhat more arcane pursuits. Darwin's ideas went on to become some of the most influential in history.

However, 20 years earlier, in fact, in the exact year that Darwin had first set sail in the *Beagle,* a Scottish gardener by the name of Patrick Matthew had already come up with a theory of natural selection. He published his ideas as an appendix in a book, which, unfortunately for him, was not widely read. Darwin did later apologise that he had not been aware of this earlier work but, like Wallace, Matthew remained doomed to obscurity (see Bryson, 2003, pp. 338-347).

So, on being asked to give an overview of the history of brief, solution-focused therapy, I approach the task with some considerable trepidation, fearful that a 50-year-old book might soon be about to be rediscovered with the title *Keys and Clues to Putting Words to Difference.* However, I will do my best to be as comprehensive as my current knowledge will allow.

Evolutionist Richard Dawkins tells the following story:

> . . . I taught a young woman who affected an unusual habit. When asked a question that required deep thought, she would screw her eyes up tight shut, jerk her head down to her chest, and then freeze for up to half a minute before looking up, opening her eyes, and answering the question with fluency and intelligence. I was amused by this, and did an imitation of it to divert my colleagues after dinner. Among them was a distinguished Oxford philosopher. As soon as he saw my imitation, he immediately said, "That's Wittgenstein! Is her surname ****** by any chance?" Taken aback, I said that it was. "I thought so," said my colleague. "Both her parents are professional philosophers and devoted followers of Wittgenstein." The gesture had passed from the great philosopher via one or both of her parents to my pupil. I suppose that, although my further imitation was done in jest, I must count myself a fourth-generation transmitter of the gesture. And who knows where Wittgenstein got it? (Dawkins, 1999, p. vii)

In any field, over time, in a similar way, often the springs, streams, and tributaries of influence will be difficult, sometimes impossible to trace. I clearly take full responsibility for the particular twists I will give to the history of what Miller and de Shazer (1998) have called the "solution-focused rumor" and also for any pioneers whose ideas and influence I have unwittingly ignored, leap-frogged over, or distorted.

MILTON H. ERICKSON

It was through BFTC's efforts to apply Erickson's methods and procedures that our approach was developed. . . .

de Shazer, 1982, p. 28

All roads have been said to lead to Rome. When considering any developments within the traditions of brief, interactional, communications-focused approaches to therapy, so many of the ideas seem to lead inexorably back to the brilliant and idiosyncratic work of Milton H. Erickson (Erickson & Rossi, 1979; Erickson, Rossi, & Rossi, 1976; Haley, 1967b, 1973; O'Hanlon, 1987; Rosen, 1982; Rossi, 1980).

Milton Erickson worked from the assumption that people already have, from within their own personal experiences and histories, the resources and areas of competence they need from which to draw in order to surmount their difficulties. He did not operate from and, in fact, sought to avoid developing a clearly articulated theory of personality or of dysfunction, although, in his lectures and writings, he often used the terminology of psychoanalytic thinking. He seemed to work from an implicit theory of therapy, of what helped people to change. Neither did he operate from a deficit model. His main concern was with people's strengths and resources and it was with these that he engaged. He believed that people made the best choices they saw as being available for themselves at any given moment, and that the therapist should listen carefully to and respect all communications from the client. He saw it as the job of the therapist to meet the client in his or her own world rather than to try to work from or to impose elements of the therapist's world.

Erickson was born with a number of handicaps that were to affect him throughout his life. He was colour-blind, tone-deaf, arrhythmic, and dyslexic. Then, at the age of 17, he was almost completely paralysed by polio. In fact, one specific day, three doctors pronounced their doubts that he would live until morning. He overheard them say this and was enraged that his mother should have been told such a terrible thing. He became determined to survive at least that long, insisting to his puzzled mother that she move the dresser in his bedroom so that, through its mirror, he would be able to see the sunrise on the following day. He clearly survived. He could hear acutely, see and move his eyes and, with some difficulty, speak. He was otherwise unable to move and was possibly paralysed for life. Then, one day, he had been sat by his parents, fastened to a rocking chair in the middle of his room, and was looking longingly at the window wishing he could be closer to it.

> As he sat there, apparently immobile, wishing, and wondering, *he suddenly became aware that his chair began to rock slightly.* What a momentous discovery! Was it an accident? Or did his wishing to be closer to the window actually stimulate some minimal body movement that set the chair to rocking? . . . This experience . . . led the 17-year old lad into a feverish period of self-exploration and discovery . . . *exercising the thought or the idea of movement could lead to the actual experience of automatic body movement.* . . . In the weeks and months that followed, Milton foraged through his sense memories to try to relearn how to move. He would stare for hours at his hand, for example, and try to recall how his fingers had felt when grasping a pitchfork. Bit by bit, he found his fingers beginning to twitch and move in tiny, uncoordinated ways. He persisted until the movements became larger and until he could consciously control them. (Rossi, 1983, p. 12)

Over the next year, Erickson slowly and painfully taught his muscles to move, primarily through the process of visualisation. Of vital importance to this process were his observations of his baby sister as she learned to stand and to walk.

> I used to stand up by watching baby sister learn to stand up: use two hands for a base, uncross your legs, use the knees for a wide base, and then put more pressure on one arm and hand to get up. Sway back and forth to get balance. Practice knee bends and keep balance. Move head after the body balances. Move hand and shoulder after the body balances. Put one foot in front of the other with balance. Fall. Try again. (Rossi, 1983, p. 13)

It is clear that Erickson learned a lot about people's abilities to overcome obstacles through his own experiences of having to surmount so many. This was perhaps particularly so because of his having had to relearn, from scratch, at 17, something as fundamental as moving his fingers, then his hands, his legs, then standing, balancing, and finally walking again. This attitude toward people was perhaps one of his most valuable legacies to the future generations of therapists he was eventually destined to influence.

Equally as important as Erickson's legendary genius for constructing brilliant and unpredictable interventions was the profound level of respect he showed for his patients, for their beliefs, for their integrity, and for their capacity to change, however chronic or acute their problems. He tells the story:

> There was one patient who said he was Jesus Christ. He was very paranoid and yet he was harmless and had ground privileges. And Worcester tried to use patients with ground privileges at useful tasks. And the Psychology Laboratory wanted a handyman. And here was this patient, wrapped up in a sheet, walking around communing with God . . . very polite and courteous. And so I was told to do something with him. I told him how desirable it was for doctors to play tennis in the recreation hour. They were using their muscles and skills and abilities that God had endowed them with. And it was imperative that the tennis grounds be kept in good shape . . . dirt court. And we wandered down to the tennis court. We made a lot of comments about the trees that God had made, the beautiful grass, the creations of the earth itself, and then I noticed that there were some rough spots on the dirt court and I told him I was sure that God didn't want those rough spots there and could he in some way succeed in having the tennis ground leveled carefully and smoothed out? He said he certainly would TRY, he was there to serve mankind. So I left him. He was an excellent tennis court grounds keeper. As for the Psychology Laboratory, they wanted some bookcases built. I happened to mention Jesus was a carpenter. So he built the bookcases. He became a handyman around the Psychology Laboratory. (Gordon & Meyers-Anderson, 1981, p. 43)

This story seems to sum up beautifully for me the way Erickson would help clients utilise any aspect of themselves, including symptoms, and their social contexts to move forward from where they were stuck. His influence on the development of the brief approaches was profound. In an interview, videotaped just a few months before his death, John Weakland, a founding member of the Brief Therapy Center, Palo Alto, California, was asked what he had learned from Erickson. He replied,

A great deal. . . . I learned something about paying close attention to clients. I learned something about change being always possible even in what appear to be desperate and fixed and concrete situations; and I learned that it's the business of a therapist essentially to take charge and influence people to make changes in useful directions. . . . It was remarkable to us to see the things that Erickson could get people to do that were different from what they were accustomed to doing. (S. Chaney, personal communication, March 15, 1995)

Lankton and Lankton (1983, p. 12) have drawn up a list of principles underpinning Erickson's approach. These can be seen as implicit in the work of most brief therapists.

People operate out of their internal maps and not out of sensory experience.
People make the best choice for themselves at any given moment.
The explanation, theory, or metaphor used to relate facts about a person is not the person.
Respect all messages from the client.
Teach choice; never attempt to take choice away.
The resources the client needs lie within his or her own personal history.
Meet the client at his or her model of the world.
The person with the most flexibility or choice will be the controlling element in the system.
A person can't not communicate.
If it's hard work, reduce it down.
Outcomes are determined at the psychological level.

Erickson's work has often been presented in ways that have highlighted the skills of "Erickson-the-clever" (de Shazer, 1994, p. 33). This aspect was to have a considerable influence of the tactical and the therapist-skill focus of a generation of therapists and writers about the brief and strategic approaches. However, the influence of Erickson's lack of interest in categories and pathology, and of his profound belief in people's resources and abilities has been perhaps his most enduring legacy.

Other Early Influences

Some of the important roots of brief therapy lie in a ferment of intellectual ideas that arose in the middle of the last century as well as in the practical experiences of therapists' becoming increasingly aware of the influence of the context in which social and psychiatric problems arose and were maintained. Central to the thinking of those early therapists and theoreticians were general systems theory, cybernetics, and, to a lesser degree, information theory and game theory.

> Born from the same tradition, Cybernetics and General Systems Theory—like the Corsican brothers of the tale—were separated at birth. This was accomplished by two equally charismatic and creative characters, Norbert Weiner and Ludwig von Bertalanffy, for reasons more of province than of progeny. Growing up as if not knowing each other, both disciplines evolved with such amazing similarities that the distinction between them seemed to be retained primarily for territorial considerations. (Sluzki, 1985, p. 26)

Systems theory outlined the properties of general systems. Cybernetics was initially concerned with the rules that govern how systems maintain themselves. Central to the development of these ideas was the pioneering work of Norbert Weiner (1948). Cybernetic explanation is negative in that any course of events is said to be subject to *restraints,* which tend to prevent that course of events from moving outside of a particular set of parameters. Thus, having a myriad of patterns—sequences that just kept repeating themselves in general, not necessarily specific, detail.

In 1952, Gregory Bateson was in New York seeking a grant for a research project into the Paradoxes of Abstraction in Communication. He was staying with a former student, John Weakland. As Weakland remembered it,

> He came home one afternoon and said, "I've got a research grant!" I said, "That's nice." And he said, "How would you like to come out to the West Coast and work for me?" Under the circumstances, I said, "Great!" We all went out and had dinner and celebrated. (Lipset, 1980, p. 200)

Joined the following year by Jay Haley and William Fry, they formed a highly creative, prolific, and influential research group, producing many of the early seminal papers in the family therapy field.

The group was very influenced by cybernetic explanation. They studied a wide range of phenomena including, for example, ventriloquism, the training of guide dogs for the blind, films, animal play, humour, hypnosis, schizophrenia, and psychotherapy. At the same time, Don Jackson, a psychiatrist, was developing ideas on the families of schizophrenics as closed systems. He had been significantly influenced in his development by the work of Harry Stack Sullivan (who was interested in interpersonal phenomena, as also were Alfred Adler and Karen Horney, an interest rare with psychoanalysts at that time). Jackson began working closely with the group and subsequently became a member. The group began to look at the multiple channels, each modifying the other, that were involved in communication, with particular reference to families of schizophrenics. Their first publication was the influential paper, *Toward a Theory of Schizophrenia* (Bateson, Jackson, Haley, & Weakland, 1956), which elaborated the double-bind hypothesis and became their first exposition of the interactional view (see also Berger, 1978; Sluzki & Ransom, 1976; Watzlawick & Weakland, 1977).

Toward a Theory of Schizophrenia was particularly important in that it proposed a new way of looking at the relationship between behaviour and communication. As John Weakland later wrote,

> First there was the beginning of a close identification of communication and behaviour, as two sides of one coin, so to speak—that the most important aspect of social behaviour is its communicative effect, and that communication is the major factor in the ordering of behaviour socially. In pursuing these connections, "Toward a Theory" certainly took a one-sided or unidirectional view at important points—for example, in seeing a "binder" imposing a double bind on a "victim." Nevertheless, even if less clearly and explicitly, the article also promoted a view of communication as pervasively and basically interactional—as a system, in which unidirectional attributions and various punctuations occur, but where these (even our own) should be seen only as aspects of the larger system. . . . What is important for understanding is to see the general pattern of communication, not specific events or messages, however dramatic or striking, in isolation. (Weakland, 1976, p. 311)

It was of considerable concern to Weakland that many who were influenced by *Toward a Theory* concerned themselves with reductionist hunts for pathological elements (whether they were trying to prove or to refute the double bind hypothesis) rather than concentrating on larger recurring patterns and seeing the hypothesis as advancing a new language. As he saw it, they thus missed the whole point. As the group were to explain in a subsequent but sadly often overlooked note several years later,

The most useful way to phrase double bind description is *not* in terms of a binder and a victim, but in terms of people caught up in an ongoing system which produces conflicting definitions of relationship and consequent subjective distress. (Bateson, Jackson, Haley, & Weakland, 1963, p. 59)

There was a time when many were pointing back to the work of Gregory Bateson as the inspiration behind the development of their ideas and approaches. It had long been a puzzle and source of frustration to me that so many in our field seem drawn to the mystical and the incomprehensible, whether it be the complexities of Bateson's writings, Maturana's tautological assertions, or, more recently, the philosophical complexities of postmodernism. I one day asked Jay Haley what he thought was the most important contribution Bateson had made toward family therapy. He replied that it was finding the money to send John Weakland and him to spend time with Milton Erickson on a couple of occasions each year. I was further relieved and my morale much lifted when I finally confessed to John Weakland that I had trouble understanding Bateson. He replied that the rest of the project had also had trouble understanding what Bateson was on about much of the time, but that he was good at supporting and encouraging people to work at and follow their ideas through.

The project's earlier researches concentrated on dyadic communication. Later, both Weakland and Haley proposed that the minimum unit of observation should be three people, which might include the therapist (Haley, 1967a; Weakland, 1960).

A further development was a move away from viewing participants in such triangles as villains or victims toward assuming that each was doing the best they could, given the way they saw things, arising from their life experiences, and from the circumstances in which they found themselves. As Fisch and his colleagues were later to comment:

. . . people often persist in actions that maintain problems inadvertently, and often with the best of intentions. . . . They follow poor maps very carefully, and this is quite expectable for people who are understandably anxious in the midst of difficulties. Belief in such maps also makes it hard to see that they are not serving as effective guides. . . . (Fisch, Weakland, & Segal, 1982, pp. 16-18)

In 1958, Don Jackson founded the Mental Research Institute (MRI) in Palo Alto, a centre for both developing and researching the clinical implications of the interactional view. The project was concerned with developing ways to intervene effectively into the patterns of interaction between people rather than trying to change what was hypothetically going on inside of a person.

Don Jackson died unexpectedly in 1968 at the age of 48. His contribution to the field of brief therapy and family therapy was significant, and yet little has been written about his work and its influence on the subsequent development of the field. A charismatic person, he was a highly gifted clinician who saw the patient/client as a ". . . family-surrounded individual with real problems in the present day" (Jackson, 1967, p. 32). His focus was always on the relationships between people rather than on hypothesised characteristics of the individual members, and on what was observable rather than inferable.

COMMUNICATION IN THERAPY

Is the glass half empty or is it half full?

Bavelas and colleagues cite a paper by Davis (1986) in which Davis,

> . . . analysed an entire first therapy session, turn by turn, and showed how the therapist, over the course of the session, transformed the presenting problem into a problem that fit his theory. If one were to read the transcript Davis provided with a bias toward his particular therapeutic approach, the interview would seem an insightful discovery of the client's problem by the therapist. Examined more closely, however, the active influence of the therapist becomes clear. Davis showed how, in three stages, the therapist *reformulated* the client's social, situational problem into an intrapsychic, personality problem; *documented* the new problem using his interpretations of the client's own words; and *organized her consent* to treatment of the newly defined problem. (Bavelas, McGee, Phillips, & Routledge, 2000, p. 54)

Bavelas and her colleagues differentiate between two fundamentally different approaches to the therapy process. On the one hand are those traditions in therapy conversations that essentially shape the therapy process toward identifying pathology and particularly move it toward the therapist's theories about problems and about solutions. On the other hand, they refer to an alternative paradigm in which the therapeutic conversation is focused implicitly and explicitly on client strengths and resources.

Bavelas and her co-authors (2000) highlight three discursive tools used by therapists; these are *formulations, questions,* and the exercise of choice over how to phrase them (*lexical choice*). *Formulation* is where a participant in any conversation "... may describe, explain, characterize, explicate, translate, summarize, or furnish the gist of what the other has just said" (p. 56). They follow Heritage and Watson's (1979) proposition that formulations can serve three functions: to *preserve, delete,* or *transform* the original statement. Therapists of Bavelas' first tradition (therapist identifies pathology) tend to preserve, delete, or transform in such a way that pathology is accentuated and their theories confirmed. Those of the second tradition (focus on client strengths) tend to formulate such that the client's past successes, their strengths and resources, and their ideas are highlighted. Obviously, the choice of which questions are asked and how they are asked will also be influential in which aspects of the client and client story are pulled into focus and given importance and which are rendered invisible and discounted.

As I have suggested elsewhere, "It is impossible to avoid influencing any interactions that we are directly involved in, albeit unconsciously, through the whole range of vocal and non-vocal channels of communication through which information is exchanged" (Cade, 1994, p. 14). All of the questions we ask as well as the questions we do not ask, our facial expressions, our changes in posture and gesture, our breathing patterns, and so on, over the subtle levels of which we have little or no control, can steer a client or family unconsciously and sometimes inexorably in the direction of our prejudices and concerns and our hypotheses, even when we truly believe we are being nondirective.

Alan Wade (2000) drew a useful distinction between approaches that operate from the assumption of personal deficiency and approaches that operate on the assumption of preexisting ability. Within this latter tradition, Bavelas and her colleagues list the Palo Alto group and those groups with a specific interest in communication and language as being central to psychotherapy that have built on those early beginnings. These include the original and subsequent Milan schools, solution-focused therapy, and White and Epston's narrative therapy (although, sadly, in their recent writings, the narrative approach seems to have chopped itself off from these origins).

There have been varied and sometimes heated debates over the similarities or otherwise between the solution-focused and the narrative approaches, including a conference debate between Steve de Shazer and Michael White. It is my view that, at the diagnostic level, there are profound differences. The narrative movement is tied in, at times almost evangelically, with a range of political and social explanations for the development of problems. The solution-focused approach is not concerned with explanations of any kind, including political, although its adherents may well have strong political opinions (often similar to those of the narrative practitioners). At the practice level, there is clearly a family resemblance between "unique out-comes" and "exceptions" in that they focus on times the client or family has handled the problem more effectively.

The difference is partly one of style. Narrative therapists build an iso-lated instant into a major celebratory event, a "sparkling moment"; the solu-tion-focused therapist sees an exception as unremarkable in that they happen all the time and thus will tend to highlight them in a way that sug-gests the therapist would expect no different. However, a more profound difference is the way that unique outcomes are used as part of the "cheer-leading" process of building up the client(s)' resources for his, her, or their battle against the problem. This is externalised and then imbued often with the most ominous and Machiavellian of characteristics to be endlessly guarded against. This not only focuses on or even builds up the problem but also keeps its existence ever present. I remember Mara Selvini Palazzoli, some time in the early 1990s, over breakfast one morning in a café in Heidelberg, likening the notion of externalization to the medieval notion of demons. In contrast, a focus on exceptions is part of a process of bypassing any need to define the problem at all (unless the client wishes to) but to look toward solutions, including times when these have already been happening, often unnoticed by clients. (This will be considered later in a section titled *Figure and Ground.*) However, I suppose both approaches can be seen as coming under the general umbrella of what Wade called the approaches that operate from *the assumption of preexisting ability.*

STRATEGISTS AND TACTICIANS

As I have commented elsewhere,

> I was once asked by Lynn Hoffman how I had arrived at my Marx Brothers style of therapy. I explained that I was on the road to Damas-cus one day when a green book called *Strategies of Psychotherapy* [Haley, 1963] fell out of the sky and hit me on the head. The freshness of Jay Haley's way of thinking about therapy, his questioning of "sacred cows" and the introduction of the "uncommon therapy" of Milton Erickson had a profound influence on me, as it did on so many. (Cade, 1999, p. 196)

In those earlier days, strategies and tactical thinking were the stuff of un-derground conversations and of an increasing volume of papers describing clever therapists and brilliant interventions. However, a fundamental, un-derpinning belief was nevertheless in evidence *that the client already had the necessary strengths to surmount difficulties.* The therapist's job was to unlock, not to cure.

In 1977, in his wonderful but sadly not-well-remembered book *Strategic Therapy: Brief and Symptomatic Treatment,* Richard Rabkin chose to write his opening chapter about the client's contribution to therapy. He used the evocative analogy of "stone soup" from an old Russian story.

> As the cook, the only ingredient you provide is a stone. To make this remarkably nutritious and filling soup you boil the stone in a pot of water. Then you suggest to your guests that, although it would taste fine as it is, it would be even better if they happened to have an onion they could donate, as well as some parsley, tomatoes, meat, and so on. By the time you are done you can serve them, to their amazement and your credit, a remarkably good meal of stone soup. (p. 15)

In the current climate, we, and perhaps he, would now probably wish to change the words "to their amazement and your credit" into "to your amazement and their credit"; however, this *was* written back in 1977. Even in perhaps my own, arguably most self-indulgent, early paper in which I described paradoxical manoeuvres in terms of such breathtaking therapeutic brilliance that Ernest Hemmingway might have been inspired immediately to have rushed to his typewriter, I ended the chapter with the following codicil about the approach: "It requires optimism about the capacity of people to change even the most seemingly entrenched of symptomatic behaviours" (Cade, 1979, p. 104). Back then, many of us wrote articles seeking to demonstrate our skills at helping bring about dramatic change. With the wisdom of hindsight, we can be criticised for that. However, my experience of the majority of my now aging brief therapy colleagues was this was more a side effect of an excess of enthusiasm and a genuine wish to help people change than some kind of self-enhancing power trip. However, as Steve de Shazer commented to me in an interview in 1985,[1]

BRIAN: One of the concerns that is increasingly preoccupying people in Britain, and it may be so here, it's the ethics of using certain techniques, particularly those defined as paradoxical.

STEVE: We have found that there is no need to invent some of those tricky things, the deceptive things that some of us used to do in the past. Our fancy techniques are now all above board and we are using material given to us by the family. In fact, looking back, I guess that all those techniques came from the families we worked with. I think the concerns that some people have, have arisen out of the way we authors wrote about what we were doing, and we wrote about it in such a way that it might not recover. If we had written it differently we could have said, "Look, my, ain't those clients clever!!"

BRIAN: Yes, when I look back at some of the tricky things we have done, they weren't totally ethical in that sometimes deception was used, for example, about what was happening behind the mirror. At the time, it seemed the only way to break through a particular deadlock, and those interventions sometimes were very effective in relieving entrenched symptoms. But, with hindsight, it's possible to see another way. At times, we became caught up in our own cleverness. (Cade, 1985, p. 97)

I still have many videotapes of my work and some of the work of John Weakland from those heady days in which we primarily focused on the tactical skills of the therapist. When I look back at them through the lens of more current thinking, I am struck with how much attention we paid even then to client strengths and achievements, although, in those days, we tended to call it positioning and positive reframing or positive connotation. In a paper in 1979 titled *Brief Therapy with Families,* de Shazer demonstrated the use of balance theory in work with families in which it is clearly the therapist who decides how to intervene; there nevertheless is a definite focus on family strengths.

> When the therapist returns to the room, he or she should compliment the family in some way. He may praise them for the amount of information they felt comfortable enough to share. Furthermore, he/she and the group may compliment the family for having tried so hard to solve the problem. He/she may praise the family for their detailed report on a complex situation, or . . . the therapist may praise the family for having decided on family therapy which he/she and the group agree might be helpful. (Cited in Cade, 1985, p. 88)

THE BRIEF THERAPY CENTER, PALO ALTO[2]

The Central Philosophy of Brief Therapy

1. If it ain't broke, don't fix it.
2. If it doesn't work, don't do it again. Do something different.
3. Once you know what works, do more of it.

The Brief Therapy Center was set up in 1966 within the Mental Research Institute, Palo Alto, California, primarily at the initiative of Dick Fisch, and included John Weakland and Paul Watzlawick. This group had a profound effect on the subsequent interest in and rapid development of the brief approaches throughout the world (Fisch, Weakland, & Segal, 1982; Ray & de Shazer, 1999; Watzlawick, 1978; Watzlawick & Weakland, 1977; Watzlawick, Weakland, & Fisch, 1974; Weakland, Fisch, Watzlawick, & Bodin, 1974; Weakland & Ray, 1995). John Weakland described the origins of the brief therapy project as follows:

> To my mind we only had two or three basic ideas, which led to everything else. One, of course, was that we would work as a group. One person would be the therapist; the others would observe, and then everything would be recorded and discussed. . . . But the two main principles that I think were responsible for the directions we took within that framework were one, that we would focus on the client's main presenting complaint and *stick to it;* not try to look around it or behind it or beneath it but stick to what's the main presenting complaint. And the other thing was that, by that time, we realised that it was not so easy to get people to change. So . . . we would try anything that we could think of that was legal or ethical regardless of whether it was conventional, or a long, long way from conventional thinking. I think things just grew out of that. (S. Chaney, personal communication, March 15, 1995)

It is difficult nowadays, with the use of teams, one-way mirrors, and video recorders being so commonplace, to appreciate how revolutionary this procedural approach was at the time. Particularly revolutionary was the decision to remain tightly focused on what the client defined as the problem, making no assumptions about the existence of "deeper," underlying issues or of the function of symptoms. The group proceeded to elaborate an approach to therapy that evolved out of the direct observation of the process of trying to help people change and from the detailed analysis of recordings of therapy sessions. No nonprovable assumptions were evoked or used. They took care not to stray too far from pragmatics, from what could be unequivocally observed and clearly described. This stood in considerable contrast to other models prevalent at the time where the therapeutic approach arose out of the dictates of the tenets of sometimes quite complex theories. One of this group's most influential ideas was the notion that problems develop from and are maintained by the way that, under certain circumstances, particular, and often quite normal, life difficulties become perceived and subsequently tackled. Guided by reason, logic, tradition, or "common sense," various attempted solutions are applied (which can include a denial of the difficulty), which either have little or no effect or, alternatively, can exacerbate the situation. A problem then becomes entrenched as *more of the same* solutions or classes of solutions become followed by *more of the same* problem, attracting *more of the same* attempted solutions, and so on . . . A vicious circle develops and the continued application of "wrong" or inappropriate solutions that lock the difficulty into a self-reinforcing, self-maintaining pattern can be seen as becoming the problem. Therapy is focused on changing the "attempted solutions," on stopping or even reversing the usual approach, however logical or correct it appears to be. The assumption is that once the feedback loops maintaining the problem are changed, a greater range of responses become available.

When asked what he thought was the most important thing a therapist had to learn, John Weakland replied,

> It's going to sound dreadfully simple, but it is also very difficult to do consistently; and that is *really* listen to what the client says and how they say it; really listen which means a number of things. One of the main things it means is, don't get into the business of being so perceptive that you know what the client says or means better than the client does . . . it is very hard to do. . . . I am afraid that a lot of training is about being perceptive and I think it is very dangerous. It is much more important to listen.

Much attention was paid by this group to the positioning of the therapist: What attitude would maximise the likelihood of clients' moving forward? They discovered that a cautious, one-down position on the part of the therapist was the best default position. John Weakland, when asked about his favourite intervention, remarked that he did not like to look at therapy in those terms, but that if there was one thing he did regularly because it seemed to have very wide applicability, it was, ". . . in some way or another to advise the client to go slow" (S. Chaney, personal communication, March 15, 1995). (To be grammatically accurate, he should have said, "Go slow*ly*.") I see this as very much the precursor to the solution-focused emphasis on clients' moving up just one place on a scale.

It was seen as important for the therapist never be more enthusiastic than a client about the need for therapy or about a particular outcome for therapy. People will only change in ways for which they themselves are customers. Often, a client can remain unenthusiastic about working on the goals of the people who have brought or sent them but develop alternative goals of their *own* that they are prepared to work toward. For example, young persons sent by a teacher because of disruptive behaviour in the classroom may show no interest in changing for the teacher but may well develop an interest in finding ways of getting the teacher off their backs. Persons believed to be anorexic are unlikely to want to put on the weight that referrers want them to but may be prepared to work toward getting the energy for completing their university assignments. People labeled "problem drinkers" or "alcoholics" may have little motivation for working on drinking habits but be quite concerned about losing jobs, in relation to which goal they may draw their own conclusions about the need to cut back on alcohol consumption.

The pragmatic effect of trying to change others, if they themselves are ambivalent about that change, is often to produce counter arguments in that person to the attempts. You can actually watch it happening in front of you. As research into persuasion techniques has shown,

> . . . individuals are active participants in the persuasion process who attempt to relate message elements to their existing repertoires of information. In so doing, these individuals may consider materials that are not actually contained in the persuasive message. These self-generated cognitions may agree with the position advocated by the source or they may disagree. Insofar as the communication elicits favorable cognitive responses, attitudes should change in the direction advocated by the source. To the extent that the message evokes unfavorable mental reactions, attitude change in the direction advocated by the source should be inhibited. (Perloff & Brock, 1980, p. 69)

Pragmatically, influencing somebody is limited by the fact that self-generated arguments are far more influential than arguments produced by others, and it appears that the more arguments are self-generated in favour of a position, the more likely it is that position will persist. It also appears that, when considering a series of persuasive messages, people remember with more clarity their own thoughts and their own arguments than the messages themselves (whether they were in favour of or against those messages). As Deborah Tannen (1991), a professor of linguistics, suggested,

> Much—even most—meaning in conversation does not reside in the words spoken at all, but is filled in by the person listening. Each of us decides whether we think others are speaking in the spirit of different status or symmetrical connection. The likelihood that individuals will interpret someone else's words as one or the other depends more on the hearer's own focus, concerns, and habits than on the spirit in which the words were intended. (p. 37)

The pragmatic effect of adopting a "not-knowing" stance in a validating relationship is often that clients seem to become more creative in considering their own options. As Milton Erickson observed, having already influenced the then fledgling brief therapy movement toward the regular adoption of the stance many years before its recent reinvention, "Not knowing and not doing are of particular value in trance work when we wish to evoke the patient's own individuality in seeking the best modality of therapeutic response" (Erickson & Rossi, 1979, p. 25).

The pragmatic effect of trying to control is usually to invoke compliance or defiance (neither of which represents a therapeutic change). And as for the ethics of control, as Erickson expressed unequivocally to a seminar in Seattle in 1965,

> Now, do you control patients? I don't think you do. I don't think you should even try. You ought to talk to patients; you ought to analyze their behaviors; and then you ought to wonder what you can do to help them. I try to utilize their behaviors in a helpful, constructive way because certainly I am not qualified to control their behavior . . . You do not work with patients to achieve your own goals. . . . I haven't got the right to force my standards, whether lower or higher, on any patient. (Erickson, 1983, p. 272)

BRIEF FAMILY THERAPY CENTER, MILWAUKEE

> From out of the soil of Wisconsin were born Spencer Tracey, Georgia O'Keeffe, Thornton Wilder, Harry Houdini, Liberace. And then . . .

Among the increasing number of professionals who began to have contact with the Brief Therapy Center in the late 1960s and early 1970s were Steve de Shazer and Insoo Kim Berg, who were to become so influential in the development of the solution-focused approaches. In fact, I understand that it was John Weakland who put the two of them in touch with each other and so can take, to some extent, either the credit or the blame for what followed. de Shazer wrote of the earlier influence on him of the work of Milton Erickson and of Jay Haley's (1963) groundbreaking book, *Strategies of Psychotherapy*:

> Until I read this book, as far as I can remember, I had never even heard the term, "psychotherapy." Certainly, this was the first book on the topic that I read. I enjoyed it perhaps more than any other "professional book" I'd read in philosophy, art history, architecture, or sociology. So, I went to the library and looked at its neighbors.

I was shocked. I was unable to finish any of the others I tried to read: After *Strategies*—which made so much sense to me—everything else was (poorly written) nonsense until I found *Advanced Techniques of Hypnosis and Therapy* [Haley, 1967b], which is a selection of Milton H. Erickson's papers. It is not going too far to say that these two books changed my life and shaped my future. Unlike so many other "professional books," the books by Erickson and Haley were well written. They were clear. (I then read everything else they had written and I followed their references to other authors and other articles and books.) Among other things, these books implicitly and indirectly (at times) suggested many of the themes that would form my career, including the idea of "brief therapy." (de Shazer, 1999, p. 2)

The Brief Family Therapy Center was set up in Milwaukee in 1978. As de Shazer commented,

Insoo and I and a group of our colleagues—who had been working together (secretly) for many years—decided to set up an independent "MRI of the Midwest" where we could both study therapeutic effectiveness, train therapists to do things as efficiently as possible, and, of course, practice therapy. (de Shazer, 1999, pp. 2-3)

The original Milwaukee group, in addition to Steve de Shazer and Insoo Kim Berg, included James Derks, Marvin Weiner, Elam Nunnally, Eve Lipchik, Alex Molnar, and Marilyn La Court. Over the next few years, the membership of the team was continually to evolve. Among later members who also made contributions were Wallace Gingerich, Michele Weiner-Davis, John Walter, Kate Kowalski, Ron Kral, Gale Miller, Scott Miller, and Larry Hopwood.

In the early days, the group was using a problem-focused model essentially similar to that of the Palo Alto Brief Therapy Center. In the early 1980s, they became increasingly interested in what clients were already doing on their own to solve problems and in clients' own ideas about what needed to be changed, about how things could be different, and what it would take to bring about such changes. A focus on the description of solutions rather than on a clarification of problems and failed solutions led quickly to the realisation that it was not necessary to know much about the problem or its origins, assuming these could ever reliably be established, to begin the process of change. They began to see the clients as the experts in their own lives.

There are those who differentiate between the MRI brief therapy approach and the solution-focused approach by defining the former as problem focused. I would profoundly disagree with this position. Clearly, there are differences in techniques (as well as many overlaps), but I would see both as essentially similar in that they are primarily focused on the future and on client resilience and resources. Bavelas and her colleagues (2000) cited a personal communication from John Weakland in which he described how the Palo Alto brief therapy project quickly rejected the usefulness of pathology and started working from the assumption that "people know how to be well" (p. 55). I believe the differences to be but a matter of emphasis. As de Shazer and Berg pointed out (1995, p. 252), following their discovery that clients often had many examples of times their complaint/problem did not occur, they changed the order of the central philosophy of brief therapy to,

1. *If it ain't broke, don't fix it.*
2. *Once you know what works, do more of it.*
3. *If it doesn't work, don't do it again. Do something different.*

KEYS TO SOLUTION:
THE WIZARD OF OZ TECHNIQUE

STEVE: We now believe that interventions need only fit the constraints of the problematic situation much as a skeleton key fits a lock.

BRIAN: People usually associate each lock with having its own unique key. So the idea of the skeleton key is presumably an important one?

STEVE: Yes. You don't need to know the precise nature of a lock to use a skeleton key, and a fairly small bunch of skeleton keys is all that is needed to be able to open a vast range of locks to help people get on with their futures—and that's how you judge your effectiveness; if the key works and you can open the door.

BRIAN: So that means that, in therapy, you don't have to be so concerned with ascertaining the precise nature of the problem?

STEVE: Correct. There are cases in which you can do the whole therapy without needing to know what the problem or complaint is. It is sometimes useful to have some ideas about how the client perceives the problem in order to know how to frame interventions but, theoretically, it is not necessary.

BRIAN: Your approach seems very similar, in some ways, to that of Milton Erickson, in that he believed that people have a vast reservoir of abilities and that therapy was not a process of putting something into people, or replacing deficiencies, but of unlocking what is already available to them.

STEVE: Absolutely. We call this the *Wizard of Oz Technique*. We don't give them anything that they haven't already got. For instance, to give you one example, a couple came in and I asked the husband what it was that had brought them here. He said that some of their fights led to physical violence. I turned immediately to the wife and asked what happens when they don't. We spent the rest of the session talking about what happens when they don't get physically violent with each other. I never found out about the fight pattern; I've no idea who got violent with whom.

BRIAN: Which, traditionally, a therapist would be primarily concerned with finding out; who did what, and to whom, and how often, etc.

STEVE: Including me, four or five years ago.

BRIAN: So you are particularly concerned with what people are already doing well. When people come into therapy, they have usually become preoccupied with what is going badly and are not aware of the many things that they are also doing quite competently.

STEVE: Yes; most of the time. (Cade, 1985, p. 96)

In 1984, de Shazer and Molnar outlined a first-session task that was routinely being given to clients regardless of the nature of the presenting problem.

> Between now and the next time we meet, we (I) want you to observe, so that you can tell us (me) next time, what happens in your (life, marriage, family, or relationship) that you want to continue to have happen. (de Shazer & Molnar, 1984, p. 298)

They discovered that, in a significant number of cases, concrete changes occurred between the giving of this task and the following session.

> With surprising frequency (fifty out of fifty-six in a follow-up survey), most clients notice things they want to have continue and many (forty-five of the fifty) describe at least one of these as "new or different." Thus, things are on the way to solution; concrete, observable changes have happened. (de Shazer et al., 1986, p. 217)

Moshe Talmon described how, working in a medical health center, he would give a suggestion similar to de Shazer's first session task to patients during the initial phone contact while a first appointment was being set up (Talmon, 1990, p. 19). Weiner-Davis, de Shazer, and Gingerich (1987) found that, in a significant proportion of cases, significant changes frequently seemed to occur prior to the first appointment even where no such suggestion had been offered. They would ask the following question: "Many times, people notice in between the time they make the appointment for therapy and the first session that things already seem different. What have you noticed about your situation?" (p. 306).

In *Keys to Solution in Brief Therapy,* de Shazer (1985) described the development of further "formula interventions" through which, it was argued, the process of building solutions could be started. He invoked the analogy of a skeleton key in that, with just one skeleton key, a whole range of different locks can be opened without the need to find the exact key that will fit the exact shape of each and every lock.

Molnar and de Shazer (1987, p. 355) elaborated a list of these formula interventions:

1. Client is asked to do more of the behaviors, which are satisfactory and different from the problem behavior.
2. Client is asked to "pay attention to what you do when you overcome the temptation or urge to . . ." (Perform the symptom or some behavior associated with the symptom).
3. Client is given a prediction assignment such as whether in the time between sessions there will be more instances of behavior that are an exception to the problem behavior.
4. Client is told, "Between now and the next time, I (we) would like you to do something different and then tell me (us) what happened."
5. Client is asked to do a structured task (such as keeping a log of certain incidents) which is related to those times when the problem behavior ceases or is not present.
6. Client is told, "The situation is very (complicated, volatile, etc.). Between now and the next time, attempt to identify why the situation is not worse."

The common theme with each of these interventions is that they are concerned with and focus the client and the process of therapy on what has worked, is working, or is beginning to work, rather than with exploring or categorizing pathology. They operate from an assumption that change is inevitable and that people are already bringing it about or have all that is necessary to do so. The group continued to seek clearer and more precise descriptions of the essence of what it takes to be therapeutic: *What works?* On the way, they dropped those assumptions, ways of thinking, or of intervening that they discovered to be unnecessary or unhelpful. Many of these latter included assumptions and approaches that are often seen as of central importance in many other approaches (e.g., clear problem definition, hypothesizing, and diagnosis).

BRIAN: I would like to change direction and talk about how your team functions. One thing that has particularly struck me is the unstructured, almost random, way in which your team seems to work. You often have two, three, or four interviews going on at the same time, and team members walk in and out of the various observing rooms, sometimes going off to do something different, sometimes wandering in just before the end of a session. The interviewer might go into the interviewing room with a particular person or group behind the mirror yet, when he or she comes out later for a consultation, a different person or group may be there, or nobody at all.

STEVE: That's true. You use a team, or don't use a team. The client or family is introduced to the idea, unless there are trainees around so that there are definitely going to be observers, that there may or may not be someone behind the mirror. I won't know until I go out there to find out.

BRIAN: So the family, at any point, doesn't know whether there is someone there or not?

STEVE: There might or there might not, regardless of which we will still take a break. We go out to develop an intervention, on our own or with a consultant or team.

BRIAN: Or it might be with someone who happens to be walking through the room at that moment?

STEVE: Right. And then we will go back and say either that there was or that there wasn't somebody back there.

BRIAN: Some people would say that this is a distracting way to work, destroying continuity, and destroying concentration. How the hell can you help with a family if you have only just walked in!

STEVE: Well, we've tried the other way. Obviously, one problem for us is that we are a private agency and have to make our bucks. However, we've tried many times to have a consistent team for certain cases and have found that we get stuck more when we work that way than with having someone just "popping in" behind the mirror. It provides us with a fresh view without any of the bias that we may have developed during the first half hour of the interview. So we consider it a virtue that Alex Molnar, for example, might pop in for a few minutes of a session, lay out some crazy idea, and then leave; but he leaves his idea behind.

BRIAN: So Alex may react to something he sees going on for which he has no frame, no prejudices, no preconceived diagnostic formulations. The others in the teams will already have begun to develop a kind of tunnel vision.

STEVE: Right. You saw me last night wandering around watching bits of three different cases. If I get bored with one, I can shift to the next one. Suddenly you can find yourself reacting to a small segment of an interview and coming up with a crazy idea that turns out to be useful.

BRIAN: What do you mean by a "crazy" idea?

STEVE: Crazy meaning not fitting the content within which things are currently being defined and explored by the client/therapist system. (Cade, 1985, pp. 96-97)

Insoo Kim Berg told a story from the early 1980s of being stuck with a client who had become overwhelmed with her problems. Her children were out of control and her husband was on the brink of being dismissed from his job because of his heavy drinking. Insoo asked her how she thought the session could help and the woman replied, "I'm not sure; I have so many problems. Maybe only a miracle would help, but I suppose that's too much to expect." Insoo asked the woman, "Okay, suppose a miracle did happen and the problem that brought you here is solved?" To Insoo's amazement, this woman, who had seemed so overwhelmed and unable to go on, began describing a vision of a different life. She said that her husband would be "more responsible, keeping his job, and managing the money better." She said her children would "follow rules at school and at home, doing their chores without putting up such a fuss." And, most of all, she said that she would be different: "I will have more energy, smile more, be calmer with the children—instead of snapping at them—talk to them in a normal tone of voice. I might even start having normal conversations with my husband, like we used to when we first were married" (De Jong & Berg, 2002, p. 77).

From then on, the team at the Brief Family Therapy Center began using what came to be called *the miracle question* with more and more of their clients. Over the past 15 years or so, it has been used in nearly every case.

I once declared that Milton Erickson was a plagiarist but was more cunning than most—he would plagiarize ideas about 30 years ahead of time. It seems to me almost impossible to do anything that he has not either done or at least in some way anticipated years ago. As Margaret Mead (1977) once wrote, "It can be firmly said that Milton Erickson never solved a problem in an old way if he can think of a new way—and he usually can" (p. 4).

Why is this relevant? Well, in 1954, Erickson published a paper in which he described several cases where he had used hypnosis to orientate patients *forward* in time and invited them to hallucinate watching themselves in the future and commenting on the changes they see in themselves. Amnesia would then be suggested to the hypnotic experience. In the cases described, the patients returned to a later appointment having made significant inroads into their problems. As Erickson suggested,

> This technique was formulated by a utilization of the general appreciation that practice leads to perfection, that action once initiated tends to continue and that deeds are the offspring of hope and expectancy. These ideas are utilized to create a therapy situation in which the patient could respond effectively psychologically to desired therapeutic goals *as actualities already achieved.*
>
> This was done by employing hypnosis and using, conversely to age regression, a technique of orientation into the future. Thus, the patient was enabled to achieve a detached, dissociated, objective, and yet subjective view of *what he believed at the moment he had already accomplished* (emphasis added), without awareness that those accomplishments were the expression in fantasy of his [*sic*] hopes and desires. (Erickson, 1954, p. 261)

I believe the miracle question is a highly effective way of doing something very similar but without the use of a formal hypnotic trance. Interestingly, a young brief therapist named Steve de Shazer wrote an article in 1978 in which he described the successful use of this same technique with eight cases. So, I imagine when Insoo's client invented the technique, it straight away found itself in extremely fertile soil.

In 1988, with his next book, *Clues: Investigating Solutions in Brief Therapy,* de Shazer summarised the basic principles behind and techniques used in the solution-focused approach that have since then been its essential features (de Shazer, 1988). More recently (de Shazer & Berg, 1997, p. 123), these characteristic features have been summarised as follows:

1. At some point in the first interview, the therapist will ask the "Miracle Question."
2. At least once during the first interview and at subsequent ones, the client will be asked to rate something on a scale of "0-10 or "1-10."
3. At some point during the interview, the therapist will take a break.
4. After this intermission, the therapist will give the client some compliments which will sometimes (frequently) be followed by a suggestion or homework task (frequently called an experiment).

de Shazer's later books (1991, 1994) and a number of books by Insoo Kim Berg, either as sole or as co-author further elaborated on the use of these ideas in different settings (e.g., Berg, 1994; Berg & Miller, 1992; Berg & Reuss, 1998; De Jong & Berg, 2002). There also are a growing number of books written by people who were members of or were influenced by the Milwaukee group. These authors include (although this is by no means an exhaustive list) Dolan (1991), Durrant (1993), Miller and associates (1997; Miller, Hubble, & Duncan, 1996), Jacob (2001), Jackson and McKergow (2002), Thomas and Cockburn (1998), and Turnell and Edwards (1999).

The approach has been critiqued as ignoring power differentials and being prey to what Hare-Mustin (1987) described as *"beta prejudice—neglecting difference."* The approach is criticised because, with respect to gender and power differentials, ". . . there is still no mechanism built into the framework of the solution-focused model to systematically deal with these issues" (Dermer, Hemesath, & Russell, 1998, p. 249). This is a difficult and sometimes an emotive issue. The solution-focused approach is basically a way of asking questions and formulating summarising-responses such that a client's agenda predominates and is addressed. It is not an explanatory model and thus is not a basis for defining how things are or should be in the world, or for making pronouncements about what should be the focus of any therapy session. I would certainly endorse the view that all therapists should be aware of political and social issues and be alert for their relevance (which can only be defined by the client) in therapy sessions, but making such pronouncements is beyond the purview of the solution-focused approach (Lipchik, 2002; Berg & Steiner, 2003; Lee et al., 2003; Nelson, 2005; Turnell & Essex, 2006; Macdonald, 2007).

WHO WANTS WHAT?

The customer is always right.

The Brief Therapy Center, Palo Alto paid close attention to who wants help, with what, and for whom, as well as asking the question, "why now?" Much of what is often seen as "resistance" in a client is the result of a therapist's failing to clarify whether somebody is a customer or not or, when she is a customer, and/or failing to clarify and respect exactly what it is that she is a customer for. Trying to "sell" something to a client who is *currently* not interested in buying anything or something other than what she has come in to buy tends not to work. It is thus important to establish at the beginning whether it is the client's concerns or the concerns of some other person(s) that have led to her being there. If the client is there because of her own concerns, then the therapy can proceed with the job of establishing what those concerns are and what needs to happen for the session to be useful. When a client comes to therapy because of the concerns of others, a respectful acknowledgement by the therapist that she is there initially out of her own choice can often lead to the beginning of a productive discussion (which might then lead to the development of an agenda for therapy or to a joint decision not to proceed). A case example:

THERAPIST (T): What brings you here?

CLIENT (C): My doctor thought it would be useful for me to come and talk about some things.

T: Did you agree with him or her that it might be useful?

C: I don't know.

T: What do you think your doctor hoped would happen by your coming here and talking?

C: He thinks I need grief counselling to help me get over the death of my mother.

T: Do you agree with him?

C: I don't know. I don't like to talk about it. (*pause*) I don't know if I want to.

T: When did she die?

C: About a year ago.

T: What do you think makes him think that you need grief counselling?

C: Well, I've been depressed and not been sleeping too well, and I burst into tears at the slightest thing. I've not been able to work since I broke down earlier this year.

T: And the doctor feels that this is related to the death of your mother?

C: I guess so.

T: Do you agree?

C: I suppose it could be.

T: Were you close to her?

C: Very. (*Client looks tearful*)

T: So, your doctor feels that talking about your mother's death might be helpful?

C: I guess so.

T: What difference is he hoping that talking about it will make?

C: Well, ultimately, that I might get off of these antidepressants and even be able to go back to teaching. I used to be a primary school teacher.

T: Do you want to go back to teaching?

C: Yes, I'd like to feel that I could.

T: So what would need to start happening differently in your life so that you could say, maybe not today but in a couple of weeks or so, "I'm glad I took the doctor's advice and went to see that therapist?"

C: If I could just wake up one morning and find that I'm actually looking forward to the day.

T: Suppose that happened. What would be the most likely small but significant thing you would start looking forward to?

C: Just something simple like going out for a walk and having a morning coffee in Eastwood. Perhaps, meeting up with my friend. I've been putting off calling her for weeks, now.

T: What else?

This woman agreed to a second appointment and eventually came for a series of sessions with the goal of gradually increasing the number of things she was doing each day that it would be possible for her to look forward to on waking up. Apart from briefly acknowledging the important role her mother had played in her life and her profound sadness about her death, very little time was spent on issues to do with grief (which is not to say that the issue of grief was not important, nor that the woman did not have grief issues to work through; grief was just not what *she* wanted to work on in therapy).

At times, a therapist can become too clearly identified with the arguments in favour of a particular change, especially, for example, when operating on the behalf of an agency with statutory powers and responsibilities. Whether that urgency is explicitly or implicitly communicated, the therapist can become the main "customer" for how a client should be or for what a client should do. It then becomes as though the therapist has colonised the arguments in favour of that change, leaving available to the client only the counterarguments to the change together with the accompanying affect produced by those counterarguments. The perceived rights and wrongs of the therapist's view of how things *ought to be* are irrelevant if the pursuit of those ends has the effect of disempowering the client, increasing "resistance," or further entrenching attitudes.

LANGUAGE AND FIGURE/GROUND

As a thing is viewed, so it appears

The Tibetan Book of the Great Liberation
(Evans-Wentz, 1969)

Brief therapy and solution-focused therapy developed within the tradition of the constructivist and constructionist thinking of the interactional view. Within these theories, in seeking to describe, understand, and explain human behaviour, there is no one reality "out there" available for objective analysis. There are as many realities as there are observers or groups of observers. Reality, in terms of the way it is experienced and reacted to, is constructed out of the way that each individual perceives, divides up, makes sense of, allocates meaning to, *and talks about* his or her world. This in turn is embedded in and powerfully affected by the negotiations about reality that continually evolve in the interactions between people from the level of dyad, family, kinship, and friendship networks; through larger and larger communities of (and means of) connection, including local, national, and international social, political, and knowledge systems; up to the instant global reach of the media and the worldwide community(ies) of the Internet.

Language is clearly the primary medium through which such realities are negotiated and, in every area of discourse and at all levels of discourse, ways of using language develop that both reflect and transmit the needs and the essences of that particular area of discourse. Particular clusters of words and phrases and ways of using them tend to be favoured and take on meanings or shades of meaning relevant to the context. The philosopher Ludwig Wittgenstein evoked the term "language game" to highlight the way that the meaning of words stands not in a fixed relation between each word and some aspect of reality that it denotes but in a local convention of usage that varies from context to context and is dependent on the spirit within which they are being used. Different language games would be used in, for example, an attempt at seduction, negotiating a loan with a bank manager, union–employer bargaining, gossiping with a neighbour, discussing a scientific theory, and engaging in an act of communal worship. Each would clearly be conducted in a different manner and the words used would be chosen and would take on conventions of meaning and association relevant to the activity and the traditions and customary expectations of those involved. We cannot move outside of language, so, in the same way that a fish can be seen as being unaware that it is in water, we can remain unaware of the particular language game in which we are immersed because it is so familiar to us. As an example of how a word can have a meaning within but be relatively meaningless outside of a "language game,"

> Take the word "good." What is common between a good joke, a good player, a good man, feeling good, good will, good breeding, good looking, and a good for nothing? There is no one common property, which the word *good* refers to. We cannot analyse the word so that we reach some essence or element from which the concept is built up. . . . But there are resemblances between the various meanings of the term. . . . The circumstances in which the words are used give the clue. Specificity does not belong to the *experience* but to the *language game* which enables us to talk about or express our desires, intentions, meanings, etc. . . . Meaning depends on articulation rather than representation. What is specific is always a function of the language game and can only be articulated within it. (Heaton & Groves, 1994, pp. 127-129)

In any field toward which our attention is drawn, certain aspects of that field will stand out in a figure/ground relation to other aspects. Which aspects of the field become figure and which become ground will relate to our expectations of the situation and to our current and most pressing preoccupations and intentions. These will also both be affected by and affect the language games through which we customarily operate. Discussing figure/ground phenomena in a chapter on perception, Adcock (1964, p. 142) commented that ". . . detail is observable in the portion regarded as figure whereas the background tends to be rather homogenous."

> A friend of mine, many years ago, bought a Victorian drawing, which was a rather skillfully executed reversible figure/ground picture of the type frequently used in works on the psychology of perception. The picture could be seen either as a naked young woman or as a collection of gaunt human skulls. The friend had only seen the former figure and was unable to see the latter until some time after it was pointed out. He was looking absentmindedly at it several days later when suddenly he was able to see the skulls for the first time. Clearly, in such a drawing, the emergence of either subject depends on two totally different interpretations of which lines and which areas of shade constitute the figure against which all of the rest then goes to make up the ground. The two subjects cannot exist simultaneously for any one observer (although they can rapidly be alternated between, once you have developed the hang of it). (Cade & Hudson O'Hanlon, 1993, p. 27)

Troubled people tend to see and remember those aspects of their lives that confirm their problem-saturated sense of themselves or each other, which thus stand out as the figure against which everything else becomes the ground. Also, whether seen as residing in the individual, the family, or in any other system, problems tend to be the focus of considerable preoccupation by the symptom bearer, his or her intimates, and often of other systems—legal, medical, school, psychotherapeutic, neighbourhood, work, and so forth. These preoccupations will be embedded in family, community, or professional language games that consist of explanatory frameworks, affective responses, and behaviours for dealing with the problem and its various effects. This will mean that particular events and attributes associated with problems will stand out as figure against which other possibilities will become ground. As the problem becomes embedded, it is as though a gestalt develops in which certain behaviours and beliefs, attitudes, and responses are continually being highlighted and repeated, and thus reinforced within an interlocking web of language games.

There is an ever-burgeoning number of models of therapy (one recent estimate puts the number as more than 250) with differing ways of explaining the development of problems; the relationship between problems and past, present, or future aspects of people's lives or their inner and outer worlds; and with sometimes widely differing ideas as to what is the proper focus of attention for the therapist and the therapy. Each approach will have its own language game and, whilst there may well be "family resemblances" between the games, it cannot be assumed, from approach to approach, that terms used in common have the same meanings and carry the same implications. Many a primary worker with a case will be familiar with the feeling of total confusion and even of paralysis that can follow the experience of discussing their client(s) in a multiagency, multidisciplinary case conference.

Miller and de Shazer (1998) differentiated between the language games that are involved in creating stories about problems as opposed to those that are concerned with helping clients construct stories about solutions. The former tend to focus on deficits and the past, on what is wrong, and to become part of a discourse that constructs and maintains a problem. The latter tend to focus on client resources available for constructing solutions and on what is possible, to emphasize what can be defined as already working, and also tend to be future-focused. In many of the former, it is also assumed that there is a direct correspondence between things and events and the words that are used to describe them: he *is* depressed; she *has* a personality disorder; this cluster of symptoms *confirms* a diagnosis of schizophrenia; this family *is* dysfunctional. The latter would show no interest in such categorization and would see such labels as saying as much if not more about the categoriser than about the categorised.

Miller and de Shazer also differentiate between the language games used when therapy is seen as a job to be done, defined by what the client specifically seeks help with, and evaluated in terms of whether it effectively does that job for the client, as opposed to those language games in which therapy is linked to an overarching explanatory theory, an ideology, or a cause such that the client is encouraged to view himself or herself differently in relation to personal, political, social, or cultural patterns identified as important by the therapist. Solution-focused therapy, with its primary concern with therapist attitudes and behaviours associated with most rapidly and effectively bringing about the sought for (by them) changes in clients' lives, clearly falls within the former group.

APPLICATIONS AND OUTCOME STUDIES

Over the last decade or so, the solution-focused approach has grown rapidly throughout the world and is used in a wide range of settings. From early on, it began to be used in residential settings and in schools. It is used in mental health settings, in public social services agencies, in hospitals, in the probation service and prisons, and in child welfare. It is used with groups, as an approach to supervision, and in institutional or business consultations. It has been used with child and adolescent problems, domestic violence, survivors of sexual abuse, drug and alcohol problems, mental illness, the physically handicapped, marital problems, multiproblem/multiagency families, the problems of aging, eating disorders, adoptive families, and family medicine. This is, of course, by no means an exhaustive list. For a continually updated list of publications (now over 1,000 items), readers are referred to Patrick Triggiano's comprehensive compilation titled, *The Solution Papers Revisited: A Compilation of the Beginning, Integration, and Ever Expanding Guide to Solution-Focused Publications,* available on the Internet at www.talkingcure.com/solutionfocused.htm.

Over the years that it has been developing the approach, the Brief Family Therapy Center has systematically followed up its clients by contacting them at between 6 to 18 months and asking whether they felt they had achieved their treatment goals or, at least, made significant progress toward them. Results have consistently shown between 70 and 80 percent answering in the affirmative (de Shazer et al., 1986; De Jong & Hopwood, 1996; Kiser, 1988). However, such subjective and uncontrolled studies, whilst providing useful early indicators, do not have the necessary rigour to allow statements that are more conclusive about the effectiveness of the approach.

There are now increasing numbers of outcome studies being published, many of them using a similar design to those mentioned earlier and reporting varied levels of effectiveness. However, in a conference paper given in April of 1999, Wallace Gingerich (an early member of the Milwaukee group) and Sheri Eisengart reported on a more recent substantial rise in controlled studies (see the following list). They identified 15 such studies, 7 of which assert that,

> SFBT (solution-focused brief therapy) equaled or surpassed the outcomes of standard treatment. SFBT sometimes produced better outcomes, and sometimes produced comparable outcomes in less time. Only one study (Littrell et al., 1995) failed to report any positive outcomes for SFBT. . . . The fifteen studies included a wide range of modalities, ranging from the individual and family therapy, to group, consultative, supervisory, and network interventions. Five of the six studies that employed individual or family therapy of two or more session duration, the modality most consistent with the original form of SFBT, had positive outcomes. However, studies that used indirect interventions such as consultation or supervision had a comparable success rate. Most of the studies used real-world clinical populations, and client problems ranged all the way from common mental health problems, to school functioning, self-sufficiency, delinquent behaviour, and work hardening. This represented an unexpectedly wide range of application of SFBT.
>
> We also find it interesting that in all but one of the studies (Lambert et al., 1998), the SFBT intervention appeared to be implemented by relatively inexperienced therapists, in many cases, just newly trained. In psychotherapy research generally, experienced therapists tend to get better results than inexperienced therapists. (Gingerich & Eisengart, 1999)

However, Gingerich and Eisengart referred to the lack of proceduralization, lack of evidence of treatment integrity, and the fact that over half of investigators were advocates of solution-focused brief therapy as important reasons for caution. They comment that, whilst ". . . providing promising evidence . . . [n]one of the studies meet accepted standards for empirically validated treatments."

Nevertheless, as Gingerich and Eisengart pointed out,

> That fifteen studies have appeared in so short a time is rather remarkable for an intervention approach that has been in existence for less than twenty years. It is all the more remarkable when one considers that SFBT (solution-focused brief therapy) evolved out of a clinical context, not a quantitative research context, and that all of the published studies were carried out by investigators outside the original Milwaukee group. (Gingerich & Eisengart, 1999)

CONCLUDING THOUGHTS

I have seen brief and solution-focused approaches used in respectful ways that have helped clients find their own answers, or to take suggestions that have fit for them, and I have seen them used disrespectfully and unhelpfully. I have seen the "not-knowing," reflectively questioning, and "non-expert" stance help clients, and I have seen it frustrate and anger them. I have seen complex, detailed, therapist-engendered tasks help clients to change, and I have seen them fail totally. I have seen reflecting teams used in ways that have validated and helped, and have seen them operate in a stilted way with all the authenticity of a seven-dollar note, leaving clients totally mystified. I have seen an eminent narrative therapist powerfully persuade a family to adopt a new story about itself with very little evidence of "co-creation" (but it seemed to be helpful for the family and so I have no problem with it, only with the therapist's denial of the use of influence). And I am talking of these approaches being used by eminent people in the field, including by their acknowledged originators (I have also, at one time or other, done all of these things myself).

Ultimately, doing our job well in the eye of the only important beholders (our clients, the only ones who can, ultimately, decide) seems to me to depend less on our adherence to "correct" models or approaches or philosophical stances, but much more to the nuts and bolts of the pragmatic effects of our interactions with them. If, after talking with us, they are influenced and persuaded through the course of the dialogue to change for the better (in their eyes), whether it be by what *we* thought, said, or suggested or by what *they* thought, said, or decided (or whether by what they or we *thought* that they or we said or heard, regardless of what was *actually* said or heard, assuming that could ever be reliably remembered or interpreted), then we have done our part of the job, whatever way we have done it.

DEDICATION

This chapter is dedicated to John Weakland, mentor and friend. In March 1995 in Saratoga, California, I was privileged to play a part in the last professional gathering John attended before he died. At the meeting was Jay Haley, another survivor of the Bateson group, Dick Fisch, and Paul Watzlawick, John's colleagues for so many years at the Brief Therapy Centre, and many others. It was a moving occasion. He was clearly ill, yet he stubbornly stayed the course and contributed fully with a typical economy of words, clarity of thought, and humour. His final advice to following generations of therapists was, "Stay curious!"

NOTES

1. From Cade, B. W. (1985). The Wizard of Oz approach to brief family therapy: An interview with Steve de Shazer. *The Australian and New Zealand Journal of Family Therapy, 6,* 95-97. Used with permission of the editors.

2. Parts of the remainder of this chapter are adapted from the following works:

Cade, B. (2001). Building alternative futures. In S. Cullari (Ed.), *Counseling and psychotherapy* (pp. 182-216). Boston: Allyn and Bacon. Adapted by permission of the publisher.

Cade, B. W. (1996). Towards a one-and-a-halfth order practice: Rehabilitating pragmatics. *Journal of Family Therapy, 18,* 243-248. By permission of the publisher, Blackwell Publishing.

REFERENCES

Adcock, C. J. (1964). *Fundamentals of psychology.* Harmondsworth, Middlesex: Penguin Books.

Bateson, G., Jackson, D. D., Haley, J., & Weakland, J. H. (1956). Toward a theory of schizophrenia. *Behavioral Science, 1*(4), 251-264.

Bateson, G., Jackson, D. D., Haley, J., & Weakland, J. H. (1963). A note on the double bind—962. *Family Process, 2,* 154-161.

Bavelas, J. B., McGee, D., Phillips, B., & Routledge, R. (2000). Microanalysis of communication in psychotherapy. *Human Systems: The Journal of Systemic Consultation and Management, 11*(1), 47-66.

Berg, I. K. (1994). *Family based services: A solution-focused approach.* New York: Norton.

Berg, I. K., & Miller, S. D. (1992). *Working with the problem drinker: A solution-focused approach.* New York: Norton.

Berg, I. K., & Reuss, N. H. (1998). *Solutions step by step: A substance abuse treatment manual.* New York: Norton.

Berg, I. K. & Steiner, T. (2003). *Children's solution work*. New York: W. W. Norton.

Berger, M. M. (Ed.). (1978). *Beyond the double bind*. New York: Brunner/Mazel.

Bryson, B. (2003). *A short history of nearly everything*. London: Doubleday.

Cade, B. (1979). The use of paradox in therapy. In S. Walrond-Skinner (Ed.), *Family and marital psychotherapy: A critical approach* (pp. 99-105). London: Routledge & Kegan Paul.

Cade, B. W. (1985). The Wizard of Oz approach to brief family therapy: An interview with Steve de Shazer. *The Australian and New Zealand Journal of Family Therapy, 6*, 95-97.

Cade, B. W. (1994). Treating the house like a hotel: From simile to metaphor. *Case Studies in Brief and Family Therapy, 8*(1), 5-14.

Cade, B. (1999). Taking humour seriously: Monty Python-focused therapy. In W. Ray & S. de Shazer (Eds.), *Evolving brief therapies: In honor of John H. Weakland* (pp. 195-208). Iowa City, IA: Geist & Russell.

Cade, B., & Hudson O'Hanlon, W. (1993). *A brief guide to brief therapy*. New York: Norton.

Davis, K. (1986). The process of problem (re)formulation in psychotherapy. *Sociology of Health and Illness, 8*, 44-74.

Dawkins, R. (1999). Foreword. In S. Blackmore, *The meme machine*. Oxford: Oxford University Press.

De Jong, P., & Berg, I. K. (2002). *Interviewing for solutions* (2nd ed.). Pacific Grove, CA: Brooks/Cole.

De Jong, P., & Hopwood, L. E. (1996). Outcome research on treatment conducted at the Brief Family Therapy Center, 1992-1993. In S. D. Miller, M. A. Hubble, & B. L. Duncan (Eds.), *Handbook of solution-focused brief therapy* (pp. 272-298). San Francisco: Jossey-Bass.

Dermer, S. B., Hemesath, C. W., & Russell, C. S. (1998). A feminist critique of solution-focused therapy. *The American Journal of Family Therapy, 26*, 239-250.

de Shazer, S. (1978). Brief hypnotherapy of two sexual dysfunctions: The crystal ball technique. *The American Journal of Clinical Hypnosis, 20*(3), 203-208.

de Shazer, S. (1979). Brief therapy with families. *The American Journal of Family Therapy, 7*(2), 83-95.

de Shazer, S. (1982). *Patterns of brief family therapy: An ecosystemic approach*. New York: Guilford.

de Shazer, S. (1985). *Keys to solution in brief therapy*. New York: Norton.

de Shazer, S. (1988). *Clues: Investigating solutions in brief therapy*. New York: Norton.

de Shazer, S. (1991). *Putting difference to work*. New York: Norton.

de Shazer, S. (1994). *Words were originally magic*. New York: Norton.

de Shazer, S. (1999). *Beginnings*. Retrieved February 10, 1999 from www.brief_therapy.org.

de Shazer, S., & Berg, I. K. (1995). The brief therapy tradition. In J. H. Weakland & W. Ray (Eds.), *Propogations: Thirty years of influence from the Mental Research Institute* (pp. 249-252). Binghamton, NY: Haworth.

de Shazer, S., & Berg, I. K. (1997). "What works?" Remarks on research aspects of solution-focused brief therapy. *Journal of Family Therapy, 19*(2), 121-124.

de Shazer, S., Berg, I. K., Lipchik, E., Nunnally, E., Molnar, A., Gingerich, W., & Weiner-Davis, M. (1986). Brief therapy: Focused solution development. *Family Process, 25*(2), 207-222.

de Shazer, S., & Molnar, A. (1984). Four useful interventions in brief family therapy. *Journal of Marital & Family Therapy, 10*(3), 297-304.

Dolan, Y. M. (1991). *Resolving sexual abuse: Solution-focused therapy and Ericksonian hypnosis for adult survivors.* New York: Norton.

Durrant, M. (1993). *Residential treatment: A cooperative, competency-based approach to therapy and program design.* New York: Norton.

Erickson, M. H. (1954). Pseudo-orientation in time as a hypnotherapeutic procedure. *Journal of Clinical and Experimental Hypnosis, 2,* 261-283.

Erickson, M. H. (1983). *Healing in hypnosis.* New York: Irvington Publishers.

Erickson, M. H., & Rossi, E. L. (1979). *Hypnotherapy: An exploratory casebook.* New York: Irvington Publishers.

Erickson, M. H., Rossi, E. L., & Rossi, S. I. (1976). *Hypnotic realities: The induction of clinical hypnosis and forms of indirect suggestion.* New York: Irvington.

Evans-Wentz, W. Y. (Ed.). (1969). *The Tibetan book of the great liberation.* Oxford: Oxford University Press.

Fisch, R., Weakland, J. H., & Segal, L. (1982). *The tactics of change: Doing therapy briefly.* San Francisco: Jossey-Bass.

Gingerich, W. J., & Eisengart, S. (1999, April). *Solution-focused brief therapy: A review of the outcome literature.* Research presentation at the International Family Therapy Association, Akron, Ohio.

Gordon, D., & Meyers-Anderson, M. (1981). *Phoenix: Therapeutic patterns of Milton H. Erickson.* Cupertino, CA: Meta Publications.

Haley, J. (1963). *Strategies of psychotherapy.* New York: Grune and Stratton.

Haley, J. (1967a). Toward a theory of pathological systems. In P. Watzlawick & J. H. Weakland (Eds.), *The interactional view* (pp. 31-48). New York: Norton.

Haley, J. (Ed.). (1967b). *Advanced techniques of hypnosis and therapy: Selected papers of Milton H. Erickson.* New York: Grune and Stratton.

Haley, J. (1973). *Uncommon therapy: The psychiatric techniques of Milton H. Erickson.* New York: Norton.

Hare-Mustin, R. T. (1987). The problem of gender in family therapy theory. *Family Process, 26,* 15-27.

Heaton, J., & Groves, J. (1994). *Wittgenstein for beginners.* Cambridge: Icon Books.

Heritage, J., & Watson, R. (1979). Formulations as conversational objects. In G. Pasathas (Ed.), *Everyday language: Studies in ethnomethodology* (pp. 123-162). New York: Irvington.

Jackson, D. D. (1967). Aspects of conjoint family therapy. In G. H. Zuk & I. Boszormenyi-Nagy (Eds.), *Family therapy and disturbed families* (pp. 28-40). Palo Alto, CA: Science and Behaviour Books.

Jackson, P. Z., & McKergow, M. (2002). *The solutions focus: The simple way to positive change.* London: Nicholas Brearly.

Jacob, F. (2001). *Solution focused recovery from eating disorders.* London: BT Press.

Kiser, D. J. (1988). *A follow-up study conducted at the Brief Family Therapy Center of Milwaukee, Wisconsin.* Unpublished manuscript.

Lambert, M. J., Okiishi, J. C., Finch, A. E., & Johnson, L. D. (1998). Outcome assessment: From conceptualization to implementation. *Professional Psychology: Research and Practice, 29*(1), 63-70.

Lankton, S., & Lankton, C. (1983). *The answer within: A clinical framework of Ericksonian hypnotherapy.* New York: Brunner/Mazel.

Lee, M. Y., Sebold, J., & Uken, A. (2003). *Solution-focused treatment of domestic violence offenders: Accountability for change.* New York: Oxford University Press.

Lipchik, E. (2002). *Beyond technique in solution-focused therapy: Working with emotions and the therapeutic relationship.* New York: Guilford.

Lipset, D. (1980). *Gregory Bateson: The legacy of a scientist.* New Jersey: Prentice Hall.

Littrell, J. M., Malia, J. A., & Vanderwood, M. (1995). Single-session brief counseling in a high school. *Journal of Counseling and Development, 73*(4), 451-458.

Macdonald, A. (2007). *Solution focused therapy: Theory, research and practice.* London: Sage.

Mead, M. (1977). The originality of Milton Erickson. *American Journal of Clinical Hypnosis, 20*, 4-5.

Miller, G. (1997). *Becoming miracle workers: Language and meaning in brief therapy.* New York: Aldine de Gruyter.

Miller, G., & de Shazer, S. (1998). Have you heard the latest about . . .? Solution-focused therapy as a rumor. *Family Process, 37*(3), 363-377.

Miller, S. D., Hubble, M. A., & Duncan, B. L. (1996). *Handbook of solution-focused brief therapy.* San Francisco: Jossey-Bass.

Molnar, A., & de Shazer, S. (1987). Solution-focused therapy: Toward the identification of therapeutic tasks. *Journal of Marital and Family Therapy, 13*, 349-358.

Nelson, T. S. (Ed.) (2005). *Education and training in solution-focused brief therapy.* Binghamton, NY: Haworth Press.

O'Hanlon, W. H. (1987). *Taproots: Underlying principles of Milton H. Erickson's therapy and hypnosis.* New York: Norton.

Perloff, R. M., & Brock, T. C. (1980). ". . . And thinking makes it so": Cognitive responses to persuasion. In M. E. Roloff & G. R. Miller (Eds.), *Persuasion: New directions in theory and research* (pp. 67-99). Beverly Hills: Sage Publications.

Rabkin, R. (1977). *Strategic therapy: Brief and symptomatic treatment.* New York: Basic Books.

Ray, W. A., & de Shazer, S. (Eds.). (1999). *Evolving brief therapies: In honour of John H. Weakland.* Galena, IL: Geist and Russell.

Rosen, S. (1982). *My voice will go with you: The teaching tales of Milton H. Erickson, M. D.* New York: Norton.

Rossi, E. L. (Ed.). (1980). *The collected papers of Milton Erickson.* New York: Irvington Publishers, Inc.

Rossi, E. L. (1983). Milton H. Erickson: A biographical sketch. In M. H. Erickson (Ed.), *Healing in hypnosis: The seminars, workshops, and lectures of Milton H. Erickson* (pp. 1-59). New York: Irvington Publishers.

Sluzki, C. (1985, May-June). A minimal map of cybernetics. *The Family Therapy Networker, 9*, 26.

Sluzki, C. E., & Ransom, D. C. (Eds.). (1976). *Double bind: The foundation of the communicational approach to the family.* New York: Grune & Stratton.

Talmon, M. (1990). *Single session therapy.* San Francisco: Jossey-Bass.

Tannen, D. (1991). *You just don't understand: Women and men in conversation.* Sydney: Random House Australia.

Thomas, F. N., & Cockburn, J. (1998). *Competency-based counseling: Building on client strengths.* Minneapolis: Fortress.

Turnell, A., & Edwards, S. (1999). *Signs of safety: A solution and safety oriented approach to child protection.* New York: Norton.

Turnell, A., & Essex, S. (2006). *Working with "denied" child abuse: A resolutions approach.* Buckingham: The Open University Press.

Wade, A. (2000). *Resistance to interpersonal violence: Implications for the practice of therapy.* Unpublished doctoral dissertation, University of Victoria, Victoria, Canada.

Watzlawick, P. (1978). *The language of change: Elements of therapeutic communication.* New York: Basic Books.

Watzlawick, P., & Weakland, J. H. (Eds.). (1977). *The interactional view.* New York: Norton.

Watzlawick, P., Weakland, J. H., & Fisch, R. (1974). *Change: Principles of problem formation and problem resolution.* New York: Norton.

Weakland, J. (1960). The "double-bind" hypothesis of schizophrenia and three-party interaction. In C. E. Sluzki & D. C. Ransom (Eds.), *Double bind: The foundation of the communicational approach to family therapy* (pp. 23-37). New York: Grune and Stratton.

Weakland, J. H. (1976). The double bind theory by self-reflexive hindsight. In C. E. Sluzki & D. C. Ransom (Eds.), *Double bind: The foundation of the communicational approach to the family* (pp. 307-314). New York: Grune & Stratton.

Weakland, J. H., Fisch, R., Watzlawick, P., & Bodin, A. (1974). Brief therapy: Focused problem resolution. *Family Process, 13*(2), 141-168.

Weakland, J. H., & Ray, W. A. (Eds.) (1995). *Propagations: Thirty years of influence from the Mental Research Institute.* New York: The Haworth Press, Inc.

Weiner, N. (1948). *Cybernetics of control and communication in the animal and the machines.* New York: Wiley.

Weiner-Davis, M., de Shazer, S., & Gingerich, W. J. (1987). Building on pretreatment change to construct the therapeutic solution: An exploratory study. *Journal of Marital and Family Therapy, 13*, 359-363.

Chapter 3

Miraculous Knowing: Epistemology and Solution-Focused Therapy

Duane R. Bidwell

INTRODUCTION

It was a question that I, like most clinicians who practice some version of solution-focused therapy, had asked hundreds of times: "In the morning, when you wake up, how will you know the miracle has happened?"

But there had never been a reply like this.

"What do you mean, 'know'?" Kyle asked, cocking his head like a schnauzer hearing a rat in the wall. "I mean, how does anyone 'know' anything? Don't we just rationalize things in a way that makes sense to us and then call that 'knowing'? What if I 'knew' the miracle had happened but my girlfriend didn't—what difference would my 'knowing' make then?"

Today, I might have some useful therapeutic responses to that question; in the moment, I took a deep breath and cursed the karma that led a twenty-something graduate student to seek therapy with me. But in the days and weeks that followed, Kyle's question began to seem increasingly legitimate: When we speak of "knowing" in solution-focused therapy, what exactly do we mean?

Contemporary philosopher Esther Lightcap Meek (2003) defines knowing as "the responsible human struggle to rely on clues to focus on a coherent pattern and submit to its reality" (p. 13). This struggle shapes not only how we perceive reality, but also our responses to the realities we perceive. Thus, our understandings of "knowledge" and ways of "knowing"—murky or clear, thought-full or thoughtless—are at the heart of psychotherapy. As

Handbook of Solution-Focused Brief Therapy: Clinical Applications
© 2007 by The Haworth Press, Inc. All rights reserved.
doi:10.1300/5135_03

healing professionals concerned with change and meaning in human lives, our assumptions about "knowing"—its nature, characteristics, and limitations—carry serious implications for clinical practice.

Consider, for example, the following questions: In creating solutions and evaluating progress toward goals, should the therapeutic process privilege the knowing of the therapist, of the counselee, or of the therapeutic relationship? Does knowledge of difference originate from concrete experiences in the "real world," from thoughts and ideas that bubble up from within individuals apart from "real world" experiences, or from a combination of the two (or, perhaps, from none of the above)? Do we, as therapists, need hard empirical evidence—the absence of depressive symptoms, a recent paycheck stub, fewer arguments—to know that a change has occurred in a counselee's life? Or do we accept a counselee's reasonable argument, or affective sense, that things are better—"We still fight all the time, but I just feel happier knowing he will call me when he's running late"—even though things seem to us as chaotic as ever? How can we know that the changes our counselees report are "true"? How do we keep from being wrong about our assessment—which is nothing more or less than what we think we know—of a particular case?

You will not find hard-and-fast answers to such questions here. My more modest goal is to clarify and categorize some assumptions about knowledge that have informed the theory and practice of solution-focused therapy—to identify, in other words, particular prejudices (in the philosophical sense) that may shape a solution-focused practitioner's response to such questions. This will require me to articulate some of the criteria that solution-focused therapists rely on when they assess and critique—both formally during theoretical reflection and "on the fly" during therapy sessions—particular claims of knowledge in particular situations, especially claims of knowledge that emerge during therapeutic conversations.

In doing so, I am not attempting to describe the "real" understanding of knowledge that informs solution-focused therapy. In fact, I question whether it is possible—and even if possible, whether it would be useful—to identify a precise philosophical perspective on knowledge that exactly matches or explains solution-focused therapy. Rather, I am providing an account of how knowing unfolds in solution-focused work—a general description that fits some of the ways in which solution-focused theorists and practitioners understand, approach, and make use of "knowledge" in the therapeutic process.[1] In shaping an account that fits, I hope to make possible new understandings (and misunderstandings) of solution-focused therapy and how it works in relation to "knowing"—thus adding one more (largely fabricated but nonetheless truthful) detail to the solution-focused rumor (Miller & de Shazer, 1998) that continues to circulate through the helping professions.

THINKING ABOUT KNOWING: A HISTORICAL SUMMARY

We are concerned in this chapter with theories of knowledge. In the discipline of philosophy, theories of knowledge are called epistemology—literally, "words about knowing." These theories describe the possibility, origins, character, development, and limits of human knowledge. In its oldest usages, the idea of episteme (knowledge) refers to "an organized body of theoretical knowledge" and/or "a body of demonstrable truths about the essences of things" (Philosophy Pages, 2003). Philosophers have sought for thousands of years to develop a comprehensive epistemology; here I want to attend briefly (and, by necessity, with much less richness than the subject deserves) to aspects of modern and postmodern epistemology that inform my account of solution-focused knowing.

In general, Western cultures have tended toward a bipolar approach to theories of knowledge, partly in response to the cultural shifts of the seventeenth and eighteenth centuries that many people call "the Scientific Revolution" and "the Enlightenment." On the one hand is the rationalism/idealism characterized by Rene Descartes, for whom the origins of knowledge could be traced to innate truths in the human mind. For Descartes and other rationalists/idealists, knowledge may precede experience. On the other hand is the positivism/empiricism/realism characterized by John Locke (1995, 1698), whose *An Essay Concerning Human Understanding* introduced the concept of the human mind as tabula rasa, a blank slate on which the world gradually imprints itself. Locke argued that all knowledge comes from experience; no thought can occur until sparked by an event.

Both of these orientations have a primary criterion for justifying claims of knowledge; one relies on evidence, the other on reason. Yet, both place the locus of knowledge within the individual human mind—a central assumption of the modernist, positivist-empiricist worldview.

From a modernist perspective, the individual is valued over and against the group, and the individual mind is understood as a mirror accurately reflecting the contents of the world. The "real," the "good," and the "true" can, from this perspective, be objectively identified and accurately described by an individual using reason, evidence, and logic. At the same time, "absolute reality" cannot be seen plainly; it is not overtly evident but hidden behind appearances. Thus, as John Shotter (1993) writes,

> A very special power resides in the nature of reflective or theoretical thought: it can penetrate through the surface forms of things and activities to grasp the nature of a deeper "form of order," an underlying order from which all human thought and activity *must* in fact spring. (p. 24, emphasis original)

This perspective can be called structuralism, the idea that what we observe (and what we know) reflects an underlying structure or essence.

By the middle of the twentieth century, however, a seismic intellectual shift began to deconstruct the primary assumptions of modernist epistemology. The "turn to language" in philosophy, initiated in part by the later work of Wittgenstein (e.g., 1974), sought the origins of knowledge in intersubjective, or relational, processes. From this perspective, all knowledge is context dependent; it originates neither in an isolated mind nor from the experiences of an individual, but from the particularities of human interaction. Thus, meaning and knowledge are aspects of an interpretative process, negotiated by participants in discourse. Knowledge does not emerge from within an individual, flowing out to influence the world, but materializes in the space between people, being simultaneously situated in, generated by, and generative of human relationships. Shotter (1984) calls this process "duality of structure."

Wittgenstein's concept of "language games" articulates this understanding of knowledge (de Shazer, 1994; Watzlawick, Weakland, and Fisch, 1974; Wittgenstein, 1974; see also de Shazer, 1988). For Wittgenstein, words did not have "meanings," fixed and essential definitions that represent or refer to concrete "things" in the world. Rather, words have "uses," and the uses of a word—and thus its meanings—are established by the rules of the particular language game, or conversation, in which the word is brought into play. In this view, the meanings of language are rhetorical and responsive to circumstance (Shotter, 1993). In the conversation that opened this chapter, for example, I asked, "How will you know the miracle has happened?" with the implication that "know" has either a concrete, given, and unchanging meaning or at least a clear, shared use for the counselee and me. But the counselee called the meaning of "know" into question. This signaled that we needed to negotiate a shared use of the word, a use particular to our conversation and governed by the rules of our therapeutic/academic language game.

This postmodern shift—from viewing knowledge and language as fixed, universal, and representing and referring to real things and the structures behind them, to viewing knowledge and language as negotiated, particular, and rhetorical-responsive—profoundly influenced the forbearers and creators of both family therapy in general and solution-focused therapy in particular. This influence can be identified tangentially in the work of Milton Erickson; it shaped the interactional views of Gregory Bateson, John Weakland, Don Jackson, Paul Watzlawick, and Richard Fisch, theorists whose work at the Mental Research Institute and the Mental Research Institute/Brief Therapy Center in Palo Alto, California shaped the ideas that led to the solution-focused approach; and it informs some central assumptions and techniques of narrative and solution-focused therapies. The writing of Steve de Shazer, an originator of the solution-focused approach, frequently references Wittgenstein. (See especially de Shazer's *Words Were Originally Magic* [1994], which explicates the importance of language to the practice of psychotherapy.)

Gradually, a different way of knowing—one attentive to the "surfaces" of life rather than to its deep structures, one inclusive of what happens between people in addition to what happens within them—became valued (Bidwell, 2004). In popular culture, this shift has contributed to an "emerging epistemology" that missiologist Leonard Sweet (2003) characterizes with the acronym "EPIC": experiential, participatory, image-rich, and connectional. In short, this postmodern way of knowing almost reverses the rational, objective, isolated epistemology of the modern period.

It is important to note that the "turn to language" in philosophy has implications beyond the theory of knowledge; it also influences understandings of being itself. Some theorists contend that "what we know" (epistemology) and "what there is" (ontology) are separate issues. Yet, questions of knowing imply that a knower exists; our epistemology reflects, in some measure, what we believe about being; and our beliefs about knowledge have ontological consequences. Remembering the symbiotic relationship between "what we know" and "what is" has been important to me as I seek to clarify the facets of solution-focused knowing.

While much about solution-focused knowing can be described through the positivist/rationalist split described earlier, the dualistic approach to knowledge in Western philosophy does not exhaust human accounts of the nature, characteristics, and limitations of knowledge. Islamic philosophy, in fact, offers a third epistemological position that can serve as a middle way between positivism and rationalism. We will explore this third position, called "knowledge by presence," later in this chapter as one way of making sense of the miracle question (see Chapter 1, this volume). Knowledge by presence may offer important insights into how a certain type of knowing occurs in solution-focused therapy, clarifying how the miracle question makes a difference in the process of therapy.

A POSTMODERN TURN IN PSYCHOLOGY:
SOCIAL CONSTRUCTIONIST THEORIES

Early solution-focused thought did not consciously make use of a particular psychological theory, but its practitioners eventually turned to constructivist (Miller, 1997) and social constructionist psychology to support and refine their ideas (Berg & De Jong, 1996; Bidwell, 2000; De Jong & Berg, 1998; de Shazer, 1991, 1994; de Shazer & Berg, 1992; Miller, 2000; Miller, Hubble, & Duncan, 1996; O'Hanlon, 1990). Social constructionist thought evolved out of the "turn to language" in philosophy and the ways in which that shift was interpreted by and applied to literary, social, and hermeneutical (interpretive) theory.

In general, social constructionist thought holds that knowledge is constructed rather than discovered, and that construction is accomplished by people in relationship rather than by an individual reflecting on the world. Thus, the process of interpreting, sharing, and correlating experience through conversation (and other forms of discourse) creates human "knowledge," placing "the locus of knowledge . . . not in the minds of single individuals, but in the collectivity. It is not the internal processes of the individual that generate what is taken for knowledge, but a social process of communication" (Gergen, 1982, p. 207). This gives rise to a "participatory epistemology" (Efron & Clarfield, 1992) that places priority on relational processes rather than cognition. Social interaction is assumed to precede and shape the individual; interdependence and interaction, rather than intrapsychic experience, are the primary focus of psychological inquiry, description, and explanation. In addition, social constructionists tend to view theory as secondary to social practices; activities, not objects, are the focus of constructionist inquiry and proposals (Shotter, 1992).

Because these inquiries and proposals seek to be inclusive rather than exclusive, there are no "essential tenets" of constructionism. The range of social constructionist thought includes many approaches. Still, most constructionist proposals share at least five assumptions, briefly outlined below (Bidwell, 2004).

First, the correspondence theory of truth, which "postulates that our mental representations mirror an objective reality 'out there,' as it truly is" (Rosen, 1996, p. 5), is assumed to be bankrupt. Instead, "knowledge, and the meaning we imbue it with, is a construction of the human mind" (Rosen, p. 5). In this view, realities are multiple; the knower and the known are inseparable, and consensus about the nature of reality occurs through linguistic activity (de Shazer, 1991).

Second, no "essential" human nature is assumed. In order to be complete, people must be situated in a specific context that allows them to make sense of the world and themselves. Consensus about the nature of reality gives social roles, processes, and structures the status of "reality," and they, in turn, further shape the "selves" of people who share those understandings. From this perspective, cause and effect cannot be separated; they comprise a seamless whole.

Third, consensus about the nature of reality evolves through relationships, which provide the linguistic tools and "cultural artifacts" (Cushman, 1995, p. 18)—that is, material objects, ideas, and actions—that humans use to make meaning of experience. Understandings of reality are correlated with the understandings of others in ways that keep people accountable to (and maintain) their social orders. Thus, as emphasized earlier, the group shapes and influences the individual before the individual influences the group.

Fourth, the ways in which people collectively make sense of the world are assumed to carry implications for the future; today's descriptions and meanings shape tomorrow's possibilities, and relationships can strengthen, undermine, and/or create new social orders and new understandings of reality. The future implications of a particular social construction are key to assessing its validity; as John Shotter (1993) points out, a central constructionist question is, "Which of a possible plurality of future next steps should we take for the best? Whose version points towards [*sic*] a best future for us?" (p. 18).

The fifth assumption is related to the fourth: particular constructions of reality are evaluated with the criteria of reflexivity, generativity, and pragmatism. Empirical validity (that is, correspondence to reality) is rejected as a criterion, and pragmatism is the primary evaluative criterion in many of the social constructionist writing. From this perspective, key evaluative questions include, what can we do with this understanding of reality? To what use can it be put? Does it lead to action? What does it help us accomplish? Does it create new perspectives or open a new vision that offers functional alternatives? Does it encourage new possibilities? Is it respectful? Does it allow for differences of perception? Does it invite people to have alternative experiences to those they usually have? Does it allow for multiple metaphors of understanding or impose a monologic metaphor?

Within these assumptions, the literature of social psychology is careful to call social constructionism an epistemological (knowledge-focused) and not ontological (being-focused) theory. That is, social constructionism makes claims about what humans know but not about the known; it describes a negotiable and contingent social reality and not a physical or essential reality. From a constructionist perspective, knowledge claims are to be evaluated "not upon validity (i.e., correspondence of an individual's beliefs to objective truth) but upon viability (i.e., the pragmatic adaptability of the individual's beliefs, so that he or she can navigate successfully within the world)" (Rosen, 1996, p. 13; see also Gergen, 2001, p. 32). This emphasizes that social constructions impact the "real world" through the social practices they inform, which include models of psychotherapy. Thus, human concepts and knowledge cannot be separated from social practices and social structures (Burr, 1998); this is a premise for the constructionist claim that knowledge is located in the space "between" people rather than within individuals.

Not everyone endorses these ideas, of course; constructionist theories are hotly contested in some psychological circles. Barbara Held (1995) has criticized social constructionist psychotherapies for an inconsistent approach to understanding how "constructions of reality" are generated. She believes these therapies (including narrative and solution-focused models) are guilty of wanting to "have it both ways"—asserting that constructions of reality emerge out of a person's subjectivity and are therefore individual, and asserting that constructions of reality are social and generated out of social processes. If constructions emerge from social processes, she argues, then individuality is compromised. This is a concession she is not willing to make. She also discounts social constructionist claims to epistemological and not ontological status; for her, many social constructionists are clearly antirealist, denying the existence of an ontic world beyond social discourse.

From a constructionist perspective, Held's discomfort with these therapies can be understood as a struggle between discourses—a primary positivist discourse about atomistic, individual selves who make autonomous decisions in an empirical world, and a secondary, constructionist discourse about human autonomy located in social processes between people rather than within individuals. While Held might have identified a logical inconsistency in these postmodern therapies (a tension between "affirming individual freedom and autonomy" while maintaining that "constructions of reality are negotiated socially"), her argument does not render social constructionist understandings of experience worthless; they maintain the reflexive and generative capacities that make them compelling alternatives to positivist-empiricist world views. In my view, Held seems to have exaggerated the ontological/epistemological dualism in the literature of social constructionism, generalizing broadly from the stance of particular therapists who are using language in casual rather than careful ways. In my reading of social constructionist literature, I do not find substantial ontological claims; in fact, I find theorists are careful to avoid such claims.

What most social constructionists do claim is a sociocritical "hermeneutic of suspicion" (Ricoeur, 1970, pp. 32-35; see also Fiorenza, 1985) which seeks to deconstruct all knowledge claims in order to identify their inherent ideological commitments and assumptions. This hermeneutic strengthens psychotherapies that promote the assumptions of social constructionism. For example, solution-focused therapy's constructionist commitments lead it to emphasize mutuality, human freedom, human responsibility, and an open-ended future (Bidwell, 2000); these aspects of solution-focused therapy suggest that it may be a step toward a practical psychology grounded in critical social theory as called for by ethicist Don Browning (1987). Pastoral theologian Christie Neuger (2001) has suggested similar strengths for the narrative counseling models rooted in social constructionist thought.

In the literatures of psychology, psychotherapy, and theology, however, social constructionist thought more often encounters criticism than praise. These literatures voice three consistent concerns about constructionist thought: the moral relativity assumed to be at the heart of constructionism; its challenge to the concept of an objective, knowable truth or reality; and a reductionism by which the most essential aspects of human experience become solely a byproduct of social processes.

The charge of "moral relativity" stems from the constructionist claim that moral choices depend on communal norms/discourses rather than on absolute or essential truths. The implication is that moral choices are relative because they are based on subjective standards rather than an objective reality. Yet, social constructionist theory does not necessarily reject an underlying "reality" in which moral claims might be grounded (see Schilderman, 2002). As an epistemological position, social constructionist theory claims only that humanity cannot know reality in full or without the overlay of social discourse. Therefore, epistemological and moral claims must be understood as partial. But even this claim of partiality does not require social constructionists to adopt a relativist stance toward morality. Social constructionist discourses do not flatten the moral landscape; rather, they view community norms as substantial and adequate ground for elevating some moral claims above others. In addition, social constructionism itself is not morally neutral; its liberationist tendencies are well known, and its evaluative criteria of pragmatism, generativity, and reflexivity are imbued with value judgments. Moral relativism is not a de facto element of social constructionism metatheory.

Similarly, the criticism that social constructionism challenges the concept of "objective truth" seems inadequate. It is an ontological critique of an epistemological stance. Social constructionism does not claim to know "the truth" about reality; rather, it positions itself as one approach to talking about how human beings know reality. Rather than making ontological truth claims, Kenneth Gergen (2002) argues, "constructionist proposals constitute a domain of intelligibility that invites, enables, or facilitates certain forms of cultural practice" (pp. 280-281). These forms of practice, as mentioned earlier, allow "constructed knowledge" to have a felt impact in the material world without necessarily making claims about the truth or reality of the material world or its ontology. Thus, social constructionism is less concerned with the truth of an underlying structure of reality than with the consequences of our various understandings of that reality as carried in particular discourses. The practical impact of such knowledge is at the heart of social constructionist inquiry.

Given these perspectives on moral relativity and objective truth, it is easier to see that social constructionist theory does not necessarily threaten to reduce the "human essence" to the status of a construct. Rather, many social constructionist theorists feel that constructionism returns legitimacy to concepts like "the sacred" and "the real" by accepting those terms and knowledges as vital, generative, communal resources equal in value to scientific or positivist-empiricist discourses. Thus, social constructionist theory works against the use of psychology "to explain away or reduce what may have profound cultural value" (Hardy, 2001, p. 25).

SHIFTING THE EPISTEMOLOGICAL FOCUS IN FAMILY THERAPY

Social constructionist thought evolved from broader conversations in the social sciences about communication, interaction, and change. These conversations were generated in part by the field of family therapy, and it was from this context that the theory and practice of solution-focused therapy also emerged (see Brian Cade's chapter in this volume). A history of these conversations could trace the epistemological shifts in Western cultures in the twentieth century (which were never as precise or as clear as they appear here).

The first major epistemological shift in family therapy occurred in the mid-1950s, when researchers at the Mental Research Institute in Palo Alto, California proposed a direct relationship between communication and behavior (Bateson, Jackson, Haley, & Weakland, 1956). They viewed communication as a complex, interactive process between participants in a closed system. A primary effect of this communicative process was to order the social behavior of the members of the system. It is difficult today to grasp the enormity of this proposal; to say that conflicting interpretations or definitions of an interaction will mutually and simultaneously influence participants in ways that create, maintain, and change social behaviors is almost mundane now. But at the time, the idea was radical. It might have been the first time that psychotherapists focused on the "surface" of human experiences (that is, observable behaviors and patterns) rather than plumbing the depths of the intrapsychic or cognitive self.

Within a decade, some of the same researchers began to focus on brief psychotherapy, pledging to focus strictly on what counselees said was the problem. This was a second major epistemological shift. There would be no digging for the "real issue" or the meaning behind the words; rather, the interpretive frames of counselees would be accepted as the only realities with which the therapist could work. Change was understood to occur as the therapist identified and altered systemic patterns of communication that created and maintained the problems that counselees carried into the therapy room. To achieve this, the therapist relied on observations and descriptions of "the surface" of the communicative system rather than on professional interpretations of what lay behind or beneath behaviors. This meant that assumptions or hypotheses that could not be pragmatically observed were rejected; hidden, structural understandings of human beings (and of reality in general) were no longer primary. For these therapists, everything that was important could be seen or heard, and therapeutic interventions had to be tailored to a particular problem. The therapist was a technician working on a closed system, much as a mechanic would tune up an engine.

Clearly, this ecosystemic model privileged empirical observation in psychotherapy, and thus a positivist epistemology, in a new way. Yet, the therapist's "expert opinion" remained essential; the approach was an explanatory model in which a therapist first articulated a particular, contextual description of how problems were created/maintained, and then intervened to change problematic patterns of communication. The criteria for inducing change were largely empirical and pragmatic (Watzlawick et al., 1974), but the new approach remained partly rationalist/idealist in its epistemology; despite placing new attention on empirical data—the "surface" of life—the model continued to privilege the therapist's individual, interior understanding as the means by which conditions for change would ultimately occur. The therapist could see things that counselees could not.

Over the next decade, dozens of mental health professionals were socialized into these ideas. A group of such practitioners, including Steve de Shazer and Insoo Kim Berg, established the Brief Family Therapy Center in Milwaukee in 1978. This group—like nearly all brief psychotherapists—was strongly influenced by the practice and ideas of Milton Erickson. In fact, it was through "efforts to apply Erickson's methods and procedures," de Shazer (1982) writes "that our [solution-focused] approach was developed" (p. 28). Particularly influential was Erickson's dual insistence that people act on the best choice they see in a given situation and that people have innate resources and skills to apply to their problems. Working from these assumptions, the Milwaukee group shifted its focus from explaining problems (the primary task of the interactional, ecosystemic model) to describing solutions.

de Shazer in particular did not believe that therapeutic interventions had to be tailored to specific problems. Rather, he sought to identify general principles that could be used to solve a variety of problems. The process of constructing a solution "from one case to another is more similar than the problems each intervention is meant to solve," de Shazer (1985, p. xv) wrote. He goes on to say:

> It is the therapist's task . . . to develop with the client . . . expectations of change and solution. In practice, this means that constructing a solution does not need to involve knowing anything about the person's past (unlike traditional therapy), nor does it need to involve knowing, in any detail, what is maintaining the complaint (unlike other forms of brief therapy and some types of family therapy). Furthermore, with an open expectation of change, the therapist can promote durable change quite quickly. (p. xvi)

In the process of developing expectations for change in the midst of a search for a general theory of solution, the Milwaukee practitioners found themselves becoming more collaborative with counselees (Miller, 1997); therapeutic conversation became oriented toward rich descriptions of how counselees would know that their problems were solved, the counselee's theory of change took on growing importance, and counselee perceptions of valid change became a key criterion for successful therapy. As de Shazer (1985) described, "A shift occurred from our being interested in 'problems/ complaints and how to solve them' to 'solutions and how they work'" (p. 45).

Through a series of qualitative shifts in understanding (rather than a progressive accumulation of knowledge), the Milwaukee group began to explore what counselees were already doing to influence and modify complaints; these already-existing behaviors became the means for solving the problems. Over time, these practitioners stopped viewing themselves as objective witnesses of interactional processes; instead, they began to understand themselves as a part of the interactional system. "All that a therapist deals with," de Shazer (1988) stated, "is his [*sic*] construction of how his [*sic*] client constructs his [*sic*] own reality; from these two constructions, client and therapist jointly construct a therapeutic reality" (p. 61). Thus, therapists are participants in the creation of therapeutic problems and solutions (de Shazer, 1985, 1988), viewing "interactions with clients as sites for self-consciously constructing social realities, not just for describing them" (Miller, 1997, p. 68). From this perspective, the therapist became an interpretive guide who participated in the construction of knowledge particular to the therapeutic conversation, rather than a technician intervening in a closed system.

This marked a third significant shift in the way knowledge was understood and used in the therapeutic conversation. First, solution-focused therapists moved away from a purely positivist/empiricist epistemology that sought descriptions of problems that were "really there"; the problems described by counselees were no longer assumed to refer to concrete realities outside of the therapeutic session but to particular (and shifting) perceptions that existed within the therapeutic conversation itself. Second, the rationalist/idealist knowing of the therapist—the expert knowledge of what was "really going on" and how to intervene to fix it—was secondary to a shared understanding of how a problem might be influenced or solved. Tentative and participatory knowing became privileged over sure and certain individual knowledge. Gale Miller (1997) calls this form of knowing "constructivist" because "it focuses therapists' attention on the relativity of their own and their clients' knowledge, and on how both forms of knowledge might be used to construct and remedy clients' troubles" (p. 59). Alternatively, I would call this a "constructionist" shift because of the emphasis on the social process of coming to new understandings through conversation.

THE CHARACTER OF SOLUTION-FOCUSED KNOWING

de Shazer's *Keys to Solution in Brief Therapy* (1985) was the first comprehensive argument for a solution-focused approach, and his later works further develop the ideas proposed there. There are many other solution-focused theorists writing today; I have chosen to focus here on de Shazer's early writing for practical and pragmatic reasons: the solution-focused literature is too vast to be addressed adequately within the limits of this project, and de Shazer's early descriptions of the model perhaps best reveal the contours of its epistemological assumptions.

From the beginning, the Milwaukee group sought to identify empirically the most effective approaches to brief therapy. As such, the work was grounded in a positivist-empiricist epistemology that valued usefulness, positive results, and a "high degree of rigor" (de Shazer, 1988, p. 15) as criteria for judging effectiveness. The project, John Weakland asserted (de Shazer), focused "solely on observable data" (p. vi), and pragmatism was at the forefront. For these practitioners, elegant theoretical explanations were not necessary; they were seeking therapeutic interventions that worked. In fact, the aphorism, "look for what works rather than what does not" is a mainstay of the model (de Shazer). The positivist-empiricist stance can be seen clearly in the Milwaukee group's use of a computer program to generate therapeutic options based on empirically established criteria (de Shazer).

As the group's orientation shifted from problems to solutions, the therapeutic benefit of focusing on differences in behavior and perception, exceptions to complaints, and presession change became clear. In identifying these general keys to solutions, the Milwaukee group did not "create" a new approach to therapy. Rather, these practitioners simply did more of what the evidence suggested was effective; as de Shazer (1988) stated, "One follows where the data lead" (p. xiv). Concrete, behavioral descriptions of change, not explanations of inner states or of outer behaviors, were the data that counted.

As the empirical evidence suggested ways to create change more quickly and more effectively than previous therapeutic models, de Shazer and his colleagues adopted an almost phenomenological approach to understanding how counselees experience solutions. Phenomenology is a philosophical method that attempts to understand the reality of a concept—such as "solution"—by creating a rich (or "thick") description of a particular, concrete occurrence of the concept without imposing theoretical explanations or restrictions. (It is unclear whether de Shazer and his colleagues intentionally adopted a phenomenological approach; it may be that I am imposing this description because it fits the available data—a move consistent with solution-focused knowing. Simply put, in retrospect, the phenomenological method fits the way the solution-focused model became clearly articulated, although it may not precisely match the method used to develop the model. My story about this process is probably different from the stories of de Shazer, Berg, Scott Miller, Eve Lipchik, and others involved in the early days of solution-focused therapy.) A phenomenological description, however, is shaped by the criteria used to choose the particular event to clarify a general concept. Given the essentially pragmatic theory of knowledge in solution-focused therapy, a single criterion reigns in its phenomenology of solutions: Does it work?

> What "works" is identified through client reports of change. Whatever the clients report, the therapist takes it at face value . . . That is, for the therapist, reported change is "change," and the relevance of talking

about change in the future is only born out by the clients, in subsequent sessions, actually reporting changes. (de Shazer, 1988, p. 11)

"Change" is identified as "new and different behaviors and/or perceptions" (de Shazer, 1985, p. 65). Thus, the issue for solution-focused therapists was never the rationalist-idealist task of uncovering "truth" or the "root" of problems, "but developing effective strategies for misreading clients' lives and troubles in change-oriented ways" (Miller, 1997, p. 70). Because therapists work only with perceptions and not with facts (de Shazer, 1988), the solution-focused approach considers self-reports of counselees' "empirical data" that offer sufficient evidence of therapeutic success (and failure).

It is at this juncture that rationalist-idealist ways of knowing become important to solution-focused therapy. A counselee's innate sense of difference—a perception that a complaint has improved or that a problem has dissolved—is trusted as empirical evidence even though its source might be understood as rationalist-idealist. By uttering a perception of change, the counselee transforms it into a "fact"; putting a sense of difference into language changes it from a certain but nonempirical perception to a concrete report of difference, and concrete reports can be supported with behavioral evidence. Solution-focused therapists rarely accept a counselee's rationalist-idealist argument that things are different as "the whole story," because a primary assumption of solution-focused therapy is that every "fact"—rational or empirical—contains unknown elements.

This is why the solution-focused therapist adopts a "not-knowing" stance (Anderson, 2005; Anderson & Goolishian, 1992; De Jong & Berg, 1998, 2002) toward the counselee; no assumption is to be made about the content or meanings of the counselee's experience; the counselee is the expert who fills in the gaps. Through careful questions and by bracketing all assumptions that have not been verbally confirmed by the counselee, the solution-focused therapist seeks to find out what else a counselee knows about perceived changes. In doing so, the therapist focuses her questions on specific and behavioral evidence for change—converting rational knowledge into empirical knowledge. Scaling questions are an excellent example of the process of translating "ideal knowing" (or an "inner sense" of something) into empirical terms; there is no logical basis for the scales used in solution-focused therapy, but scaling a felt sense of something makes it concrete enough to measure improvement or degeneration. Thus, rationalist-idealist knowledge is important but always secondary to positivist-realist knowing in solution-focused therapy.

This new knowledge, however, is not located in an individual mind, and therefore, it is neither purely positivist-empiricist nor rationalist-idealist, as Western philosophy traditionally has understood these terms. Rather, solution-focused knowledge results from the interaction between therapist and counselee, manifested in the space between them through joint action (Shotter, 1984). In social constructionist terms, the knowledge that emerges from solution-focused conversations is a shared resource initially located in the zone between action ("what people do") and events ("what happens to people"). de Shazer (1985) recognized this early in the development of the solution-focused model; "solutions," he writes, "do not depend entirely on either the creativity of the therapist and/or therapy team or of the client. The source of the creativity 'lies' in the cooperative relationship between the two subsystems" (p. 171). Thus, solution-focused knowing cannot be initiated solely by the therapist or by the counselee; it is primarily a product of the conversation and only secondarily the "property" of the participants. The product of such joint action, John Shotter (1993) writes, is "something first created only in the spontaneous, contexted [sic] activities between people, . . . later 'privatized' or 'internalized' by individuals, for use under their own personal, decontextualized, deliberate control" (p. 75).

The idea that knowledge, as joint action, is negotiated in conversation illustrates another aspect of solution-focused knowing: It is hermeneutical, or interpretive, in nature. Solution-focused therapists use questions to direct a counselee's attention to parts of their experience that they might not have noticed. As counselees become aware of "new" aspects of their experiences—such as times when the complaint is not happening or is not troublesome—they must reinterpret their stories about those experiences. (Consider, for example, how quickly the story that a problem "always happens" can change when a solution-focused conversation creates knowledge of times when the complaint is not happening.) The assumption, de Shazer (1988) stated, is "that a change in the way clients construct their experience, as reflected in how they report it or talk about it, will promote their having a different experiences [sic] which, in turn, will prompt different depictions or reports in subsequent sessions" (p. 77). For solution-focused therapists, then,

> . . . constructing exceptions is not about making up fictional stories about clients' lives, but about creating stories that make it possible for clients to see and learn from what is already there. The new stories make it possible for clients to learn from their own successes and for therapists to better utilize clients' abilities and resources in helping them solve their problems. Thus, in constructing exceptions, solution-focused therapists and clients create progressive stories that assert that clients have already begun to realize their miracles. (Miller, 1997, p. 197)

Miller concluded that the interpretive process in solution-focused therapy

> . . . encourages clients to assume that their lives will get better and provides them with interpretive 'lenses' for seeing how their lives are already better than clients had previously assumed. In this and other ways, brief therapists subvert the conventional Western distinction between fact and fiction. (p. 214)

Miller's (1997) statement highlights an essential element of solution-focused knowing: the assumption that positive change will occur. This assumption seems to be another way in which rationalist-idealist knowing has been important to solution-focused therapy. In a given therapeutic encounter, expectation of change is a stance, not a fact; it is something initially known by faith rather than by evidence (no matter how quickly evidence is discovered to support the assumption). By whatever means it is known, however, expectation of change is essential to the process of solution-focused therapy. "Since expectations help to determine the nature of subsequent events," de Shazer (1985) wrote, "it seems clear that the behavior will change when the expectation changes" (p. 94). Therefore, a primary responsibility of the therapist is to create an expectation of change (de Shazer, 1985, 1988); influence "in the therapeutic context," de Shazer (1985) wrote, "needs to be constructively used to create for the client the expectation of noticeable change—which is what the therapist is paid to do" (pp. 69-70).

Some have named this, "the placebo effect" (Hubble, Duncan, & Miller, 1999); I prefer to call it hope. But whatever we call it, the expectation of change is essential to solution-focused therapy, and it places hope and possibility at the forefront of the model (Bidwell, 2000) by turning the collaborative, interpretive process of solution-focused conversation toward "progressive stories," those that "emphasize how clients are moving toward desired goals" (Miller, 1997, p. 61). Solution-focused conversations seek to create knowledge of both a positive future and the ways in which that future is already breaking into the present (Bidwell, 2005).

Solution-focused knowing, then, is pragmatic in nature. It is interpretive and partial rather than definitive. It is progressive, and it is the result of joint action rather than of an individual mind or experience. Philosophically, it is primarily positivist-empiricist; even when rationalist-idealist knowing is introduced into solution-focused conversations, it is "fleshed out" with supportive empirical evidence. Above all, solution-focused knowing is future-oriented—which suggests a facet of its epistemology that reaches beyond traditional Western concepts of knowledge.

MIRACLES OF BEING

One way that solution-focused therapists generate expectations of change is to ask the miracle question. As an imaginative exercise, the miracle question invites counselees to describe in detail their experiences on the day after a miracle resolves the complaint that led them to therapy. Taking a not-knowing stance, the therapist continually elicits ever-richer descriptions of the miracle day, including behavioral and empirical evidence by which the counselee would recognize that a miracle had occurred. Images, explicated in language, are an especially potent aspect of a counselee's response. In the process of describing their miracles, something happens to counselees; as de Shazer (1988) has written, "Simply describing in detail a future in which the problem is already solved helps to build the expectation that the problem will be solved and then this expectation, once formed, can help the client think and behave in ways that will lead to fulfilling this expectation" (p. 50).

Certainly, creating an expectation of change is one of the strengths of the miracle question. The technique is also an indirect way of eliciting counseling goals (Bidwell, 2005), and de Shazer (1994) has cited its ability to strengthen the therapeutic alliance. Both de Shazer (1988) and Miller (1997) note that the miracle question shifts the counselee's orientation in time, allowing the future to become as (or more) salient than the past. In fact, the change imagined by counselees, Miller states "is often as useful to solution-focused therapists as their direct observation of it. Both [observation and imagination] contribute to the development of progressive stories" (p. 191). But the intent of the miracle question is not merely to imagine change. Once a clear description of a redeemed future—one free of the problematic complaint—has been obtained, therapist and counselee can jointly construct knowledge of ways in which aspects of the miracle day already exist in current experience.

All of these benefits of the miracle question—creating expectation of change, clarifying therapeutic goals, strengthening the therapeutic relationship, increasing salience of the future—seem important. But I wonder if, taken together, they are not a too-meager description of what occurs in the process of imagining a miracle day? These accounts are pragmatic descriptions of the technique's effects, but do they fully account for the power of the miracle question to evoke tremendous changes in the lives of counselees? Further, how is it that counselees can imagine or "know" problem-free futures seemingly beyond their previous experiences and unconnected to their complaints?

These, of course, are leading questions; I believe there is a richer description of the miracle question's contribution to the therapeutic process than those given so far, and that description relates to the process of knowing. So, at this point, my peculiar account of solution-focused knowing shifts from pragmatic description to theoretical explanation—a move not exactly consistent with the therapeutic model, but nonetheless necessary to fully account for the many facets of its epistemology.

As mentioned earlier, Islamic philosophy includes an account of knowing called "knowledge by presence" (Ha'iri Yazdi, 1992), which may bridge the epistemological/ontological split (the divide between "what we know" and "what exists") in postmodern philosophy. The concept is deeply implicated in Islamic mysticism, where it is considered a category of empirical knowledge that can be verified through experience. It arises not from an innate capacity of the mind to create knowledge that corresponds with reality nor through an empirical encounter with sense-data (sight, smell, touch, taste, sound); knowledge by presence does not "match" the physical world (although it might "fit" the physical world), nor is it akin to imagining how a chicken feather might feel against your arm because you know the feeling of a pigeon feather you picked up in the park. Rather, knowledge by presence occurs when the infinity and fullness of Being, the realm of limitless possibility, asserts itself—or "knows"—through a finite human being. The process introduces possibilities that are beyond the individual's own capacity to know or imagine; at its fullest, knowledge by presence can become a living dialogue between a human being and Being itself.

I do not pretend to fully understand this concept. Nor do I intend to explore its mystical implications. What intrigues me is its ability to account for a counselee's knowing that change is possible—and knowing what changes to make—by imagining future experiences. In the process of imagining a problem-free future, might Being itself disclose possibilities previously unknown to the counselee? Ha'iri, a Persian philosopher who seems to be the first to have written in English about knowledge by presence, explicitly states that this type of knowing can occur through dreams, imagination, and intuition—the sort of experiences the miracle question implicitly invites. In fact, the miracle question evolved from the crystal-ball technique of Ericksonian hypnosis (de Shazer, 1988) and seems most successful when introduced with elements of trance induction (although the Milwaukee group explicitly avoided using hypnotic trance with the technique).

Islamic philosophy allows for different levels of knowledge by presence, acknowledging that different people may be more or less open to being "known through" in this way. The ability to know by presence seems to depend on an individual's awareness of Being itself and of the ways in which Being and individual consciousness participate in one another. Various levels of openness to knowledge by presence may partially explain why the miracle question is more successful for some counselees than others. Whatever the mechanism, it is an intriguing thought that descriptions of problem-free futures constructed through the miracle question are in part the result of knowledge by presence—a beneficent *reality* asserting itself through the conversation to point the way toward a fuller and more satisfying life.

Admittedly, this idea straddles the theoretical realms of philosophy and theology, the technical realm of clinical practice, and the experiential realm of practical wisdom, which transcends both theory and technique. But if knowledge by presence fits the sort of knowing that occurs in solution-focused therapy as well or better than rationalist–idealist and positivist–empiricist theories of knowledge (which I have already suggested are insufficient for accounting for the knowledge that emerges from solution-focused conversations), the idea might be worth exploring. If the concept is useful for understanding the theory of knowledge implicit in solution-focused therapy, it certainly raises important questions for solution-focused practice. How, for instance, can solution-focused conversations help create the conditions through which counselees might be "known through" by Being in ways that lead to ever faster and more effective solutions? What practices can facilitate the invitation of Being to assert itself in the therapeutic process? What clues might suggest a particular counselee has a greater or lesser capacity for knowledge by presence? And how might therapists nurture their own capacities for knowledge by presence?

CONCLUSION: POINTING TOWARD THE FUTURE

Again, these are questions that are beyond the scope of this project. My conclusion so far is that engaging the epistemological category of knowledge by presence might offer one way for solution-focused theorists and practitioners to respond to criticism that postmodern epistemologies, and the social practices built on them (including solution-focused therapy), have lost touch with "reality."

The idea that we cannot know what is real, but only our accounts of it—an idea that pervades the solution-focused literature—has been increasingly troublesome in contemporary philosophy. In response, a school of thought called "critical realism" (Lopez & Potter, 2001) has attempted to reconnect "what we know" to "what there is," asserting that reality "is far broader and much more complex" (p. 75) than our knowledge of it. These philosophers want to preserve the partiality of our historically contingent knowledge, while nonetheless making ontological assertions. Meek (2003) suggested that a sense of rich possibilities indicates that our knowledge is in touch with reality. Who understands better than solution-focused therapists do, the rich possibilities that people may encounter together?

To my knowledge, philosophers of knowledge in the Western hemisphere have not turned to knowledge by presence as a bridge across the epistemological/ontological divide. Perhaps, solution-focused practitioners who see my account as a fitting and useful description of "knowing" in clinical practice can lead the way to a richer description of how humans know and encounter "possibility" as both an aspect of reality and a type of knowledge.

NOTE

1. This distinction between "fit and match," as articulated by Ernst von Glasersfeld (1984), has been important to the development of solution-focused thought and its ways of knowing (de Shazer, 1985; Miller & de Shazer, 1998).

REFERENCES

Anderson, H. (2005). Myths about "not knowing." *Family Process, 44*(4), 497-504.
Anderson, H., & Goolishian, H. (1992). The client is the expert: A not-knowing approach to therapy. In S. McNamee & K. J. Gergen (Eds.), *Therapy as social construction* (pp. 25-39). London: Sage.
Bateson, G., Jackson, D. D., Haley, J., & Weakland, J. H. (1956). Toward a theory of schizophrenia. *Behavioral Science, 1*, 251-264.
Berg, I. K., & De Jong, P. (1996). Solution-building conversations: Co-constructing a sense of competency with clients. *Families in Society: The Journal of Contemporary Human Services, 77*(6), 376-391.
Bidwell, D. R. (2000). Hope and possibility: The theory of culture inherent to solution-focused brief therapy. *American Journal of Pastoral Counseling, 3*(1), 3-21.
Bidwell, D. R. (2004). Real/izing the sacred: Spiritual direction and social constructionism. *The Journal of Pastoral Theology, 14*(1), 59-74.
Bidwell, D. R. (2005). Working miracles: Goaling for short-term spiritual care. *Healing Ministry, 12*(2), 31-36.
Browning, D. S. (1987). *Religious thought and the modern psychologies: A critical conversation in the theology of culture.* Philadelphia: Fortress Press.
Burr, V. (1998). Overview: Realism, relativism, social constructionism and discourse. In I. Parker (Ed.), *Social constructionism, discourse and realism* (pp. 13-25). London: Sage.
Cade, B. (2007). Springs, streams, and tributaries: A history of the brief, solution-focused approach. In T. S. Nelson & F. N. Thomas (Eds.), *Handbook of solution-focused brief therapy: Clinical applications* (pp. 25-64). Binghamton, NY: The Haworth Press.

Cushman, P. (1995). *Constructing the self, constructing America: A cultural history of psychotherapy.* Reading, MA: Addison-Wesley.

De Jong, P., & Berg, I. K. (1998). *Interviewing for solutions.* New York: Brooks/ Cole.

De Jong, P., & Berg, I. K. (2002). *Interviewing for solutions* (2nd ed.). Pacific Grove, CA: Brooks/Cole.

de Shazer, S. (1982). *Patterns of brief family therapy: An ecosystemic approach.* New York: Guilford.

de Shazer, S. (1985). *Keys to solution in brief therapy.* New York: Norton.

de Shazer, S. (1988). *Clues: Investigating solutions in brief therapy.* New York: Norton.

de Shazer, S. (1991). *Putting difference to work.* New York: Norton.

de Shazer, S. (1994). *Words were originally magic.* New York: Norton.

de Shazer, S., & Berg, I. K. (1992). Doing therapy: A post-structural revision. *Journal of Marital and Family Therapy, 18*(1), 71-81.

Efron, J. S., & Clarfield, L. E. (1992). Constructionist therapy, sense, and non-sense. In S. McNamee & K. J. Gergen (Eds.), *Therapy as social construction* (pp. 200-217). London: Sage.

Fiorenza, E. S. (1985). The will to choose or to reject: Continuing our critical work. In L. M. Russell (Ed.), *Feminist interpretation of the bible* (pp. 125-136). Philadelphia: Westminster.

Gergen, K. J. (1982). *Toward transformation in social knowledge.* New York: Springer-Verlag.

Gergen, K. J. (2001). *Social construction in context.* London: Sage.

Gergen, K. J. (2002). Reflecting on/with my companions. In C. A. M. Hermans, G. Immink, A. DeJong, & J. van der Lans (Eds.), *Social constructionism and theology* (pp. 273-289). Leiden, Netherlands: Brill.

Ha'iri Yazdi, M. (1992). *The principles of epistemology in Islamic philosophy: Knowledge by presence.* Albany, NY: State University of New York.

Hardy, D. (2001). Theologians of a kind: Trinity Church conference speakers on what it is to be human. *Research News and Opportunities in Science and Theology, 2*(4), 24-25.

Held, B. S. (1995). *Back to reality: A critique of postmodern theory in psychotherapy.* New York: Norton.

Hubble, M. A., Duncan, B. L., & Miller, S. D. (1999). *The heart and soul of change: What works in therapy.* Washington, DC: American Psychological Association.

Locke, J. (1995, 1698). *An essay concerning human understanding.* Amherst, NY: Prometheus.

Lopez, J., & Potter, G. (2001). *After postmodernism: An introduction to critical realism.* London: Athlone.

Meek, E. L. (2003). *Longing to know: The philosophy of knowledge for ordinary people.* Grand Rapids, MI: Brazos.

Miller, G. (1997). *Becoming miracle workers: Language and meaning in brief therapy.* Hawthorne, NY: Aldine de Gruyter.

Miller, G. (2000). From "how" to "what" questions. *RATKES: Journal of the Finnish Association for the Advancement of Solution and Resource Oriented Therapy and Methods, 2,* 24-29.

Miller, G., & de Shazer, S. (1998). Have you heard the latest rumor about . . .? Solution-focused therapy as a rumor. *Family Process 37*(3), 363-377.

Miller, S. D., Hubble, M. A., & Duncan, B. L. (Eds.). (1996). *Handbook of solution-focused brief therapy.* San Francisco, CA: Jossey-Bass.

Neuger, C. C. (2001). *Counseling women: A narrative, pastoral approach.* Minneapolis, MN: Fortress.

O'Hanlon, W. H. (1990). A grand unified theory for brief therapy: Putting problems in context. In J. K. Zeig & S. G. Gilligan (Eds.), *Brief therapy: Myths, methods, and metaphors* (pp. 78-89). New York: Brunner/Mazel.

Philosophy Pages. (2003). επιστημη *(episteme) and epistemology.* Retrieved December 31, 2003 from http://www.philosophypages.com/dy/e5.htm

Ricoeur, P. (1970). *Freud and philosophy: An essay on interpretation* (trans. Denis Savage). New Haven, CT: Yale University Press.

Rosen, H. (1996). Meaning-making narratives: Foundations for constructivist and social constructionist psychotherapies. In H. Rosen & K. T. Kuehlwein (Eds.), *Constructing realities: Meaning-making perspectives for psychotherapists* (pp. 3-51). San Francisco, CA: Jossey-Bass.

Schilderman, H.. (2002). Personal religion. In C. A. M. Hermans, G. Immink, A. DeJong., & J. van der Lans (Eds.), *Social constructionism and theology* (pp. 211-237). Leiden, Netherlands: Brill.

Shotter, J. (1984). *Social accountability and selfhood.* Oxford: Basil Blackwood.

Shotter, J. (1992). "Getting in touch": The meta-methodology of a postmodern science of mental life. In S. Kvale (Ed.), *Psychology and postmodernism* (pp. 58-73). London: Sage.

Shotter, J. (1993). *Conversational realities: Constructing life through language.* London: Sage.

Sweet, L. (2003, November). Lecture before Grace Presbytery at Austin College, Sherman, TX.

Thomas, F. N., & Nelson, T. S. (2007). Assumptions within the solution-focused brief therapy tradition. In T. S. Nelson & F. N. Thomas, *Handbook of solution-focused brief therapy: Clinical applications* (pp. 3-24). Binghamton, NY: The Haworth Press.

Von Glasersfeld, E. (1984). An introduction to radical constructivism. In P. Watzlawick (Ed.), *The invented reality* (pp. 17-40). New York: Norton.

Watzlawick, P., Weakland, J., & Fisch, R. (1974). *Change: Principles of problem formation and problem resolution.* New York: Norton.

Wittgenstein, L. (1974). *Philosophical grammar* (A. Kenny, trans.). Oxford: Oxford University Press.

SECTION II: APPLICATIONS

In which we present situations for which Solution-Focused Brief Therapy may be useful.

Handbook of Solution-Focused Brief Therapy: Clinical Applications
© 2007 by The Haworth Press, Inc. All rights reserved.
doi:10.1300/5135_P2

Chapter 4

Solution-Focused Therapy with Couples

Phillip Ziegler
Tobey Hiller

HISTORY AND IDEAS OF OUR APPROACH

Couples therapy is challenging, and not for the faint hearted. It is a constant work-in-progress to find effective, elastic, and creative ways to meet the complex and sometimes confusing charge of helping two people who are at odds—or sometimes, at war—to sort out and improve their relationship along the lines that make sense to them. Primary among the therapeutic imperatives is finding a way to establish an inclusive rapport; that is, to connect with both partners, respecting and integrating what are often sharply differing points of view. To show why we think solution-focused therapy (SFT) offers an effective way of dealing with this and many other problems and questions that can confound both novice and experienced couples therapists, we want to give a brief account of the evolution of our own thinking about couples therapy.

We first began to work with couples in the early 1970s. Until the early 1990s, we were generally guided by ideas about what makes long-term intimate relationships flourish or deteriorate, by various models of normative relationships, and by scattered research findings about what distinguishes functional from dysfunctional relationships. We felt our helping role included identifying and helping to change people's troubled thinking and destabilizing interactions, and we focused on both intrapsychic and systemic sources of marital discord and dissatisfaction. Guided also by a rather vaguely outlined normative model of healthy relationships, we tried to teach

Handbook of Solution-Focused Brief Therapy: Clinical Applications
© 2007 by The Haworth Press, Inc. All rights reserved.
doi:10.1300/5135_04

couples how to relate better as intimates and partners. This meant, among other things, modeling respectful relationship, introducing new ways of handling conflict, and teaching good communication skills.

Whatever techniques we used, we intended to foster emotional and cognitive breakthroughs that could lead to greater mutual understanding, respect, and affection in the couple. We were often quite successful in helping couples turn around their troubled relationships. But over the years, we continued to look for more effective and efficient ways of working, and although we assessed ways we were becoming more effective, we often talked about our failures, and where we, our models, and our techniques had not worked very well or produced much positive change.

In our practices and our conversations, we began to notice certain landmarks and recurring features in the couples counseling therapy landscape, landmarks that might make navigation more precise. We became increasingly interested in the important roles that perception and meaning-making play in relationship life, and, significantly, we noticed a strong correlation among positive changes in people's perceptions, the meanings they ascribed to each other's gestures, and their eventual success at the end of our work together. It seemed that the sooner this took place, the better the outcome. We also noticed the therapeutic power of highlighting of a couple's positive bond and their various strengths and assets throughout the therapeutic process. In other words, we were trying to distinguish exactly what we were doing in our work with couples that seemed to contribute to the success of the therapy. Gradually, we found ourselves moving away from a theory of couples therapy based on the eradication of dysfunction in behalf of a template model of intimate relationship toward a quite different view of how to conduct couples therapy. We were being guided by a different question: instead of focusing on *what makes relationships fail*, we focused on *what makes marital therapy work.*

Reflecting back, over 20 years of experience in working with couples, we were able to pick out a few patterns that seemed to correlate with our successes. When we were able to create a safe place for the couple to "talk things out" and come to some greater mutual understanding, things usually got better. In an atmosphere of safety, partners were frequently able to shift from an adversarial stance primed for blame and defense to some form of teamwork, finding renewed pleasure in working as allies for mutually desired changes. In this shift, partners also became better able to take in each other's differing perceptions and explore misunderstood and blocked meanings, which tended to lower the incidence of conflict. A better alliance between the partners produced more emotional leeway and fewer trigger-happy reactions. This zone of safety, collaboration, and receptivity or respect was just as important for couples who decided to part, making it more manageable to work through the painful process of separation in a spirit of cooperation.

In hindsight, we realized that our natural tendency to highlight peoples' assets, bond, and special qualities as a couple (an emphasis on their competency and efficacy) had a positive effect on a couple's ability to maintain their alliance and generate hope and motivation to work collaboratively, and that this orientation helped the couple draw on their strengths and resources in behalf of the daunting work of change. We also saw that immediacy counted: When we were able to generate hope and a collaborative atmosphere with our couples right away, preferably in the first session, these early changes made them enthusiastic and energetic in their commitment to change and supported therapeutic success.

Looking at our work through this evolving new lens, we noticed that a few specific techniques, tools, or perspectives seemed to be particularly effective in creating the kind of collaborative and safe environment we were finding ideal for effective therapy; we'll mention three important ones here. When used appropriately, all these techniques can contribute to the therapist's ability to be responsive to the partners' differing needs and points of view and establish an inclusive rapport. Although couples therapy is never simple, we have found these tools to be reliable and flexible, and almost always appropriate in the early and ongoing sessions of couples work. These tools include the reframing techniques of *normalizing* and *mutualizing* as well as what we call *the "good story" orientation,* which highlights a couple's successes and builds evidence of the partners' effectiveness in dealing with the challenges of relationship life.

Normalizing is a reframing technique in which the couple's problems are redefined as common rather than unique. This has two effects: first, it implies that the couple and the individual partners are not strange, abnormal, or deviant and that their problems are experiences familiar to many couples. Second, it defines conflict and differing points of view as part and parcel of relationship life. This kind of problem-definition reframe can go a long way to reducing divisive feelings of shame, isolation, and desperation, and support a sense that the couple's issues/problems/concerns are manageable. Problems that are viewed as unique and complex seem by nature potentially defeating or insoluble, while common problems, defined simply, are perceived as much easier to solve.

Mutualizing is another reframing technique in which the problem is defined as something that exists between the partners in a fluid relational context rather than as a defect, situation, or trouble caused by one or both of them. Mutualizing reframes the problem definition in a way that promotes a shift away from adversarial positions and puts both partners on the same side so that they can work together against a common problem or external force that is now seen as making trouble for them both, sometimes in different but related ways. It opens a space for partnership revitalization. Michael White and David Epston (1990) have refined this kind of reframing technique in Narrative Therapy, calling it "externalizing the problem." Mutualizing also leads to another important contextual shift: It supports an inclusive rapport in therapy. Instead of adjudicating or taking sides, this shift makes it possible for the therapist to position herself or himself as a collaborator in exploring ways to solve a shared problem *with* the couple while also understanding the impact(s) that problem may have for each partner as an individual.

The third important element, a hallmark of our own couples work (Ziegler & Hiller, 2001), is not so much a technique as an orientation. *The "good story" orientation* involves approaching the couple's relational life together as a set of holistic narratives or stories on a continuum of "good" (relationship-supportive) to "bad" (relationship-destructive). All couples have mutual and individual conceptions of their lives together that range from the very positive to the very negative. Over time, events—especially emotionally charged experiences—and repeating patterns of interaction give gravitational weight to these polar narratives that have both perceptual and interpretive power. When a relationship begins to deteriorate (for whatever reason), there is a tendency for the influential shaping power of the *bad story* narrative to begin overshadowing the perceptual and interpretive powers of the couple's *good story* narrative. This can set in motion a downward spiral in the couple's relational life and the bad story thickens, growing in influence. When couples therapy is undertaken without regard to these experience-defining narrative contexts, changes made at the level of behavior, cognition, and emotion are often ignored or eroded because, when the bad story is still exercising its influence over what the partners notice about each other's actions and the meanings they ascribe to them, even positive or reparative acts are not received as constructive.

Further, the bad story context is inherently a conflictual, divisive, or distanced one in which the partners are at odds or remote from each other. As the therapist works with a couple to reinvigorate the good story and helps them to find ready exits from it (without reducing the importance of the bad story), the pressure on the therapist to take sides or desert the multiperspective point of view diminishes. Differences are likely to be viewed as tolerable or creative when couples are living more within their good stories. Helping a couple caught in their bad story to create bridges back to their good story involves (a) listening for, asking about, and identifying positive themes in the various problem stories related by the partners; (b) looking for signs of the good story context; and (c) searching for pathways back into the positive set of assumptions and ideas about the partner and relationship. Even as we listen and try to understand each person's experience of the difficulties, we are alert to narrative bits and pieces that might be woven into stories that reveal partner and relationship strengths and resources.

The use of these three tools, which all involve conversation using generative and curious questions by the therapist, will go a long way to reducing confusion and alliance difficulties therapists face when working with couples. Asking questions that come out of these framework orientations helps make it possible for a therapist to hold and respect varying and even opposed perspectives from the partners and to proceed toward exploring individual meanings and ways to find common ground with everyone on-board. In addition, focusing on goals helps to bring out shared perspectives and decrease the time that a couple spends in argument about who is to blame and in trying to triangulate the therapist into getting the partner to change.

As our work became increasingly couple-contextual, collaborative, and strength-based, we came to see that we could help couples design and carry out their own uniquely applicable therapy—a custom-built program of change, respecting both *what* changes needed to happen and *how* to bring them about. Our job as therapists became helping couples clarify their goals, finding the shared space in those pictures, helping them figure out for themselves what could help them realize those desired changes, and reminding them of their successes as we went along.

It was at this time we began hearing about other theoreticians and clinicians who were thinking along similar lines and were developing ways of working that sounded like they would fit nicely into our own evolving approach. We were most intrigued and excited by Steve de Shazer and Insoo Kim Berg's Solution-Focused Brief Therapy (de Shazer & Berg, 1985) and Bill O'Hanlon's Possibility Therapy (Hudson & O'Hanlon, 1991). We also drew from Narrative Therapy developed by Michael White and David Epston (White & Epston, 1990) as well as Harry Goolishian and Harlene Anderson's Collaborative Language Therapy (Anderson, 1997; Anderson & Goolishian, 1992), but solution-focused therapy (SFT) was, for us, the best fit. Recreating partnership couples therapy (RPCT) is our integration and adaptation of these three constructionist therapies into our own work, with a special emphasis on SFT (Ziegler & Hiller, 2002). The following is our formulation of the assumptions of a solution-focused approach to couples therapy:

• Change is occurring all the time. Experience is always varied. By the time most couples come to therapy, they are frozen in a troubled perspective of their relationship. The therapist's job is to help them get unstuck from these constraining, relationship-harming pictures as efficiently and effectively as possible.

- Couples therapy, like all therapy, will be more effective, efficient, and creative when the enterprise is goal- or outcome-directed; that is, when the couple and therapist have worked out a shared agreement regarding what will tell everyone that therapy has been successful.

- Couples therapy will be more effective and time-sensitive when it is strength-based, and change- and success-attuned. The orientation centers on the couple's strengths and resources and on positive experiences and changes. This orientation extends from before the first session through every point during therapy into the described post-therapy future. SFT conversations flesh out both "exceptions" (times the problem was in some way less of a problem) as well as successes and positive experiences. Such conversations generate hope and feelings of self-efficacy and establish the basis for the development of a couple's individually designed solutions.

- The solution-focused therapist essentially serves as a consultant who influences, leading from one step behind (De Jong & Berg, 2002). Through the use of transformative questions, particularly the "miracle question" (c.f., Thomas & Nelson, this publication), the therapist creates opportunities in which the partners can begin to view their encounters in new ways, give new relationship-supportive meanings to their interactions, and discover and create new possibilities of change.

- Apart from any model or technique, flexibility and sensitivity to the needs of the moment are a therapist's greatest resources. Like any approach, SFT can be practiced badly when the clinician is more interested in doing what the model dictates rather than in listening closely, responding sensitively, and working flexibly with each client.

- Therapy conversation is always by invitation. Clients are continually inviting us into certain kinds of conversations and we are accepting or declining their invitations. We also invite clients into certain kinds of conversations and they accept or decline our invitations. All therapy takes place in this context of continual and subtle conversational interplay, and if the therapist is not aware of the differing types of conversation that can occur between therapist and partners in a couple, many well-meaning efforts at helping will go awry. Traditional brief therapies (including SFT) use the terms "visitor," "complainant," and "consultant" to describe the nature of the therapeutic relationship at a given point in time. We have found it more helpful to adopt the following bipersonal terms, using them to describe therapeutic conversation: *visitor/host, complainant/sympathizer,* and *customer/ consultant* (Ziegler & Hiller, 2001). Being able to recognize what kind of conversation is occurring is crucial to excluding of the kinds of therapist-couple interactions that support triangulation, wandering, and getting stuck.

CASE EXAMPLES

The last section of this chapter focuses on two couples cases. We are presenting two cases for a number of reasons. First, because each case was handled by a different therapist, we hope readers will get a sense of how a therapist can express his or her unique style within the framework of RPT or SFT techniques. Second, by presenting two cases, we hope to show how a solution-focused approach with couples can orient the therapist when couples confront the therapist with certain clinical challenges that can baffle even highly experienced couples therapists. The first case is a good example of the importance of taking the time to establish a good working relationship with both partners, avoiding triangulation, and not assuming everyone is on the same page when the first meeting begins. The second case presentation contains an important discussion of the importance of goal-building in couples therapy and provides an example of how a therapist can go about helping the couple develop well-formed therapy goals.

Case 1: A Marital Crisis

We present a case from Phil's practice that contains a number of typical challenges that can overwhelm a beginner couples therapist. We want to demonstrate how Phil uses a number of solution-focused interventive questions to meet these challenges, how he guides the subsequent conversations to thicken the couple's good story, and how he collaborates with the couple to generate ways to work through the crisis in their marriage.

This particular case conveys the importance of establishing rapport with both partners and finding common ground when members of a couple bring very different perspectives about being in therapy and arrive with different initial goals and opposing ideas about how therapy might be helpful. It also demonstrates that a collaborative, nonexpert stance does not preclude giving some advice about how a couple might solve a presenting problem or find pathways toward solution. And it is our hope that this case will show that SFT, when practiced with a focus on the collaborative, is not solution-forced therapy, as some critics suggest (Nylund & Corsiglia, 1994).

Gail, who first called to set up the couple's appointment, said she and her husband needed help with a marital crisis. When Phil welcomed them into his office, Gail and Alan both looked visibly nervous; Gail was hesitant, and

Alan somewhat stiff. They were attractive, well-dressed people in late middle age. Phil introduced himself, asked them to make themselves comfortable, and (as is our general practice) said he would like them each to tell him how he could help with whatever was bringing them to his office. Phil explained that all he had heard from Gail was that they were in the middle of some kind of marital crisis. (We always want to reveal whatever either partner has told us over the phone, which we present in a very matter-of-fact way no matter how potentially explosive it might be.) Note that Phil did not specifically ask for information about the crisis, nor did he limit his question only to the crisis. He wanted to keep the field open so that when he moved into helping the couple establish their goals for therapy, important concerns and themes would not be locked out of consideration by the "marital crisis" frame. This is one of the ways we are attentive to the invitations and directions inherent in therapeutic questions.

GAIL (*with tears welling, which she tried hard to stop*): Alan was having an affair.

ALAN (*immediately*): It's over; I told her it's over. And that it didn't really mean a thing. I keep telling her I'm sorry, that it's over, and that I love her very much. (*Despite their apparent nervousness, they have plunged right in, as often happens.*)

GAIL (*now looking and sounding angry, firing back*): Yeah, sure. You think all you've gotta do is say you're sorry and that it's over and that's supposed to be the end of it, huh? Well, my trust in you and in our marriage has been totally destroyed. Totally destroyed! (*Alan looks pained and grim. The atmosphere in the room has become, in a flash, quite tense.*)

PHIL: Wow. This is pretty serious—I can see that you're struggling with a very hard situation. I'm glad you've taken the step to come for help. (*Validating that both have strong feelings, acknowledging the crisis without blaming anyone, and highlighting that both must have felt strongly enough about getting through it that they came for help.*)

ALAN: Well, I gotta be honest here. I'm really not the kind of guy who believes in therapy. She's a big one for pouring out your troubles to someone you pay a lot of money to, but I'm pretty private, and I like to solve my own problems. Don't take it personally or anything. You seem like a nice enough guy, but that's how I feel.

PHIL: Hey, I don't take it personally, Alan. Believe me: I don't think therapy is right for everyone. Who knows, maybe, by the end of this session we'll agree not to schedule another appointment. But how about this? How about we spend this hour with my learning more about what's happened for you folks and maybe see if we can come up with some ideas about how the two of you can work through this tough time and come out the other end ready to move on? We'll only consider making another appointment if all three of us think it's a good idea. How's that? (*Phil's response is based on his knowledge that so far he is in a visitor/host conversation with Alan, meaning Alan so far has not bought into the idea that therapy could be helpful or seen as a goal to be achieved by coming, and like a mandated client, he is only there because a third party—in this case, Gail—has convinced him he should or must. Proceeding to invite Alan into "therapeutic" conversation that doesn't take into account his current lack of interest or confidence in the therapeutic project would not build a collaborative context.)*

ALAN: That seems fair, but I gotta warn you, Gail and I have been through a lot together and we've always found a way to solve our marital problems—hell, all couples have marital problems—without any outside help. I pretty much think we can get through this on our own, too.

PHIL: Okay. Sounds like you two have faced some challenges and done pretty well. That says a lot about your relationship. How long have you been together?

ALAN: Twenty-three years. We have two grown kids and three grandchildren. Gail can't get enough of those grandkids.

PHIL: (*interested in building on the "good story" material Alan is presenting, but also being concerned not to discount Gail's feelings about the seriousness of the affair's impact on her and the relationship. Building rapport with both partners in a couple or maintaining what we call "active neutrality" requires that the therapist include and validate both partners' perspectives.*) You know, I don't know the two of you very well, but the sense I get is that this crisis is pretty serious and it's really important that you find a way through it. But I also hear that you've been together a long time, been through a lot, and love the family you've built. And, let me know if I'm on the right page here, it seems like you both love each other a lot and want to save this marriage if it's at all possible. (*Both Alan and Gail are nodding and even glancing at each other with small smiles, and Phil would not have said these things had he not had a strong sense that both would agree with his comments.*) But I have to tell you, I've worked with a lot of couples over the years where one partner's affair was the issue, and while couples can and do come through it, many don't, and it's never easy or fast. But, with hard work, lots of couples do make it through. Maybe, at some point, you would like me to share what I've learned from some of these successful couples. (*It's quite helpful, as you approach goal-building in couples work to both name the possibilities for success and suggest that success will entail very hard work; it may be that this makes people feel both hopeful and respected in the gravity of their situation. Note also that Phil is normalizing their problem by talking about other couples who have faced it and alluding to their ability to move through the difficulty.*)

GAIL: Yes. Maybe that's what we need, some guidance about how to get through this. We just keep getting into fights. Over and over. You know, I start getting upset, thinking about stuff, you know, and then I can't help myself, I start asking questions. I know I shouldn't, but I can't help it. Then Alan clams up, gets all upset, and won't talk. Or he gets pissed and says what's he gotta' do? Slit his wrists, nail himself to the cross?

PHIL (*normalizing further*): You know, in my experience, this is pretty common. See if this fits how it goes with you two: Usually when an affair is discovered, if the partners still really love each other and don't want to end the marriage, the one who discovers the affair has lots of plaguing thoughts and fantasies. They drive that person nuts. (*Gail nods her head.*) And, Gail, like most people in your position, you can't stop wanting the details even though it's painful to hear them, and you want more than anything for the pain to stop. (*Gail is nodding and tearful; Alan is looking unhappy and a bit irritated toward Phil.*) And, Alan, the person who's had the affair, and who suddenly realizes what he's jeopardized, wants more than anything to save the marriage, to make clear how bad he feels, and how hard he wants to work to make it up to his partner and prove his love. Now that he's clear about it, he wants to move on and make things better. (*Alan relaxes a bit but still appears wary. Phil has validated both partners' experiences, normalized their differences, and begun a process of mutualizing in which the problem can be seen as common to them both and their responses as more in reaction to the problem than in reaction to the other person.*)

PHIL (*continuing*): So, for what it's worth, in my experience, what you two are going through and how each of you is handling things is pretty normal. The problem is that you're both in pretty different places, and your feelings and needs make each of you do things that are understandable but only make things worse and don't always fit with the other person. Does this seem right? (*Checking with partners to build collaborative sense of situation.*)

BOTH: Yes, exactly.

PHIL (*Continuing to frame the problem as mutual and normal and beginning to work on what the goals of therapy might be—building a future picture and some steps leading to that picture that would serve as signs that the couple is moving forward, on track toward the changes they want*): So, do you suppose you'll be on your way to getting through this crisis when you can find a way that both of your needs can be met—that is, Gail's need to be able to ask for details when she needs to and have Alan answer even though it's pretty painful . . .

GAIL: Yes.

PHIL: . . . and also Alan's need to know that, in time, Gail won't need to ask so often, and he can sometimes say he doesn't want to talk about it for the moment? (*Alan is nodding.*) And, that with time, the two of you will find ways to rebuild Gail's trust?

BOTH: Yes. (*Now that all have joined in a collaborative effort to delineate general goals, both Gail and Alan have entered solidly into customer/ consultant mode with Phil.*)

PHIL: Okay then. Let me ask you both this: It's sort of a strange question and I don't mean in asking it that I think this can all be solved overnight, but I'd like to ask you this: Suppose when you go home tonight . . . and, after dinner and whatever you do in the evening, you go to sleep. . . . and, . . . while you're both asleep, a miracle happens and somehow this crisis is resolved; it's behind you both. And tomorrow morning when you both get up, you begin to notice something's different. But since you were asleep, you don't know the miracle happened—but you can see signs of it, that the crisis is behind you. When you feel ready, I'd like each of you to tell me, as you imagine the day after the miracle, what you notice that will tell you the miracle happened (*This is the "miracle question"* [Thomas & Nelson, 2007]. *The point of the miracle question is to elicit a number of signs and signals of a desired relationship, bits and pieces of a well-imagined future solution-accomplished picture with the idea that formulating those concrete signs will make them more likely to happen and be perceived. Any well-formed goal, in addition, whether elicited by the miracle question or by other questions, begins the process of thickening the good story right in the in-session moment.*)

GAIL: I won't have that awful knot in my stomach. That woman's face won't be in my mind and I won't be having fantasies about her and him in some motel room.

PHIL (*using Gail's initial answers as a starting point for developing well-formed goals—experiential signs indicating positive changes toward the desired ends and experiential bits and pieces of the desired future picture itself. Notice Phil goes step-by-step helping Gail develop goals that satisfy all the criteria of being therapeutically well-formed. One criterion is that goals be stated in the presence of something, not the absence. Another is that they be stated in terms of small, observable actions. Here, Phil seeks to move from absence to presence while still in the realm of nonobservable changes—feelings and thoughts*): What will you be feeling and thinking about that morning instead?

GAIL: Well, I guess I might still have some bad feelings . . . It'd have to be some miracle for all the bad feelings to be gone (*smiles*); but anyway, I'd probably be feeling glad Alan and I are still together. Sort of more confident that even though he had the affair he still loves me and we have a good marriage (*Alan smiles at her*), and that we can make our marriage even better if we get through this. Oh, yeah, and I would be feeling confident that he isn't going to have any contact with her ever again.

ALAN (*jumping in*): How many times do I have to tell you?—I love you more than you can know. And, I swear to God, I will never see or talk to her again. I told you I can't stop her from leaving voicemails and sending e-mails, but I no longer want any of that, I mean it: I don't want anything to do with her. I don't respond to her e-mails or voicemails. I just erase them. It's over. All I want is for you to see you are the only woman in the world for me.

PHIL (*aware that Alan is getting into the pattern of "selling," a pattern he assumes has caused downward spirals before, Phil wants to interrupt Alan while still validating his positive intentions*): Alan, I get the clear sense that you're doing everything you can to assure Gail the affair is over and that you feel bad about it. But, from what you both say, your assurances and apologies, while sincere, aren't always making a difference; in fact, sometimes they seem to make things worse. (*Both nod in agreement.*) So I want to ask you, if I could, a different kind of question before we go back to the miracle morning. If you put yourself in Gail's shoes, what do you think she would say would make her get a little more confident that she can trust you about this? (*This is a reflexive question, which asks one partner to imagine the other's reactions or feelings. It can be used to highlight the empathic bridge between people. Notice that Phil does not ask about bad story or negative feelings—why Gail doesn't like his protestations, for instance—but about what she might desire and receive warmly, what would move her—in other words, toward their goal picture.*)

ALAN: Well, I don't know really. I try to reassure her. (*Phil waits quietly.*) Just time, maybe.

PHIL: Anything else? Maybe something you're already doing sometimes, or some little step—something, remember, she'd say she wanted—that would tell her how much you really care?

ALAN: Well, maybe she'd say if I answered her questions patiently sometimes, without getting mad, including the ones, I guess, about whether I was thinking about the affair or not. Which I'm not! She's the one who has it on her mind all the time! (*Despite Alan's last relapse into his own perspective, Gail is smiling and nodding her head. Obviously, his understanding of her point of view has positive meaning for her.*)

PHIL: Great. I see Gail nodding her head here, so I guess you must have gotten it right.

GAIL: He did!

PHIL: Okay, so now I'd like to ask you, Gail, a few more questions about the postmiracle morning. (*Now inviting Gail again to imagine the small observable signs that will reflect changes in her feelings and thinking.*) Taking a look, now, at a few more things . . . what do you suppose Alan will notice different about you that morning that will tell him your feelings are different and you're having more positive thoughts? (*This is also a reflexive question; in answering it, Gail will be detailing not only her own behavior when she's feeling happier and more confident, but conveying to Alan that she understands what he's likely to notice and value. It's also a question about behavior, making concrete what positive change would look like.*)

GAIL: I don't know. (*Phil waits, and eventually Gail comes up with something; when asking a "picturing" question that gets an initial don't-know answer—as earlier with Alan, also—silence can be quite fruitful, giving people's imaginations time to work.*) Well, I guess he'll notice that I wake up and look at him with a smile—that hasn't happened for a while. (Both Alan and Gail are smiling somewhat mischievously at the moment.) And, maybe he'll notice me roll over and give him a kiss, cuddle a bit.

ALAN (*notice his response in light of his initial reluctance to try therapy*): Wow! That would sure say a lot. You wouldn't have to do much more than that to give me a lot more hope.

GAIL: Gee. I realized something just now. I don't want you to feel like you can get off the hook so easily. You caused me a lot of really awful pain. I want you to suffer for it. I want you to have to feel bad when you have to admit to what you've done. I don't want to forgive you yet.

PHIL (*going with this as important information for developing the solutions rather than continuing for the moment to explore the details of the post-miracle morning*): That's a really important thing to realize. Probably that doesn't come as a big surprise to you, right, Alan?

ALAN: No, I know about it. It's hard to take, but I know she wants me to hurt 'cause I hurt her so badly. I understand that. I don't always like it and I try to protect myself sometimes. But I don't blame her, I guess. But I would like her to see that I've been hurting real bad, too. Not as bad as her. But I feel pretty crummy about it, believe me.

PHIL (*sensing grounds for mutualizing and potential good story material*): So, I get that both of you see that part of what Gail needs is to know that—really know that—Alan is paying a price for the pain he caused her—that he doesn't get off easy. And maybe, if Alan's patient about that, that's something he could do that would really make a difference to reduce both your pain and get you back on track.

GAIL: That's true. Maybe it's kind of screwy, but it's true.

PHIL: Just let me ask, Alan, if, knowing Gail as you do, you could say what it might be you would be doing that would tell Gail you understood about this "paying a price" thing, that you were willing to be patient. (*Another reflexive question; the action of these, because they highlight empathy and mutually imagined pictures, is to thicken the good story.*)

ALAN: Gee, I don't know. (*Phil waits.*) Well, maybe I could just tell her, you know, instead of getting pissed, I could just tell her I understand it will take a while, to get over this, to get over the hurt. That I know that. That I accept it. (*Gail tears up again; Alan looks at her tenderly.*)

PHIL: But I also sense that at some point, when the time's right, things have to move to another stage. I'm not sure what that stage will look like, but my guess is that some of the things you notice the day after the miracle will be part of it (*reaffirming the steps forward toward the goal of greater trust and closeness*).

ALAN: Yeah. I can see that. I guess I'm wondering how long we have to go before we can move on, though.

GAIL: Well, I didn't want to tell you this before because I didn't want you to come here just to get me to give up my feelings, but the fact that you came here today—I know how much you didn't want to—the fact that you came really made a difference. I didn't want you to do it just to win points, so I didn't say anything. (*Starting to cry once more.*) But I know how much you hate letting other people know about your troubles and how much you don't believe in counseling. But, you came and you're actually opening up. It means a lot to me, Alan.

ALAN: Well, I don't want to spoil a good thing, I mean, yeah, I did come, and all, but this guy [Phil] is okay. I expected him to get all over my case and tell me all sorts of stuff about what the problem with me is and what I have to do and not do, stuff like that. He's said some right-on things—a few things I didn't particularly like hearing, but all in all, I think coming here was a good idea.

PHIL (*taking the opportunity to learn more about what Alan thinks has been helpful and also acknowledging that he might have said some things that bothered him*): Alan, I'm not sure what I said that bothered you. I know I didn't pull my punches, but I didn't intend to say anything that didn't sit right. Could we take a moment so you can tell me both what I said that you didn't like and what we've done here that makes you say coming here was a good idea? (*As part of a collaborative process, Phil asks specifically about what helps and what works and doesn't for people.*)

ALAN: Well, I like it that you don't use all that psychobabble talk and that you just say what you mean. I didn't really like hearing that it's natural for Gail to want to see me hurt for all the pain I caused her, but I know that's true. Mostly I think talking with you, finding out that we're not the only ones you've worked with that have had some of the same problems, finding out that there are some things that can help and some stuff we need to be careful about, those have all been good things. Sometimes I sort of feel you're on Gail's side, but then I see you're pretty neutral. I like that you can see we really care for each other and love each other, that we're just in a hard place right now but we can get through it.

GAIL: How do you feel about coming back? I think Phil can help us.

ALAN: Well I don't want to get into some long-term thing, you know, digging into every aspect of our relationship, going on and on for years.

PHIL: Well, Alan, could you say what you would want—what you think we could do in maybe four or five sessions—that could really make a difference? (*Focusing on goal-building, specific signs that therapy is helpful in order to see whether coming back would be worthwhile.*)

ALAN (*thinks for few moments and then says something surprising*): Well, I don't know if we can fix this in a few sessions, but I gotta' say that part of why I had the affair—I'm not blaming you Gail, it's been both of us—but we haven't been really very close for a long time. I come home from work and you're out a lot and when we're home in the evening I just want to veg in front of the TV for a while and you go into the living room and read by yourself. We weren't even going to bed at the same time; we hardly had sex. (*Looking at Phil*) Actually since this all came out, we've been having the best sex in years. Then Gail gets pissed about something or I get defensive and that's the end of that. I guess my point is that maybe my having the affair and you finding out and our coming here is a chance to make some changes, you know—get our groove back. (*As happens not infrequently, Alan is defining a new goal now that he feels safe about and effective in working with the presenting problem in therapy. Goals often evolve. The conversation with Alan has moved thoroughly into customer/consultant mode from its initial visitor/host mode.*)

GAIL: I can't believe my ears! Are you finally admitting that things haven't been so good with us for a while?

ALAN: Yes, I admit it. It's just that you kept pestering me to go to counseling so I didn't want to admit I was unhappy. I know, I know, I probably should have. But now that all this has happened, I'm up for doing some work with Phil, not just about the affair but ways we can get closer again.

GAIL: Talk about a miracle! And, you know what? I believe you. I can tell you're telling me the truth about how you feel.

PHIL: Wow. We've come a long way today. In about an hour you two have talked about how much you want to save this marriage, how much you understand each other, and now how willing you are to work to get through this crisis—which might take time and patience. And you're also talking about working to improve your relationship, which you both recognize was in trouble even before the affair. Well, if you both feel like working with me, I would love the opportunity. I've been very moved by the honesty and courage you've both shown here. It's been my experience that when couples come in and work as hard as you two have in the first session, the chances are pretty good they'll get what they came for. (*Phil is validating and complimenting this couple, who have worked hard and come a long way. Noticing assets and diligence highlights the good story and draws attention to people's competence, effectiveness, and resourcefulness in solving problems.*)

At this point, the hour was coming to a close. The couple made another appointment for a week later. They came to the second session saying that overall, things were much better. They had had only one fight and they were able to cut it off without either feeling bad. Gail reported feeling more confident in their future and pleased that Alan seemed to get that he couldn't rush her to trust him fully. Alan was feeling better able to answer Gail's questions with patience, knowing that this was a natural part of the process of her rebuilding trust and even that part of her motivation was to make him squirm— he was seeing that by and large as a justifiable punishment. They decided to schedule the third session several weeks away so they could see how things went on their own.

They came to the third session saying they had decided to make Thursday evening a romantic night—going out for dinner or doing something special together. Alan agreed he would leave work early on Thursdays so he would have the energy to make the night a nice event. At the end of the third session, Phil and the couple talked about whether they felt on track and both said they did. He used progress-scaling questions and both Gail and Alan said they were somewhere between 8 and 9 on how much progress they felt they had made toward putting the affair behind them and rekindling the romance in their marriage. Phil then scaled how confident each partner was that she or he could keep making things better on her or his own. Both said 9 to 9.5. They both agreed that since their confidence was not a 10 that they would schedule a session for a month later with the option to cancel if both of them felt things were still going well.

Gail called about a week before the scheduled appointment and said she and Alan were doing great and that they were going to take a break for the time being. However, she assured Phil that both of them, particularly Alan, wanted to know that they could come back if they ran into any difficulties. Phil called back and said how pleased he was to hear they were doing well but that he was a bit sad that he was not going to have the pleasure of seeing them now that things were so much better, and he assured Gail that if they ever felt the need for a minor or even a major tune-up they should not hesitate to call.

Case 2: Incompatible Goals

Our second case demonstrates the challenge couples therapy presents when the partners arrive with apparently incompatible goals. This is a common situation in couples therapy and all too often the therapist proceeds without addressing this problem, sometimes without even noticing it. This makes true collaboration with the clients impossible and means the therapy often bogs down without achieving productive results. The therapist may blame the couple for being unmotivated or difficult when in fact what has happened is that no shared goals have been delineated. (In this case, the couple we reported that they had been to five or six couples therapists during a three-year period before coming to see Tobey.) In this example, we focus on the importance of constructing therapeutically well-formed goals; and, in couples work, one criterion of well-formed goals is that they be mutually meaningful, entailing a future picture that both partners are willing to work to achieve. In Recreating Partnership terms, this shared future picture is a return to the *good story* context.

This couple came to Tobey referred by the husband's individual therapist. He had referred them as a couple because the husband was increasingly upset about the fact that he and his wife had no sex life. The husband had reported that in her own therapy, his wife was discovering that she had been molested as a child and now she felt she needed to learn to maintain her boundaries, and until she was able to do that she did not want to have sex.

In the first session, the partners began by talking about their individual positions, confirming that there was, in fact, a serous division between them: he said he wanted regular sex with his wife, and she said she wanted to feel safe and entitled to protect herself and her body from sexual activities she experienced as triggering her fear and anxiety. As Tobey began a goal-development discussion, she asked Gordon (the husband) whether he thought it might help to try and be more patient with Lillian (the wife), supporting her in her need to be able to say "no" clearly, but Gordon said that he had been patient for three years and that he had run out of patience. Lillian, for her part, explained that in her individual therapy, it had become clear that she had never been able to decide for herself in this arena, whether or not she was going along with someone else or making her own decisions and that until she worked out those issues even the idea of sex was abhorrent to her. She wanted Gordon to be more understanding and back off. These goals/ desires were in sharp conflict, and Tobey saw that before going forward, it was essential to develop some agreed-upon, shared meta-goal with the couple (an inclusive, overarching goal). This might provide a foundation for developing step-by-step signs of progress that could move the couple toward a shared and mutually attractive future picture while meeting each partner's individual needs to some degree. This change would entail moving the conversation from complainant/sympathizer mode to customer/consultant. Most couples begin their first sessions in complainant/sympathizer mode, where each partner's hope is that the therapy will bring about desired changes in the other. They may conceive of the therapist as an adjudicator or sympathizer who will verify their complaints and lay down the law about who is to blame. If the therapist is unaware of this conversational mode, it is quite easy to get caught in triangulation or confusion, ending up in an unhelpful alliance with one partner or an inability to formulate a pathway forward. Goal development is a process that moves the couple toward customer/consultant conversations, where each partner becomes interested in taking action in behalf of a mutually satisfying future with the collaborative help of the therapist and all three, therapist and partners, can embrace an overarching perspective.

During the hour, Tobey initiated conversation about increasing intimacy as a goal they could both share, but by the end it was fairly clear that, at least for the time being, their ideas of increased intimacy still came up against conflicting individual pictures, and no therapeutically well-formed goals had been established; each partner kept returning to the restatement of their differences about sex and their complaints about the other's lack of compliance with their needs. Tobey asked if there might be other issues and goals they could agree to work toward in therapy. Both Gordon and Lillian said this difference was a major problem and that the other therapies had been a waste of time precisely because they never got anywhere on this issue; thus, there were really no other issues they wanted to work on currently.

As the first session came to a close, Tobey complimented both partners for their willingness to persevere on such a challenging issue and for being so clear that the sexual issue was really their focus. She also offered them a choice: either they could make another appointment and in the meantime see if they could come up with an agreed-upon goal or they could give it some time, and if they discovered a common goal or desire they wanted help to achieve, they could call her. This was something of a shock to this couple, who said they had never had a therapist suggest they might want to wait before doing therapy; in a sense, Tobey was making it hard, not easy, to get her to agree to work with them. Most importantly, she was drawing attention to the need for a partnership orientation. About a month later, Lillian called to schedule a second appointment, saying they had come up with a shared goal and wanted Tobey's help.

When they came in, they explained that they had been to a couples encounter weekend where they had learned the "mirroring" technique. It had been pretty useful to them during the workshop and they were excited about it, but when they got home, they could not do it very well. Both said that they wanted Tobey's help in practicing their mirroring skills. Tobey saw this as a good start; improving their mirroring skills was a mutual goal and might serve as a means to some greater ends and she wanted to explore this possibility. In this context, she might be able to help the couple develop some experiential and interpretive signs that their relationship was improving. So, when the couple came in, she used the conversation about the value of mirroring as an entryway into solution–and goal-building conversations that could strengthen partnership and develop a shared desired future.

TOBEY: It sounds as though we have a good starting place: You've agreed that if you can improve your mirroring skills, if you can use this technique during challenging conversations, you'll both feel this will be an important sign you're getting somewhere in making your relationship happier. It would be helpful to me to get a sense about how well you think you're using mirroring and how you'll know, you're getting better. So let me ask you kind of a strange numbers question. On a scale from one to ten, with one being the lowest score you would give to your ability to use mirroring and ten being that you're both great at it, where would you say you are currently as a couple? (*She wants them to rate their relational, not individual levels so that she can flesh out interpersonal changes. Scaling questions are a very good way both to focus on the incremental steps that make change happen and to set a positive perceptual frame.*)

LILLIAN: Well, if you mean, "together," I would say we're at maybe three. I'm not good at it really, and Gordon isn't either, so that seems about right.

GORDON: Well, I try, but no matter how much I try, you always complain I don't do it right and you keep adding stuff that makes it really hard. (*Gordon is still hovering in the complainant mode, hoping for a sympathizer response, but Tobey will decline this invitation and invite him again into customer/consultant mode.*)

TOBEY: Okay, Gordon I hear that, but for now I just need to get a sense about where you see yourselves, as a couple, on your ability to use mirroring together. (*Declining an invitation into a bad story conversation and redirecting Gordon to come up with a number.*)

GORDON: Well, overall, I'd agree with Lil, about a three.

TOBEY: Okay, so we have a place to start. Can each of you tell me what will be different in your mirroring conversations that will tell you both that you've moved up to say a four or four and a half? (*This incremental step question is meant to elicit concrete signs and signals that can then be noticed and at the same time, prefigure or shape an imagined future.*)

LILLIAN: Oh, that's easy. We could tell the other person what we heard without adding a lot of our own stuff. We both have a hard time with that.

GORDON: Well, I agree, but I would add that Lillian wouldn't go on and on, so I could follow her and be able to summarize what she was trying to say without forgetting it.

TOBEY: Okay, let's see if I could put this together in a way you would both agree on. You would both listen and just feed back what you heard without adding your own thoughts and reactions. And in order to help you do this, Gordon, it would make a difference if Lillian would try and limit the length and range of her statements so you could follow and reflect back what she's said. Have I got that? (*This is an example of mutualizing a picture of progress and coincidently model-mirroring.*)

BOTH: Yes.

TOBEY: Well, do you think it would be a good idea to have you try and talk now about some issue using mirroring? And, if you want, I can jump in now and then and help when it looks like you guys are going off track or are having trouble. How does that sound? (*Please note that while mirroring exercises are a pretty standard part of much couples therapy, this exercise situation came up specifically because the partners requested it after Tobey had planted the idea of a shared goal. Also, the couples weekend had helped them to move forward. Part of being a collaborative therapist is realizing that couples can find useful resources and opportunities—many of them extra-therapeutic—in many places and therapy can make use of that.*)

LILLIAN (*with Gordon nodding agreement*): That's a good idea, and, yeah, better jump in if we get into trouble. Gordon, I'd like to talk about how we could work together to get the house cleaned up and get the kids to help so we can get to bed together at a reasonable hour.

GORDON: That's a good one. We always get into a fight about this.

At this point, having developed signs of progress with respect to using the mirroring technique, Tobey has prepared the ground for the couple to practice mirroring around a contentious issue with clear ideas about what will tell each partner they are doing a "better job" at the mirroring project. Each partner knew what to do and what to look for. In fact, they have the conversation, and, by the end, they have reached several agreements about how to get the house cleaned up and agreed that when they did this they would have a chance to get in bed together at a reasonable hour, which both wanted so long as Gordon agreed to not make immediate sexual advances. At the end, they each gave the conversation a high 6 or 7. As the session came to a close, Tobey suggested that they could either practice mirroring at home or, if they thought it was better to do their practicing with her help, they could wait until the next session to take up this or another issue. Notice that Tobey makes very open-ended, flexible suggestions, letting the couple decide how they will change and how to use therapy and their mirroring practice in a way that is productive for them. These kinds of questions leave plenty of room for the couple's own creative and idiosyncratic pathways toward change.

It should also be noted that the initial issue concerning the couple's sex life has been set aside for now because the couple and Tobey have agreed to work on mirroring skill-building. Nevertheless, Tobey is cognizant of the husband's earlier-stated objection to former therapies, which he said had been sidetracked. Thus, she remains attentive to possibilities for inviting the couple into conversations that might form the basis for mutual goal-building around that thorny and (so far) intractable issue.

At the beginning of the third session, Gordon and Lillian come into the room smiling and holding hands. Tobey said it looked like they had a good week and enthusiastically invited them to tell her all about it.

LILLIAN: Well, I think the most important thing is that I woke up about three in the morning this morning feeling horny. I was too tired, and I knew Gordon was too, so I didn't want to wake him up. But this is the first time in a long time where I felt really sexual and wanted Gordon.

TOBEY (*wanting to convey a positive response without being overeager to reframe their goals in light of this announcement*): Huh! That's pretty interesting. Let me ask you something about this, Lillian. When you first came in, Gordon said his goal was to have a sex life again with you, and you said your goal was to get Gordon to back off. Am I hearing you right, here, that even though you may still want him to be patient you also may want to be sexual with him, too? And it sounds like maybe this means you're starting to get in touch with your own sexual desires again?

LILLIAN: Yes, I do want that too. It's just that if Gordon keeps pushing at me and telling me over and over how much he wants sex, it's a complete turn-off. It feels like he just wants to use me and doesn't get it that I have old issues on this. And I hate it when he begs; it makes me feel guilty and pisses me off at the same time.

TOBEY (*declining the invitation to investigate bad story material and instead asking about the positive changes that brought on the experience she's describing*): Huh! So something must have changed to allow you to have this sexual feeling early this morning. Did Gordon know about this?

LILLIAN: Well, I told him when we got up this morning.

TOBEY (*to Gordon*): When Lillian told you about this, did it make a difference to you? Maybe it told you that things were heading in the right direction for you around your goals for having a sexual life with Lillian?

GORDON: Well, I liked hearing it but I'm not so sure if it will ever really lead to anything. This kind of thing has happened before.

TOBEY: Hmm, okay Gordon, so let me ask you: Do you know what Lillian might have been noticing different about you this past week that might have contributed to her feeling sexy toward you? (*Now Tobey is building a relational context for Lillian's change of feeling. By asking Gordon a reflexive, role-reversal question she's building agency: suggesting to them both that Gordon can have a positive influence on Lillian's interest in sex.*) And do you have any idea about what Lillian might say you could do more of that might help her get even more in touch with feeling desire toward you? (*Continued reflexive questions, inviting Gordon to see himself through Lillian's eyes, not to see what he has done wrong but what he has done right, and what he might want to do more of. This is a solution-focused approach: identify what made the difference, amplify agency, and ask people to identify what they can do more of to move further toward the future they want [De Jong & Berg, 2002, 1998].*)

GORDON: I'm not sure. Maybe it's just that I stopped talking about wanting sex. Maybe it made a difference that we worked together to get the house cleaned up and got the kids to pitch in . . . that took my being pretty clear with them that we wanted them to help . . . I don't know what else, really.

LILLIAN: Well, I can tell you this. You seemed more manly to me this week. I don't know exactly what it was, but you did.

TOBEY (*picking up on this good story material and building possible links between Lillian's observation about the different Gordon, the meaning to her of this difference, and Gordon's and Lillian's individual goals regarding their intimacy*): It might be really helpful, Lillian, if you could sort of think back over the week and see if you can discover what Gordon did that made him seem more manly? (*Both talking about his sexual needs and not talking about them have been equally ineffective ploys for Gordon in influencing Lillian to be more sexual; but now Lillian is saying that she wants to feel more sexual toward Gordon and that the key may have something to do with how he might appear rather than whether or not he presses her for sex. So, Tobey wants to flesh out what "more manly" means to Lillian and what the signs of this might be.)*

LILLIAN: Well, the first thing that comes to mind is that he really pitched in getting the house cleaned up. And when he talked to Gabe and 'Lissa about helping, he wasn't so wimpy, he just said they had to help and he didn't want any excuses. Wow. I have to tell you that really was different. I liked it. Felt like he was really my partner on this. Now that I think about it, watching him with the kids and seeing him like that made me feel a lot more intimate with him, somehow in a physical way, too. (*Note that, in terms of goal-building, the pathway to sexual intimacy for this couple seems to be through building partnership around family functioning rather than, as the couple first envisioned it, through mediated negotiations around how to have sex. As stated in Thomas and Nelson in this volume [2007], the solution is not necessarily directly related to the problem.*)

TOBEY: This is intriguing, Lillian. Do you suppose if you saw Gordon helping more and talking to the kids more that way, kind of keeping on that track somehow, it might help you feel more like being intimate with Gordon? And, maybe over time, move back into a sexual life with him?

LILLIAN: Yes, I think so. But I still don't want him to push me. You know like, "Well, now that I'm helping more around the house, how about us having sex."

GORDON: I understand.

TOBEY: Well, it seems like you two have built another element into your change program: Gordon helping more, taking more charge with the children, the two of you getting to bed together at a reasonable time, Gordon avoiding pressuring Lillian, and Lillian paying attention to times when she's feeling more sexual toward Gordon are all part of the plan at the moment. Does that make sense?

BOTH: Yes!!

TOBEY: So having talked about this, I'd like to check in on where we are right now and how we're doing.

TOBEY (*At this point, both Lillian and Gordon were smiling at each other and leaning together tenderly on the couch. Although the indicators about whether the session was on the right track seemed good, Tobey wanted to make sure the couple felt they were guiding the process and knew where they were going, so she moved toward scaling progress. This was also a move, given the obvious positive feelings in the room, to thicken the good story.*): Well, then, I'd like to ask a few more of those numbers questions to get a sense of where we are in our work together. First, let me ask you both, on a scale from one to ten, where would you say you folks are on the general issue of how well you two are doing?

BOTH (*one after another, looking at each other*): Eight!!

TOBEY: Wow! That's terrific. You guys have worked hard and made real progress. So, let me ask this then: how confident, again using the scale, one being no confidence at all and ten being absolutely sure, how confident are the two of you that you're developing the tools to allow you to keep moving toward your shared and individual goals for this relationship?

GORDON: Well, in general I would say eight or nine, on the sex issue maybe six or seven.

LILLIAN: I would say eight or nine on all the issues (*smiling at Gordon*), including sex, smarty.

TOBEY: Well, this sounds pretty good then. Lillian, is it still important to you that Gordon not push you on the sex issue?

LILLIAN: Yes.

TOBEY: Well, then, my guess is that he might need some idea about how he's to know you want to make love, as you approach that time. (*Gordon nod.*) Since he isn't going to initiate sex, what do you think you might do so he knows when you're beginning to feel more receptive? (*Notice that Tobey is using a lot of gradual and going-on-into-the-future terms to keep the idea of change incremental as a trend toward something, not an absolute state of being.*)

LILLIAN (*in a flirty way, looking at Gordon*): Oh, he'll know!

TOBEY: Well, if you don't want to put it into words in front of me, I can understand that. But will you be willing to tell him after you leave this session?

LILLIAN: Uh huh!

This session ended soon after this interchange. The couple came in for their fourth session reporting that Lillian had initiated sex and both agreed they had had a good time. Even though by the end of this session both partners said they were confident they were on their way, they both, particularly Gordon, felt cautious about their ability to maintain progress, and they said they also felt it was important to keep coming for awhile so they could deal with other issues that they'd had on the back burner, issues that included finances and possibly selling their home and moving to a more rural community. Tobey had seen this couple for eight more sessions spread out over four months, and they had a future session scheduled at the time of this writing. Both Gordon and Lillian feel that, although it remains a struggle sometimes to maintain closeness and good feeling, they've made significant progress in reestablishing intimacy and have built new confidence in their ability to feel like a team.

SUGGESTED READINGS

Berg, I. K. (1994). *Irreconcilable differences: A solution focused approach to marital therapy* [Videotape]. Milwaukee, WI: Brief Family Therapy Center.

Bertolino, B., & O'Hanlon, W. H. (2001). *Collaborative, competency-based counseling and psychotherapy.* Boston: Allyn and Bacon.

de Shazer, S. (1988). *Clues: Investigating solutions in brief therapy.* New York: Norton.

de Shazer, S. (1994). *Words were originally magic.* New York: Norton.

Duncan, B. L., & Miller, S. D. (2002). *The heroic client: Doing client-directed, outcome-informed therapy.* San Francisco: Jossey-Bass.

Eron, J. B., & Lund, T. W. (1996). *Narrative solutions in brief therapy.* New York: Guilford.

Friedman, S. (1993). Possibility therapy with couples: Constructing time-effective solutions. *Journal of Family Psychotherapy, 4*(4), 35-52.

Friedman, S. (1996). Couples therapy: Changing conversations. In H. Rosen & K. T. Kuehlwein (Eds.). *Constructing realities: Meaning-making perspectives for psychotherapists* (pp. 413-453). San Francisco: Jossey-Bass.

Friedman, S., & Lipchik, E. (1999). A time-effective, solution-focused approach to couple therapy. In J. M. Donovan (Ed.) *Short term couple therapy* (pp. 325-339). New York: Guilford.

Gottman, J. M. (1999). *The marriage clinic.* New York: Norton.

Gurman, A. S. (2002). Brief integrative marital therapy: A depth-behavioral approach. In A. S. Gurman & N. S. Jacobson (Eds.). *Clinical handbook of couple therapy* (3rd ed.) (pp. 180-220). New York: Guilford.

Hoffman, L. (1993). *Exchanging voices: A collaborative approach to family therapy.* London: Karnac.

Hoyt, M. (Ed.) (1994). *Constructive therapies.* Vol. 1. New York: Guilford Press.

Hoyt, M. (Ed.) (1996). *Constructive therapies.* Vol. 2. New York: Guilford Press.

Hoyt, M. (Ed.) (1998). *The handbook of constructive therapies.* San Francisco: Jossey-Bass.

Hoyt, M. (2000). *Some stories are better than others: Doing what works in brief therapy and managed care.* New York: Brunner/Mazel (Taylor and Francis).

Hoyt, M. F. (2002). Solution-focused couple therapy. In A. S. Gurman & N. S. Jacobson (Eds.). *Clinical handbook of couple therapy* (3rd ed.) (pp. 335-369). New York: Guilford.

Hoyt, M. F., & Berg. I. K. (1998). Solution focused couple therapy: Helping clients construct self-fulfilling realities. In F. M. Dattilio (Ed.), *Case studies in couple and family therapy* (pp. 203-232). New York: Guilford.

Johnson, C. E., & Goldman, J. (1996). Taking safety home: A solution-focused approach with domestic violence. In M. F. Hoyt (Ed.), *Constructive therapies* (Vol. 2, pp. 184-196). New York: Guilford.

Johnson, L. D. (1995). *Psychotherapy in the age of accountability.* New York: Norton.

Lipchik, E. (2002). *Beyond technique in solution-focused therapy.* New York: Guilford.

Walter, J. L., & Peller, J. E. (2000). *Recreating brief therapy: Preferences and possibilities.* New York: Norton.

Walter, J. L., & Peller, J. E. (1992). *Becoming solution focused in brief therapy.* New York: Brunner/Mazel (Taylor & Francis).

Walter, J. L., & Peller, J. E. (1988). Going beyond the attempted solution: A couple's meta-solution. *Family Therapy Case Studies, 3*(1), 41-45.

Ziegler, P. B. (1998). Solution-focused therapy for the not-so-brief-clinician. *Journal of Collaborative Therapies, 6*(1), 22-25.

Ziegler, P., & Hiller, T. (2001). *Recreating partnership: A solution-oriented, collaborative approach to couples therapy.* New York: Norton.

REFERENCES

Anderson, H. (1997). *Conversation, language, and possibilities: A postmodern approach to therapy.* New York: Basic Books.

Anderson, H., & Goolishian, H. A. (1992). The client is the expert: A not-knowing approach to therapy. In S. McNamee & K. J. Gergen (Eds.), *Therapy as social construction* (pp. 25-39). Newbury Park, CA: Sage.

De Jong, P., & Berg, I. K. (2002). *Interviewing for solutions* (2nd ed.). Monterey, CA: Brooks-Cole.

de Shazer, S., & Berg, I. K. (1985). A part is not apart: Working with only one of the partners present. In A. S. Gurman (Ed.), *Casebook of marital therapy* (pp. 97-110). New York: Guilford.

Hudson, P., & O'Hanlon, W. H. (1991). *Rewriting love stories: Brief marital therapy.* New York: Norton.

Nylund, D., & Corsiglia, V. (1994). Becoming solution-focused forced in brief therapy: Remembering something important we already knew. *Journal of Systemic Therapies, 13*(1), 5-12.

Thomas, F. N., & Nelson, T. S. (2007). Assumptions within the solution-focused brief therapy tradition. In T. S. Nelson & F. N. Thomas (Eds.). *Handbook of solution-focused brief therapy: Clinical applications* (pp. 3-24). Binghamton, NY: The Haworth Press.

White, M., & Epston, D. (1992). *Narrative means to therapeutic ends.* New York: Norton.

Ziegler, P. B., & Hiller, T. (2001). *Recreating partnership: A solution-oriented, collaborative approach to couples therapy.* New York: Norton.

Ziegler, P. B., & Hiller, T. (2002). Good story/bad story: Collaborating with violent couples. *Psychotherapy Networker, 26*(2), 63-68.

Chapter 5

Looking Beyond Depression

Teri Pichot

INTRODUCTION

Depression has been described as a blue mood, a deep hole, a dark tunnel, and countless other analogies in an effort to capture the dark emotion that is the hallmark of depression. The commonalities among all these descriptions are aloneness or emptiness and an intense sense of sadness that has a perceived suffocating grip. Depression has a way of making its victim start to believe that there is no way out, that no one could possibly understand, and that there is something fundamentally flawed that is beyond repair. This belief, if unchecked, can even lead to suicide. For those who are struggling with depression, there is often the belief that there is no point of looking beyond the depression. It is for this very reason that Solution-Focused Brief Therapy (SFBT) is such a powerful approach to working with those who are afflicted with depressive symptoms. SFBT offers the very hope and future vision that is frequently lost by those who struggle with this condition.

Estimates are that approximately 9.5 percent of the adult American population is affected by some form of depression (National Institute of Mental Health [NIMH], 2003). According to the World Health Organization's 2001 World Health Report (cited in NIMH, 2003), "depression was the leading cause of years lived with a disability among men and women of all ages in the United States and worldwide." Sources estimate that approximately 12 million women in the United States experience depression each year (NIMH, 1999). Experts have discovered that depressive disorders affect roughly twice as many women as men, and "this two-to-one ratio exists regardless of racial and ethnic background or economic status" (NIMH, 2000).

Handbook of Solution-Focused Brief Therapy: Clinical Applications
© 2007 by The Haworth Press, Inc. All rights reserved.
doi:10.1300/5135_05

Clients who present with symptoms of depression are well known to mental health professionals. These symptoms include depressed mood, feelings of hopelessness, diminished interest or pleasure in previously enjoyed activities, significant weight loss/gain or decrease/increased appetite, insomnia/hypersomnia, psychomotor agitation/retardation, fatigue or loss of energy, feelings of worthlessness, feelings of excessive or inappropriate guilt, diminished ability to think or concentrate or indecisiveness, and recurrent thoughts of death or suicide (American Psychiatric Association, 1994, pp. 162-163).

In addition to these symptoms, medical conditions can be exacerbated by mood, because what one thinks has an influence on one's health (Kemper, Healthwise Staff, & Smith, 1997). Clients who have positive outlooks on their medical conditions frequently recover more rapidly than those who do not. Medications can even be more effective when the client believes that the medication has positive potential (the placebo effect). Clients have been known to attribute benefits to medications before the pharmacological effects are possible. The mind has a powerful influence over our mental and physical well-being, so much so that a field of science now exists (psycho-neuroimmunology) to study the mind/body connection (Kemper et al., 1997). Lastly, when one is experiencing a clinical depression, diet, exercise, and other elements that impact one's health can be compromised, further exacerbating the physical and mental condition.

The exact cause of depression continues to be researched, but as yet, it is not completely understood. According to many sources, "most major depressions involve problems with chemical messengers (neurotransmitters) in the brain" (Kemper et al., 1997, p. 298). Because of this, most health insurance plans now must recognize major depressive disorders as physiological conditions qualifying for medical benefits. Depressive episodes can be triggered by a negative life event (such as a death or loss of employment); however, this is not always the case. For some, depressive episodes seem suddenly to appear without warning or cause.

There are many approaches to treating depression including antidepressant medications, psychotherapy, or a combination of both. Psychotherapy often includes cognitive and behavioral interventions (approaches that are frequently encouraged by insurance companies) and they are now the "most widely practiced forms of therapy in the world" (Burns, 1999, p. xxxi). David Burns (1980, 1999) described cognitive-behavioral therapy as a clinically proven drug-free treatment for depression. This approach seeks to change the client's thinking by challenging and modifying "self-defeating" thoughts, resulting in the alleviation of one's depressed mood and ineffective behaviors. One of the first steps of this approach is to delve into one's thinking. Clients are repeatedly encouraged to thoroughly understand the connection between their negative thoughts and their negative feelings. This basic tenet is further echoed in the advertisement slogan for the antidepressant medication, Zoloft (Understanding Depression, 2003): "When you know more about what's wrong, you can help make it right." This cause and effect approach is at the foundation of most problem-focused approaches, yet it is in direct contrast to one of the fundamental tenets of SFBT, which assert that there is no necessary connection between the cause of a problem and its solution.

In many ways, this traditional cause and effect approach encourages clients to remain in their dark place longer so that they can explore and understand it better. Although this approach has been very helpful for many, others cannot tolerate this dark space any longer and become increasingly discouraged as they explore these negative aspects of themselves, thereby only deepening the depressive state. For them, an alternative approach that gives immediate hope and a vision of what is possible is much more effective. That is where SFBT can make a difference. According to this approach, "problems are problems and they can best be understood in relation to their solutions" (de Shazer, 1988, p. 7). Miller and de Shazer (1988) further state that therapists have a "responsibility to encourage their clients to notice how clients are already managing their problems and to identify personal and social resources that clients might use to take greater control of their lives" rather than to further their clients' "victimization by continuing to direct attention toward clients' powerlessness and hopelessness" (p. 373).

At times, SFBT is confused with the more commonly taught cognitive and behavioral approaches because all focus on here-and-now changes (including behaviors, cognitions, and resultant feelings), are goal-driven, and challenge clients' thoughts and assumptions. However, SFBT fundamentally is different in at least three key areas. The first is in the therapist's position in relationship to the desired solution. In traditional treatment such as cognitive-behavioral therapy, the therapist problem-solves with the client to explore possible solutions (from the present or past looking into the future). A common part of this is the need to understand at least some elements of the problem in order to brainstorm possible solutions. This is very different from SFBT, because, in this approach, the therapist strives to ask questions from a place in which the problem is resolved: the future. This results in a more curious stance and a future orientation (from the future looking back to the present). Second, in most traditional treatment models, the therapist is in the role of an expert. The therapist's opinions and recommendations are paramount to the direction of treatment. In SFBT, the clients are viewed as the experts on their own lives. This is extremely empowering for clients who are struggling with depression, because they frequently view themselves initially as powerless and hopeless. Third, traditional cognitive and behavioral treatments focus primarily on a client's cognitions and behaviors as key to changing the client's affect. Although SFBT incorporates clients' ways of thinking and frequently asks questions about behaviors and resultant feelings, it does not take this linear, cause and effect approach. Solution-focused therapists ask questions about all aspects of a client's life from the context in which the problem is resolved. However, there is no assumption about what elements the client must change in order to achieve success. The client ultimately determines the targeted change. For more information about what makes SFBT unique and for a detailed description of each commonly used intervention, I invite you to refer back to the chapter on *Assumptions of SFBT* in this volume. I will now build upon those basic assumptions to describe how the specific interventions commonly used in SFBT effectively address and resolve the characteristic symptoms of depression without the need to rehash and relive the negative thinking that typifies this disorder.

MIRACLE QUESTION

I often have been asked about the appropriateness of using the miracle question[1] when a client is experiencing intense emotional pain (such as the pain characterized by depression). At first, I was taken aback by this question. I believe that the client is in such intense emotional pain that the miracle question is relevant and even necessary. In these times of pain, something is needed that generates hope that the pain will end. Suicide frequently is considered by clients only as a way to get the pain to stop. Offering a client an immediate, alternative focus is necessary and healing to clients who are experiencing depression. However, I also have observed inexperienced therapists when they are learning to use SFBT and noticed the unintentional coldness that this approach can have if the therapist is not well trained in listening to the clients and in communicating to them that their pain is very real. This must happen prior to inviting them to move past the pain through the use of the miracle question.

De Jong and Berg (1998) speak to this when they state that it is only after a client has been validated and the client's pain has been acknowledged that the therapist can "move on to explore what the client is doing to mobilize his or her strengths in order to get through this difficult time" (p. 38). Although they emphasize the importance of this validation, they also caution to avoid amplifying negative feelings. They state, "We have found that such statements tend to drive clients further into those aspects of their lives that are least useful for generating positive change" (p. 37). Clients have a way of knowing when therapists hear and accept their emotional pain.

It is important to note that this kind of validation is very different from the therapist having to relate to this pain through a shared or common experience. A skilled therapist is able to communicate empathy without relying on self-disclosure. Common or shared experiences (although we all have them with clients from time to time) do not necessarily give helpful insight into what solution is best for the client and can therefore be distracting in this process. In problem-focused approaches, a direct correlation between problems and solutions is often assumed. Therefore, a common experience logically points to a possible common solution. However, a cause and effect connection is not part of SFBT. Therefore, shared problems do not necessarily correspond to shared solutions. In addition, the therapist's disclosure of shared experiences risks the client's interpreting the therapist as the expert, thereby missing the opportunity to assist the client in redefining himself or herself as the expert and potential source of solutions. This balance of validation and acknowledgement of the client's pain with skillful avoidance of overemphasizing the problem is a key factor in determining the most effective timing of the miracle question for clients who are struggling with depressive symptoms. Once the client's pain or other emotions are validated, it is time for the miracle question.

Therapists who utilize traditional methods tend to ask clients questions about the problem. They often explore the symptoms of depression, thereby directing the clients' attention to the most painful areas of their lives. In contrast, the miracle question directs the client's attention to a place in which the depression and related symptoms are resolved. When asking the miracle question with clients who are struggling with depressive symptoms, it often is helpful to personalize the format rather than asking it in the traditional form ("the problem that brought you here is resolved"). By defining the miracle, the therapist is able to better tailor the intervention to the client and avoid many of the arguments that the therapist can predict, given the client's previous disclosure. For example, for a client who has just stated how hopeless change is and that no one could possibly understand, then the intervention might be worded as follows:

> Now I'm going to ask you a strange question. Suppose that when you go to bed tonight, a miracle happens . . . and the miracle is that even though life seems so incredibly hopeless and like no one understands, all these problems you have mentioned . . . including your feelings of depression . . . are resolved. Change happens anyway! People are now

able to understand! Unfortunately, you are asleep, and you don't know that this miracle happens. So, what will be the first signs that you will notice in the morning that will let you know that this miracle happened?

This modifies the wording, assisting the client in remaining focused on the purpose of the intervention and demonstrates that the therapist really understands the client's feelings of hopelessness and emotional isolation. This frees the client to hear the question and begin to formulate an answer. The miracle question shifts the client's focus from the feelings of depression and hopelessness to a place beyond the depression. The form of the question implies that this place exists and is therefore worth discussing. The challenge of looking at such a place is the first step of healing. Clients are generally very polite and will play along with the therapist's interventions even when they do not yet believe the supporting suppositions. However, their participation frequently leads to their imagining themselves in the miracle and gradually accepting the underlying tenets as well. These are the first sprouts of hope. It is this hope and alternative vision that slowly begin to combat the heart of depression and the feelings of aloneness and hopelessness. Clients are able to envision themselves reengaging in previously enjoyed activities, enjoying friendships, getting a good night's sleep, having the needed energy and desire to get through the day, and so on. It puts the depression back into perspective as a temporary and manageable problem.

SCALING

Clients who are struggling with depression often fall prey to black-and-white thinking: "No one understands," "This is how it always is," "I'm never happy," and so on. Negativity becomes the lens through which they view the world. One of the solution-focused principles that can be very helpful when working with clients who struggle with depression is, "No problem happens all the time" (Pichot & Dolan, 2003, p. 13). Without this principle, the clients' statements that they are "always" depressed can become a self-fulfilling prophecy and can then become their identity. As Berg and Miller (1992) write, "Clients typically view the complaints that they bring into treatment as being constant in nature; any and all such exceptions go unnoticed" (p. 12). Through the use of scaling, therapists gently challenge the clients' beliefs of constancy. It is important to mention that therapists must skillfully anchor the scale through their definitions of "1" and "10." Without this, the client might use the scale to further validate the lack of existence of any exceptions. For example, the following scale might be used with a client suffering from depression who attended a session with a therapist:

> So, on a scale of one to ten, with one being that you can't even get out of bed to attend any appointments, no matter how important they are, and ten is that you are able to go on with your life despite your feelings of depression, where would you put yourself today?

In this scenario, the therapist purposefully defines "1" as the client is "unable to attend any appointments" because the therapist knows that the client did somehow attend the appointment with her. Therefore, the client is very unlikely to scale himself or herself as a 1. This provides a nice starting point for exploring exceptions that the client initiates. The conversation might unfold as follows:

CLIENT (C): Well, since you put it that way, I guess I would have to say that I am a three.

THERAPIST (T): Wow! A three! That's pretty high, given all you have described! What is going on that lets you know that you are so high?

C: Well, I'm here. It was really hard to come, but I did. I even took a shower before I came. And I also attended an appointment at my daughter's school last week. I couldn't miss that.

T: It's very impressive that you have made sure that you attended these two appointments and even showered despite how you have been feeling. How did you push yourself to do it?

Through the use of scaling, clients frequently identify additional times in which they were able to make small steps that they otherwise would not disclose to the therapist. In preparation for therapy, clients often mentally review what is wrong to ensure that they don't forget to highlight these points, similar to when one takes a vehicle into the shop for repair. When addressing mechanical problems, it is wise to find the right words to describe the particular clunk or rattle, to pinpoint when exactly the noise occurs, for how long, and so on. Most of us think that without this precise knowledge, the expert will not be able to accurately diagnose and correct the problem. Clients who struggle with depression are desperate for the therapist to help them find a solution, and they diligently gather information to assist in this end. Unfortunately, change in human beings is much more complex than automotive mechanics, and the details of the problems are not what solution-focused therapists find useful. Clients are often surprised to learn that the information that solution-focused therapists find most valuable is in relation to those times in which the problem is just a little bit better. Scaling is an excellent tool to gently teach clients this important lesson and to begin to shift their focus.

Scaling also can be a valuable tool when therapists are faced with clients who are experiencing suicidal ideation. It is tempting to abandon SFBT when clients are in crisis, believing that these interventions can only be used effectively when clients are more stable. I have seen therapists who, in these circumstances, reverted back to traditional interventions and began suicide assessment, delving into the thoughts and symptoms of the depression to determine the level of the client's lethality. Although there is no doubt that the client's level of safety must be quickly assessed, traditional methods are not the only ways to proceed. As previously mentioned, the therapist's goal is to shift the client's focus away from the problem toward a place in which this problem is resolved. Hope is most vital when clients are suicidal. The following interaction demonstrates how a scale can be very useful to maintain the shift to a future focus while providing the needed assessment information.

T: So, on a scale of one to ten, with ten being that even though times are very tough right now, you are able to get through them, and one being that you are going to leave this session and kill yourself, where are you today?

C: I would have to say that I'm a four. I'm not going to go kill myself. I have too much to live for, but I have a long way to go.

T: Wow! A four is pretty high! What lets you know that you are a four and not a three?

C: Well, my daughter is very important to me. I could never let her grow up without a mom. No matter how hard times get, I've got to get through it for her. I may think of offing myself, but I never really would. Not now. That was an option a few years ago, but I've got responsibilities now.

T: I can tell you really love your daughter! What helps you remember how important she is to you during these difficult times?

C: I carry her picture with me on my key chain, so I see her whenever I use my keys. Seeing her picture makes me smile. (*She smiles as she speaks, looking at the picture on her key ring in her hand.*)

This interaction provides valuable information to the therapist about the client's level of safety. The therapist learned that although the client has thoughts of suicide, she does not have a plan nor does she envision her killing herself; she has someone (her daughter) to live for and she has an effective way to remind herself daily of her reasons to live. This safety information was gathered without the need to shift the focus to the problem. This allows the therapist to maintain the solution-focused stance while listening for signs of client safety, thereby allowing a smooth transition from safety assessment to therapeutic work without distracting the client by asking problem-focused questions.

Over the course of treatment, the therapist must skillfully craft scales that match where the client is in the process, carefully creating additional scales that evolve as the client progresses in treatment. In this way, scales provide the ladder by which the clients climb from the depths of their depression into the miracle.

EXCEPTION QUESTIONS

Scaling is a natural way to highlight times in which the client is doing just a little bit better, so it serves as a perfect lead-in for a discussion about exceptions—times when the problem is not there or is not as severe. Exceptions to problems are everywhere, and it is the therapist's role to notice them and to gently challenge the client to exchange his or her worldview for a more w ell rounded one, one in which both positive and negative events are noticed. However, a word of caution is important at this point. I have seen well-intentioned therapists become overzealous when using exception questions. One telltale sign of this is when therapists use what I call, "yeah, but-ing." This happens when a therapist attempts to combat every negative client statement with a previously stated fact that on the surface appears to contradict the client's negative statement ("yeah, but you mentioned that you were able to get out of bed yesterday"). It can have a discounting effect on clients, and clients frequently become frustrated, believing that the therapist does not really as understand or accept what they are saying. Because clients who struggle with depression can be very challenging due to their frequent, pervasive negativity, I have found it most effective to avoid directly asking for exceptions and rather find exceptions through scaling (e.g., "what lets you know you are at five and not four"). This allows the client to slowly excavate exceptions while reminding the therapist to walk slowly beside the client and not become more excited about exceptions than the client indicates. This slower pace also has the added benefit of validating the client's feelings by not overtly highlighting positive aspects mentioned by the client. Once the client's feelings of depression lessen, the client may be more receptive to more blatant exploration of exceptions.

Despite the word of caution, the power of exception questions cannot be overstated. It is through the use of these questions that clients often find additional signs of hope, seeing that change is already underfoot. Peter De Jong and Insoo Kim Berg (1998) state, "Whenever you and a client bring an exception to light, both of you become aware that some good things are happening in the client's life and, consequently, you can both feel more hopeful about the client's future" (p. 98).

RELATIONSHIP QUESTIONS

As depressive symptoms deepen, clients frequently feel more isolated because they believe that no one understands or could be helpful to them. A sense of guilt or a belief that they are bothersome to others is commonplace. Relationship questions are a valuable tool to challenge these notions and to broaden the client's current and future reality to include those who love them and matter the most. Using the previous client example, the following demonstrates the power of relationship questions once the therapist has discovered who matters most to the client:

T: May I see the picture of your daughter?

C: Of course (*beaming as she hands the therapist the picture*)! She's four. Her name is Tracey.

T: She's quite a cute little girl! I can see why you are fighting so hard to get through all these problems.

C: Yeah, she's great!

T: So, I'm curious . . . In that miracle that we talked about, what difference will all these changes make to Tracey?

C: They will make a big difference! I will be able to really focus on her and be the kind of mom that she deserves!

T: And what will that look like on this miracle day?

C: Well, I will be making her breakfast, really listening to what is important to her, taking the time to play and spend the time doing things she enjoys . . .

T: And how will this change her world?

C: She will know how much she is loved. And if she really gets that, she will have the confidence she needs to be a strong woman when she grows up.

T: Wow! That's quite an important role that you play in her life!

By exploring the client's relationships and the positive impact that her changes will make on those around them, the therapist is able to understand how these changes will impact the client's system long-term, thereby making a meaningful difference. This is extremely important when working with those who struggle with depression. Without a solid understanding of this positive systemic impact and without hope that changes (even the smallest of changes) will make a significant difference, the depressive symptoms can go unchecked. As clients explore the impact that their changes will make on those whom they love, they are able to see an immediate benefit of their work even before they may experience a change in their mood. One of the most common symptoms of depression is self-absorption or a narrowing of one's perception. This solution-focused intervention provides a direct intervention that targets self-absorption as the focus shifts to those who matter to them.

DIFFERENCE QUESTIONS

Difference questions can be used in combination with any solution-focused intervention (this is also true about all of the other interventions discussed in this chapter) and have the function of exploring the meaningfulness of a past, current, or proposed change. This is particularly helpful with clients who struggle with depression because they often have not noticed how the small changes they have made are part of more meaningful differences. Difference questions might be used to explore a possible difference for the client or for those who matter most to the client (as previously mentioned in the discussion about relationship questions). Steve de Shazer (1988) said, "Once something different is noticed, then the excitement builds again as the observers look for similar events and patterns" (pp. 2-3). This excitement increases the energy that is frequently very low in clients who are struggling with depressive symptoms. Additionally, it gives meaning and purpose for the work that lies ahead.

COMPLIMENTS

Hearing a compliment can be difficult for someone who is struggling with the symptoms of depression. This is another intervention that must be used with sensitivity to ensure that the client's feelings are validated and not minimized. Otherwise, the client might misunderstand the therapist's statements as indicators that the problem is not being perceived as severe as it feels to the client. (Although a significant component of depression is that the client's feelings are disproportionate to the client's reality, it is most effective when the client comes to this conclusion rather than the therapist's pointing it out.) One of the most effective forms of complimenting is a two-step process compliment described in Pichot and Dolan (2003, p. 26):

> Express positive surprise in reaction to one of the client's accomplishments.
> Ask the client how she or he did it.

Clients frequently mention times when things are just a little better. In doing so, they are providing the therapist with opportunities to discover what they did that resulted in a small change. This form of complimenting is most effective with these discoveries because clients frequently have neglected to take credit for instigating the change. By expressing positive surprise and then inviting the clients to further explore how they achieved this, therapists help clients discover behaviors they previously overlooked. This further increases client hope and provides needed energy to continue to make changes.

Clients' perceptions of their behaviors and situations are gently challenged by experiencing the therapist's different perceptions and by witnessing the therapist express surprise or give a genuinely expressed compliment. Through this way of complimenting, clients are subtly encouraged to discover what the therapist appreciated that the client previously overlooked. This often results in a sense of curiosity on the part of the client and a new-found appreciation for previously neglected resources.

CASE EXAMPLE

Susan was initially referred to me through her insurance company. She was in her early thirties and had just discovered that she was pregnant. Although it is commonly thought that this event should trigger feelings of happiness and joy, this was not the case for Susan. Susan was happily married and her husband was ecstatic about the pregnancy, but Susan was filled with dread. I talked with her so that I could better understand what brought her to my office, and she told me about years of battling with symptoms of depression, an eating disorder, and prescription pain medication abuse. She knew herself well, and she had already gone to her primary care physician to obtain antidepressant medications. As she described problem after problem, I was struck by her wisdom in acting so quickly in obtaining the medication and by her awareness of the importance of talking to her primary care physician about her pregnancy as well as her depressive symptoms. Because of this, I asked permission to interrupt her unsolicited history to get further clarification about how she did that. She politely gave me permission, and then gave additional information about how she knew she should go to her physician to get the medication, the changes she had noticed since starting the antidepressants, and how much better things had been since she made the phone call to schedule the appointment with me. The following dialogue demonstrates how compliments and further exploration of this exception were used with Susan during this initial session:

THERAPIST (T): Really! They have already started to work! (*Referring to the antidepressant medications*) That is amazing. You have a good handle on how to begin to manage this.

SUSAN (S): Yeah. I've been dealing with this for years, so I know when things are getting out of control, and what I need to do.

T: That is very impressive. What else have you learned about yourself and about what works?

S: Not a lot. That is why I'm here. I've got to understand what is causing these feelings to come up. I shouldn't feel this way. I should be happy like my husband.

T: So, suppose we have been able to figure all this out and you have all the understanding that you need to resolve your depression. . . . What all would you understand?

S: Good, good (*Susan nodded as she spoke, seemingly relieved that I was really getting that she really was here to gain insight in order to control her depression.*) Well, I would understand why I'm not happy about the pregnancy, why I feel suffocated by it, and I guess why this keeps coming up every few years. I'm sure it has something to do with my mom, don't you think?

T: Well, I don't know yet. That's quite a list. It seems like you have put a lot of thought into this.

S: Yes! It's important to me that we figure this out.

T: I can tell that you are the type of person who really works hard to solve problems, and that you spend a lot of time analyzing problems to find the right answer. Is that right?

S: Yeah! I think you are right. I never looked at it that way before! (*Smiling; seeming to be gaining some pride in herself for the first time during the session.*)

T: Well, that trait will sure come in handy in our work. I tend to give a lot of homework that requires a lot of noticing and analyzing. Are you up for that?

S: Sure! (*Her mood seemed to have shifted; almost eager to be given her first assignment and hopeful that therapy might help. Susan was no longer focused on regurgitating years of problematic history and seemed poised for my next question.*)

T: Okay. Just so I really understand what you want and what difference this will make, I have a question for you. Suppose that when you go to bed tonight, a miracle happens, and the miracle is that you have this understanding of what is causing your depression, and so on. But, because you were asleep, you are unaware that this miracle happened. What would you notice first thing in the morning that let you know that this miracle occurred?

S: Well, I guess I would be happy about the pregnancy, I'd be talking about the baby with Matt [her husband] and not afraid that I'm going to end up a bag lady.

T: Oh! You have "bag lady syndrome!"

S: You've heard of it? (*Susan looked suddenly relieved that she was not crazy, and that her feelings might have been seen before.*)

T: Well of course! That's when a person fears she might lose her job, and if she loses her job, then she might not be able to pay the bills, and then if she can't pay her bills, she will lose her home. If she loses her home, she will soon be on the street pushing a grocery cart stolen from the parking lot. . . . She will be a bag lady. (*Although this interaction may not appear on the surface to be very solution-focused, it was quite effective in communicating to the client that her deep fears were heard. In addition, it gave the needed perception of insight that she had told me was her purpose of coming to therapy.*)

S (*Laughing*): That's it! I'm terrified of that! I then get so scared that I get depressed! I want this baby; I am just afraid of what will happen if I can't work as much and of changing my life. I have worked so hard to get my career going, and now all that will be changing. Will we be able to live with less money?

T: So, if we were able to get rid of the bag lady syndrome, would that be a miracle and a good use of our time?

S: Totally! That's my problem! I have to somehow trust that I'm not going to end up a bag lady!

T: Okay! So let me change that miracle question a little. So, when this miracle happens tonight, the miracle is that you have complete confidence in your ability to make good decisions and to prevent becoming a bag lady. Your depression is miraculously gone! What lets you know that this miracle happened?

S: I would have peace! . . .

Susan's case is not that uncommon. She presented with multiple problems and had spent considerable time analyzing the problems and determining what she believed she needed (in her case, it was insight). Unfortunately, in doing so, her depression only deepened. However, she had done some things that resulted in positive changes, and she would have quickly ignored those actions had I not stopped and explored them further.

Susan's multiple problem history could have become a distraction in this case. Her current pregnancy, combined with her history of an eating disorder and prescription drug abuse, could easily have tempted a therapist to explore that history in a more problem-focused manner. Should this have occurred, Susan might have become more overwhelmed with the possibility of a relapsed to either drug abuse or her eating disorder; this increased focused might even have triggered a relapse due to increased fear of the possibility. Instead, by focusing on Susan's wisdom to seek medical consultation and by discovering what would be different when this problem was resolved, her positive decisions and resources were the focus of conversation. It is important to note that despite my solution-focused treatment approach with Susan, I did not neglect these potentially significant problems. Throughout treatment, I listened intently for clues that Susan's eating and other health-related decisions remained sound, however, this was done while maintaining Susan's future focus. If Susan did not readily reveal needed safety information, I would craft a scale that would invite Susan to rate her progress in an area that was related to the area of concern. By explaining why she was as high as she was on the various scales and what would indicate to her in future sessions that she was just a little higher, Susan provided all the information I needed to ensure that her eating remained stable and that she was not relapsing on prescription medications. My vigilance to these matters prevented Susan from having to divert her attention from her important work of obtaining her desired sense of "peace" and trust.

As Susan's case highlights, antidepressant medications are a common intervention with depressive disorders. Although these medications are helpful to some, they are not helpful to others. I find that clients often have decided prior to seeking psychotherapy whether antidepressant medication would be helpful to them. The knowledge of the possible benefits of these medications is widely available, and clients rarely need this information from me (however, if it was ever apparent that the client was unaware of this technology and might benefit from psychotropic medications, I would certainly provide the needed education). By supporting clients' decisions in this matter, we can focus on what they need from psychotherapy. Ironically, I have found that the client's decision in these matters is most often correct, including times in which clients have changed their minds about this matter midtreatment. Consistent with this notion, I have not seen good success when clients have allowed themselves to be externally pressured regarding their use of medication one way or the other. However, on occasion, clients may initially decline the use of medication and then appear to make minimal progress in treatment. By refocusing the client on his or her miracle, (a place in which the depression is resolved) and by using scales to measure progress toward this miracle, the therapist can easily and gently explore with the client if changes are needed. It may be that the client is aware of progress that he or she has not yet shared with the therapist, or the client might decide to reevaluate the use of medication.

Supporting the client's belief about all aspects of the desired solution is a key factor. In Susan's case, she believed that insight was the missing piece. The spontaneous creation of the "bag lady" syndrome was a playful way to let her know that I really heard her fears and respected this. Once she understood this, she was able to make needed insights, and we were able to refocus on a place in which the problem was resolved. This was the only insight on which Susan needed to spend time during our sessions. Due to Susan's analytical nature, she discovered many other insights between sessions. However, we spent our time in session exploring the changes that she made as a result of these newfound ideas and how these changes helped her to get closer to her miracle.

I met with Susan three more times over the next few months. During those sessions, we scaled her confidence, progress, and numerous other things. I also encouraged her to imagine how her life would be once she was able to sustain her confidence in her ability to manage change once the baby was born. She wrote it all down and stated that she planned to review it in a year to see how close she had come. Her excitement over her pregnancy grew, and she was able to identify skills that she had that would help to prevent future problems as her family changed. Her eating disorder and prescription drug abuse remained only part of her history. During the last session, she playfully stated, "So as long as I'm not looking at which cart I would steal as I drive past the grocery store, I think I'm doing okay." Bag lady syndrome was defeated as she enjoyed her vision of her future.

CONCLUSION

Depressive disorders are a common presenting complaint seen by therapists, and the effects of these disorders, if left untreated, can have devastating consequences for clients, their families, and for society as a whole. In addition, these disorders are frequently intermingled with other challenging problems. Although many approaches are available to treat these disorders, they frequently emphasize exploring dysfunctional behavioral or cognitive patterns, which may unintentionally deepen the very feelings of hopelessness and despair they are seeking to relieve. SFBT is a powerful and effective approach to treating depressive disorders. This approach's value of a future focus and lack of need to explore and understand the presenting problem or the existing cognitive distortions allows the client to benefit from the hope that is immediately generated from these interventions, thereby providing the energy and internal motivation needed to envision life without the symptoms and move beyond depression.

NOTE

1. For an example of the miracle question in this volume, see Thomas & Nelson (2007), pp. 3-24.

REFERENCES

American Psychiatric Association. (1994). *Quick reference to the diagnostic criteria from DSM-IV.* Washington, DC: Author.

Berg, I. K., & Miller, S. D. (1992). *Working with the problem drinker: A solution-focused approach.* New York: Norton.

Burns. D. D. (1980). *Feeling good: The new mood therapy.* New York: Signet.

Burns, D. D. (1999). *The feeling good handbook.* New York: Plume.

De Jong, P., & Berg, I. K. (1998). *Interviewing for solutions.* Pacific Grove, CA: Brooks/Cole.

de Shazer, S. (1988). *Clues: Investigating solutions in brief therapy.* New York: Norton.

Kemper, D. W., Healthwise Staff, & Smith, T. (Eds.). (1997). *Healthwise handbook: A self-care manual for you* (13th ed.). Boise, ID: Healthwise.

Miller, G., & de Shazer, S. (1998). Have you heard the latest rumor about . . .? Solution-focused therapy as a rumor. *Family Process, 37*(3), 363-377.

National Institute of Mental Health. (1999). "The numbers count: Mental illness in America," *Silence on our minds fact sheet series.* Retrieved August 5, 1999 from http://www.nimh.nih.gov/publicat/numbers.cfm.

National Institute of Mental Health. (2000, August). *Depression: What every woman should know.* NIH Publication No. 00-4779. Retrieved November 14, 2003 from http://www.nimh.nih.gov.

National Institute of Mental Health. (2003, March). *Depression: A treatable illness.* NIH Publication No. 03-5299. Retrieved November 14, 2003 from http://www.nimh.nih.gov.

Pichot, T., & Dolan, Y. M. (2003). *Solution-focused brief therapy: Its effective use in agency settings.* Binghamton, NY: The Haworth Press.

Thomas, F. N., & Nelson, T. S. (2007). Assumptions and practices within the solution-focused brief therapy tradition. In T. S. Nelson & F. N. Thomas (Eds.), *Handbook of Solution-Focused Brief Therapy: Clinical Applications* (pp. 3-24). Binghamton, NY: The Haworth Press.

Understanding Depression. (n.d.) Retrieved November 14, 2003 from http://www.zoloft.com/index.asp?pageid=2.

Chapter 6

Solution-Focused Treatment with Domestic Violence Offenders

Mo Yee Lee
John Sebold
Adriana Uken

INTRODUCTION

This class was very different in a lot of ways. I had been through a class in Sacramento and it seemed more like school all over again, which might be good for the students but unfortunately for the majority of people. . . . I think most people in life need to learn by practice instead of by someone telling you what is right or wrong. The people who taught this class make sure that you did the work outside of class. They wanted you to do something positive and very achievable. What this did for me was one, I found out that you can start a positive cycle in your life almost as simply as a negative one. Everyone knows that when something goes wrong, everything goes wrong. What I didn't know is when you change a simple thing for the better, it can snowball into a lot more better things. (Program Participant)

In this chapter, we will share the collaborative work of our research and clinical team. Our conjoint efforts date back to 1993 when Mo Yee Lee offered to conduct a wide variety of research on the Plumas Project, a solution-focused domestic violence treatment program for offenders. The Plumas Project Domestic Violence Treatment Program, which originated in 1991, represented a radical departure in thinking and application from the treatment

doi:10.1300/5135_06

models of the 1970s and 1980s and continues to challenge the largely unchanged societal/clinical approaches to this problem. Perhaps, the most controversial aspect of the program is that there is no direct, solicited discussion or instruction related to domestic violence, anger management, or conflict resolution throughout the total scope of the program. In addition, the program is brief, totaling 8 sessions over 10 to 12 weeks. In spite of (or perhaps, because of) its unique design, it has had impressive researched results.

We begin by presenting a brief academic review of the research associated with domestic violence treatment programs followed by descriptions of how our approach evolved, why the approach makes sense, and the core features of the program. The chapter also includes participant perspectives in their own words, describing how the program influenced them and changed their lives. These perspectives are typical rather than unique examples of this program's participants' views. Please keep in mind that a complete description of the how the program works, particularly how language is used to facilitate change, cannot be fully expressed in the allotted space (see Lee, Sebold, & Uken, 2003 for a more detailed description of the program).

THE BIG PICTURE FROM A RESEARCHER'S PERSPECTIVE

There have been a number of approaches developed in an attempt to end domestic violence in intimate relationships. This complex problem has resulted in great misery, deeply hurting families and children. The early efforts of the battered women's movement in the 1970s to protect victims and their children have been expanded to include legal sanctions with most states' mandating treatment programs for offenders (Roberts & Kurst Swanger, 2002; Schechter, 1982). Currently, the design of most treatment programs for domestic violence offenders has been based on a cognitive-behavioral approach that mainly targets individual characteristics or problems contributing to violent behaviors (e.g., Geffner & Mantooth, 1999; Saunders, 1996) and/or a feminist perspective that focuses on the sociocultural roots of domestic violence (e.g., Martin, 1976; Pence & Paymar, 1993; Walker, 1984). Such treatment designs are influenced by the predominance of individual and sociocultural factors in understanding the etiology of domestic violence. Proponents of the individual pathology perspective usually take a mental health view: offenders have mental health, substance abuse, and/or personality issues that must be addressed in order to stop violent behavior (e.g., Dutton, 1995; Gondolf & White, 2001; Holtzworth-Munroe & Stuart, 1994; Kantor & Straus, 1987). The feminist perspective focuses on sociocultural factors and maintains that male dominance and misogyny based on patriarchal beliefs and social structure constitute the root of violence against women. The goals of pro-feminist treatment programs are to raise offenders' consciousness about sex role conditioning and to resocialize men to work toward gender equality and to take responsibility of their abusive behavior (Mederos, 1999; Pence & Paymar, 1993). These treatment approaches usually assume that domestic violence offenders have deficits in knowledge and/or skills that create tendencies to batter (Geffner & Mantooth, 1999). Building on such assumptions leads to a treatment orientation that views the behaviors of domestic violence offenders as changeable through a reeducation process. Consequently, the core components of these treatment programs generally include direct education about violence, anger management, conflict containment, communication training, stress management, (Geffner & Mantooth, 1999; Russell, 1995) and raising awareness of patriarchal power and control (Pence & Paymar, 1993). The resulting psychoeducational programs usually focus on confronting participants in an effort to help them recognize and admit their violent behaviors, take full responsibility for their problems (Lindsey, McBride, & Platt, 1993; Pence & Paymar, 1993; Russell, 1995), learn new ways to manage their anger, and communicate effectively with their partners (Geffner & Mantooth, 1999; Sonkin, 1995; Wexler, 1999).

The significant contributions of feminist-cognitive-behavioral treatment approaches in the advancement of treatment for domestic violence offenders can never be overestimated. At the same time, questions have been raised regarding the effectiveness of such programs from both clinical and outcome perspectives. A major therapeutic hurdle when working with this population is motivation (De Jong & Berg, 2002). Most domestic violence offenders are involuntary, court-mandated clients who are not self-motivated to be reeducated. Many practitioners working with court-mandated domestic violence offenders are only too familiar with defensiveness commonly manifested in constant evasiveness, silence, phony agreement, and vociferous counterarguments when participants are confronted with their problems of violence (Murphy & Baxter, 1997). Many mandated individuals never begin treatment and others stop attending programs before program completion. According to a survey of program directors, nearly half of the treatment programs faced dropout rates of over 50 percent of the men accepted at intake (Gondolf, 1990). Cadsky, Hanson, Crawford, and Lalonde (1996) reported a 75 percent noncompletion rate of participants who were recommended for treatment at male batterer treatment programs in Canada.

In addition, some professionals have begun to question how a focus on confrontation and deficits can be conducive to stopping violence or initiating positive changes in offenders (Edleson, 1996; Lee et al., 2003; Uken & Sebold, 1996). Because blaming is one of the major strategies used by offenders to intimidate victims and to justify their abusive acts, using confrontation and assigning blame as a treatment strategy only mirrors and perhaps inflames this aggressive dynamic. The effectiveness of a deficit perspective and/or a blaming stance in treatment is also dubious if one looks at the characteristics of domestic violence offenders. The most consistent risk markers for violent males have been identified as experiencing and/or witnessing parental violence, frequent alcohol use, low assertiveness, and low self-esteem (Hotaling & Sugarman, 1986; Saunders, 1995; Straus, 1996). As a result, a high percentage of domestic violence offenders are likely to be insecure individuals at the margins of society who victimize others to boost their low self-esteem. Studies on personality further indicate that many domestic violence offenders fit the personality profile of narcissistic or borderline personality disorder (Dutton, 1995; Hamberger & Hastings, 1990). It is well documented that persons who are narcissistic or borderline have a very fragile sense of self and do not, in general, respond well to confrontation and criticism (Kernis & Sun, 1994). Such individuals may perceive and experience instruction and skill training as criticism and rejection.

In spite of research efforts that attempt to develop an abuser profile, existing literature also indicates that domestic violence offenders are not a homogenous group of people who can be easily characterized by any single profile. Some offenders may have experienced or witnessed abuse as children (Saunders, 1995; Straus, 1996); others may have problems with alcohol abuse (Kaufman Kantor, 1993). Some are violent outside homes and have criminal records while others are only violent in their "havens" (Holtzworth-Munroe & Stuart, 1994). Some have a *Diagnostic and Statistical Manual of Mental Disorders* (DSM-IV) (American Psychiatric Association, 1994) diagnosis while others do not. Some offenders suffer from the effect of poverty while others are the "haves" in our society. In other words, treatment programs are dealing with a wide range of people who come to violence through a variety or even infinite number of pathways. Thus, it would seem clear that programs that offer a "one size fits all" intervention and fail to respect and accommodate for the individual characteristics and responses of participants are unlikely to be successful.

Empirical studies on the effectiveness of current treatment programs are not conclusive but clearly, results are less than desirable. Reviews of domestic violence offender treatment programs generally report recidivism rates ranging from 20 percent to 50 percent within one year after completion of programs (e.g., Edleson, 1996; Rosenfeld, 1992; Tolman & Edleson, 1995). The rates of early dropouts from these treatment programs have been fairly high (Cadsky et al., 1996; Edleson & Syers, 1990). The recidivism rate of the Duluth Domestic Abuse Intervention Program and programs based on the Duluth Model was 40 percent (Shepard, 1992). The Duluth model is the most widely used treatment approach for treating domestic violence offenders that adopts a feminist-cognitive-behavioral perspective. Saunders (1996) also reported a recidivism rate of 45.9 percent for the feminist-cognitive-behavioral treatment models. Two recent experimental evaluations have found batterer treatment programs to be largely ineffective in that there were no significant differences in offender attitudes, beliefs, and behaviors between those who received group treatment and those who did not (Feder & Forde, 2000) or in the victims' reports of new violent incidents (Davis, Taylor, & Maxwell, 2000).

Hanson (2002) suggests that the field of treatment of domestic violence offenders is political as well as empirical. The inconclusive research and practice evaluations should serve as an invitation to service providers and researchers to revisit the existing paradigm of treatment for domestic violence offenders and to challenge some of the basic assumption regarding treatment.

A NEW BEGINNING

I've learned a great deal from this class. I learned a lot about caring and respecting others. I learned that other people have similar situations and that by speaking to each other openly and honestly, we all benefit. I learned that I could set goals and reach them simply by committing myself to the thought. I learned that others care about me also. I learned that life doesn't have to be so serious and stressful all the time. I learned that if you give a little of yourself the return is excellent. I believe that with the help of this class and my classmates and the instructors I have become more easygoing and friendly because of the shared personal stories. John and Adriana are great people and I am truly thankful for the chance to have participated in this course. I believe, on a scale of one to ten, my chances of making my goal work for me are a ten. I know my life will be happier and healthier. Thank you and God bless you. (Program participant)

Fourteen years ago, authors Sebold and Uken began an exploration of domestic violence treatment just as many other service providers had begun: by using a psychoeducational model. We were initially confident about our ability to apply a psychoeducational model in part because we were both experienced therapists who had achieved considerable success in working with a wide variety of participants, many of whom presented with serious difficulties. After using a psychoeducational model for over two years, we became disenchanted with the effects it had on us as well as the lack of positive impact it had on the participants. In time, it became our opinion that a psychoeducational approach created little, if any, change or actually created distance between participants and us in a manner that replicated their dysfunctional solutions. We were, in our own assessment, part of the problem. As a result, we stopped using the traditional model and conducted a much less technical review by Mo Yee Lee than that presented earlier. Our simplified review offered three important observations about the traditional treatment models available in 1991. First, a very high percentage of mandated individuals were not attending the first and subsequent appointments in many traditional programs; second, a high percentage of the individuals, if not most, who started programs were not completing them; and third, of the individuals who were completing programs, most continued to act out in some form of violent behavior. This is most profoundly pointed out by Edleson and Syers (1991). Unfortunately, when individuals were attending programs, the spouse or partners of these individuals typically assumed that their mates were being helped or cured and as a result were more likely to return to these individuals (Gondolf, 1988).

It was striking to us that once the no-shows and dropouts were accounted for, the traditional model programs for which research exists were serving a very select group of offenders—offenders who were motivated and who had the resources to stay in long and difficult-to-complete programs. In spite of this, the results were dismal, often no better than applying no treatment at all. It also seemed to us that many attempts to modify programs were actually expansions of the same approach such as lengthening treatment, adding more education, or combining approaches. These findings, combined with our unwillingness to provide services that were not helpful and our unwillingness to walk away from this issue, led us to conclude that we needed to do something diametrically different. We believed strongly that the research should be respected and it was clear to us that the research was suggesting that new and perhaps radically different approaches should be attempted. It struck us that a most important contribution of the traditional models and the research associated with them was that they provide clues as to what not to do and as such might provide clues as to what to do differently. Fortunately, at the same time we were searching for a viable new approach, beginning to utilize solution-focused approaches to treat other problems, and finding it extremely useful and efficient. It was clear to us that applying a solution-focused approach would, in many respects, result in a treatment approach that was virtually the opposite of the traditional model programs. For example, traditional programs are typically long (26-52) weeks, very problem-focused, instructional, expert-led, and unilaterally focused on male offenders. Our program is brief (8 sessions over a 12-week span), almost totally solution- versus problem-focused with no instructional elements, facilitated rather than expert driven, accepts that both males and females can be the aggressor, and includes both males and females in the same group sessions. We essentially broke most, if not all, the established core traditional rules regarding the treatment of offenders. Our research strongly supports the effectiveness of our approach with high attendance rates, extremely low drop out rates, and very low recidivism rates over long periods of follow-up. There is limited program participant selection bias in our program and the associated research because we have never rejected a referral and because the population of individuals served reflects the diversity of the communities we serve.

THEORETICAL EXPLANATIONS OF A SOLUTION-FOCUSED APPROACH

For many years, we described our approach as having no theoretical basis. We remained largely uninterested in *why* a solution-focused approach might be more effective than other models. We also believed that current theories resulted in a solidifying and closing of the field rather than facilitating a search for new and better answers and, as a result, we were cautious of introducing ideas that only further contributed to the notion that the dynamics of domestic violence are understood. We also resisted and continue to resist the notion that problems as complex as those encompassed by the term "domestic violence" can be explained by an all-encompassing theory.

This lack of a basic theory has proved frustrating for many clinicians because they understandably want to know why something works. We recognize that people believe that if they understand something, they think they will be able to change it, or make it work better. Perhaps even more important is that it is extremely difficult for people to accept that something works unless they either experience its working or create a reasonable explanation for why it works. In the balance, we have decided to offer our own ideas for why this approach works, which also may provide insight into why traditional approaches struggle to be effective. We hope that offering these ideas will expand rather than constrict the search for better approaches.

In our practice, the core element that virtually all offenders present with is a lack of connectedness to people and a subsequent lack of focused meaning in their lives. They either have not been able to connect or have lost a sense of connectedness to others. The shape and form of this lack of connectedness is varied and includes problems with shyness, immaturity, drugs and alcohol, and a variety of personal inadequacies. These inadequacies are exacerbated when relationship failure is feared or actively occurring. Traditional approaches aggravate the offender's lack of connectedness by treating offenders as if their total identity is that of an offender. The expert/educator role expands the gap between helper and offender by failing to respect the offender's unique personal characteristics, making it challenging (if not impossible) for the helper to engage the offender. Our solution-focused model respects that the individual is an offender but focuses 99 percent of the attention on connecting with and expanding the participant's other qualities, qualities that in the short- and long-run lead to their engaging with other people more effectively. The focus on building solutions that are unique to each participant allows the participant/offender to connect and engage quickly with the facilitators. The process creates an environment in which participants maintain control of critical choices regarding their treatment goals and expands the participants' expectations that they can connect successfully with other individuals. It always has been fascinating to us that in spite of the fact that we provide no sex-role psychoeducation or cognitive behavioral skill building, that many group members develop, use, and refer to these and other skills when referencing what they do differently that is effective for them. Most striking is that virtually every letter we receive from participants who complete the program speaks to their new or renewed sense of being connected to the people about whom they care.

SHIFTING TO A SOLUTION-FOCUSED APPROACH

When I first started this class, I was very doubtful that it would do any good for me. Now that I have finished my class, I have realized in some unexplainable way I'm a lot calmer. I don't blow up at the littlest thing. I'm able to think before I react. Now I think before I react to the situation and usually things work out a lot easier. I've always had a problem being able to talk to my dad about what is or was bothering me. Now I'm able to talk to him, tell him my feelings and thoughts. Since I can sit down and talk to him and my step mom we

have been able to start to become a family that can sit down and
discuss everything. It's made all of us, including my wife, kids, and
father a lot closer together. (Program participant)

We began our shift in treatment by making two important changes in our
group design. First, we agreed that we no longer were going to focus on or
talk about "the problem," and second, we decided to require that participants develop concrete, behaviorally defined personal goals that *they* believed, when acted upon, would positively impact important relationships
in their lives. Further, we insisted that participants show evidence of working on their goals by describing in detail what they were doing from session
to session in their effort to make progress on their goals. Literally, every
programmatic aspect of our approach follows and supports these basic elements. This structure creates an environment that requires that the treatment team and each participant focus solely on solution-building while in
the group context. The structural elements of our group process as well as
the manner in which language is used to facilitate change has been inspired
by the work of Insoo Kim Berg, Steve de Shazer and their associates at the
Brief Family Therapy Center in Milwaukee (Berg, 1994; de Shazer, 1991).
The program uses a treatment approach that holds domestic violence offenders accountable for creating and constructing solutions within a group
process, rather than for them to admit to their problems, be reeducated, and
complete a program.

It is often difficult for clinicians initially to comprehend such a radical
approach to domestic violence treatment when virtually every other approach
emphasizes a direct and persistent pursuit of the problem. Clinicians have
been taught that after admitting to the problem and properly understanding
the problem, offenders will be able to discover and apply solutions. We
would suggest that once we effectively learn how to assist our clients in creating solutions, we may have some clues as to what the problems really are
to those experiencing them.

Solution-Focused Assessment

The first step in beginning treatment is to complete what we refer to as a
solution-focused assessment. Similar to conventional models, we believe
that a good assessment sets the stage for positive outcomes. However, our
view of assessment is notably different from conventional models. In conventional models, the therapist acts as an expert who has specialized diagnostic skills regarding the problem and uses an assessment to determine
what treatment model or approach fits each particular individual as well as
to determine whether or not an individual can benefit from treatment. Our

solution-focused assessment involves a different set of assumptions. We view treatment and assessment as closely intertwined and we make every effort to build a positive, cooperative rapport and to activate a change process at the initial contact. There is no attempt to diagnosis for treatment purposes or to determine whether an individual is an appropriate treatment candidate. The actual assessment is usually brief, lasting 30 to 50 minutes. It offers prospective participants the opportunity to assess their readiness and interest in attending the program. Also, it provides an important opportunity for potential participants to step toward group attendance, a task that may be intimidating to them. Finally, it helps participants to resolve any fears or worries about how they will be treated and to develop a clear understanding regarding the expectations of the group. We believe that many offenders are very intimidated by the prospect of being in a group and that focusing on their strengths and reinforcing their ability to choose to attend or not to attend the program sessions greatly helps them to become engaged in the program.

We believe it is important to emphasize choice even when participants are mandated to attend. In this way, we emphasize and respect the participants' most basic right to assess what is best for them from the very beginning. In the few cases where participants decided not to attend the program, we have complimented their decision to go back to the judge and argue their case. This led to a better commitment and rapport when the individual returned, requesting admission into the program.

We believe that it is therapeutically beneficial to view the participant, not the facilitator, as the assessor. In other words, the assessment is client-centered instead of professional-driven. Consequently, the process is differentiated by the establishment of a nonhierarchical dialogue with the participant by maintaining a nonexpert stance. During assessment, the facilitator looks for client strengths and resources, and uses compliments to develop a collaborative relationship. An effort is made to set a positive tone that invites potential participants to view us as partners in working with them.

There are four major goals that must be addressed during the solution-focused assessment. These include (a) initiating a collaborative relationship, (b) building initiative for change, (c) planting seeds for immediate and future change efforts, and (d) defining the expectations for the group. The following are examples of questions that allow the participant and facilitator an opportunity to begin assessing potential strengths and resources in offenders:

- What are some of your recent successes?
- What have you done that you are proud of?

- What have you done that required a lot of hard work from you?
- Have you ever broken a habit that was hard to break?
- What kinds of things do people compliment you on?

There is no exploration of the history of the problem of violence at intake or during treatment. We also do not screen and/or exclude potential participants based on severity of violence, substance use, or DSM-IV (APA, 1994) diagnoses. From a solution-focused perspective, we are more interested in assessing the observable "surface" behaviors or cognitions of individual participants that may be relevant to future goal development or that might motivate the individual to do something different and useful. Discovering and exploring an individual's accomplishments and previous successes not only assists the prospective group member in shifting their focus to solution-building, but it also helps the facilitator to see the individual from a perspective of budding potential and hope. This creates an enriched environment where both participant and facilitator are ripe for developing goals that are meaningful and connected to the participant's strengths. This is in significant contrast to traditional diagnostic approaches that tend to focus on problem categories that revolve around a person's deficits. We contend that labeling can inadvertently sustain a problem reality in that the facilitator begins to make assumptions based on a diagnosis rather than the broader reality that reflects who the person is and what the individual is capable of (Berg & Miller, 1992).

When participants present with anger, agitation, or fears, we sometimes find it useful to help them assess how they will manage their emotions when they are in the group. We approach them directly with questions that help them devise their own solutions to these issues. We do not minimize the challenge they face or attempt to solve the challenge for them. We are patient and calm, expecting that they will discover resources within themselves to manage their emotions in an acceptable manner. In such situations, it is often important for the facilitators to do less rather than more. It is particularly important that the potential group members understand that they will be expected to solve their problems and that the facilitator fully believes that they are capable of doing so. Effectively addressing such issues during the intake process sets the stage for effective group process. Conversely, implications that the facilitator has special knowledge and/or special skills that can *directly* solve the individual's problems invariably lead to a self-defeating pattern for both the facilitator and the potential group member. The following example provides insight regarding how to approach such situations.

F: So, now that you have an idea of how the group is structured and the expectations of the group, do you have any questions?

NATE: No, I just don't think I should have to do this class and I wouldn't even be here if my wife wasn't a drunk. Why isn't she here . . . tell me why she isn't here?

F: I don't know . . . I guess the judge ordered you to come.

(The facilitator refuses the opportunity to make judgment and keeps the response simple and factual.)

NATE: That's right; you don't know, do you? You're just making money, right?

F: I can see that you're angry about the judge's ordering you to come and I can understand that. I think it's important to know that you don't have to come to this program if you don't think it will be helpful to you.

(The facilitator respectfully notes Nate's anger and brings awareness to the choice. Note that there is the subtle implication that should Nate choose to come to the group it will be helpful.)

NATE: Just where am I going to go? All the way to Reno, all the way to Chico, or Sacramento?

F: I don't know, perhaps you could talk to the judge or your attorney about your options.

(The facilitator makes a suggestion but it is obvious rather than insightful. This allows Nate to maintain the initiative and keeps the responsibility for change and decision making with Nate.)

NATE: Right, it's jail or here.

F: Those are tough choices.

(Again, emphasizing choice is critical.)

NATE: Yeah, real tough, and you don't care one bit and my wife's out there doing exactly what she wants.

F: Nate, I'm curious: have you ever had to do something you really didn't want to do and still made it work?

(The facilitator makes a shift to initiate a search for competencies.)

NATE: Like, what does that mean?

F: Well, you're facing this incredible challenge and pressure. I was wondering if you've ever been able to get through something this difficult before?

Nate's question allows the facilitator to frame the current situation as an incredible challenge, thus elevating his ability to manage it to a heroic level.

NATE: (*Pause*) I used to come home from school and all there was, was a jar of mayonnaise in the fridge. I don't want my kids' coming home to that. They deserve better than that. You know what I mean?

F: Yeah, I definitely do. You want something better for your kid. You're a man who really cares about his kid.

NATE: Yeah, I am . . . so, when does this group start?

F: In two weeks. Are you ready?

NATE: Yeah.

The facilitator respects Nate's question about the group start date by simply telling him the start date, confirming his desire to attend, and saying good-bye. This ending may seem a bit unconventional to the reader, given that Nate has also shared some dramatic and revealing personal information about his childhood. It is tempting for some facilitators to ask a question that elicits more information from him about his childhood misery. Our impression is that Nate has developed a level of connectedness that will enable him to come to the group. He is saying, "I'm ready to get on with it" and we simply respect his message. If Nate had expanded his thoughts about the challenges he faced as a child, we would have followed his lead and explored how he was able to survive and what he learned that might help him now.

Getting to Work: Group Meetings One to Three

Our experience has affirmed that a group of between 8 and 12 participants is the optimal size for successful treatment. Working with 8 participants is very manageable, and it requires significantly more discipline, teamwork, skill, and focus to manage groups that exceed 10 members. We generally work as a male/female team; we occasionally work alone but not until after the fourth group meeting is completed. We find it highly advantageous for the female facilitator to complete the majority of the intakes. This allows the female facilitator to develop rapport that translates to a more relaxed and effective presence during the first few groups. We do not fully understand the dynamic involved in this but are confident that it is helpful to approach the process in this manner.

During the first group, facilitators set some rules, define the structure of the group, and initiate goal development. After the facilitators introduce themselves, the group rules are handed out, and it is suggested that participants read the rules, one at a time out loud, so that the whole group can hear the rules and ask questions for clarification. The rules are designed to be transparent with no hidden agendas and are, for most participants, obviously reasonable. They outline straightforward expectations and limits. The final rule outlines the expectation that *"You must have a goal by the end of the third session. The goal must be something you choose to do differently that improves your life and something that other people can notice and be positively affected by. If you don't have a goal by the third session, you will not be able to continue in the group."* The facilitators emphasize that group members will need to work hard both in and out of group meetings to develop workable goals if they are to remain in the group. We note that we should begin working immediately so that at least one or two participants can leave the first group with a well-defined and workable goal. This process underlines that the group will require focused work for participants and facilitators, that participants will be accountable for creating goals for change, and that the clock is ticking for each group member and the treatment team. Once the treatment team and group have made the transition to the goal development process, the treatment team moves methodically from one participant to the next, assisting each participant in developing a well-defined goal. This complex process requires an understanding of what an acceptable goal is and the ability to provide the appropriate level of guidance for the participant to progress successfully. The following section provides insight into this process.

Developing Useful Goals

During the last few months, I have been involved in the domestic violence class. The basic class required setting goals and learning to work through or deal with issues in new ways. I learned that I can do nothing about other people. I cannot change the way anyone thinks, feels, or acts. The only person I can do anything about is myself. If we look toward change, we will often find we have the answer within and may see it when we are willing to quit looking at the problem and consider what we may do to respond in different ways. Often, the small changes will make a dramatic change in response from others. If our changes don't affect the other individuals, we have to work things out accordingly.

The goal I determined to pursue was to look at my wife in a different way much as when we were young and dating. I also decided to quit having expectations of what she would do or become. If I see or receive anything good I just need to be thankful and in appreciation.

The current results of this change appear to make the effort of continuing well worthwhile. I believe the goals established are changing our life together in a major way and will continue throughout our life. This is not dependent upon my wife or whether she continues to respond. I have seen enough to know that if I continue to set goals of positive input with people, I will, with some, get more results that are positive. If it doesn't work with certain individuals, my life is better spent for the changes I have made. (Program participant)

Goals for change as determined by clients have important and pervasive impact on therapeutic process (Elliot & Church, 2002; Foster & Mash, 1999). When goals are defined as a major focus of treatment, accountability for changing one's behavior can be effectively achieved. The use of goals shifts the focus of attention to what can be done as opposed to what cannot. It moves participants away from blaming others or themselves and holds them accountable for developing a better and different future. Goals also increase the participant's awareness of choice and offer an opportunity to play an active role in treatment (Lee et al., 2003; Locke, 1996). Consequently, clients' goals influence how they orient to treatment, participate in the process, and evaluate the effectiveness of the treatment efforts (Elliot & Church, 2002).

Useful goals come neither easily nor effortlessly. Participants would not need treatment if they had clear visions of the solutions to their complaints and ways to realize them. Arriving at a useful goal is the first and most important step to help participants to get on the right track. In our program, we describe the parameters of a useful goal as (a) useful: the goal must be personally meaningful and useful for the participant that will improve his or her life; (b) interpersonal: the goal should be one that is interpersonal in nature; when participants work on goals, others will be able to notice the changes they have made, and potentially they could be affected by the change in how the clients behave; (c) new: the goal needs to be something different, a behavior that the participant has not generally done before; and (d) regular: the goal has to be a behavior that the participant can practice on a regular basis (Lee et al., 2003). Participants are required to develop goals by the third session and share their goal efforts in each successive session. In addition, Berg and Miller (1992) described the characteristics of useful goals as personally meaningful and important to the participants; small enough to be achieved; concrete, specific, and behavioral so that indicators of success can be established and observed; and positively stated so that the goal represents the presence rather than the absence of something.

In this approach, a major portion of therapeutic work revolves around assisting participants in developing a useful goal. While a few participants readily develop well-formed, clear, and specific goals, many others experience this process as challenging. More often than not, we work with participants who initially propose vague goals; complex, undefined goals; BIG goals; and "politically correct" but personally unhelpful goals. Some have difficulty coming up with goals while others are the "everything is great clients" who do not need goals because their lives are perfect (Lee et al., 2003). Such initial goal suggestions by participants are to be expected and represent challenges that can be successfully overcome with a persistent and thoughtful approach. It is most helpful that the solution-focused facilitators view all forms of "resistance" as typical responses that individuals make when faced by pressure to make changes in their lives. When facilitators approach participants from this perspective, they do not become distracted by the participants' lack of clear focus and proceed to ask useful questions that will assist participants in developing, clarifying, specifying, and reformulating the initial efforts of well-formed and attainable goals.

The following transcription provides an example of how facilitators can help participants move from complex goal descriptions to simplified, workable goals.

GARY: I think I need to work on communication, you know, communicating better.

F1: What would we *see you doing* if you were communicating better?

(*The facilitating team wastes no time in pursuing observable goal behavior.*)

GARY: Well I don't really know, I just think that communicating would be better, I mean my girlfriend and I don't really talk a lot any more.

F2: Was there a time when you and your girlfriend were talking more and things were better?

GARY: We used to go for walks, but I've been coming home and watching TV. Just crashing in front of it, drinking a beer, and I don't really hear much after that.

F2: When you went for walks, was that better?

GARY: Yeah, I had more energy and did more things.

F1: I'm curious, what do you think was most helpful about what you did, I mean for you?

GARY: I don't know, but I know things were a lot better when we just did things together, like the walking. I had forgotten about that! I think I need to work on doing more things.

F2: Doing more things?

GARY: Well, about two weeks ago, I went for a walk by myself after work, I mean before I went home and I really felt relaxed when I got home.

I think that helped a lot because she was stressed by the kids and I was okay with it all and usually I would be all worked up and saying stupid things to her.

F1: Wow, it was that helpful to walk after work?

GARY: Yeah, it made a big difference, me being calm. When we talk a lot about problems, things get pretty messed up, so I'm not so sure about this communicating.

F1: What about the walking helped?

GARY: I think I'm so intense about work and I bring it right home and I treat her like she's one of my employees. That just isn't going to work. I mean, I can see that even if I don't like what she's doing that, that won't work.

F2: So what little thing will you start to begin doing different . . . something that we or someone else might see you do?

GARY: I think I'm going to exercise or walk before I come home from work. I know that works and I need to not treat her like an employee. That would go a long way.

(Gary has become clearer about what he will do and the facilitating team is interested in defining the possible benefits in as much detail as possible.)

F1: So what would your wife see you do, that was different after you come home from your walk?

GARY: I would just be calmer.

F2: How would she know that?

(Notice how this question helps Gary assess what his wife really wants from him in a very practical way.)

GARY: I would take the time to just listen to her; I think, sometimes that's all she wants. I mean I don't even have to really listen to her. I just need to sit there and nod my head until she settles down.

F1: Do you think you can actually do this?

GARY: Yeah, I'm sure I can.

F1: Well, I'm really impressed by how you've thought this through and I can see how this will be helpful to you. When will be the first time you will begin making these changes?

Typically, we pursue the details of, how, when, where, and how often a goal behavior will need to occur for a benefit to be noticed. This gives the participant the opportunity to not only evaluate the task but also to do the task for the first time in his or her imagination. We also often use a scaling question to assist the participant in evaluating an aspect of the task and/or to define their commitment to do it. For example: "On a scale of one to ten, ten being you absolutely believe doing the dishes will make a significant difference in your relationship with your wife and one being it will make no difference, where would rate this?"

(Continuing the interview . . .)

GARY: Tomorrow, I don't see why I can't begin right away.

F1: How often do you think it makes sense to do this? I mean to get the maximum benefit?

GARY: I think I should shoot for every day but I don't know if, you know, sometimes it might be impossible. I think most days I will do it.

F2: So, your goal is to do this walking or exercise most days after work, and to listen to your wife and nod your head until she seems to be more settled down. Is that what you think will be the most helpful?

GARY: Yeah

F2: We will be very curious about how your wife responds to this. Can you keep track of how this affects her . . . whatever you notice?

GARY: I think she's going to notice the difference.

F1: So you're sure you're on the right track here.

GARY: Yeah!

Gary begins searching for a goal by telling the facilitators what he thinks counselors want to hear in very general terms, but the facilitators pursue the details, which leads to a goal that defines a clear set of behaviors that he believes will actually assist him to be involved with his wife in way that they both can potentially enjoy. The facilitators let Gary know that they are interested in how this works and will expect the details. They also prompt Gary to notice his wife's response so that he becomes sensitive and connected to her responses.

Participants often feel a sense of accomplishment in developing a well-defined, doable goal. They know what they want to accomplish and how they are going to do it. They begin to feel that the group process is doable and as a result are often relieved in knowing that they can be successful in meeting the requirements of the program. They sense that they are taking control of their lives by working on one small step at a time. The experience of having a team focus totally on them and their plan to make their life better is both subtle and powerful. They begin to recognize that the treatment team is working for and with them to accomplish their goals. They begin to feel connected not only to the drama of their own transformation but gradually become connected to the successes and transformations of other participants.

Utilizing Goals in the Process of Change: Group Meetings Four Through Six

Because our program utilizes goals to create a context for change, therapeutic interventions revolve around utilizing goal accomplishment to expand, amplify, and reinforce solution behaviors in real-life context. By the end of the third session, all participants have developed a well-formed goal, which they report on at each session. Our focus is to (a) encourage and compliment all goal-related efforts, (b) optimize the goal efforts by helping participants attach as much meaning as possible to their goal work, and (c) help participants evaluate and notice what is working. We often encounter one of two responses to this process: Participants report positive experience as a result of their goals, or participants report no change, or that the goal is not helpful.

When participants report and share positive goal results, it is important to use these reports as opportunities to expand the meaning and value of the goal and to encourage their efforts. We do so by becoming very curious and interested in what happened and by collecting as many details as possible. Great detail is requested so that all possibilities and meanings of the goal behavior can be examined and explored in the group's presence. We focus on helping participants evaluate the impact their behavior has had on others who may have directly or indirectly experienced the changes. This process of discovering the details and exploring the full impact of the goal behavior magnifies its importance and expands the meaning that is attributed to it. We often reflect on the courage that it takes to do something new and on the participant's wisdom in picking a goal that is already proving to be beneficial. Direct and indirect compliments are critical to this process, not only because they offer important feedback but also because they set a positive tone of expectation for change.

Working with participants who do not notice benefits from their goal work presents a stimulating challenge. It is critical to keep in mind that a participant's response to his or her goal work is just a response. There is no good or bad response and the participant's response always has great potential to be useful. Beginning therapists tend to feel more comfortable when participants share with them that things are much better. Yet, there is a very old saying that reminds us that a cup is at its most useful state when it is empty. When participants report that something did not work, they are often much more open and available to creating new ideas. From our point of view, all goal-related behavior is helpful, even when a participant states that a goal effort has failed to produce the desired results. At the very least, knowing that a goal is not working helps the participant to discover what is and is not a solution. It encourages the participant and the facilitator to look in other directions that will likely hold more promise. It is also important to keep in mind that if a goal does not improve a relationship, it can still have unanticipated benefits and remain useful. The question is whether the participant is able to notice how the goal is useful and whether the therapist can help the participant to do so.

In our experience, participants' descriptions and statements are extremely flexible and constantly changing. Treating participants' descriptions as if they are solid objects creates a distinct disadvantage if change is the desired outcome. Language is a creative medium with few boundaries or limitations, and the flexible aspect of language can be used to create transitions from one description to another very quickly. Goals that were described as useless can be dramatically transformed to being very helpful when language is used to focus attention in a search for the useful aspects of the participants' efforts. When participants share with us that a goal was not helpful, we routinely ask them to first state the goal and review details of behavior before dismissing the goal as not helpful. We do so for the following reasons: (a) people often fail to notice secondary benefits or do not recall the positive results of their goal work until they carefully review it; (b) sometimes participants become distracted from the original goal and benefit by refocusing on it; and (c) some participants attempt to accomplish too much at first, causing them to miss small but important changes. It is our job as facilitators to help clients notice what they have overlooked that may be useful to them and to assist them in attaching meaning to those diamonds in the rough.

On rare occasions, participants experience no benefits from their goal efforts or even view them as making things worse. In those situations, we help them carefully evaluate whether changing goals would be helpful. We do so by asking detailed questions regarding their goal work, help them search for unnoticed benefits, and evaluate potential benefits of the goal work. If once this is accomplished the participant can find no benefit in the goal, we do not pursue the goal further even if we suspect that continuing with the goal might be beneficial. We assume that participants know what is best for them. Our role is to help them self-evaluate what might be helpful to improve their lives. In such situations, it is far more important to stay connected and to convey to the participant that we will follow his or her lead than to argue for continuing with a goal that they have no confidence in.

The Future: Group Meetings Seven and Eight

As a result of developing and accomplishing self-initiated, personally meaningful goals, most participants have a positive outlook about themselves and their life during the latter part of the group treatment process. They often feel significantly connected to other group members as well to others who were the focus of their goal-related efforts. The pertinent question, however, is whether they will be able to follow along the path that they have started. A major challenge in the field of treatment of domestic violence offenders is the reduction of the reoccurrence of violent behaviors after completion of treatment. For this reason, it is important that we help participants firm up and consolidate changes as well as solidify the implied meanings associated with those changes by developing a road map for the future. From a more basic perspective, it is important to help increase participants' awareness of what they are doing that works so that they continue to be successful. To do this, we focus on the following: (a) creating a futuristic extension of how each participant's goals will continue to be helpful, (b) defining and consolidating what participants believe about the changes they have made and how those changes have changed their ideas of who they are, and (c) developing a blueprint for staying connected with others.

Future Perspective

We find that as the group moves toward completion, participants have a receptiveness to evaluate what they have accomplished. We use this natural tendency not only to help them evaluate the immediate impacts of their efforts, but also to encourage them to project into the future how and in what way their goal work will remain important. To accomplish this, we ask questions that nudge participants into conversations about the future, exploring what they will be doing in as much detail as possible. Questions may include:

- "What will you continue to do to be successful in the future?"
- "What is the most important part of what you are doing now that you will keep doing later on?"
- "How will you go about continuing to do_____?"
- "Your children are now playing with you for the first time in their life, what will you do to keep this going?"
- "On a scale from one to ten, how important is it that you keep doing this to assure that you stay connected with your children?"

- "If we were to visit you six months from now, what would we see you doing that makes your life better with you and your partner?"
- "How will doing this make an important difference?"

Our basic process is to ask questions that focus the participant's attention on postgroup behaviors that they believe will make a difference. We use language that presupposes they will continue working long after we are "out of their lives" and that the work they do will be dramatically beneficial for them and the people they love. We often use language that directs the attention of the participant to the perspective of a person that they care about

- "Your son is now two years old. . . . What will he say about your efforts when he is seven?"
- "How will those efforts make his life better?"
- "What difference will it make for your son if you continue to visit him every Saturday over the next three months?"
- "As you keep working on this goal, what will you be most proud of one year from now?"
- "If we were to go out for coffee with your wife one year from now, what would she say that you are doing that makes the biggest difference to her happiness?"
- "When your son is your age, what would like him to say about you and what you did to make his life better?"

As facilitators, it is important to remain mindful that some participants are able to reach further into the future than others, and it is critical to listen to what the participant is saying about the future. For example, if, after asking, "How will you expand your goal in the future?," a participants states, "I just need to keep taking a deep breath and walking away from my boss, because that really works for me," it is important to respect that the participant needs to keep it simple and in the present. At the same time, we still want to push gently into the future and might respond with, "Of course, that really is working great for you. As you keep taking that deep breath and walking away, do you think it will become easier or harder to do that in the future?" This type of response appears simple but is actually complex. For example, it fully affirms the participant's statements, restates the participant's behavioral commitment regarding his goal, and uses presuppositional language to extend the participant's behavior into the future, "As you continue to. . . ." implies continuing. It also contains a subtle presuppositional bind by creating the assumption that the behavior will either be harder or easier in the future, which assumes it will occur. Perhaps as important, is that there is no assumption that continuing with the goal behavior will become easier. The fact that it could become harder is respected. We find this particularly important when working with mandated participants who can be sensitive to issues of control and choice.

In most cases, the participants are ready to converse in significant detail regarding their future goal behavior and how it will evolve. The facilitator must only invite the future into the conversation with questions that evoke the participant's participation and fertilize the process with well-placed compliments.

Consolidating

A second major theme of the final groups is that of consolidating new participant beliefs about who they are and who they are becoming. Many participants recognize that they have changed in some fundamental manner and, as a result, describe themselves with new thematic labels. The development of such thematic labels establishes that they have changed and offers further confirmation that the change is now part of the individual's self and social context. A woman who accomplished a goal to connect with her estranged daughter may now view herself as a "caring mother" where before she saw herself as a "failed mother." A shy, isolated man who now talks to and does projects with his elderly neighbor may see himself as a "good community member" as opposed to "the loner." As these changes evolve, we find it helpful to recognize the new labels and descriptors people ascribe to themselves as well as to offer thematic labels that are consistent with new sets of behavior. The following transcript provides a brief consolidated example of this process.

FACILITATOR: So what did you do when your wife was in such pain?

ED: I just told her it would be okay and took her to the hospital . . . I just hate that stuff, you know, when she is all upset . . . I just wanted to go and get in my truck and get away . . . I mean, I don't hang around for that stuff.

F: Sure, but you decided to stay?

ED: I held her hand, you know, even though it makes me feel real uncomfortable . . . I've been working on my goal to say something nice to her and I just thought she sort of needed me to hold her hand.

F: So you've become more aware of what she needs from you.

ED: I think I knew but I've always been a pretty tough guy, you know, let the women take care of that stuff . . . all that crying and stuff.

F: Do you think she noticed this change?

ED: Oh yeah! She just kept thanking me and squeezing my hand and I just said it was okay.

F: So, what do you think this says about you and who you are?

ED: I don't know . . . (*Facilitators wait and look expectantly*) I think I was kind of gentle with her.

F: You're becoming a gentle guy?

ED: I guess I am . . . it's not easy for me.

F: It's a big challenge for you and you're doing great. We are very impressed.

When the facilitators move the act of being gentle to becoming a "gentle guy," the change is attributed directly to the character of the individual. We believe this helps to solidify the change process. This process is the antithesis of diagnostic labeling in that it labels and consolidates change descriptions into phrases that encapsulate an aspect of the participant's strengths as opposed to an individual's deficits. Once thematic labels are introduced and accepted by a participant, we use them with repetition to affirm the participant's new self-description.

At times, new descriptions result in internal conflicts for participants in that they may have to modify previous ideas of who they are to accept the new descriptions. For example, one participant noted that she would have to become a "soccer mom" to achieve meaningful change, but she thought that becoming a "soccer mom" would inhibit her ability to speak her mind and dress in the manner she preferred. When asked to evaluate what being a "soccer mom" would mean for her and her children, she saw that the description contained many of the benefits that she wanted for herself and her children, yet she perceived that her choice was between being a "soccer mom" or being "herself." The interview team remained curious and "not-knowing" (Goolishian & Anderson, 1987), posing questions that helped her evaluate whether it was possible to be a "soccer mom," and, at the same time, speaking her mind and dressing in the way she felt most comfortable. As a result, she was able to consolidate the two roles into an all-encompassing description that she could "try on for size." This example emphasizes the importance of exploring participants' surface descriptions and assisting them in transitioning from one description to another.

Developing Personal Connections

The third major theme of the final two groups is that of developing blueprints of important personal connections that have the potential to help sustain and expand participants' change efforts. In many cases, participants have shared information about people who have helped them be successful in their goal efforts. We utilize questions that help participants identify these relationships, that assist them in evaluating their future importance, and that initiate development of a plan for their continuing. We have found it particularly helpful to give participants a one-page writing assignment after group six that requires them to write about someone in their life who has had a positive influence on them. This creates a rich opportunity for questions that assist participants in evaluating what they can learn from people that they admire and it further offers a platform for discussing people that are currently supportive of them.

Once a participant identifies a person who is currently helping make a difference in their change process, we pursue details regarding what they will do to stay connected with this person. We also often suggest that the supportive person believes in and recognizes the potential of the participant. A question such as, "What do you suppose they see in you that compels them to remain supportive of you?" This question has the dual benefit of complimenting the group member and the supportive person. We directly compliment supportive relationships and challenge participants to maintain relationships with statements such as, "This is a great relationship that clearly has been helpful to you . . . do you think _____ realizes how much she (or he) means to you?" It is important to recognize that even though such questions are often directed to one person in the group, other members reflect on how such questions relate to them.

Program Modifications

Because there has been enormous political pressure as well as a strong historical trend to address the treatment of offenders with longer and more complicated programs, we are often asked to share our thoughts about the potential value of lengthening our approach or integrating a solution-focused approach into other models. Our current thinking is that there may be benefits to increasing the length to between 10 and 12 sessions. We believe that exceeding 12 sessions is likely to decrease effectiveness and would also result in fewer offenders' participating in programs and fewer successful completions. Offenders must view programs as feasible and, once in the program, of value to them. We strongly support legal accountability for offenders but believe that relying on the sheer force of the legal system will not in and of itself effectively change compliance, completion rates, or success rates of programs that exceed 12 weeks. Treatment approaches that fail to account for the energy and resource limitations of offenders only decrease treatment attendance and treatment compliance. The overall result is that offenders as a group receive less rather than more treatment.

Our current thinking is that adding two to four group sessions to our model may have potential benefits. Some participants seem to need more sessions to solidify the changes they have initiated. This may be particularly true of individuals who have concurrent substance abuse problems and/or organic brain disorders. However, it is important to note that the current eight-session format creates a high degree of pressure on facilitators and participants to use time effectively. This results in focused and intentioned work by the facilitators and participants. This aspect of our work is not always obvious when reading a transcript but is evidenced in the relatively quick pace and intensely focused process. We believe that short treatment duration conveys the message that the facilitators believe in each participant's ability to make positive changes within a short period of time if they are willing to work with commitment. In addition, research that examines the relationship between time and therapeutic change generally indicates that change occurs as a linear function of the logarithm of the number of sessions, with the greatest gains produced early in treatment with diminishing returns thereafter (Howard, Kopta, Krause, & Orlinsky, 1986); most therapeutic gains occurring within the first eight sessions (Garfield, 1989).

Substance Abuse

Substance abuse is a significant factor for many offenders. For a number of years, we avoided focusing on substance abuse issues with the exception of requiring participants to be sober when attending group sessions. We believed strongly that it was counterproductive for substance abuse issues or related conversations to consume the attention of the group process. This approach was in fact effective because participants often found that their new behaviors and evolving lifestyle did not leave room for alcohol and drugs. Previous substance abusing participants would comment on the many benefits of stopping their use. We have gradually come to recognize that many offenders benefit from an exploration and expanded conversation regarding their substance abuse issues. We still reject "stopping drinking/substance use" as a goal because it represents a process of not doing as opposed to doing an observable behavior. We do listen intently when participants share information regarding this issue and help them evaluate the impacts on themselves and the people they care about. We also listen intently to their success stories regarding substance and alcohol use and assist them in exploring how their future will be different as a result of their efforts and changes in this area. In addition, we help them create a brief plan to attain additional treatment and support if they believe this will be helpful. We redirect participants when they wander into stories of substance abuse "drama" that draw focus away from solution building. Concurrent treatment of participants with alcohol and substance problems may increase the overall effectiveness of our approach.

WORKING WITH OTHER SYSTEMS

We believe that coordinated efforts of different social-political-cultural systems are crucial in the process of eradicating domestic violence. Consistent with the philosophy of our program, it is important to look for common goals, small changes, and connections between and among different institutions that can create a positive difference in the process. In our experience, we have found it very useful to develop cooperative relationships with certain players in the broader system. Empirical evidence indicates that combined interventions of arrest, incarceration, legal advocates, victim services, courts' criteria for batterer programs, and the courts' responses to noncompliant participants contribute to the reduction of recidivism and/or program effectiveness (Edleson, 1991; Kaci & Tarrant, 1988; Steinman, 1988). In our work, we maintain connections with the district attorney, probation departments, and judges because all of these people play important roles in assuring that offenders are held accountable for their behavior. We suspect that most group participants would never voluntarily seek treatment for their problems. They come to our program only because they are mandated to do so. In this way, the "positive therapeutic impact" of our group treatment program is made possible only by the strong backup of the legal system. In other situations, we recognize that punishment including limited incarceration sends an important message that in some cases reduces or prevents further violent behavior, not just with offenders but perhaps with otherwise potential offenders as well.

EVALUATION OF THE TREATMENT PROGRAM

We have used a one-group pre- and posttest study design with a six-month follow-up to evaluate the effectiveness of the treatment program based on multiple reporting sources that include program participants, their partners/ spouses, and official arrest records. Data analyses were based on data of participants of 14 groups that were conducted between October 1996 and January 2002. Respondents consisted of 90 program participants: 77 males

(85.6 percent) and 13 females (14.4 percent). Findings of the outcome study provided initial empirical evidence of the effectiveness of a solution-focused approach for treating domestic violence offenders. The recidivism rate of 16.7 percent for our program, as based on official records, is considerably lower than that for most other treatment programs for domestic violence offenders. It was comparable to the recidivism rate of 13.5 percent reported by spouses and partners at the six-month follow-up interviews. Similarly, the program completion rate of 92.8 percent was impressive compared with rates for most other programs. We believe that the relatively low program dropout rate of 7.2 percent can largely be attributed to the respectful and engaging qualities of this approach and the fact that the majority of participants discover that the program provides identifiable benefits that they find useful. Among the 50 percent of program participants who were involved in intimate relationships, findings indicated a significant improvement in their relational skills in intimate relationships as evaluated by their spouses and partners. The improvement in participants' relational skills from pretreatment to posttreatment was maintained six months after completion of the program. In addition, participants and their spouses and partners perceived a significant decrease in participants' verbal and physical violent behavior six months after participants' completion of the program. Based on self-reports of participants, findings indicated a significant increase in their self-esteem from pretreatment to posttreatment. The increase in participants' self-esteem was maintained six months after their completion of the treatment program (for detailed description of findings, please refer to Lee et al., 2003).

CONCLUSION

Helping professionals are constantly in search of effective ways to provide treatment for domestic violence offenders. Our approach is a radical departure from the traditional treatment paradigms; it challenges many of the core assumptions that have become part of the legislative responses of many state governments to domestic violence. We do not view our approach as a singular answer to this complex problem but we do hope that it offers new avenues for exploration and further research.

A solution-focused approach holds domestic violence offenders accountable for building solutions rather than focusing on their problems and deficits. Our solution-focused model utilizes goals to provide an immediate and relevant context for participants to discover viable solutions for their problems. Through developing useful goals, utilizing goal accomplishment to identify, amplify, and consolidate beneficial behaviors, participants are offered opportunities to develop alternative, new, beneficial descriptions of themselves that eliminate and exclude violence from intimate relationships.

Our view is that it is our central, moral, and ethical responsibility to protect victims and potential future victims. This can never be accomplished unless we develop and utilize therapeutic techniques that effectively and quickly create changes with offenders. We must never forget that untreated or unsuccessfully treated offenders continue to propagate misery until meaningful change occurs within them.

We firmly believe that government must hold treatment programs accountable for producing results, not simply for providing mandated classes or services. Having a response is not the same as having an effective response. Specifically, treatment programs should be accountable for increasing participant compliance, increasing completion rates, and improving upon the current dismal recidivism rates of many programs. This, of course, implies that the crucial connection between researchers and service providers must be strengthened. We strongly believe that it is overwhelmingly productive for service providers and researchers to work directly together to answer questions that move the field forward. Without the feedback loop provided by research, service providers find it difficult, if not impossible, to assess whether or not meaningful change is occurring. Worse yet, service providers may believe that what they are doing is working when, in fact, it may not be working. By sharing expertise and pulling resources together, partnership between researchers and service providers enhances society's ability to improve treatment programs and expand knowledge regarding these programs.

REFERENCES

American Psychiatric Association (1994). *Diagnostic and statistical manual of mental disorders* (4th ed.). Washington, DC: Author.

Berg, I. K. (1994). *Family-based services: A solution-focused approach.* New York: Norton.

Berg, I. K., & Miller, S. (1992). *Working with the problem drinker: A solution-focused drinker.* New York: Norton.

Cadsky, O., Hanson, R. K., Crawford, M., & Lalonde, C. (1996). Attrition from a male batterer treatment program: Client-treatment congruence and lifestyle instability. *Violence and Victims, 11,* 51-64.

Davis, R. C., Taylor, B. G., & Maxwell, C. D. (2000, January). *Does batterer treatment reduce violence? A randomized experiment in Brooklyn.* New York: Victim Services.

De Jong, P., & Berg, I. K. (2002). *Interviewing for solutions* (2nd ed.). Pacific Grove, CA: Brooks/Cole.

de Shazer, S. (1991). *Putting difference to work*. New York: Norton.

Dutton, D. G. (1995). Intimate abusiveness. *Clinical Psychology: Science and Practice, 2,* 207-224.

Edleson, J. L. (1996). Controversy and change in batterers' programs. In J. L. Edleson & Z. C. Eisikovits (Eds.), *Future interventions with battered women and their families* (pp. 154-169). Thousand Oaks, CA: Sage.

Edleson, J. L., & Syers, M. (1990). Relative effectiveness of group treatments for men who batter. *Social Work Research Abstracts, 26,* 10-17.

Elliot, A. J., & Church, M. A. (2002). Client-articulated avoidance goals in the therapy context. *Journal of Counseling Psychology, 49,* 243-254.

Feder, L., & Forde, D. R. (2000, June). *A test of the efficacy of court-mandated counseling for domestic violence offenders: The Broward experiment.* Executive summary of final report. Washington, DC: National Institute of Justice.

Foster, S., & Mash, E. (1999). Assessing social validity in clinical treatment research: Issues and procedures. *Journal of Consulting and Clinical Psychology, 67,* 308-319.

Garfield, S. L. (1989). *The practice of brief psychotherapy.* New York: Pergamon.

Geffner, R., & Mantooth, C. (1999) *Ending spouse/partner abuse: A psychoeducational approach for individuals and couples.* New York: Springer Publishing Company.

Gondolf, E. W. (1988). The state of the debate: A review essay on woman battering. *Response to the Victimization of Women and Children, 11*(3), 3-8.

Gondolf, E. W. (1990). An exploratory survey of court-mandated batterer programs. *Response to the Victimization of Women and Children, 13*(3), 7-11.

Gondolf, E. W., & White, R. J. (2001). Batterer program participants who repeatedly reassault: Psychopathic tendencies and other disorders. *Journal of Interpersonal Violence, 16,* 361-380.

Goolishian, H., & Anderson, H. (1987). Language systems and therapy. *Psychotherapy, 24,* 529-538.

Hamberger, L. K., & Hastings, J. E. (1990). Recidivism following spouse abuse abatement counseling: Treatment implications. *Violence and Victims, 5,* 157-170.

Hanson, B. (2002). Interventions for batterers: Program approaches, program tensions. In A. R. Roberts (Ed.), *Handbook of domestic violence intervention strategies: Policies, programs, and legal remedies* (pp. 419-448). New York: Oxford University Press.

Holtzworth-Munroe, A., & Stuart, G. L. (1994). Typologies of male batterers. Three subtypes and the differences among them. *Psychological Bulletin, 116,* 476-497.

Hotaling, G. T., & Sugarman, D. B. (1986). An analysis of risk markers in husband to wife violence: The current state of knowledge. *Violence and Victims, 1,* 101-124.

Howard, K. I., Kopta, S. M., Krause, M. J., & Orlinsky, D. E. (1986). The dose-effect relationship in psychotherapy. *American Psychologist, 41,* 17-22.

Kaci, J. H., & Tarrant, S. (1988). Attitudes of prosecutors and probation departments toward diversion in domestic violence cases in California. *Journal of Contemporary Criminal Justice, 4*(3), 187-200.

Kantor, G. K., & Straus, M. A. (1987). The "drunken bum" theory of wife beating. *Social Problems, 34,* 213-230.

Kaufman Kantor, G. (1993). Refining the brush strokes in portraits of alcohol and wife assaults. In *Alcohol and interpersonal violence: Fostering multidisciplinary perspectives* (NIH Research Monograph No. 24, pp. 281-290). Rockville, MD: U.S. Department of Health and Human Services.

Kernis, M. H., & Sun, C. R. (1994). Narcissism and reactions to interpersonal feedback. *Journal of Research in Personality, 28,* 4-13.

Lee, M. Y., Sebold, J., & Uken, A. (2003). *Solution-focused treatment with domestic violence offenders: Accountability for change.* New York: Oxford University Press.

Lindsey, M., McBride, R. W., & Platt, C. M. (1993). *AMEND: Philosophy and curriculum for treating batterers.* Littleton, CO: Gylantic Publishing Company.

Locke, E. A. (1996). Motivation through conscious goal setting. *Applied and Preventive Psychology, 5,* 117-124.

Martin, D. (1976). *Battered wives.* San Francisco, CA: Glide.

Mederos, F. (1999). Batterer intervention programs: The past and future prospects. In M. F. Shepard & E. L. Pence (Eds.), *Coordinating community responses to domestic violence: Lessons from Duluth and beyond* (pp. 127-150). Thousand Oaks, CA: Sage.

Murphy, C. M., & Baxter, V. A. (1997). Motivating batterers to change in the treatment context. *Journal of Interpersonal Violence, 12,* 607-619.

Pence, E., & Paymar, M. (1993). *Education groups for men who batter: The Duluth model.* New York: Springer.

Roberts, A. R., & Kurst Swanger, K. (2002). Court responses to battered women and their children. In A. R. Roberts (Ed.), *Handbook of domestic violence intervention strategies: Policies, programs, and legal remedies* (pp. 127-146). New York: Oxford University Press.

Rosenfeld, B. (1992). Court-ordered treatment of spouse abuse. *Clinical Psychology Review, 12,* 205-226.

Russell, M. N. (1995). *Confronting abusive belief: Group treatment for abusive men.* Thousand Oaks, CA: Sage.

Saunders, D. G. (1995). Prediction of wife assault. In J. C. Campbell (Ed.), *Assessing dangerousness: Violence by sexual offenders, batterers, and child abusers* (pp. 68-95). Thousand Oaks, CA: Sage

Saunders, D. G. (1996). Feminist-cognitive-behavioral and process-psychodynamic treatments for men who batter: Interaction of abuser traits and treatment models. *Violence and Victims, 11,* 393-413.

Schechter, S. (1982). *Women and male violence: The vision and struggles of the battered women's movement.* Boston: South End Press.

Shepard, M. (1992). Predicting batterer recidivism five years after community intervention. *Journal of Family Violence, 7,* 167-178.

Sonkin, D. J. (1995). *The counselor's guide to learning to live without violence.* Volcano, CA: Volcano Press.

Steinman, M. (1988). Evaluating a system-wide response to domestic violence: Some initial findings. *Journal of Contemporary Criminal Justice, 4,* 172-186.

Straus, M. A. (1996). Identifying offenders in criminal justice research on domestic assault. In E. S. Buzawa & C. G. Buzawa (Eds.), *Do arrests and restraining orders work?* (pp. 14-29). Thousand Oaks, CA: Sage.

Tolman, R. M., & Edleson, J. L. (1995). Intervention for men who batter: A review of research. In S. Stith & M. A. Straus (Eds.), *Understanding partner violence: Prevalence, causes, consequences, and solutions* (pp. 262-274). Minneapolis, MN: National Council on Family Relations.

Uken, A., & Sebold, J. (1996). The Plumas Project: A solution-focused goal directed domestic violence diversion program. *Journal of Collaborative Therapies, 4,* 10-17.

Walker, L. (1984). *The battered woman syndrome.* New York: Springer.

Wexler, D. B. (1999). *Domestic Violence 2000: An integrated skills program for men: Group leader's manual and resources for men.* New York: Norton.

Chapter 7

Solution-Focused Brief Therapy in Public School Settings

Cynthia Franklin
Beth Gerlach

INTRODUCTION

Although public schools' primary task is to educate students, they also are a major provider of child and family mental health support. The complexity of school systems requires that school-based mental health therapists seek innovative and effective approaches that complement the unique practice demands found in school settings. Solution-Focused Brief Therapy (SFBT) is flexible and creative and is easily adaptable to schools. This chapter is written to help school-based therapists effectively implement SFBT in schools. Information in the chapter also will be useful to solution-focused therapists who work outside of schools, but who want to engage school systems in order to further their practices. In this chapter, we provide an evidence base for SFBT in schools and discuss advantages of using SFBT in schools. We suggest strategies for introducing SFBT to schools in situations where the therapy is unknown and provide examples to illustrate how SFBT can be used when working with students, parents, and administrators, and teachers.

EVIDENCE BASE FOR SFBT IN SCHOOLS

Today's school environments are becoming increasingly evidenced-based. Fortunately, to gain credibility with school professionals, solution-focused therapists can offer research support for the effectiveness of SFBT

Handbook of Solution-Focused Brief Therapy: Clinical Applications
© 2007 by The Haworth Press, Inc. All rights reserved.
doi:10.1300/5135_07

in schools. Although more research is needed on the efficacy of SFBT, a growing number of studies support its effectiveness with children and adolescents. Findings suggest that solution-focused therapy results in positive outcomes for students on self-esteem and coping measures (LaFountain & Garner, 1996), a reduction in acting-out and other behavior problems (Corcoran & Stephenson, 2000; Franklin, Biever, Moore, Clemons, & Scamardo, 2001; Franklin, Corcoran, Nowicki, & Streeter, 1997; Moore & Franklin, 2005; Newsome, 2002), reaching goals (LaFountain & Garner, 1996; Littrell, Malia, & Vanderwood, 1995; Newsome, 2002), and improved social skills and academic achievement (Franklin & Streeter, 2004; Newsome, 2002).

Improving Outcomes for SFBT in Schools

Franklin et al. (2001) indicated that SFBT is more effective in schools when the teachers and staff are trained in the techniques. Moore and Franklin (2005) and Franklin & Streeter (2003, 2004) demonstrated that teachers can be trained in the approach, and that the approach can have positive effects with special education students using a teacher consultation framework and on teachers in an alternative school for dropout prevention. In order to maximize the effectiveness of SFBT in school settings, the entire school culture, norms, and practices need to change and to follow the strengths and empowerment orientation of the solution-focused approach. Gonzolo Garza High School in Austin, Texas is an example of an alternative public school that trained all school staff to use SFBT (Franklin & Streeter, 2003, 2004).

ADVANTAGES OF USING SFBT IN PUBLIC SCHOOLS

Public schools may be one of the best places to apply SFBT for helping children. First, schools provide the majority of mental health services for children and adolescents and are the only source of mental health services for many of the most at-risk students (Harris & Franklin, 2003; Roans & Hoagwood, 2000). Hispanic and African American children, for example, have the highest rates of need for mental health services and are most likely to go without care without the attention of public schools (RAND, 2001). Many homeless teens, immigrants, and teen parents also are in great need of therapeutic support and may receive care only through institutions such as public schools or the criminal justice system. SFBT originally was developed working with high-risk populations (Insoo K. Berg, personal communication, March 17, 2004) and offers excellent clinical tools for engaging these youths and families in a change process.

Second, therapy in public schools needs to be brief and efficient, and to offer immediate solutions to the problems presented. Schools have little time or money for therapy and require very practical solutions to the day-to-day issues that may prevent student success. The solution-focused practice of defining small, concrete goals is realistic in school situations in which those involved have limited time and resources (Murphy, 1996).

Third, SFBT emphasizes active listening and focusing on strengths, which facilitates collaboration with others who are involved with the students. SFBT works well because it helps build relationships, increases hope and motivation, and offers strategies for working with "uncooperative" students. SFBT also is very flexible and encourages the use of tools from other therapeutic models when used thoughtfully to accommodate students' goals. SFB therapists adopt a stance that there are many approaches that may result in solutions and respects the unique ideas, beliefs, and styles of other therapists, counselors, students, parents, and teachers (Murphy & Duncan, 1997). Solution-focused therapy uses compliments similar to encouragement or positive reinforcement, and works to alter restraining beliefs, which also makes the approach compatible with learning approaches used within schools.

Fourth, schools can be stressful environments and students may respond to this stress by developing behavioral problems that become concerns for teachers and other members of the school community. Common behaviors that concern schools include mood changes, impulsivity, inattention, aggression, poor eating and sleeping habits, decreases in academic achievement, preoccupation with sexual issues, school absences, and substance use or abuse (Center for Mental Health in Schools, 2003). SFBT focuses on the importance of changing social interactions, and assembles human resources to discover solutions to stressful social interactions. For example, the clinical process provided by SFBT may increase coping skills of students, teachers, and others in the school community, as will as address behavior and relationship problems.

Finally, students referred for therapy in schools can be considered mandated clients. That is, they are sent by someone else for help and typically do not seek help on their own. SFBT is a therapy that offers effective interviewing skills for engaging reluctant or skeptical students and for this reason it also may be especially useful in a school setting (Franklin & Hopson, in press).

INTRODUCING SFBT IN PUBLIC SCHOOLS

School professionals seldom have been trained in the SFBT approach. Educating professionals about how solution-focused therapy has become a promising therapeutic approach that is being used in schools is one way of opening conversations with such teachers and administrators. For example, it may be helpful to discuss some of the current trends in helping students and to suggest that SFBT has shown promise for working with school dropouts, classroom management, and school-related behavior problems (Franklin et al., 2001; Franklin & Streeter, 2003). It also might be helpful to provide readings on SFBT and to offer to answer questions. Fortunately, a considerable number of solution-focused resources now are available for working in schools (Franklin et al., 2001; Franklin & Streeter, 2003; Kral, 1995; Metcalf, 1995; Murphy & Duncan, 1997; Sklare, 1997; Thomas, 1997; Webb, 1999). These authors provide excellent examples and strategies for using SFBT with students, parents, teachers, and administrators.

Solution-focused therapists can maximize their work if they can become consultants and trainers in SFBT. One strategy is to volunteer to do in-service training or to provide staff training on the solution-focused approach. For example, the following exercise can be a meaningful way to introduce the perspective of SFBT to teachers and have them begin to look at problem-solving in a different way.

Divide the teachers into two groups. Tell them that each group will receive a referral for a student that they will review and discuss. Each group will recommend a plan to address the student's issues. Although both groups will have a referral describing the same student, one uses traditional problem-focused language and one uses solution-focused, strengths-based language. Bring the groups together and have them present their recommendations. Facilitate a discussion about how the language of the referral shaped their perceptions of the student, the possible plan for intervention, and their expectations.

Specific Strategies for Introducing SFBT

Franklin and Streeter (2003) suggest that the following activities are useful in introducing SFBT in school settings. Some of the strategies mentioned include:

- Obtain support from administration;
- Identify one person to be primarily responsible for training and adherence;

- Create strong partnerships with selected school staff;
- Assess what the school already is doing to build solutions;
- Introduce the model through an interdisciplinary team structure;
- Seek input from all constituents, especially students;
- Maintain a focus on the school in solution-building conversations;
- Provide opportunities for training by an expert in solution-focused therapy; and,
- Support educators in shaping the model with their own unique philosophies and approaches.

When a therapist is coming from the outside of the school system, it also may be helpful to first establish alliances with the principal, management team, and key school-based mental health professionals before introducing SFBT. We suggest that therapists build teams of interested professionals, train them, and then proceed to other staff training, using these persons as cotrainers.

SUCCESSFULLY WORKING ON SCHOOL CAMPUSES

Working conditions frequently are different on school campuses than in therapists' offices or mental health clinics (Streeter & Franklin, 2002). Therapists coming from outside of the school often are unfamiliar with these working conditions and must prepare themselves for these differences. For example, school-based therapists may meet with students and teachers on the playground and lunch room. Additionally, therapists in schools often face the challenge of fulfilling multiple roles. Social workers, family therapists, and other counselors often wear many hats in schools, ranging from student advocate to disciplinarian, and these competing roles and corresponding goals must be considered. The therapist must be a good negotiator and balance the goals of schools with the diverse needs of students.

Competing roles may not always create an ideal situation for applying SFBT. Solution-focused therapists must see multiple roles as opportunities to engage and influence complainants and clients at multiple levels. Solution-focused therapists who can negotiate complex situations and competing tasks will be the credible and effective in schools.

The school context sometimes makes it more challenging for SFB therapists to be fully integrated into the school culture. For example, some therapists visit campuses only one day a week or are co-located from another agency for a small amount of time. On a school campus, a solution-focused therapist might be the only or one of only a few trained mental health professionals on staff. Furthermore, the role of a therapist of any kind may be met with some skepticism by school staff.

Example of Negotiating Multiple Goals on a School Campus

Joey Smith is a 17-year-old student who was skipping school, using alcohol and marijuana, and living part of the time with his friends and part of the time with his grandmother. The school is most concerned about his increased absences, alleged drug use, and failing grades. Joey's personal situation is of great concern to the school social worker. His mother is addicted to crack cocaine and she disappears for weeks at a time. There have been reports that she is involved in prostitution. When she emerges, she stays with her mother for a few days at a time but is not involved in Joey's care. Joey's father is in prison and Joey has little support from his other family members. He has a 22-two-year-old sister who is reported to have moved to Las Vegas to pursue her career as a dancer, and he has not seen or heard from her in two years. He has three younger half siblings, ages 5, 7, and 10, who are in custody of Child Protective Services.

In this case, it might be important for the solution-focused therapist to increase student safety at home and help the family tackle the problems in living, including the substance abuse. The school goals, however, must be agreed upon by other school professionals who have certain behavioral expectations and demands for Joey within the school. The school professionals' goals may not be as family-focused as the therapist's goals. For example, school professionals such as teachers and administrators might be happy that a parent entered substance abuse treatment as a result of the therapists' interventions or that a student is staying at home every night and not with friends. But, what is more important in the school context is how an intervention helped the student's attendance, grades, and performance in the classroom. In cases that involve multiple challenges and goals, solution-focused therapists, like all school mental health professionals, are faced with the daunting task of linking mental health interventions with school values and outcomes.

In the situation with Joey, the solution-focused therapist negotiated goals that had a common theme of safety and cooperation and that related to Joey's behavior at school. The goals were specifically shaped to meet the demands of the school context. The goal of Joey's teachers, for example, was for Joey to come to class sober and to finish the work for that day. He also needed to turn in late assignments. Teachers agreed to give him extra help until he could catch up, without referring him to the principal, if he came to class sober and participated. One teacher agreed to act as a buddy and tutor to Joey. The goal of the principal was for Joey to attend school regularly, cooperate with the teachers, and be clean of drugs when on the school campus. The principal agreed to not refer Joey to the truant officer and juvenile court, even if he occasionally missed a day, as long as he attended 90 percent of the time for each grading period. The goal of the grandmother was for the school to stop calling her to complain about Joey's absences and to stop sending the truant officer who imposed fines that they could not afford to pay. She wanted a week of peace without calls from the school. The grandmother agreed to help Joey more financially if he lived with her all the time during the school week and went to school every day for a week. After that time, if he continued to live with her on school days and maintained the 90 percent rule of the principal, she would continue to support him and add additional privileges that he wanted.

Joey's goals were to avoid arrest and juvenile detention. He did not want to end up in prison like his father. He specifically wanted to avoid court involvement. Joey also indicated that he wanted to do well enough in school to make passing grades but he did not like the strict attendance rule. His goals were to attend class for one week, catch up on three critically important assignments, and to stay free of visits from the juvenile authorities that week. He agreed he could follow the 90 percent rule and stay with his grandmother.

BUILDING COLLABORATIVE RELATIONSHIPS

The collaborative stance is, perhaps, one of the most useful SFBT techniques for schools. This approach acknowledges that each member of the school team brings her or his own meaningful expertise into the solution formation, rather than the therapist's providing a solution for others to follow. Leading in this way works well in schools where mental health professionals must engage and work with other school professionals in order to work out solutions. Solution-focused therapists who can lead processes that include everyone's input and validates their care and concern for students are more likely to gain greater buy-in from the school staff. For example, principals do not want to be told how to run their schools and teachers do not want to be told how to fix their classrooms. However, school professionals may welcome collaborators who will listen closely to their concerns and offer strategies that seem practical and workable in their day-to-day routine.

Strategies for Building Collaboration

To be effective in forming collaborative relationships in schools, practitioners must know how to include key stakeholders in the collaboration and be adept at understanding the sociopolitical and organizational environment of the school. Practitioners can ask questions such as:

- Who might share certain views? Who might disagree? Why?
- Who is easiest to influence toward your interventions and how?
- Who are the decision makers that you must influence to make needed changes?
- Is this a problem that you can influence directly? With others?
- What interventions need to be delivered and how can they be delivered with the most impact and to whom and from whom?
- Who is best to involve in the intervention to get results?
- Who should show support for your intervention if it is going to be followed? (Cashman, 2006)

Harris and Franklin (2004) provide additional information for how to work collaboratively in school systems.

Building Collaboration and Cooperation with the Principal

One key solution-focused strategy for collaborating with administrators is to adopt their points of view and join with them in their goals and visions. Principals establish the climate and vision of schools and it is important for therapists to use the language of the schools instead of the language of therapy. For this reason, we suggest using the term *solution-building conversations* instead of *Solution-Focused Brief Therapy*. Solution-building is a term used by De Jong and Berg (2002) to describe the use of solution-focused therapy in interviewing. Of course, every therapist should use whatever language works best for a particular setting. However, our experience in schools indicates that principals and administrators are likely to respond favorably to the use of *solution-building conversations* that can empower teachers and staff to be more effective with students who display at-risk behaviors. For example, empowering staff to reflect on the assumptions of solution-building while using the techniques to prevent problems from increasing can allow for minimal disruption of the learning environment. Most principals will support any therapy that delivers such an outcome.

WORKING WITH STUDENTS

SFBT uses a helping process that puts change in the hands of students instead of schools, which can ease the pressure for behavioral control that both schools and students often feel. The need to control students and get them to cooperate with the rules of the school often can alienate students and work against building relationships and cooperation. Part of the reason this often happens is because schools tend to use coercion and punishment techniques. Solution-focused techniques help students develop concrete, achievable goals to work toward rather than getting stuck on problems and issues of control. For example, a therapist can work with a student to take small steps forward. Using a small-step approach offers faculty hope because they can see some change, even if it is small, and positive belief that students are able to improve their behavior, thus relieving the pressure to use punishment and coercion to control students.

Focusing on Small Steps

Rita is a tenth grade student who is reported to be asocial. She is an average student, making mostly Cs and some Bs. Rita does not speak to others and does not make eye contact. She occasionally keeps poor hygiene and often does not follow through on tasks. With prompting, however, she usually accomplishes tasks and even improves her hygiene. Her teacher finds the continual prompting to be annoying but states that she is concerned most about her isolation from the other students and lack of social adjustment.

RITA: I just hate my teacher and especially this school. It sucks!

THERAPIST: What specifically do you not like about the school?

RITA: Lots of things.

THERAPIST: Name the most important one.

RITA: I do not have any friends in this school. I guess you can say I am a loner.

THERAPIST: Have there been times in the past you had friends?

RITA: Yeah, before I moved to this school when I was in the eighth grade, I had a friend I used to do things with.

THERAPIST: So, you have not always been a loner?

RITA: I guess not.

THERAPIST: So, in the past, did you like spending time with your friend?

RITA: (*Silence*)

THERAPIST asks the question again and waits.

RITA: Yeah, we had some fun times.

THERAPIST: On a scale of one to ten, how much are you dissatisfied with not having a friend in school right now? Think of one as, "I do not have many friends in school right now," and ten as, "I have as many friends as I could ever want."

RITA: One. There is nobody and I will never have a ten.

THERAPIST: Sure, ten would be pretty amazing for anyone. So, what would two look like?

RITA: I guess if I felt like I had one friend I could talk to at school I might feel like I had a two.

THERAPIST: What could you do to feel like you have one friend?

RITA (*Silence therapist waits for answer*): I don't know. You're the counselor.

THERAPIST: Well, just pretend for a moment that you did know. What might you say? (*Waits*)

RITA (*Pause*): I guess I could talk to this girl in my English class that I think could be a friend. She likes poetry like I do. I think she hates the teacher, too.

THERAPIST: Well, that sounds like a good start. When is your next class? Wednesday, right?

RITA: Yeah, Wednesday.

THERAPIST: So, I am curious, how will you talk to her?

RITA: Maybe in the hall before class, I could say hi. She smiled at me once by the lockers. When we are standing by the lockers, I could invite her to work on a class project with me. But, I don't know if I can. I don't like to start talking. I'd rather she ask me.

THERAPIST: It would be easier if she would talk first. But that might be hard for her, too. Sure, it is not easy to start a conversation with someone you don't know. So, what will you say to her?

RITA: Just, "Hi, how are you?" And then I'll ask if she might like to work on the project.

THERAPIST: Okay, I'll pretend to be her and you pretend you're asking me.

RITA (Hesitates): Okay, I guess so, but that sounds stupid because you are not her.

THERAPIST: Of course, but try it anyway.

RITA: Okay.

Developing Well-Formed Goals and Exploring Exceptions

Students often have experienced goal setting, but lack skills in developing concrete and behaviorally focused goals as suggested in SFBT. Scaling questions are powerful tools for developing goals that are defined by small increments that represent movement up one point on the scale (Franklin & Streeter, 2003). Scaling questions strive to lead students to create visions of the future without the problem. Constructing goals is enhanced by using the miracle question as described in Chapter 1 of this text. The miracle question asks students (or parents or teachers) to describe in specific detail what would happen if the difficulty were to disappear while they slept one night. Fleshing out this vision in as much detail as possible not only enhances motivation for change, but also provides clues for constructing first steps toward solutions. By asking, "Walk me through the day," or, "You are getting on the bus; describe what is happening," therapists can lead students through every class or situation in vivid detail.

Another approach is to use a journalistic style of describing a day after the miracle to the therapist. In this approach, therapists might ask students to fill in a log with times for each hour of the day with descriptions of what is happening that says the miracle happened. Video talk[1] and asking "What else?" can help to bring a vision of the future to life for the student. Students also can be asked to draw solutions or act them out. A follow-up question is to ask what part of the miracle already is happening, even if just a little bit. This yields a possible avenue for students to do more of what they already are doing and to illustrate that no problem exists in the same intensity all the time. Exploring exceptions to the problem and reviewing in detail those instances when the difficulty is absent or even a bit better provides clues to the direction to take in building a solution. Students already have experienced some changes and successes, and these can be carried forward by the momentum of the success.

Something Different and Homework

The main goal for school meetings with students is to end the meeting with plans to do something different. Meetings should include compliments that reflect the strengths and commitment of the students and enthusiasm for the changes to come and then to make suggestions for action. Homework assignments arise out of the vision of a future without the problem and include exceptions that already are occurring. Homework often includes the student's observing a part of his or her life to report back. Homework assignments also can direct the student to act for part of the day as if the miracle has happened.

Using a technique such as creating surprise endings can lead to specific steps to be tried for a week. For example, the student is asked to describe the typical outcome in a class in which he or she is having trouble. Details of that account are provided. The counselor then asks the student to write, draw, or act out the details for a totally different, surprise ending. The student can be instructed to pick a class period to make this surprise ending happen and report back the results.

STUDENT: Arrgh! Ms. Wilson just sent me to the assistant principal again— she hates me and is always picking on me.

THERAPIST: What happened?

STUDENT: Well, I was just talking to my friend and she told me to stop talking. I told her that it was really important and that I was done with my homework anyway and, like always, she totally got in my face and told me I was disrespecting her. I tried to tell her that she was the one that was acting rude and disrespectful because she was yelling at me in front of the class. And then I walked out of the class because I wasn't going to let her talk to me like that, and she told me to go to the principal's office.

THERAPIST: Hmmm—it seems like this has been happening a lot this past month.

STUDENT: Yeah, I know—she totally hates me.

THERAPIST: It seems like you almost expect to be sent to the principal's office by Ms. Wilson now.

STUDENT: Yeah—it is like no matter what I do, she is in my face about something.

THERAPIST: I wonder if you would be willing to think of a totally different ending to your class with Ms. Wilson, one that would totally surprise you and Ms. Wilson. Like, she would not even believe it could happen with you.

STUDENT: Like she and I hug and become best friends? Yeah, right, that will never happen.

THERAPIST: Well, that would certainly be an enormous surprise for all of us . . . but what about some other ending that you could imagine but would still be a surprise to everyone.

STUDENT: Like, if I stayed in class the whole period and she did not get in my face about anything and she smiled at me when the class was over?

THERAPIST: That would certainly be an unexpected outcome! I wonder if you could find a way to totally surprise Ms. Wilson and make that happen.

STUDENT: It could happen—but it would not be easy since she practically always wants to send me to the principal's office. But I bet I could come up with something to shock her into smiling at me.

THERAPIST: Hmmm—you are really good at coming up with creative stories. How about you take the last fifteen minutes of our meeting and write how you are going to create this surprise ending—like an everyday story with a twist at the end!

STUDENT: I guess I could do that—although it sounds kind of stupid. Would anyone else have to read it?

THERAPIST: No—no one else has to read it. How about sometime this week, you just plan to totally surprise her by making this ending happen. You can even surprise me about when you are going to make it happen. When we get together next week you can tell me how you surprised her by not having to go to the principal's office—and maybe even got her to smile at you!

Making Use of Breaks in Schools

SFBT therapists often take breaks during or near the end of sessions in order for both the client and the therapist to collect their thoughts and reflect on the session. This sometimes is done differently in schools, but can still be a useful strategy. A break for gathering one's thoughts is highly respectful of students. Furthermore, in school settings, taking breaks can accommodate the difficulty for both students and teachers in setting aside large blocks of time. For example, a break might occur naturally between morning and afternoon or before or after lunch. However, taking a too-long break might negate the impact of goal-setting activities, especially the vision of a future without the problem. Breaks can match the normal routine of a parent-teacher conference and can be especially useful for increasing the comfort of the participants. That is, students and parents often are overwhelmed when sitting in rooms with teachers, counselors, and administrators, discussing the student's difficulty; the break can be used to offer relief and focus.

WORKING WITH STUDENTS AND PARENTS

SFBT can be very empowering for students and parents. It can be especially encouraging for those students and parents that routinely interact with the school due to problems. These parents and students come to expect complaints, criticism, and constant struggle over school. SFBT moves away from a problem-focus and allows both students and parents to see hope for improvement. The therapist works to remind families of their resources and times that the problems have exceptions. This communicates that the school sees strengths in both parents and students. It also communicates that school personnel believe that problems can get better, and that they are not willing to give up on the student. Using this approach, SFBT helps facilitate partnerships between families and schools and, even if schools and families define problems in different ways, the ultimate goal for both is what is best for the student.

Breaking Problem Patterns

SFBT techniques can encourage families to break their routines and try something different, and can be powerful for families that are stuck in problem patterns.

MOTHER: Tabitha refuses to get up on time in the morning and she is late to school every day.

THERAPIST: Tell me about the days that she does get up.

MOTHER: There are no days. I am telling you that there is no getup in that girl. She is the laziest thing I have ever seen. That is why she is getting absences: because of the [*accumulated*] tardies.

THERAPIST: Of course, many teenagers are hard to get up. Drives parents crazy!

MOTHER: Uh huh, it sure does.

THERAPIST: What happens in the morning when she does not get up?

MOTHER: I yell up the stairs at her to get your butt up!

THERAPIST: Does that work?

MOTHER: Well, no, I guess not. But, what else can I do?

THERAPIST: I'm not sure I know yet. What is something that Tabitha enjoys that she might be willing to work toward?

MOTHER: Well, let me think . . . She is really into her music. She does like her music.

THERAPIST: I'm not sure, but I'm wondering if you can use music in any way to get her up.

MOTHER: You mean like taking it away from her? Now, that does make her mad when I take her CD player. She threatens to skip school when I do that . . . We can get in some big fights. One time, we almost came to blows.

THERAPIST: So, that doesn't get her to get up on time?

MOTHER: No! No! She is too stubborn. I have taken away lots of things and I can't watch her all the time and she just sneaks and finds a way to listen or get the stuff back when I'm gone to work. I work in the evenings, you know.

THERAPIST: Of course, you try and watch her but you can't do that all the time. I can see why that wouldn't work, then. What does work with her?

MOTHER: Well, even though she can be lazy about getting up, she will work for her allowance but I can't just pay her for everything. I don't have that kind of money.

THERAPIST: Oh, so she likes to work for privileges. Great! I know it sounds strange, but how about instead of yelling and taking her music away for not getting up if you give her something to work toward; maybe do something really different that will both shock her and motivate her?

MOTHER: Like what?

THERAPIST: Well you said she likes music; maybe buy one of her favorite CDs and play it in her room at wake-up time in the morning. Because she likes to work for privileges, tell her she can only listen to the CD in the mornings before school, but if she gets up and makes it to school on time for five days in a row that, you will let her have it for keeps. Maybe this would get her started on a habit of getting up?

MOTHER: Now, that is different. I don't know? Maybe?

THERAPIST: Do you think you could give it a try?

MOTHER: Sounds crazy, but I guess so. She does like music.

As illustrated, although SFBT focuses on small, simple, behavioral changes for families, it also aims at helping parents and students get "unstuck" from perpetual problem patterns that repeat and reinforce themselves.[2] Getting unstuck can help parents and students change their perspectives of possible solutions and motivate them to try new things.

WORKING WITH ADMINISTRATORS

All experienced solution-focused therapists understand how language and personal perceptions are created through social interactions, and hold the view that changes in talk, beliefs, and behavior happen simultaneously. Principals, however, may be more skeptical of this *believing is seeing* philosophy.[3] Most principals are trained as administrators and have a practical, bottom-line perspective. Their jobs also are performance-oriented and they are held accountable to outcomes such as attendance of their students. They want to *see* before they *believe* and what they want to *see* is results as they define them. As one principal at a solution-focused school said, "Show me the money."

So, it is important to demonstrate to administrators how the solution-building techniques work. Observing a teacher or counselor using a technique from solution-building may convince a principal that solution-building is beneficial. At Gonzolo Garza High School in Austin, Texas, a school social worker demonstrated the formula first-session task (de Shazer, 1982), described in Chapter 1 of this volume, at the end of a staffing with a student as a prelude to meeting with the student later in the week. The results of this task intrigued the principal so much that she became receptive to adopting the process schoolwide. Of course, what helped most is that the student improved his attendance. In another school in Ft. Lauderdale, Florida, a school psychologist helped three teachers in a special classroom to observe what the students with at-risk behaviors were doing right and to learn how to use compliments for those behaviors. He also taught the teachers to use scaling questions to help the students to see their progress. The result was that those classrooms improved in attendance and other outcomes (Berg & Shilts, 2004). These changes were noticeable to the principal, who tracked data on the classroom performances, and then asked for more teacher-training in these techniques.

Evaluating Progress

Principals and other school administrators appreciate therapists who evaluate progress of students. In schools, evaluating progress can be fairly informal, with teachers' asking students how things are going or asking where they are on the scale. Scaling questions often reveal that changes have been more than one step. Scaling also can be used to rate students' levels of confidence in their ability to maintain changes and, with permission of the students, the confidence ratings and changes that have been achieved can be reported back to the principal.

Another evaluation strategy is for therapists to generate stories that communicate "before and after" pictures of the students' progress. Students can be brought into this process by describing differences in their behavior. Teachers can be coached on this approach and encouraged to write comments on sheets of paper in "before and after" columns that describe the differences they see in students. These comments can then be developed into narratives that can be communicated back to the principal and others. For example, one teacher reported,

> When Tim first came to my class in the fall, honestly, I did not know if he could make it or not. But, I will say that I am amazed at how much progress Tim has made and how much he has grown up. When Tim

first came to class, he sat in the back with his arms folded and did not talk, but now Tim is one of the most courteous students in this class. He helps me and volunteers to help the other students. I even heard that he was asked to be PAL [Peer Assistance Leader]. Nothing surprises me anymore. His grades have improved from Ds to Cs and Bs and he even mentioned college. Does that surprise you about Tim as much as it surprises me?

A third option for evaluation is to develop a solution-oriented report card that can be given to the principal and others. On this report card, goals for behavioral improvement can be listed along with input from teachers and students, and letter grades can be assigned, starting with where the students were at the time of the referral and moving forward in time. That is, students might start with D or F, move to C, and make even more progress to B or A. Quick glances, then, are all that are needed to monitor progress.

WORKING WITH TEACHERS

Teachers must welcome collaboration with therapists and must be courted even further if they are going to be responsive to learning how to use solution-building techniques themselves. For this to happen, it is important for school counselors and mental health professionals to support the teachers. Training teachers to use basic solution-focused techniques with students in the classroom can help minimize problem behaviors in school. Teachers must agree, however, to learn and use solution-building conversations, and, in our opinion, it is not a good idea to mandate the use of the techniques. We think it is best when the principal and the mental health professionals support the effort; the therapist may start with some in-service training and volunteer follow-up training that supports the individual teachers' concerns and goals for their classrooms. One-to-one consultation and help with the students also can be used with individual teachers or classes if a more schoolwide approach is not immediately feasible. In working with teachers, solution-focused therapists might take roles of consultant, collaborator, and coach in discovering solutions for teacher's concerns. The coach role empowers teachers to handle behavior concerns on their own and to see that they can use solution-building conversations with favorable outcomes.

When teachers encounter mental health and social problems, they often feel powerless. Many students live with serious difficulties every day of their lives and it is not unusual for these difficulties to intrude upon their time at school. For many students, school provides a haven where they can learn and work away from their problems. Solution-building conversations can be used to empower teachers to respond to students in distress, while, at the same time, keeping a clear school focus. The question to keep foremost in mind is, "What can we do at school to make things better and make you more successful?" It is very tempting to become deeply involved in a student's situation outside of school, but that is not the intention of empowering teachers or equipping them with the skills of solution-building. Teachers can be encouraged to provide first aid and triage, and part of triage is to reduce unnecessary referrals and to be able to effectively advance students to the next level of care.

For example, a solution-focused approach between a student and teacher about turning in homework could sound like this:

TEACHER: Ricky, I am concerned because you have not turned in your homework for the past two weeks.

RICKY: I'm sorry, but my mom got put back in jail a couple of weeks ago and I've been trying to work more hours so we can pay our rent.

TEACHER: I'm sorry to hear about your mom and it sounds like you are trying to be very responsible. Next time, please let me know what is going on, okay?

RICKY: Yeah, okay.

TEACHER: You're being a very good son and brother to do the extra work. I know that it's important for you to pass this class. So, what can we do to help you be responsible about your homework, too?

RICKY: Well, I almost have the homework done from last week.

TEACHER: That's great—how did you manage to do that with all your other work?

RICKY: I don't know. I did it on breaks and late at night. Just a little at a time.

TEACHER: Really . . . that shows how much you really want to finish. How about you turn in what you have so far and I can grade it in parts?

RICKY: Yeah. I can do some of the homework during breaks at work or at lunch time every day and then turn those parts in to you.

TEACHER: I am impressed that you've been able to work on your homework a little bit. I mean, with everything else going on! Can you get more time to focus on school with your mom gone?

RICKY: Not really. I thought I might even have to drop out and work for a while.

TEACHER: Of course, you have to take care of your rent. But, I know you want to stay in school. We can modify the homework for now but what else would help you be able to have more time for school?

RICKY: I think a cheaper place to live or some kind of help like that.

TEACHER: Yeah, I can see how that would make it easier because you would not need as much money to pay rent. What have you done to try and solve this problem?

RICKY: Not much . . . Well, I talked to some friends, but that's about it.

TEACHER: What did your friends say?

RICKY: They said I should either drop out or get a cheaper place. One friend told me to forget school until my mom could get out of jail but another one said I might be able to get some kind of help with my rent, but I do not see how.

TEACHER: Have you talked with Ms. Rogers? She has ideas for getting help with rent and stuff like that.

RICKY: No, I didn't know that.

TEACHER: She might have some ideas.

RICKY: Thanks—I think I'm going to have to keep working, but it would be okay to get some help with the rent. How do I see that lady?

TEACHER: Here is her phone number and I will fill out a slip so you can get an appointment. Maybe, when you see her, you can work out something so you can have more time for schoolwork.

RICKY: Yeah, maybe.

TEACHER: Let me know how it goes. I look forward to getting part of your homework tomorrow. Okay?

RICKY: Okay.

Supporting the Solutions of Classroom Teachers

SFB therapists can model solution-building conversations with classroom teachers when discussing students, at meetings, and when providing other support. For example:

TEACHER: Renee is such a behavior problem—I wish they could transfer her out of my class! I just don't know what to do with her.

COUNSELOR: She can be quite a challenge! I'm not sure I know what to do yet, either. I'm amazed that you have succeeded in keeping her in your class for this long—not everyone has been able to do that. How do you manage to deal with her every day?

TEACHER: Sometimes I just don't know how I do it. But, I have found that if I stay calm, give her a little bit of time, and try to make her laugh, she can often get her behavior under control.

COUNSELOR: Wow! That sounds like a great strategy. How often does that work?

TEACHER: Well, when I can stay patient and give her enough time, she almost always improves her behavior. But, she goes too far.

COUNSELOR: Of course, she goes too far. But what you are able to do is great! It sounds like she can be challenging, but that you know what to do to help her change her behavior. I am impressed—that must be why she has had some success in your class. Of course, you recognize the success in your class that she has? I know other teachers have told me that you can get her to cooperate.

TEACHER: Yes, she seems to like me despite everything. But, I can't say that it always goes both ways. I get tired of her and she disrupts the other students.

COUNSELOR: That is why I'm even more impressed with you: because you keep being patient with her. You know how to keep her in your class and help her improve her behavior even when you want to throw her out.

TEACHER: Yes, I guess I do know how to do that, but I'm not sure it's always best.

COUNSELOR: Of course, you have your days that you doubt your effectiveness and whether she is worth the effort. But, you have not given up. You're not only patient, but also consistent and that works.

TEACHER: Yeah, I never thought of it just like that but I guess that is why she has hung on in my class so long when she got sent out of other classes.

WORKING WITH OTHER MENTAL HEALTH PROFESSIONALS IN SCHOOLS

It is important for therapists using SFBT to work with the other therapists in the school. Bridging solution-focused strategies with familiar approaches such as family systems models and cognitive-behavioral therapies is a good way to facilitate collaboration among these professionals. One promising method that has been used in schools involves developing a team of learners who want to work together to apply SFBT (Franklin & Streeter, 2003). In this approach, novice learners are paired with expert solution-focused therapists who coach them and illustrate how to use the method.

Using the Team Approach in Schools

Time constraints and limited resources can make it difficult to use a team approach in schools. However, a team can be used in situations that require conjoint meetings between students, teachers, parents, and others. Identifying one person to conduct the interview and using the rest of the professionals as "reflectors" can counteract the students' or parents' feelings of being in the hot seat. At Gonzolo Garza High School, the reflecting team approach is used when students continue to present challenges after standard interventions have been used. Students are interviewed by a solution-focused therapist and the team (e.g., assistant principal, counselors, and teachers) provides reflections and suggestions. Students also are asked to choose advocates to be on their side and offer support to them; these individuals also participate on the team.

CONCLUSION

School-based interventions are badly needed to help students succeed and to help the teachers and administrators who work with them. Solution-focused brief therapy is uniquely suited for this work because it is goal-oriented and fits within the time and space constraints of the settings. Teachers and administrators easily can learn the basics of the approach, which helps them to be more effective and can produce faster, better results than can be provided by school counselors or therapists alone.

NOTES

1. Video talk is a variation of filmstrip talk described by the promulgators of the strategic approach at the Mental Research Institute (Weakland & Fisch, 1992). In this technique, the therapist asks the clients to describe life situations as though they were describing a film or video. The client is asked for graphic details from beginning to end with questions such as, "What would I see?" "Who is doing what/ when?" "Then what happens?" "What else is happening?" and "What is this person doing when you are doing that?"

2. Editors' note: Many would consider this to be a strategic move a la the MRI approach (Watzlawick, Weakland, & Fish, 1974). In this case, it might be used to help the mother think of exceptions, or it might be used to gather information about positive change that occurs as a result of the suggestion, which would lead to more solution-building talk.

3. Editor's note: This idea is discussed by Heinz von Foerster (1984) in his seminal work on constructivism.

REFERENCES

Berg, I. K., & Shilts, L. (2004). *Classroom solutions: WOWW approach.* Milwaukee, WI: BFTC Press.

Cashman, J. (2006). Influencing policies in legal education authorities. In C. Franklin, M. B. Harris, & P. A. Meares (Eds.), *The school services source book: A guide for social workers, counselors and mental health therapists.* New York: Oxford University Press.

Center for Mental Health in Schools. (2003). *Guidebook: Common psychological problems of school aged youth: Developmental variations, problems, disorders, and perspectives for prevention and treatment.* Retrieved January 25, 2005 from http://smhp.psych.ucla.edu

Corcoran, J., & Stephenson, M. (2000). The effectiveness of solution-focused therapy with child behavior problems: A preliminary study. *Families in Society, 81*(5), 468-474.

De Jong, P., & Berg, I. K. (2002). *Interviewing for solutions* (2nd ed.). Pacific Grove, CA: Brooks/Cole.

de Shazer, S. (1982). *Patterns of brief family therapy: An ecosystemic approach.* New York: Guilford.

Foerster, H. von (1984). On constructing a reality. In H. von Foerster (Ed.), *Observing systems* (2nd ed., pp. 287-312). Seaside, CA: Intersystem Publications.

Franklin, C., Biever, J. L., Moore, K. C., Clemons, D., & Scamardo, M. (2001). Effectiveness of solution-focused therapy with children in a school setting. *Research on Social Work Practice, 11*(4), 411-434.

Franklin, C., Corcoran, J., Nowicki, J., & Streeter, C. L. (1997). Using client self-anchored scales to measure outcomes in solution-focused therapy. *Journal of Systemic Therapies, 16*(3), 246-265.

Franklin, C., & Hopson, L. (in press). Involuntary clients in public schools: Solution-focused interventions. In R. H. Rooney (Ed.), *Strategies for work with involuntary clients* (2nd ed.). New York: Columbia University Press.

Franklin, C., & Streeter, C. L. (2003). *Solution-focused accountability schools for the twenty first century: A training manual for Gonzalo Garza Independence High School.* Unpublished manuscript, the Hogg Foundation for Mental Health: The University of Texas at Austin.

Franklin, C., & Streeter, C. L. (2004). *Solution-focused alternative schools: An evaluation of Gonzalo Garza Independence High School.* Unpublished manuscript, the Hogg Foundation for Mental Health: The University of Texas at Austin.

Harris, M., & Franklin, C. (2003). Effectiveness of a cognitive-behavioral, school based group intervention with Mexican-American pregnant and parenting adolescents. *Social Work Research, 27*(2), 71-84.

Harris, M. B., & Franklin, C. (2004). The design of school social work services. In P. A. Meares (Ed.), *Social work services in the school* (4th ed., pp. 277-294). Boston: Allyn & Bacon.

Kral, R. (1995). *Solutions for schools*. Milwaukee: Brief Family Therapy Center Press.

LaFountain, R. M., & Garner, N. E. (1996). Solution-focused counseling groups: The results are in. *Journal for Specialists in Group Work, 21*(2), 128-143.

Littrell, J. M., Malia, J. A., & Vanderwood, M. (1995). Single-session brief counseling in a high school. *Journal of Counseling and Development, 73,* 451-458.

Metcalf, L. (1995). *Counseling toward solutions: A practical solution-focused program for working with students, teachers, and parents.* San Francisco: Jossey-Bass.

Moore, K., & Franklin, C. (2005). The effectiveness of solution-focused therapy with school-related behavior problems. Manuscript submitted for publication.

Murphy, J. J. (1996). Solution-focused brief therapy in the school. In S. D. Miller., M. A. Hubble, & B. S. Duncan (Eds.), *Handbook of solution-focused brief therapy* (pp. 184-204). San Francisco: Jossey-Bass.

Murphy, J. J., & Duncan, B.S. (1997). *Brief interventions for school problems.* New York: Guildford Publications.

Newsome, S. (2002). *The impact of solution-focused brief therapy with at-risk junior high school students.* Unpublished doctoral dissertation, Ohio State University, Columbus, Ohio.

RAND health research highlights: Mental health case for youth (2001). Retrieved January 30, 2005 from www.rand.org/publications/RB/RB4541

Roans, M., & Hoagwood, K. (2000). School-based mental health services: A research review. *Clinical Child and Family Psychology Review, 3*(4), 223-241.

Sklare, G. B. (1997). *Brief counseling that works: A solution-focused approach for school counselors.* Thousand Oaks, CA: Sage.

Streeter, C. L., & Franklin, C. (2002). Standards for school social work in the 21st century. In A. Roberts & G. Greene (Eds.). *Social worker's desk reference* (pp. 612-619). Oxford University Press.

Thomas, F. N., (1997, August). *What you see is what you get: Competency-based techniques with couples, families and other earth units.* Workshop at the Texas Network for Children, Austin, TX.

Thomas, F. N., & Nelson, T. S. (2007). Assumptions within the solution-focused brief therapy tradition. In T. S. Nelson & F. N. Thomas (Eds.), *Handbook of solution-focused brief therapy: Clinical application* (pp. 3-24). Binghamton, NY: The Haworth Press.

Watzlawick, P., Weakland, J., & Fisch, R. (1974). *Change: Principles of problem formation and problem resolution.* New York: Norton.

Weakland, J., & Fisch, C. (1992). Brief therapy-MRI style. In S. H. Budman, M. F. Hoyt, & S. Friedman (Eds.). *The first session in brief therapy* (pp. 306-323). New York: Guilford.

Webb, W. H. (1999). *Solutioning: Solution-focused interventions for counselors.* Philadelphia, PA: Accelerated Press.

Chapter 8

Solution-Focused Work with Children and Young People

Paul Hackett
Guy Shennan

INTRODUCTION

Our starting point, and the single most crucial principle in our work with children, is that you have to treat what they say seriously and convey that what they say is of importance. Now this may seem so obvious that you are considering skipping this chapter, but bear with us. Just cast your mind back to when you were a child. What did you do if you felt that people were not listening to you? Or what did you do as an adolescent when you felt slighted by those in authority? Did you try harder to make them understand or did you just feel more misunderstood? Imagine if you can, the adults in your childhood whom you felt most understood you or who conveyed that they respected your wishes. Imagine sitting with a stranger who began to convey that and now imagine sitting with a stranger who conveyed the opposite. Take a minute or so to do that. All the work that we do with children and adolescents, whatever techniques, tools, or tricks of the trade we employ has to be built upon this firm foundation of respect for whom they are, for what they want, and for what they have to say.

When we work with children, starting where the client is, poses a particular challenge. As adults, we need to make a creative leap of the imagination to enter the child's world, resisting the tempting illusion that, having once been children ourselves, we know this world. However, the attempt to

Handbook of Solution-Focused Brief Therapy: Clinical Applications
© 2007 by The Haworth Press, Inc. All rights reserved.
doi:10.1300/5135_08

make this leap can be full of excitement and wonder, and if we can convey here a fraction of our own excitement at making this attempt, then we will feel that we have succeeded.

SFBT FOR WHICH CHILDREN?

In conversations about Solution-Focused Brief Therapy (SFBT), (for example, when running training courses), we are often asked about for which children the model is most helpful and if there are any types of childhood difficulties for which it is not suitable. The first thing we would say in response to this is that the literature is now abounding with accounts of SFBT's being applied to a wide range of childhood issues. To list only a selection, there are examples of the approach being used with children with behavioral problems (Berg & Steiner, 2003; Selekman, 1993; Stringer & Mall, 1999), with adolescents who are depressed and suicidal (Selekman, 2002; Sharry, 2004), with anorexia and other eating disorders (Berg & Steiner, 2003; Jacob, 2001), with children and young people who have been abused or neglected (Durrant & White, 1990; Lethem, 1994), in situations where children are bullied (Young, 2002), with ADHD (Berg & Steiner, 2003; Dielman & Franklin, 1998; Prosser, 1999; Sharry, 2004), with children on the autistic spectrum (Berg & Steiner, 2003; Prosser, 1998; Sharry, 2004) and with wetting and soiling problems (Berg & Steiner, 2003). Our second response would be to allude to what the research so far tells us, which is that there is no client group or type of problem for which SFBT is never effective (Gingerich & Eisengart, 2000; Macdonald, 2003).

In our basic response to the question of the potential client population for our solution-focused work with children, we, as is our habit, aspire to simplicity. The earlier list of applications of solution-focused practice with virtually the full range of childhood mental health disorders attests to the potential usefulness of the approach for any helping professional working with children and young people. However, providing such a list can be misleading and not in the spirit of a strengths-based approach such as SFBT. Strengths-based approaches move us away from a preoccupation with categorizations based on pathology. We take a simpler view of our potential client group. Working with adults, we view our potential clients as being that group of people who would like something to be different in their lives and who are prepared to talk to someone as one means of trying to achieve this. In other words, the characteristics of the client population can be summed up as simply as "people who want help."

It is slightly different in the case of children, who are rarely active seek-ers of help in the way that adults are, with this becoming increasingly so the younger the child. We have never had a preadolescent child come to us ask-ing if we could provide him or her with counselling. Requests for help with children and adolescents normally come from others such as parents or teachers. Given the power relations at play and the positions they are in rel-ative to these adults, children can usually be seen as involuntary clients (Berg & Steiner, 2003), at least at the beginning of a piece of work. In some cases, as the child's understanding of what is happening increases and as the worker's relationships with the child and adults significant to the child develop, the child may become more active in wanting the help we offer and hence move toward a more voluntary client status. So, in our work with children, we could characterise our client population as "children who somebody wants us to help and/or who want help themselves." The patho-logical labels and categorizations can simply fall away.

We were careful to say that we "*could* characterise our client population as. . . ." While this is the way we think about the children we see, we do not tend to see the child as our primary *client*. It makes more sense to us to see the person who has made the request for help as our client, and in our work setting, this usually means a parent or parents (Shennan, 2003a). If we were working as educational psychologists, it is likely that we would usually re-gard the teacher who referred a troublesome child as our client, *whether or not the person we more often saw directly was the child.* Working in settings where parents make contact and ask for help for their children, we try to resist the pressure sometimes placed upon us to see a child alone, at least initially. We are keen to avoid a situation whereby a child is sent to us to be "fixed." We do not wish to seem critical of parents who want to send their children to us and not be involved in the work themselves. We understand how they can come to the idea that this is the best way forward, because it is a viewpoint shared by therapists operating within the traditional and still hegemonic expert model, but also is due to the effects of the frustration caused by their children's behaviour. We have expressed this in the, "I can't see why they do it" equation (Hackett, 2003):

FRUSTRATION + HOPELESSNESS = PATHOLOGY

This can be translated as, "We've tried everything plus nothing works equals there is something wrong (biologically, mentally, physically) with the child."

So, to avoid feeding in to this, our standard practice in the first instance is to offer to see the parents, either alone or with whomever they wish to bring.

This could be including the child about whom they are concerned, the whole family, or anyone else whom the parent wishes to attend. So, in practice, our work with children and adolescents usually takes place as family work and it is rare for us to see younger children separately from their parents or caregivers. We are more likely to do individual work with older children and adolescents who can have a more informed involvement in their treatment and have greater ability to independently affect change for themselves. However, a large part of our work with this age group still takes place in a family context.

Engaging Children and Young People

Working with the family and having parents or other significant adults present together with the child has a particular usefulness at the beginning of the work. There are a range of views within the solution-focused world about whether engaging or joining with the client needs to be seen as a distinct and separate stage in itself. The idea that there does not need to be an opening, rapport-building stage is based on the belief that "rapport is there from the beginning; it is the therapist's job not to lose it" (de Shazer, 2002). Others have been concerned that SFBT has not paid enough attention to building the relationship (Lipchik, 2002) and that joining with the client(s) is an essential part of the therapy (Sharry, Madden, & Darmody, 2002). We believe that when working with children, who are likely to be anxious and possibly reluctant participants, it is important to spend time at the start in building rapport. We begin by trying to explain what is going to happen in as simple and straightforward a way as possible, and as part of this, we say that we usually ask quite a lot of questions. We do not assume that children and young people will want to answer our questions, and we attempt to respect their involuntary status by asking for their permission to ask questions of them as well as their parents. In our experience, it is extremely rare for a child to say "no" to this, but it can happen, as in the case of David, a 13-year-old brought along by his mother (Shennan, 2003b). In these cases, we try to help young people keep their options open by responding in as inclusive a way as possible (O'Hanlon & Beadle, 1996) along these lines: "That's okay. So, you can either sit here and just listen to what is being said, listen to what is being said and join in when you want, or listen to what is being said and ask to join in" (Hackett, 2001). This can remove the pressure on young people to speak and to help them do so when they are ready. We hope it also conveys a message to the parents that they do not need to cajole their children to talk. David did not say a word in the first two sessions and was complimented at the end of each one for sticking to his decision not to speak (yet), when he may well have felt under some pressure to do so. He started talking right at the beginning of the third session and joined in throughout and so was complimented at the end for knowing when would be the right time for him to speak and for acting on this.

The main way solution-focused practitioners begin to engage with an individual or family is by instigating what is often described as "problem-free talk" (George, Iveson, & Ratner, 1999; Sharry et al., 2002). We find this a rather neutral label and prefer to think of "competence talk" (O'Connell, 1998) or "strengths talk" (Shennan, 2003b). As with SFBT, more generally, we should not let the simplicity of this idea obscure the powerful effects it can generate.

Mandy, age 14, had been kicked out of her mother's house and gone to live with her father, his second wife, and their two young children. Shortly after this event, Mandy's father contacted Social Services, saying that Mandy might have to go into [foster] care. He reluctantly agreed to try some family sessions first, and came to the first one looking rather ill-tempered, with Mandy in tow looking sulky and apprehensive. It is unlikely that either of them expected that Mandy's father would initially be asked, "What is Mandy good at?" Taken unawares, he struggled a little or perhaps was reluctant to answer the question, but with some gentle persistence on the part of the worker, he mentioned Mandy's skill at sport at school, and then he said that she was good with her young half-brother and sister. The worker encouraged Mandy's father to be specific about this and he ended up talking about how she could look after the younger ones responsibly so that he and his wife were confident about leaving them in Mandy's care. This in turn led to a discussion about Mandy's caring nature. The worker also asked Mandy what she liked about her Dad and, despite a little difficulty she had in answering the question initially, she also talked about her Dad being caring, which the worker followed up by asking what he did that was caring and by noting that they seemed to have something in common. A thawing between them was apparent, the atmosphere becoming less strained and tense.

Beginning by exploring the problems that had led to the session would in all likelihood have had the opposite effect. In meetings of this type, young people will probably be expecting to receive a lot of negative attention and this expectation will decrease the likelihood that they will contribute. Beginning with strengths talk is aimed at relaxing the young person, encouraging positive interactions between the different family members in the room, and making explicit some of the strengths of the family members at a very early stage. It is more likely that a 14-year-old girl who is caring and a father who is caring will take part in a constructive conversation than a sulky daughter and angry father. Moreover, the positive impact of Mandy's hearing that she is caring is enhanced by the fact that it is her father she has heard say this. A further potential advantage of seeing Mandy with a parent also present is the modeling that the worker is doing by initiating a discussion about strengths.

Goal Negotiation

The negotiation of goals with children and young people needs a bit of careful thought. Here, we go back to our thinking about who our client is and, in the case of children, we usually see the adult or adults who requested some work to be done as our primary client. As well as being the ones whose request led to the work being done in the first place, it is the parents or other responsible adults who will usually decide when the work is finished. So we believe it is essential that we elicit their goals for our involvement in a clear fashion, how they will know that the work is done. In fact, the work cannot proceed until we know what it is that the primary client wants from it. Having said this, we do try to ascertain the individual hopes of everyone we are seeing for their involvement with us, including children and young people. While many of the children we see do articulate a goal, a significant number seem to find this difficult or, perhaps with the more involuntary ones, are unwilling to do so.

We try always to be alert to the possibility that the difficulty is arising from our inability to communicate in a way that can be understood. For example, in our experience, the "getting down to business" question that seems to best help our adult clients articulate what they want is, "What are your best hopes from seeing us?" But this does not seem to work for children below a certain age and so we might try a variety of other questions: "What are you hoping could be different for you by coming to talk to us?" or a closed question such as, "Do you want things to be better for you?" with a positive answer being followed by, "What would you like to be better?" or "What would make things better?" We might also investigate more specifically and concretely: "Is there something about school (home, the way you get on with . . .) that you would like to be different?" In the past, we would have felt that we had "failed" if we could not elicit a goal statement from everyone present in the first session and we would do all we could to help children to make one, perhaps ending with a leading question along the lines of:

WORKER: I guess you may not be all that happy with how things are at the moment?

CHILD: No (*or "dunno," or shrugs, or says nothing*).

WORKER: So, if coming here helped you to feel happier, would that be useful for you?

A particular leading question might be aimed at eliciting that classic goal of the involuntary client: "It seems like you don't really want to be here. I guess what you might be hoping for is that you don't have to come here anymore, that we all get off your backs?" Our practice is shifting as we become less concerned to push for goals in this way. If young people do not voice hopes of their own, we are likely to ask what they think about their parents' hopes for the work before moving on.

The ideal situation for therapy seems to be when all the individuals present have volunteered their clear hopes for the work to be done and we like this when it happens. However, as long as our primary clients have stated what they want from us, then it feels to us like the work can begin. Of course, in those cases where the child or young person has been the one actively seeking the help, which in our experience can be the case with some adolescents, it is essential that we establish with them what they want from us.

Creating Miracles with Children

However, when the overall goals for the work have been established, we want to encourage everyone to look forward and to be engaged with us in future-focused conversations (bearing in mind that we are working with children in other modes of communication, as we shall see shortly). The miracle question (de Shazer, 1988) is central to this part of our solution-focused practice with children as well as with adults. It opens up possibilities in the most entrenched situations. For younger children, it can require adapting or using in a slightly different way, but we find that it is comprehensible and works down to an age range of about 8 or 10 years. Miracles in SFBT are usually mundane in our experience; our clients' desired futures tend to be down-to-earth, everyday affairs. Children and adolescents are normally no different but are more likely to occasionally surprise us with flights of fantasy. The most useful response on our part is to enter their frame and show an interest in whatever answers the child gives. A question about miracles is, after all, inviting a fantasy response. At the same time, the worker can attempt to ground the miracle in the everyday by being curious about the hoped-for differences an initial fantasy-type response might bring. Some children we have worked with have begun their miracle with, "We'd have won the lottery." As with any answer, this could simply be sidestepped by the follow-up, "What else would be different?" But, if the theme persists, the worker can ask, "And if you did win lots of money, what difference would that make to you?" The idea is to elicit differences, particularly in behaviour, that are more within the client's control.

Sometimes the response to the miracle question can be a little more perplexing, but it is still best to stay with it. For example, something slightly unexpected was brought in by Rosa, age eight, but the worker's subsequent questions brought it back to the everyday.

WORKER: What would be the first thing you noticed when you open your door on the way out to school that would tell you that the miracle has happened?

ROSA: There'd be a big white horse on the doorstep.

WORKER: Really?! What would the big white horse notice about you that would tell it the miracle had happened?

ROSA: I'd be smiling.

WORKER: And what would happen next?

ROSA: I'd walk with the white horse to school.

WORKER: And, on the way to school, what would the white horse notice different about you?

ROSA: I wouldn't be running off.

WORKER: What would you be doing instead?

ROSA: Walking nicely.

WORKER: Who else would see you walking nicely?

ROSA: My Mum of course!

WORKER: Would your Mum be pleased?

ROSA: Yeah!

WORKER: How would you know your Mum was pleased?

Then there was the 13-year-old boy who said that the first thing he would notice after he woke up would be that he would have his head in a bowl of cornflakes! The worker was unsure how to follow this up, the consensus in the team later being that the question, "What brand, Kellogg's?" might have best fit the bill.

Breakfast cereals seem to crop up with some regularity in our sessions. The following example (Shennan, 2003b) illustrates the benefits of parents' hearing their children's miracles. In a first session with two girls and their parents, a tiny aspect of 10-year-old Sarah's miracle, unremarked upon at the time, was, "eating my Mum's cereal" for breakfast. A week later, the family members were describing significant improvements in how they were getting on and in Sarah's behaviour in particular. Her mother, reflecting on how the improvements had occurred, said that they had not realised how the muesli had been perceived as hers and the Rice Krispies as the children's, and she had since made a point of ensuring that Sarah could have any of the cereals. It seemed that, by her actions, Sarah's mother was demonstrating to Sarah how much she was listening to her.

With younger children who might not understand "miracle," we sometimes ask them to imagine that something magic has happened and things are just like they want them to be. Or we might simply ask about the best day they could have or, less dramatically, about if things became a little better for them. Bearing in mind that there will be someone else, usually a significant adult, who has an agenda for the work, we sometimes use the idea of including this agenda together with the child's in the miracle question or its variant (Iveson, 2003). For example, "Suppose, when you go to school tomorrow, you're going to have just the sort of day that you want to have, and you're going to behave in a way that your teacher will be pleased about. Tell me about this day. What sorts of things would you do?" Finally, it is important to bear in mind that younger children are less likely to be able to conceptualize the future so that discussions of good days they have experienced will be more meaningful than hypothetical good days to come.

Drawing

With younger children, we have also had success by asking them to draw what a good day would look like or has looked like and allowing the supplementary questions to flow from that. The power that a picture can have, even worked on over several sessions, is remarkable. Sometimes we help the child to write bits of narrative to accompany their pictures, like captions in a cartoon. Such techniques can be used at any stage in the work, and a nice example arose in a first session where there had been lots of presession change.

Ben, age 10, came along with his mother, and the worker duly began by asking what Ben was good at and what he liked to do. It emerged that Ben was an avid reader and that he enjoyed reading newspapers. When asked about her hopes, Ben's mother started talking about the improvements Ben had made in the past two weeks. The worker probed for specific details of these improvements and learned about the differences in Ben's behaviour at home and at school. The worker then put together a newspaper front page with Ben, the main headline reading, "Great Improvements in Ben's Behaviour!" next to a "photograph" Ben drew of himself. Details of the improvements were written as a news report, including quotes from Ben's mother and teacher (Ben's mother had recently spoken to the teacher and reported her positive comments in the session). Other, smaller headlines included, "Ben Plays Nicely with Sister," "Smith Family Go out Together," and, "Ben Gets Top Marks!" Ben designed the page, deciding where to place the various headlines and articles, and took several photocopies to give to his father, his teacher, and others. Each of the subsequent sessions (there were three in total) was built around the production of a newspaper front page devoted to reporting on Ben's progress.

Given the use made of art in some schools of therapy, we should clarify here that we do not interpret drawings or artwork, just as we do not interpret our clients' verbal communications. We use drawing simply as an alternative mode of communication, which children often find easier than talking. It is for the child, if anyone, to explain what a drawing means. We see the drawing and artwork done in our sessions as being the property of the children who have made it, and who therefore get to keep it or to give it to significant others of their choosing, as with Ben in the case study.

Scaling with Children

Our experience also suggests that children from around the ages of 8 to 10 years are comfortable with a scale from 0 to 10; indeed, children tend to be closer to the malleability of numbers than adults are. With most children, therefore, we simply begin with a numerical scale and use it to develop a dialogue about achievements and progress as we would with adults. However, we are also likely to introduce a lot more variety into scaling with children and young people and to use alternatives to numbers, especially with younger children. One reason for playing with the scale is that by the time we introduce it, 20, 30, or 40 minutes may have passed, and children may begin to fidget, grow restless, and even bored. A more active segment to the work can strike the right balance that will allow smooth progress toward the break.

We frequently use drawing techniques with scaling. Having the child draw the scale can be beneficial for several reasons. It helps to maintain the child's attention and interest, makes the scale more personal and potentially more real for the child, and allows the worker to gauge how much of the scale is understood. Putting scales on paper means that they can also be given to children as both a record and celebration of progress. If you are fortunate to work in an office with a large whiteboard, the scale can become a more expanded intervention of where children believe significant others would place themselves on the scale and a pictorial representation of what one point higher may mean. With younger children, we often use a succession of more or less sad and happy faces and, again, drawing the faces with them or having the children draw them gives this a greater resonance. Other pictorial scales have included climbing a mountain, climbing up a ladder, and stepping-stones across a river.

Involving the child in determining how to represent the scale helps to make it meaningful to them. A colleague of ours (Black, 2004) had been working with Amy, age eight, for several sessions, when he decided to review with her the progress she had made. They had established the very general goal of Amy's becoming happy. The worker asked Amy to remind him of her interests and her favourite activity turned out to be swimming. The worker then drew a "map" on the flipchart, where there were two countries, "Happyland" at the top and "Unhappyland" at the bottom, with the sea in between. Amy was asked to draw herself swimming in the sea toward Happyland, indicating how far she had swum. All the things that had helped Amy swim that far—making some friends, seeing her Dad, and so on— were written on the flipchart under where Amy was swimming. She was asked what would help her swim a bit closer to Happyland and her answer of "having more fun at home with [her] Mum" was written on the chart just ahead of her.

When using scales, it is always important to be clear what the scale means by defining its endpoints. It is particularly important to check that a child understands what is being scaled. Children can be good at defining the endpoints for themselves, often better than the worker, as the following two examples show.

Paul and His "Normal Self"

Paul was a very bright eight-year-old boy who had been referred by the school nurse because of his temper tantrums. Paul's parents came alone to the first session and the second session—Paul's first—focused on ways that Paul already had for dealing with "the anger," as Paul called it. The following is an extract from the latter part of the third session, the first part having looked at further progress made by Paul in managing the anger and at other improvements within the family.

WORKER (*to parents*): Is Paul good with numbers?

DAD: Yes.

PAUL: I can count up to 200!

WORKER: You should be able to do this then. This just goes up to ten, so you should be okay with this. So, just think, between zero and ten, where ten is things are at their best (*starts to demonstrate endpoints with hands*), things are really good, that you stop the anger coming all the time, okay? And zero is at the bottom, that's when things are really bad, and the anger is coming in all the time, okay? What number do you think things are at the moment?

PAUL: Er . . . about four or five.

WORKER: Four or five. Okay, are you pleased with that?

(*Paul nods.*)

WORKER: Has it been hard to get to four or five? Have you had to work hard, would you say?

(*Paul looks at Mum and Dad, unsure how to answer.*)

MUM: Has it been hard, keeping your temper?

DAD: You do struggle with it, don't you, but you do good.

The worker went on to ask the parents where they would settle for on their scales and about their confidence that the family would get there. While they were thinking about their confidence scales, Paul, who looked like he had been thinking hard, reentered the conversation.

PAUL: You know, if I get my anger down to 300, like, it's going downer and downer (*starts to demonstrate with hands*) and my normal self is going upper and upper, up to 300, I think that will be better for me.

WORKER: You've got a different scale than us, haven't you? You've got zero to 300. So, the higher the better?

PAUL: Well, the higher my normal self, the better, because I don't get angry on my normal self.

WORKER: I see. So, do you think you've been more your normal self?

PAUL: Well, I think I've been my normal self every day, sometimes.

WORKER: That sounds great, Paul. Next time we meet, we will have to hear more about when you are being your normal self!

The worker's 10 had been defined in a negative way, by the absence of anger, whereas Paul had turned this into a positive aim, becoming more like his normal self. Paul is helping the worker to become more solution-focused—there is no longer any need to refer to the anger. Discussion about Paul's normal self will suffice because he does not "get angry on (his) normal self."

Another example involved a seven-year-old boy, Jack, whose mother had allegedly held a knife to his throat before a neighbour called the police because of the noise and the mother was arrested. As part of his assessment, the social worker wanted to know how safe Jack felt if his mother were to return. Scaling safety (Turnell & Edwards, 1999) did not seem to work because Jack appeared to be confused by what safety meant. Taking a step back for a second, the worker took some time to find out what Jack's understanding of "safe" was. Jack picked the words "scared" and "happy" to define his continuum, and the worker drew a mountain and asked Jack to place his words where he thought they should go. He put scared at the bottom and happy at the top. The worker asked him, "Whereabouts are you on the mountain today?," and he was about halfway up. When he was asked, "How come you're about halfway up?," Jack said that he knew his "Mum was a good Mum," and that what would make him go higher would be if his Mum were to come in and say that she should not have done it. Whilst this was not the only component of the safety package, telling Jack's mother what her son had said, the compliment he had paid her in particular, helped to elicit a full narrative of events that she had not told the police. She also recognized that she required help, agreed that her mother would come and stay for a while, and said that the worker could visit any time he wanted. On seeing the boy a day later, the worker learned that he had gone some way further up the mountain.

Another good way to represent the scale is to use the space within which you are working as the boundaries of the scale. One corner of the office to another can quickly represent the scale and allow for a participatory and playful interaction. If you are working with a family, you can have parents place where they are on the scale and where they think their children are. Whilst confusion is quickly possible with larger groups, it can provide useful information and model how families can work together. One of the authors worked in an office that had stairs leading to it and the stairs became a scale for a six-year-old girl who had struggled with both verbal and pictorial scales. She clearly understood the difference between top and bottom, and when, after six sessions, she got to the top of the stairs-scale, her mother was there to give her a hug. For some children, numbered squares to stand on are useful. A nice variation is to cut footprints increasing in size out of paper and place them on a chart, walking and growing bigger toward a goal.

Show Me!

A wonderful technique with younger children, whether asking about the desired future or about progress toward it, is to ask them to show rather than tell you about constructive behaviour (constructive in this context tending to mean behaviour desired by significant adults in their lives) they can imagine themselves doing or have done already. Children love to respond to the injunction, "Show me!" Showing is a very useful activity because it is both a clear example of the ability to behave in a certain way and a rehearsal for future behaviour of this kind. It invites positive feedback in the form of compliments on the child's performance; there is immediacy to this feedback that is not quite there for compliments based on reported behaviour. If there are parents or responsible adults in the room with you, you can set them the task of looking out for examples of what they have seen to report back to you in the next session. We frequently have children who report that they would walk nicely to school, sit properly at the dinner table, or play a game with their siblings, showing us what this would look like by acting it out in the therapy room.

CASE EXAMPLE

Carl, age seven, and his Mum, Rebecca, had had a couple of sessions due to Rebecca's concerns about Carl's aggressive behaviour and bedwetting. They turned up for their third session accompanied by Carl's five-year-old sister, Kylie. Rebecca explained that she had brought Kylie because she had no one to look after her, but she went on to discuss her worries about the way Carl and Kylie were always falling out with each other. This was turned into a goal statement when Rebecca answered, "Yes," to the question, "So, you'd like them to be getting on better with each other?" Asked to give a specific example of Carl and Kylie getting on better, Rebecca answered, "If Carl wants something, not to lash out at Kylie and Kylie not to be so mardy. I would rather that if Kylie's got something and Carl wants it and she won't give it to him that he was able to ask for it politely." When asked if she had ever noticed Carl doing this, Rebecca said, "Yes, but very rarely." Very rarely was enough! The worker surmised that Carl could do this and invited him to "show me" how he could. Fortuitously, the worker was videotaping the session, and an elaborate play was devised, codirected by Carl, Kylie, and the worker in which Carl and Kylie could demonstrate and rehearse their ability in getting on with each other. The worker harnessed Carl and Kylie's wonderful imaginative abilities and they constructed a domestic scene where the children were watching television (the video camera!) together. Kylie had an apple from Mum and Carl wanted some, too. He asked Kylie for some politely and then, when she refused, he asked his Mum for one for himself. They did several "takes" and were able to get immediate feedback from watching playbacks on the video camera. The worker also encouraged their mother to tell Carl and Kylie what she liked about how they did. The whole session was based on showing rather than telling in a very playful way. The children were thus completely engaged in the process in a way that would have been hard to imagine if there had been only a conversation that was taking place.

"I Don't Know"

Adolescents tend to be expert at conserving their energy and often will not answer questions or to follow some rule of adolescent etiquette. A case in point is the answer, "I don't know." In our experience, this probably is the single most common response from teenagers in SFBT. This response can agitate both workers and clients. One of the most frequent questions we are asked in training, especially in follow-up sessions, is, "What do you do when the client says, 'I don't know'?" Parents also can become frustrated to hear their offspring proffer "dunno" after "dunno." We think of this answer differently; we see it as the adolescent client's unique way of cooperating (de Shazer, 1982). We do not assume that "I don't know" means literally that the young person does not know (although it might well be). It might mean, "I need more time to think about that," or, "That question does not make sense," or, "I cannot be bothered to answer that at the moment," or, "It is too difficult to answer that (at the moment)." We certainly do not wish to be put off, so we choose to not translate it as, "Stop asking me questions" and to treat it both seriously and playfully. For instance, a good tactic when faced with "don't knows" is simply to wait a while before speaking again. Around six seconds will usually suffice.

WORKER: So, what are your best hopes for this meeting?
CLIENT (*age 13*): I don't know.
WORKER (*counting in head: one and two and three and four and five . . .*)
CLIENT: Just for her (*points at her Mum*) to get off my back.
WORKER: Uh-huh. And what will your Mum be doing instead when she gets off your back?
CLIENT: She'll get out of my face.

Another way to handle the "don't knows" is to put the onus back on yourself as the worker. The 10 Daft Questions rule is one way to do this, and it also increases the amount of information you receive about the pitch of your questions. This rule is another, more surreptitious request for permission to engage with a young person; its acceptance gives the worker at least 10 questions. Following a sequence of the "don't knows," a worker can say, "Okay, sometimes my questions might not make much sense. If that happens just say 'daft question.' If we get to ten in a row, we'll take a break to let me think of some other ones." We have found it helpful for the ninth question (yes, we have gotten that far!) to be, "So, what would be a good question to ask you next?"

When there are other people in the room, it can be helpful to include them in countering the "don't knows," as in this exchange with Johnny, age nine, and his Dad:

WORKER: You know what I mean by confidence?

JOHNNY: Yeah, it's like when you know you can do something.

WORKER: Exactly. So, on a scale from zero to ten, how confident are you that things will get better?

JOHNNY: Don't know.

(Worker waits.)

JOHNNY: I don't know.

WORKER (*to Dad*): Whereabouts do you think Johnny would be?

DAD: About eight or nine.

WORKER: About eight or nine. (*Pauses for a couple of seconds, then, to Johnny*): Are you surprised that your Dad puts you at eight or nine?

JOHNNY: Yeah.

WORKER: Where would you put it?

JOHNNY: About six.

Finally, in dealing with a case of the "don't knows," we have found certain phrases helpful:

WORKER (*asks any question*)

CLIENT: I don't know.

WORKER: Have a guess.

Or: What do you think?

Or: Suppose you did know?

Or: Suppose there was a "you" sitting next to you who did know. What would she (or he) say?

We feel that it is most useful and most accurate to view the "don't knows" as being a function of the interaction between worker and client as opposed to reflecting some failing of the young person. The onus is as much on the worker to ask a useful and relevant question as it is on the young person to answer it.

Utilizing Media Literacy

An idea we have been developing particularly in our work with teenagers is to utilise their media literacy as a way of framing solution-focused questions (Hackett, 2002, 2003). By media literacy, we mean the knowledge young people have of television, films, and popular music. This taps into and utilises the knowledge they have of the argot of their peer and reference group. The competence teenagers can show in these exchanges can come as welcome surprises to besieged parents and allow them to reconsider how the actions of their teenage offspring are framed. Having teenagers talk about their futures in a hypothetical frame might be the beginning of a renegotiation of the rules and expectations that bound family life. Our essential aim is to evoke competence and possibility through the resources that the media have given us. These are a collective pool, if you will, of shared experiences that can be utilised to promote change. The first two examples were developed as alternatives to the miracle question.

Example 1: Who Wants to Be a Millionaire?

This example was used with a 13-year-old boy who had decided he would not answer the miracle question. Our involvement was based on the boy's behaviour becoming extremely difficult.

A 13-year-old boy had stolen his father's car, crashed it into a wall, and then threw the keys away, pretending he had not stolen it (he was spotted driving it by a teacher from his school). The worker had asked his father and elder sister about their miracles and turned to the boy and asked him if it was going to be okay to ask him the same question. The boy said it was not okay. After checking that he knew the format of *Who Wants to Be a Millionaire,* the worker asked, "If you were on *Who Wants to Be a Millionaire,* whose phone numbers would you give to help you with the question of how you would get through this difficult time?" The boy gave three names and he was then asked these follow-up questions:

> What is it about these people that would lead you to pick them?
> What do you think they would say to help you get through this difficult time?
> What effect would hearing them say that have on you?
> When you start doing that, what will you notice different about your Dad?

The worker continued this analogy by asking a scaling question that ran from £100-£1,000,000 and then wondered what would be happening when things moved up to £32,000. These types of questions have been used with children from the age of six upward and have proved to be a useful frame to stimulate dialogue in situations where a stand-off would otherwise have been likely. In one instance with a very intelligent 12-year-old girl, "millionaire questions" were able to prick the ennui that had been engulfing the interaction. It was the first time a smile crept over her face in six sessions.

Example 2: This is Your Life

A 14-year-old boy, Steve, who had been sleeping on his sister's couch since his mother had thrown him out for using drugs and stealing from her, said that the miracle question was "stupid" and "pointless." Present during this home visit were Steve, his mother, his sister, and her two children. The worker changed tack and asked whether he knew what *This is Your Life* was, which he did. *This is Your Life* was chosen because celebrities and those whose lives have been exemplary or interesting are taken through their life stories in the studio. The worker was hoping to elicit competence and confidence by inviting Steve to imagine that he could be on the programme in the future:

WORKER: Imagine that in twenty years' time, you are on *This is Your Life*. Who would you like to have on the programme with you?

STEVE: My Mum, sister, some friends, other people in the family.

WORKER: What would you hope they would say about you?

STEVE: Doing well, working as a security guard like my sister's boyfriend.

WORKER: Suppose we got round to talking about this difficult time, what would you hope they would say they did to help you get through?

STEVE: Talked to me, for my mum to spend more time with me.

WORKER: What would they say that you did to help yourself get through?

STEVE: Stuck at it, not got expelled from school, came in on time.

The most surprising thing from Mum's point of view was that her 14-year-old son wanted to spend time with her! The worker was able to compliment Steve on having the maturity to articulate this. A plan was agreed that Steve and his Mum would spend some time together at home watching videos and having a pizza. This would also give his sister some respite.

Example 3: Big Brother

There are many ways to use teenagers' familiarity and expertise in popular culture. *Big Brother* has provided a range of options: Suppose you were in the *Big Brother* house. What would you need to do to stay in? Who would you want to be in the *Big Brother* house with you? If you were in the *Big Brother* house and the viewers saw you at your best, what would they see you doing? Imagine that you are in the diary room and big brother has asked you to report on when you have been pleased with yourself this past week, what would you say?

Example 4: Trailers

Big Brother questions typically are used to encourage young people to describe their progress between sessions. Another addition we have made to the basic, "What's better?" opening in subsequent sessions is the "trailers" question (Hackett, 2002) that developed out of work with a 12-year-old girl and her family.

A 12-year-old girls' behaviour had become increasingly difficult to manage: she had destroyed her room, was refusing to go to school, and increasingly was hanging around with the "wrong crowd." Her father had a diagnosis of bipolar disorder, symptoms of which the parents believed the daughter was displaying (she had seen a psychiatrist who did not share the parents' diagnosis). During the first two sessions, we discovered that she loved watching videos and going to the cinema. At the third session, to elicit what had been better, the worker asked, "So, you know, at the cinema, yeah, before the main film, they have all those trailers on showing you the best bits of films so you might go and see them next time? If you were going to show me a trailer of your last week, what would we see on the tape?"

This allowed us to focus on the positives that had occurred in the last week in such a way that further detail was added by the supporting cast members of the family. At closure, five sessions later, confidence was high that "her growing up" (the parents' goal) would continue. We have used this intervention with many children since and its effect has always been to stimulate conversation.

These are just a few of the examples of our use of television and films. Whilst it can be very useful to draw on current programmes to engage children, the surprising breadth of their media literacy means that we are limited only by the extent of our own creativity.

CAUTIONARY NOTES

In this chapter, we have highlighted some of the ways we adapt and vary the techniques of the solution-focused approach when working with children. Being contrary types, we will end by saying that we usually try to do it with children just the same as with anyone else. We have been excited by our use of television and film metaphors and other child-centred frames and modes of communication. We like to think that they help us to fit our thinking to children, whose minds are less dulled by the daily grind. By this, we mean that their thought patterns are less bounded, their imaginative ability less bridled than us poor "a-dolts," to use a *Simpsons*-ism. However, while it can be of much therapeutic benefit to develop techniques from the particular abilities and expertise of children and adolescents, we do not feel that this should be at the expense of good, basic solution-focused practice. Although a large part of this chapter has described variations of the SFBT model, it is worth stating that our successes with children have overwhelmingly utilised that mundane, humane blueprint first developed in Milwaukee (de Shazer et al., 1986) and usually in its most minimalist forms (Ajmal, George, Iveson, & Ratner, 2003; George et al., 1999, 2001).

In keeping with the SFBT principle of parsimony and its debt to William of Ockham (de Shazer, 1985), we believe that over-elaboration should be avoided at all costs. If you are leaving a session excited about a wonderful media frame or scale you have used and cannot remember what the child has said, then it would have been better to leave the frame or scale out. We were working with a four-year-old boy who talked about beyblades (a kind of fighting spinning tops) and we built an increasingly elaborate and confusing scale based on that. The scale continued throughout the next couple of sessions until the child plucked up the courage to tell the worker that he actually liked the Hulk more. Whilst some media frames are more malleable than are others, we have found that our excitement for them can get in the way of good solution-focused practice as we aspire to practice it.

Children and adolescents are quick to spot phoniness, and workers need to be wary of this coming from two opposite directions. They will soon be caught out if they try to be like "one of the kids." Unfortunately for those of us experiencing midlife crisis, we can never know what it is to be a contemporary adolescent, however much we know about youth culture in a factual sense. On the other hand, we would caution workers against displays of disingenuousness. An honest dialogue around an aspect of a child's life you genuinely know little about is fine, but pretending you do not know anything about soccer, basketball, or grunge music when you actually do to encourage a young person to talk is likely to hamper the work. For example, when one of us (PH) worked playing sports with children with learning disabilities in our school, we were asked by the coordinator to not try so hard during basketball. During the game, one of the children asked why I was not playing well because he had seen me play for the school team. In our experience, as we said at the beginning, treating children seriously means beginning and ending where they are.

REFERENCES

Ajmal, Y., George, E., Iveson, C., & Ratner, H. (2003, September). *Beyond solutions*. Paper presented at the European Brief Therapy Association annual conference, Berlin, Germany.

Berg, I. K., & Steiner, T. (2003). *Children's solution work*. New York: Norton.

Black, R. (2004, May). *Engaging the imagination*. Workshop at Solutions with Children and Adolescents conference, Brief Therapy Practice, London, England.

de Shazer, S. (1982). *Patterns of brief family therapy*. New York: Guilford.

de Shazer, S. (1985). *Keys to solution in brief therapy*. New York: Norton.

de Shazer, S. (1988). *Clues: Investigating solutions in brief therapy*. New York: Norton.

de Shazer, S. (2002, May). Live demonstration workshop, Brief Therapy Practice, London, England.

de Shazer, S., Berg, I. K., Lipchik, E., Nunnally, E., Molnar, A., Gingerich, W., & Weiner-Davis, M. (1986). Brief therapy: Focused solution development. *Family Process, 25,* 207-222.

Dielman, M., & Franklin, C. (1998). Brief solution-focused therapy with parents and adolescents with ADHD. *Social Work in Education, 20,* 261-268.

Durrant, M., & White, C. (Eds.). (1990). *Ideas for therapy with sexual abuse*. Adelaide, Australia: Dulwiche Centre Publications.

George, E., Iveson, C., & Ratner, H. (1999). *Problem to solution* (2nd ed.). London: Brief Therapy Press.

George, E., Iveson, C., & Ratner, H. (2001, September). *Sharpening Ockham's Razor*. Workshop presented at the European Brief Therapy Association annual conference, Dublin, Ireland.

Gingerich, W., & Eisengart, S. (2000). Solution-focused brief therapy: A review of the outcome research. *Family Process, 39,* 477-498.

Hackett, P. (2001, September). *Surviving teenagers*. Workshop presented at the European Brief Therapy Association annual conference, Dublin, Ireland.

Hackett, P. (2002). Solution-focused work with young people: Thank goodness for the telly! *Context, 61,* 24-25.

Hackett, P. (2003). Utilising media competence. *Journal of Family Psychotherapy, 14,* 101-104.

Iveson, C. (2003). Solution-focused couples therapy. In B. O'Connell & S. Palmer (Eds.), *Handbook of solution-focused therapy* (pp. 61-73). London: Sage.

Jacob, F. (2001). *Solution focused recovery from eating distress*. London: Brief Therapy Press.

Lethem, J. (1994). *Moved to tears, moved to action: Solution-focused brief therapy with women and children*. London: Brief Therapy Press.

Lipchik, E. (2002). *Beyond technique in solution-focused therapy*. New York: Guilford.

Macdonald, A. (2003). Research in solution-focused brief therapy. In B. O'Connell & S. Palmer, Stephen (Eds.), *Handbook of solution-focused therapy* (pp. 12-24). London: Sage.

O'Connell, B. (1998). *Solution-focused therapy*. London: Sage.
O'Hanlon, B., & Beadle, S. (1996). *A field guide to possibility land*. London: Brief Therapy Press.
Prosser, J. (1998, September). *Solution-focused brief therapy and autism*. Workshop presented at the European Brief Therapy Association annual conference, Salamanca, Spain.
Prosser, J. (1999, September). *Solution-focused brief therapy and ADHD*. Workshop presented at the European Brief Therapy Association annual conference, Carlisle, England.
Selekman, M. (1993). *Pathways to change: Brief therapy solutions with difficult adolescents*. New York: Guilford.
Selekman, M. (2002). *Living on the razor's edge: Solution-oriented brief family therapy with self-harming adolescents*. New York: Norton.
Sharry, J. (2004). *Counselling children, adolescents and families*. London: Sage.
Sharry, J., Madden, B., & Darmody, M. (2002). *Becoming a solution detective: A strengths-based guide to brief therapy*. London: Brief Therapy Press.
Shennan, G. (2003a). The Early Response Project: A voluntary sector contribution to CAMHS. *Child and Adolescent Mental Health in Primary Care, 1*, 46-50.
Shennan, G. (2003b). Solution-focused practice with families. In B. O'Connell & S. Palmer, (Eds.), *Handbook of solution-focused therapy* (pp. 38-47). London: Sage.
Stringer, B., & Mall, M. (1999). *A solution focused approach to anger management with children*. Birmingham, UK: The Questions Publishing Company.
Turnell, A., & Edwards, S. (1999). *Signs of safety: A solution and safety orientated approach to child protection*. New York: Norton.
Young, S. (2002). *Solutions to bullying*. Tamworth: NASEN.

Chapter 9

Tips and Tricks for Working
with Children

SOLUTION-FOCUSED BRIEF THERAPY
IN A GERMAN CLASSROOM

Sabine Tolksdorf

I started learning this approach near the end of November 2004. I had neither heard of the solution-focused approach nor had ever heard of Insoo or Steve. But I participated in a seminar with Steve on a friend's advice and he told me that his wife had written a book on solutions for the classroom (Berg & Steiner, 2003). I was immediately interested and ordered the book from the United States.

I teach 18 first-graders with 10 girls and 8 boys in my classroom. I teach at a countryside school, and having only 18 children is a blessing. Normal class sizes here in Germany range up to 30 students. I'm 27 years of age and currently in my second teaching year.

Editors' note: This chapter is unlike others in this book. Rather than repeat theory and philosophy, the authors of this chapter were asked to contribute their experiences of working with children and adapting the Solution-Focused Brief Therapy model to work with young clients. The first section is contributed by Sabine Tolksdorf, a teacher in Germany. She first shared her creative work with young children in her classroom on the solution focused e-mail list and was subsequently invited to contribute to this chapter. The second section was contributed by Mark Mitchell of Los Angeles, California, and reflects some work he did with difficult children in a parochial school.

Handbook of Solution-Focused Brief Therapy: Clinical Applications
© 2007 by The Haworth Press, Inc. All rights reserved.
doi:10.1300/5135_09

Why did I think about starting this approach in my class? The key that caught my attention was that this approach "takes the focus off the problems." In my own life, I've tried to solve anything that looked like a problem, and I hate the deficit view of children's (dis)abilities, especially those of little ones. They will soon enough learn what they can't do, so it is *essential* for them to gain self-confidence and strength in the first years of school. They need to learn what they can do really well, what they're good at instead of what they can't do.

When first-graders enter school, they come with completely different expectations. Some are very keen and open; others are very quiet or even skeptical. The step into school is a big one when they come from kindergarten. Some children already know from elder brothers and sisters what school is like while some are really "entering unknown space." It seems to me that supporting them so that they gain self-confidence and discover their abilities and possibilities is most important.

Following the WOWW (working on what works) approach (Berg & Shilts, 2005), the first step is goal-setting. There are two goals in my work. On the one hand, there is a goal for me and my work, which is to support my children in learning about their abilities and strengths, and through this to help them gain self-confidence. The second goal is for the children to gain self-confidence, to find a positive approach to school, and to love to come to school. These goals are quite different from those in the original WOWW approach, which focuses on children with behavioral problems. I find the approach helpful in my classroom, however, even without "problems." What follows are some tools described by Ben Furman (2007) that seem suited for my kids as well, to which I have added some of my own.

Letters

I write encouraging letters to the children. In the letters, I write what the children can do really well in their general behavior. From my notes, I take facts such as, "X is behaving really well in school and helps other children out; please, do more of that" or "Y greets me every morning with a bright smile; I look forward to more of that" or "Z comes to school with a friendly smile; I really love that. Please do continue." Each letter is written especially for the child. These letters do *not* contain any comments on how the kids perform in the subjects.

Pride Round

At the end of each day, I introduce a pride round to the kids. I tell them that I am really proud of them and instead of me telling them all the time, I'd like them to choose something they have done well in school and are proud of and to tell the class. Comments include, "I'm proud I got a stamp" (which is my stamp for well-done homework. It reads, "Well done" in German.) Or, "I'm proud I've received a star" (for outstanding homework. Children collect 10 to get a sticker in a book I made for them. When they have three stickers, they get some chocolate as a reward).

Compliments

"If something works, do more of it." I started complimenting the children on work and actions they managed well. For example, a shy little girl who wasn't talking at all at the beginning of the year greeted me every morning with a warm smile. And she *repeated* this behavior.

Parent-Teacher Day

On a parent-teacher day, I receive parents with or without their children one by one. Before the meeting, I prepare a compliment sheet for each child on which I write down compliments for that child that comes to my mind. Further, I designed a parent sheet that is meant to collect information about the children.

Step 1. I start each meeting by asking the parent(s) questions such as:

- What is the child's day like when he or she comes home from school? (daily routine and TV habits)
- Who are the child's friends? (Does the child have friends in class?)
- What are the child's favorite hobbies?
- How much time does the child spend on homework?

Step 2. I compliment the child and the parent using the compliments chart and watch the parents' faces flash with pride.

Step 3. If there is a problem, I don't tell the parent that their child has one at this meeting. Rather, I ask them to actively participate in assisting the child to perform well in school. I ask the parent for his or her support and assistance and encourage them. I tell them that their child is getting acclimated in school. I try to assure the parents that they and their children are safe and in good hands.

Step 4. I inform the parents about the letters their children will get from me. I tell them that I want to focus my attention on what the children can do because they'll encounter problems early enough when it comes to subjects, and then I show them the letter. These letters are not "usual" in school and so I find it helpful to inform the parents before handing them out.

Second Parent-Teacher Day

On the second parent-teacher day, a new challenge appears. For the first time, I have to come to grips with the fact that the children are not all performing well in class and that I still want the parents to walk out feeling safe and unconcerned. This was a gap that seemed unbridgeable. I solved it this way:

Here in Germany, we have an official school report handed out to children and their parents at the end of the first, second, and third school year. No half-term reports are given. I decided to write unofficial little reports about how the children were performing in class and in social contexts with peers. Of course, those weren't always positive. No matter how solution-focused you might be, you'll still have to face the facts. How was I going to solve this?

Because I had been practicing "positive input" for a while with my students and found it rewarding, I thought about using it with the parents as well. Positive input means that instead of saying, "Don't run in the corridors," I'd rather say "Walk slowly in the corridors, please" (An idea borrowed from Ben Furman's "Kids' Skills") (Furman, 2007). And I was surprised how well this worked.

So what I did was that I let the parents come in, shook hands, and asked them, "So, what's your impression about school and _____ (child's name)?" I also like to call this the "first associational cue." They simply start telling anything that they associate with school and their child; they tell me that their child likes to go to school, how they get on with homework, what troubles there might have been.

I then respond to their view by presenting my own view. I also tell them where I see some problematic behavior, but immediately afterward, I tell them what ability their child needs to learn. So then, the parents often ask what they can do in order to help their child achieve this skill or ability.

Example 1: Boy, Age Seven

The mother came to me and responded to my first associational cue by telling me that her boy sometimes liked to go to school and sometimes didn't. I asked her to explain this, because I had seen no signs of the boy's unwillingness in school. She told me that she forced the boy every day to finish all the pages of reading that he hadn't finished in school, which, as she explained to him, had to be done in order to "practice." She also told me that the boy often was more than reluctant, resisting her attempts so that she had to put a lot of pressure on him. This was curious to me because I did not assign reading homework for the children.

I suspected that the boy did not understand why she was doing this because I didn't tell him to do any extra work. I suggested to the mother, in order to save energy from the fights and to make the boy come to school more happily, she could agree with him that they would "train" once a week, on the weekend, for 45 minutes, and also tell him why they were doing it. The insight that additional practice helps is known to children even that age, but it has to be encouraged, not forced upon them. I told her to also reward him for his good work.

Example 2: Twin Boy, Age Seven

The difficulty with twins in the class is that they'll often compete with each other and one will ultimately be the loser. The twins were a girl and a boy, and I had recognized not very long before that the boy's behavior showed many signs of insecurity and the need to gain more self-confidence. He was terribly afraid of making mistakes; every "mistake" brought him close to tears both in school and at home, as his parents confided. I discussed this with the parents, who wanted to help their child gain self-confidence.

At one point, the father asked me whether I had any tips for how they could make it easier for the boy, and I came up with this idea: They should take some time separately with each twin because the boy obviously subordinates himself to his sister's abilities. So the father took the boy with him to spend some father-son time, just for him to practice reading some words while shopping without his sister, who is always outrunning him because she reads faster.

In addition, I suggested that they ask the boy whether he had an idea about what could help him when he's feeling so close to tears. Should the boy have no ideas, I suggested to the father that he introduce the idea of a "power toy" that the boy could choose freely, without his sister's knowing. This would be a secret toy that would help him gain strength and security (Furman, 2007, keyword: power animal).

Compliments Chart

I tried to compliment each child every day. I even designed a special sheet where I make a check mark next to the child's name to see whether I was consistent. This is very difficult to do, but the chart helps me to remember to compliment each child some time during the week.

Children's Chart

I have a class folder in which I keep pictures from my children and self-designed scale charts. When I first designed them, I used a scale, scaling from 1 to 10. I chose "rules and behavior" as the topic: How well did the children behave in school and pay attention to our class rules? I wrote this topic on each child's sheet.

Some children needed a second scaling because they had some specific behavior I needed to pay attention to. Examples include a boy who moved constantly up and down, forward and backward, and could not sit still. In his second chart, I chose the topic, "psychomotor." Also, two boys were very insecure in their self-confidence and quickly started crying when they felt they couldn't solve a set task immediately. For them, I wrote down "self-assurance." I wanted to see when they felt safe and if the level of well-being increased over time. Finally, one girl did not talk very much and did so with her hands in front of her face. For her, I wrote down "talking and interaction." Every two days, I scaled the children. I have decided that scaling from 1 to 10 is too much and have adjusted the scale sheet to 1 to 5.

Five Minutes

I introduced this in the Monday morning circle. I told the children that the school day just did not give me enough time to talk to each of them, but that I strongly wished I could spend time with every single one of them. So, I would give each one five minutes of my time and they, in exchange, would give me another five of their time. In the five minutes I give them, they are free to choose whatever activity they like to do (play a game, have a book read, or simply talk).

In the five minutes the child gives me, I do the "strength and ability hands" (Berg & Steiner, 2003). I sketch the outline of their hand and they choose a finger (Figure 9.1). When they are ready, I ask them to think about something they can do really well, which can be in or outside of school. I then write it next to the chosen finger. The child colors the finger and writes his or her name on top of the sheet. This gets hung up next to the child's picture on my wall.

This activity takes up about 15 minutes each day. The other children draw pictures during that time. They know that during the five minutes, I do not want to be disturbed. ·

Medals

In year one, there is no midterm report, just year-end reports. This is a fairly long time for parents and children to wait for some feedback. So I decided to come up with some kind of "midterm-surprise": medals. Each child gets a medal (Figure 9.2), one with silvery glittering and a paper

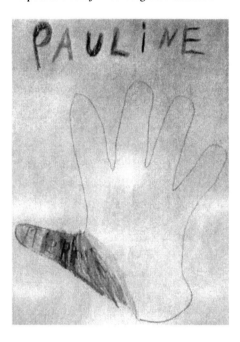

FIGURE 9.1. Pauline's strength and ability hand.

pictogram on it. I carefully thought about compliments I might pay each child and chose a special picture for each one. I wrote the name of the child and the compliment on the medal.

Compliments contain titles such as "little math king," "little reading princess," "little musician, artist, scientist" or behavioral compliments such as, "very helpful and supporting pupil." Believe me, I celebrate the medals!

The first time I did this, I told the children they would receive a surprise the day before. They were very eager and the next day, when I entered class, they all shouted, "surprise" at me. The last lesson of the day was the "surprise" lesson.

When the surprise time came, they were all really excited and looking forward to it. I had them put their hand into the medal bag without looking, and they could identify it as something "round" and "spiky." When we had finished with this, I asked them what they thought it could be, and you should have heard the answers! Their responses ranged from "hedgehog" to "cactus" and amused me very much—I was all smiles! Then I showed them the backside of one medal, and soon they had figured it out.

FIGURE 9.2. Children's medals.

I was sitting on my chair in front of class, took a medal out of the bag, and said the first letter of the child's name. The others guessed the child's name. And one by one, they came to the front, really nervous. I had explained to them that they were now in school for half a year already, and that they had deserved themselves a BIG reward for working SO well! So I hung the medals around their necks and read aloud to the others what the medal read. They were so happy, smiling brightly (but some were a bit shy) and jumping up and down back to their chairs. And we all applauded each and every child for the achievements.

The cutest thing was this: when I had given out all the medals, several children demanded where MY medal was, for working so hard with and for them. And I said, my reward is that they work so well with me. And then one of the kids said: "Well, then let's give Ms. Tolksdorf a BIG HAND!" . . . and they did, and that was so so so so SO rewarding!

The Scale

I built a beautiful wooden scale all my own. I painted a tile of wood dark green and attached five big yellow faces to it (Figure 9.3). This was a suggestion from Insoo Kim Berg: that I should visualize the scale for the children. The faces range from smiling to unhappy. I have a thread with an arrow attached to it, so it can be clipped to the face of the day.

I took the scale to class and the children unwrapped it after having received their medals.

At first, they were confused. "What's that?" But soon they found out that with this funny "wooden board" they would be able to see how they performed.

FIGURE 9.3. Scaling faces.

Topics are the same, like in the scale chart: "rules and behavior." The children repeated, together with me, the rules we had made out already. Then they made suggestions as to what the faces represented. And they were completely right. To the very unhappy face one child said,

"This face we get when we don't behave well at all." I added, "Exactly. This is when you fight all day, when you talk during lessons all day, when you interrupt other children each and every day," and they laughed. Children need to see that school can be fun, and teachers can be fun as well.

After that, I asked them where they would find themselves on the scale. I assisted them only in finding the right face and they put themselves from 3 to 5. The first child said, "The face on top." And I asked the others what they thought, and one girl answered, "I don't think we have deserved a five. I think a four is more like it." I requested a reason from her and she said, "Well, when you went outside for a minute, we were too loud." This, as Insoo said, was the best part.

REFERENCES

Furman, B. (2007). *Kids' skills in a nutshell.* Retrieved February 4, 2007, from http://www.kidsskills.org/english/index.htm.
Berg, I. K., & Shilts, L. (2005). *Classroom solutions: WOWW approach.* Milwaukee, WI: BFTC Press.
Berg, I. K., & Steiner, T. (2003). *Children's solution work.* New York: Norton.

SOLUTION-FOCUSED BRIEF THERAPY WITH CHILDREN

Mark Mitchell

The hallmark of the solution-focused (SF) approach frequently includes techniques of scaling, miracle question, coping question, and exceptions. However, these "maps" are used primarily with adults and some need to be adapted to the "territory" of children. In the spirit of SF, the use of curiosity, respect, and creativity are central to working with children. It is that spirit that is necessary to therapeutic work with children. It is important that most children be viewed as visitors and should receive compliments. The adults are more likely to be the customers for change and more likely to do tasks, although children will do tasks to please. They like to please adults and answer a question in order to get a positive adult response. The counselor needs to be aware that the child is answering frequently in order to please and frequently looks for the right answer to please.

For the past several years, I have been a supervisor and trainer at an inner city Catholic school in south central Los Angeles (St. Raphael's) near the center of the 1991 riots. I asked to help establish a counseling/coaching program for children and families at the school. The challenges of the school were quite evident from the first parent meeting when several parents approached me claiming that their children need to be "whipped" more in order to behave. The climate of negativity and punishment is pervasive. We helped change that culture and the children through a variety of solution-based interventions.

"The Principal Wants to See You" Technique

Kids are often afraid to be called into the principal's office. The education team, the principal, counselor, or other adults would call the children in for five minutes and tell them what they were doing right and then send them back into the class. They usually expect to be in trouble and are always surprised and encouraged.

The Singing Question

This technique came as result of my work at a high school during the 1991 Los Angeles riots when the students were rioting and the National Guard was at the school site. It is an extension of the miracle question. "Supposed a miracle did happen and you were to start singing a song. What song would you be singing that would tell you a miracle had or was happening?" or, "What song would make you feel good that things were getting better with the teacher?" This technique works well with all school ages. Historically, singing has always helped people cope in difficult times, especially in the African American community. Many children come up with songs like "the Barney song," "zippidy do daa," "itsy bitsy spider," and, of course, they often make up their own. Singing creates the "feeling" of a miracle and helps create thoughts that are different for the child. Asking, "What new thoughts did you have during or after the song that are helpful?" is also a helpful question. "When you feel bad, can you keep singing to feel good?"

Promises

In this technique, the counselor asks the child to promise to try the new behavior in a very short time frame. Children take promises very seriously. They know to promise something means they will do it. "Can you promise to do your work in class for the next hour?" The task has to be realistic for the child to take the promise seriously. Small amounts of time are better than large. Remember, for a child, time drags and seems endless.

Are You Strong Enough?

Children like the idea of being strong, especially boys. This polite invitation to strength and behaving can help a lot. Follow up with, "What will you tell yourself to be strong in doing your homework?" "What have you told yourself in the past to be strong enough to do your homework?" "That's amazing!"

Certificates of Achievement

This simple technique of making certificates of achievement, given to for children for behaving one or two hours, can be very powerful. They love to get certificates. We found for children with strong behavior problems that catching them doing something right for very short periods was more helpful than trying to give them feedback after a week's performance.

Relationship Question

This technique of getting kids to think of others who they perceive as more powerful or higher status can be very helpful. Some of the examples we have used are the following: "What would Jesus say to you to help you be strong?" "What would your mother say to you to help do your homework? Can you hear her voice now?" "What would Kobe Bryant (an NBA basketball player) say?" "What would Britney Spears (a pop singer) say to help you feel the miracle?" The relationship objects need to be meaningful to the child's world, so the counselor needs to ask for the representatives of the world that the child admires.

Finally, these interventions are helpful for change with children, but interventions with adults are frequently more important because they are the ones in positions of power and influence. The counselor needs to be very careful, politically, in working with these individuals to help the children's miracles continue.

Chapter 10

Solution-Focused Brief Therapy in Faith-Based Communities

Daniel Gallagher

Where you stand determines what you see and what you do not see; it determines also the angle you see it from; a change in where you stand changes everything.

Steve de Shazer (1991)

INTRODUCTION

Suppose you have finished reading this chapter. What needs to happen here—in my writing and your reading, together—so that you know that reading this chapter has been worth it to you? What will your best friend notice you doing after you finish reading this chapter that will tell him or her it was useful?

This chapter is about how to hold solution-focused conversations in various contexts of what might be called pastoral care and counseling. It is about how we as pastors[1] can work collaboratively with those who come to us to talk about their concerns and problems important to them and important to people in their lives. It is about building solutions instead of solving

---

I want to thank Steve de Shazer and Insoo Kim Berg for their bringing Solution-Focused Brief Therapy to life for me and countless others. I also thank my colleagues Janet Campbell and Margaret Kornfeld for reviewing versions of this chapter and for making many useful suggestions.

Handbook of Solution-Focused Brief Therapy: Clinical Applications
doi:10.1300/5135_10

problems. Solution-focused pastors are most interested in helping people describe a clear picture of what they will be doing when things are better, and helping them identify, from the context of their own lives, existing and available resources such as skills, experiences, relationships, behaviors, and perceptions that will help them construct their solutions.

This usually involves describing what one does, has done, and will be doing when the problem is gone from life, or is happening less or a little bit. For example, when a person feeling the loss of a loved one describes occasions when she does not feel the pain of the loss, feels it less acutely, or feels it less frequently, we ask for more details about that occasion and others when the problem is absent from her life. Such exceptions then become part of what the person wants to be doing as a result of our talk and as part of her solution. Describing exceptions tends to bring hope; progress in solution-building can be seen as having already started before the person even speaks with the pastor (de Shazer & Isebaert, 2003).

The most useful question I have found (so far) to help people develop a clear picture of what they want to be different as a result of our meeting(s) with them is the "miracle question." I use this question in virtually every meeting with someone seeking help. I usually ask it in a way similar to this (de Shazer 1985, 2005):

> Suppose, after you leave here today and you go on with your day as usual—eat, maybe watch TV, and then go to bed, and go to sleep. And, while you are sleeping, a miracle happens. And the problems and concerns that brought you here to talk with me are gone. Just like that! But this happened while you were sleeping, so you don't know it happened. When you wake up in the morning, how will you discover that this miracle has happened? What else? What will others notice you doing that will tell them that something different is happening? What else? How is this happening, even a little, already?

I then use what are called "scaling questions" to help people assess their progress as a good-enough first step toward their life as they described it in their answer to the miracle question, with "10" standing for the way things will be the morning after the miracle and "0" being the way things were when they decided to talk with me. Scaling questions further establish the idea that people are already "somewhere along the way" to a good enough solution. These questions are individualized, based on the person's answers. Say, for example, the person says things are at "4" on the scale in terms of the problem that brought him to see me and on the way to further progress. Consistent with the miracle question and based on his answer,

I ask what he and others close to him will be doing when he is at "5." The person's answers tend to provide clues that can be built into detailed interactional descriptions with the skillful use of solution-building questions. What is more, the person's answers suggest what scaling question to ask next.

FINDING OUT WHAT THE PERSON WANTS

We ask for as clear a picture as possible of what the person's life will be like when the problem that brought him to see us is gone. As the person describes such a picture, the pastor can hear what the person wants to be doing differently, which usually changes over time. The pastoral care worker can listen for what the person is already doing that is useful so that, when they do more of it, things are more like the way they see their lives with the problem gone.

We have several useful tools for directing the conversation toward building such a picture. They are questions we can ask that help the pastor construct more potentially useful follow-up questions based on the person's answers.

The first of these is what de Shazer called the "best friend" question. The best friend question involves asking the person what others will see the person doing after our conversation today that will tell the person that this meeting was worthwhile. "Others" include anyone who is important to the person in her life, especially those who are stakeholders in seeing useful change.

The following case examples are taken from work that would probably be considered within the range of what pastoral care providers could do. However, in each case, with a different approach, these situations could require the assistance of a professionally accredited pastoral counselor after one or two meetings with the pastor.

GRIEF: THE LIFE OF THE PARTY

A couple requested a consultation with their pastor. The pastor, who had known them for several years, had helped them through some troubled times after their 18-year-old son had been killed in an automobile crash five years before.

Instead of making her own assumptions about what they wanted from meeting with her, however, the pastor decided to listen for what they wanted. The pastor had learned that it is crucial to find out what the people want instead of assuming that she knows what they want or need. All too often, what people want and need and what the pastor thinks they want and need may be two different things. For example, the pastor may have assumed that they "had unresolved grief," that they had "not completed the grieving process," and that there was "no closure"—all things that were not happening, without even asking them what they envisioned themselves doing instead.

What Others Will Notice

PASTOR: Before we begin, I'm curious about something. After we have talked here today, what will others who know you well, such as your best friend, see you doing that tells them that this discussion was useful for you?

CHARLES: Well, let me tell you something about what has been happening. As you know, our son was killed five years ago, and we thought we had been handling it pretty well until just recently. It seems to us that every year when his birthday comes around, it just gets harder and harder to get past it. Polly cries all the time now and we just get this cloud of gloom over our heads. Then there's Christmas.

PASTOR: You managed to handle it pretty well until just recently? How did you do that?

POLLY: We have a close family, as you know, and we have usually been with them on special occasions that remind us of our son. But this year we weren't able to be with them and I felt very depressed—and it has been with me ever since.

PASTOR: So, what will you be doing when things are better again that you aren't doing now? What will your family see you doing?

The best friend question led to some speculation on their part about what might be helpful based on what has been helpful in the past. You may be thinking that the pastor was ignoring some very important issues such as exploring Polly's feelings of depression and unresolved grief, but she had learned from training and experience to go slowly, first gathering facts about what the couple wants to be different as a result of their talk with her. A conversation has been opened about what they want, but the pastor and they still do not have a clear picture of what they will be doing, what others will see them doing, and what difference that will make—for the two of them, and between them, and their friends, family members, colleagues, and acquaintances. But without a clear picture from them of how things will be in their lives when things are better, they may not have a clear reference point for noticing and continuing progress. Yet, they do have experience making things better on which they can build their solutions. They have been doing well, more or less, for the five years since their son's death. So the pastor decides to encourage them to construct a detailed picture of what they will be doing when the problem they came to talk with her about is gone. She uses this question in every first meeting with people consulting with her, regardless of the problem.

The Miracle Question

PASTOR: I have a strange question for you that's going to take some imagination. . . . Suppose . . . you go home after we finish talking, and go about the rest of the day, and later on, you go to bed and sleep . . . and while you are sleeping, a miracle happens. . . . But you don't know it because you are asleep . . . and the problem that brought you here is solved . . . just like that. . . . So when you wake up tomorrow morning, how will you notice that this miracle has happened to you?

The pastor waited for them to answer the question. Silence is important here (as are the pauses in the Miracle Question).

POLLY: We will take our time getting out of bed. We usually get up with the alarm and hurry on about our business. We will take our time, make ourselves a nice breakfast, and talk about what we want to do together. Tomorrow is Saturday so there is no rush to get on with things.

CHARLES: Yes, and she'll be smiling, feeling better, not dragging herself through the day like she usually does.

PASTOR TO POLLY: What will he be doing that tells you that he notices that a miracle has happened?

POLLY (*laughing*): Oh, that's easy. He'll tell me how beautiful and radiant I look! (*All laugh*) He'll give me flowers. We'll go out for dinner and a movie. He hasn't done that for a long time.

PASTOR TO CHARLES: And what will she be doing that tells you that she notices?

CHARLES: I have tried doing that from time to time and she just says she isn't interested. Doesn't have the energy. Tomorrow morning? After the miracle? She'll give me a big hug and start planning where she'd like to go.

PASTOR: And what difference will that make to you?

CHARLES: It would make my day.

PASTOR: Tell me more about that.

As you can probably see, the best friend question is similar to the Miracle Question. In fact, it is part of it. So are the questions that follow, all based on the person's answer to the previous question (Iveson, Ratner, & George, 2001).

The couple mentioned earlier that their family was very important to them. Family members may be crucial for reinforcing feeling better. Since this is important to the couple, it may be useful to find out what other family members will be able to see them doing that tells them things are better.

When the pastor asked, Polly and Charles thought it might be difficult for them to tell since they have not seen other family members much lately. They spoke about inviting Polly's sister and her husband to go out to dinner with them the next day. They also talked about how much fun they used to have together and how members of Polly's family were always ready for a party. Responding to the pastor's questions, Charles and Polly described what her family saw her doing when she was having fun, like laughing and joking around.

CHARLES: She's the life of the party when she's in the mood. She gets everybody laughing. Do you remember the Christmas pageant last year when she was supposed to be Mary? (*Polly laughs*) She was perfectly dressed for the role except for those pink sneakers?

When Were Things Somewhat Like This Miracle?

PASTOR: When's the last time that happened, even a little?
CHARLES: We did stop at a yard sale last Tuesday. You seemed to enjoy that a lot.
POLLY: I did. But lately something always happens that reminds me of Jimmy and brings me down.

Life after the miracle has already started to happen. The pastor, basing her next question on Polly's answer, is more curious about a detailed description of how Polly manages to get over feeing down than details of what triggered the feelings.

PASTOR: Tell me more about that. How do you begin to pull yourself up when that happens?
POLLY: I don't. It usually starts getting better after an hour or two if I can get my mind off it.
PASTOR: You can get your mind off it?

POLLY: Oh, if I get a call from my girlfriend, something like that.

PASTOR: Okay. Talking to her helps?

POLLY: Yes, we usually end up laughing about something. It doesn't take long. We've been like that since we were in school together.

Clearly, the problem Polly and Charles came to talk with the pastor about does not happen all the time. After the miracle question, they were remembering more times when the problem that brought them to see the pastor was solved or gone. Even if it seems like the problem was only gone for a little while, what they were doing instead increases in prominence and importance in the conversation due to the pastor's questions and their detailed descriptions of what they have already done that works. The chances are better that they will remember more and more things they are already doing that are useful in some way. To find out, the pastor must keep asking about those things throughout the conversation. For example, she could ask, "What else?" after they have described something they did that was useful for them, or ask what others have noticed them doing when things were better or during better times. These kinds of questions help them build more confidence that they can get back to and do more things like her smiling, their going out and doing things together, and friends' enjoying her or them like they used to. To even have an idea of this, it was crucial for the pastor to ask the kinds of questions that would direct the conversation toward what the couple wanted to be doing when the problem that brought them to see her was solved, and have them begin assessing where things were in that regard in relation to where they wanted them to be.

Solution-Focused Scaling Questions

So far, Polly's and Charles' brief descriptions of what was troubling them that led them to consult with the pastor have changed to descriptions of what they will be doing when things are better and how they are doing some of that already. It may be that by imagining what they will be doing when things are better, they can better remember what they already have accomplished, which gives them something to describe from their experience upon which to build. Accepting the couple's problem at face value, the pastor has invited them into a conversation about getting better instead of expanding on what is wrong, of possibilities instead of more of the painful story.

Scaling questions can be useful as ways for measuring "better." There are, however, no objective measures of what is better in solution-focused pastoral work. There are no right or wrong answers, only answers that are more useful than others. The scales that the person and solution-focused pastors construct are not linear measures of progress toward a goal. What we are asking about is not in the future. Instead, we are asking about what has already started happening that, when a person continues building on it, he (or she) will be closer to what he imagines things will be like when the problem that brought him to see the pastor is gone. Somewhere along the way, things usually are better enough that there is no need to talk about them with the pastor.

PASTOR: So, suppose we have a scale from zero to ten, where zero is the way things were when you decided to talk to me and ten is the way things will be the day after the miracle—where do you put things on the scale today?

POLLY: You mean right now?

PASTOR: Yes.

POLLY: Oh, I'd say four or five, right Charles?

CHARLES: At least four or five.

PASTOR (*To Polly*): Four or five? How come four or five and not zero?

It is more important that they are somewhere on the scale than the exact position between 0 and 10. There is a wealth of information about what is working in the gray area between 0 and 4.

POLLY: When we decided to speak with you, things were looking pretty bleak. But now I can see that there is good stuff going on, too. Like, I still have my friends and Charles to lean on. I am pulling myself up. I'm good at that.

CHARLES: She is! It was quite a blow when our son died and we have been through a lot since then, but in a sense, I wouldn't have it any other way. We loved him. We miss him. We will never forget him.

Charles put progress at 6 or 7 on the scale. The pastor was curious about why he was so optimistic. This question, a response to Charles' last answer, prompted Charles to say that Polly's crying makes sense to him. Although he gets worried about her crying sometimes, like recently, "she always pulls out of it. I deal with it more to myself, but that doesn't mean I don't miss him as much."

PASTOR: Wow, that's amazing! You two must love him a lot.

Polly and Charles described various things about their son they loved and miss. Both shed tears, but now they seemed to accept them as a normal part of remembering him.

PASTOR: (*To Polly*): So when things are at five on the scale, what will Charles and your girlfriend see you doing?

POLLY: As I said before, I'll be doing more with my girlfriend and stop at yard sales, stuff like that.

PASTOR: So, at five, what will people see you doing first?

POLLY: I think I'll invite my sister to come with us tomorrow.

PASTOR: And Charles, when things are seven or eight for you on that scale, what will be the first thing Polly will see you doing?

CHARLES: Maybe I'll be planning that fishing trip I've been putting off. My buddies have been going without me. I've been so worried about Polly. But now I think we can get on with our lives. At least we have made a pretty good first step.

The pastor continued by asking about how confident they were that they would get on with their lives, where 10 was "all the confidence in the world that the progress you have made will continue" and 0 was the opposite. "Where are you on that scale now?"

Polly said, "Eight," based on her confidence that Charles, friends, family, and God are there for her. Charles said, "Ten," indicating that they are closer to each other because of the experience of missing their son. He said they have been enriched by it and can sense God's presence with them as a result.

The pastor made it a practice to take a short break to think alone before sharing her thoughts with the people she met with pastorally. As usual, she thought of the many things the couple had told her about themselves that she thought were especially impressive. She also thought about what she might suggest they do after the meeting to continue their focus on how they keep and share the memories of their son while getting on with their lives. Then she returned to them and told them this:

PASTOR: Polly and Charles, I have had the privilege of knowing the two of you for several years and I have always been impressed with how you manage to keep your feelings for your son alive, even when they are at their most painful. Clearly, you both love him very much. And your own relationship means so much to you that you want to keep it on track even when one or the other of you is missing him especially acutely. What's more, you are very aware that you have friends and family that you want to include in your lives. What you may not know as well is how much all those people look up to and admire you as examples of how to keep loving someone who is not with you otherwise. I know people here in the church sure do. And that includes the down times, too. So I have a suggestion for you. Each of you pick a day in the next two weeks and pretend that the miracle has happened. It doesn't have to be the same day. And don't tell the other which day you chose. Polly, you try and catch Charles pretending his miracle day, and Charles, you do likewise with Polly. Then, two weeks from now, make a date to go out for dinner somewhere fancy. While you are eating dessert, compare notes about this and see if your guesses were right.

Polly and Charles did not make another appointment to talk with the pastor about this, so the pastor did not pursue the issue with them either. It was clear that they could call for a meeting if they thought it necessary. One of the advantages to working in communities like churches, synagogues, and mosques is that pastoral workers get to stay involved with many of the people they meet in the day-by-day activities of their community.

SPIRITUAL ISSUES

Naturally, in the flow of everyday activities, pastors and pastoral care workers are frequently asked about spiritual issues. These serious concerns people bring to pastors are matters that may be addressed from a variety of perspectives depending on the customs of the religious stance of the faith community. One of the most enlightening examples of how solution-focused brief approaches can be helpful whenever a person comes with a problem happened in a graduate course I was teaching for international students in pastoral counseling. One of the students was a Muslim imam from Saharan Nigeria. In an interview with him about what he was learning that might be useful for the people in his faith community back home, he told me excitedly, "It works! We believe in miracles! Miracles are in the Koran!" He went on to tell me more about how solution-focused questions fit the work he was doing with persons in his faith community.

So, when someone tells me that the morning after the miracle, she or he will know the meaning of life, find God, or believe in life after death, I can say, "Okay. So, suppose that happens. You wake up tomorrow morning and know the meaning of life, and so on. What will your best friend (colleagues, family members, Bible study group, and so on) see you *doing* that tells her or him that you have found the meaning of life (or God, or belief in life after death)? Tell me more about that. What else? How is that happening already, even a little? When others see you doing that, what do they say is different about you? What do you see different about them? On a scale from zero to ten, where zero is you have no idea of the meaning of life and ten is your concerns about that are gone, where are you now? Three! How come three and not zero? When you are at four, what will your best friend see you doing?" And so on. Instead of exploring such issues according to certain prescribed formulae, the solution-focused pastoral counselor can "cut to the chase," as one trainee described it, and "get to the results." Look for the difference it will make when the person's concerns about that issue (e.g., finding the meaning of life) are gone. People frequently tell me during such conversations that very little will change because they are already doing the best they can. This is a marvelous opportunity for the pastoral worker to ask for detailed descriptions of the things the person is already doing and what she will be doing when those things are happening a little more (use scaling questions liberally).

GOD'S JOB

Pastors tell me that they frequently hear people answering the miracle question by saying that the only way they can solve their problem is to trust that God will fix it. Even if human fixers (therapist, clergy person, or programs) cannot fix it, God can. If only they have the right faith and follow the rules, God will take care of them. If there is little or no improvement, they end up blaming themselves or blaming the pastor for misleading them. Following the quote from de Shazer at the beginning of this chapter, I would not stand in that position. I would change where I am standing. For example, I might leap right over that answer by saying, "Okay. Suppose a miracle does happen and God solves the problem for you tonight while you are asleep. What will *you* be doing tomorrow morning after you wake up that tells the first person who sees you that your life is different? What will others see you doing? What will you see them doing?"

A closely related example is common: a person's miracle answer is that the person will have an amputated leg back or that a loved one who died will be alive again. You could tell them that their thinking is unrealistic, probably making them feel even worse. Or, instead, you could accept their desires and say, "Well, suppose (have your leg back/your son is alive), what would you be doing that you are not doing now? What part of that can you do anyway? What would your best friend see you doing that would tell her that there is something really different about you? What would be different with her?"

So far in this chapter, I have been making an effort to provide enough narrative to give you an idea of how a solution-building conversation can be developed between pastor and people consulting the pastor. Since these are whole conversations, it is very difficult to summarize them and still give a sense of how the solution-focused approach works (de Shazer, 1991). In the next example, note how a solution-focused conversation is established and develops.

TO DIVORCE OR NOT TO DIVORCE: IS THAT THE QUESTION?

Alice and John, both in their thirties, had been married for 10 years and had three children ages nine, seven, and five. Alice said she had insisted on staying home with the children during the early years while John worked. He was a successful building contractor. About 18 months before coming to see the rabbi, Alice had decided that she wanted to get out of the house more and found a part-time job with a florist. She loved the work and began finding out that she was a valuable part of the business. As that happened, the couple told the pastor, they found themselves disagreeing more and more. Alice said that John had lost interest in her and she did not want to be married to him anymore. According to her, she had not left because previously, she was not making enough money to support herself and the children without John's help, and John would not agree to help her out financially if she left. John complained that Alice had broken her agreement to be home and he wanted her to come home. He said he still loved her and did not want her or the children to leave. They said they each had strongly religious childhoods and had drifted away from their congregation. When Alice asked John for a divorce, John found the rabbi's name in the yellow pages of the phone book and called for an appointment.

The couple arrived together. After they chatted with the rabbi about their jobs and explained what they had come to see him for, the rabbi asked them the miracle question. After a long pause, John answered first.

JOHN: She will look me in the eye and reach out to me. She'll come to bed when I go to bed.

RABBI: And when she looks you in the eye and comes to bed with you, what will you be doing?

JOHN: Well, we'd make love like we used to. We haven't made love in a long time. She waits until I'm asleep and then comes to bed.

ALICE: Well, he'll reach out to me first. He'll pay more attention to me. He'd say, "You look happy" instead of criticizing my clothes. And I'll be smiling. I'll have a sparkle in my eyes. I'd know he's genuinely interested in me. He'd change the cat litter without my asking. We'd do something fun. He'd suggest something to do with the family instead of my always nagging him to join us. We'd set up a schedule for our activities a month ahead.

The rabbi, building his next question on their last answer, decided to ask for a more detailed description of how their lives would be different (better) when even a small piece of the miracle happened. Both said they could hardly remember because it had been so long.

RABBI: How are parts of the miracle already happening, even in small ways?

JOHN: They haven't been happening in a long time.

RABBI: So, what makes you think it can happen?

JOHN: Wishful thinking, I guess.

RABBI: Well, suppose it does. What will the kids see different about you that, without your telling them, they would be able to say their parents are getting along better?

JOHN: Alice and the kids will still be at home.

RABBI: How come the two of you are still together now?

JOHN: What do you mean? The kids need us both. I am a believer that parents stay together for the kids. I don't want to pay for Alice and my kids to live with someone else. And we have had some good times together. We were very much in love. I think we can do that again.

ALICE: I've asked John why he would want to live with me when I don't love him anymore. He thinks that all he has to do is expect it to work and it will work.

JOHN: Like I said, I love her; she's my wife and the mother of my children.

RABBI: John, suppose that ten means that you are willing to do anything it takes to reach out to Alice and zero stands for the opposite: you are just sitting there waiting for Alice to decide to stay. Where are you today?

JOHN: I'm around a five. I want our marriage to work. I asked her out for a date last winter. We had a terrible time. I need to know that she will at least try.

RABBI: And what will Alice see you doing when things are at a six that tells her things are a little better with you?

JOHN: Well, I'd ask her about her day when I come home instead of sitting in front of the TV waiting for supper.

RABBI: And Alice, where are you on the same scale?

ALICE: If it weren't for the kids and mother's guilt, I would have left by now. I'm at about a one.

RABBI: Let me ask you this. Let's say that ten is you are enough in love so you both want to stay together, and zero is you can't stand each other for another ten seconds, where are you on that scale?

JOHN: I'm at ten. I want Alice and the kids at home with me. No question.

RABBI: Okay, and Alice?

ALICE: Oh, I'll say three, or somewhere between two and three. I need to get out soon. It took me several years to decide and now I have. It's time for me to do something.

In their mutual negotiation of the solution picture, it seems as though each person has a goal that conflicts with the other's. Yet, their answers to the miracle question seemed to show some hope that their living together was still possible somehow.

RABBI (*To Alice*): When things are at four on your scale, what will John see you doing?

ALICE: I'll be packing. I will live locally so the kids can stay in their schools and John can see them.

RABBI: Just four? That sounds like a ten.

ALICE: Oh, I will know for certain whether John will support me financially in this or if I will have to do it all on my own.

RABBI: And how will that be useful to know?

ALICE: It will make a big difference how soon I can move.

RABBI: John, you say you are at ten on that scale. Is that something new, being that high?

JOHN: No, I've always been there with Alice and my family. I just love them, that's all.

RABBI: And how will you keep that ten going, regardless of what Alice does?

ALICE: He will. He is always positive about us. That's one of the things that make this so difficult.

RABBI: Say more about that. There must have been times when things were better between the two of you? (*Both nod yes.*)

ALICE: We used to have a lot of fun together. We would go out for dinner and a movie, or we'd go to a club dancing with friends. We had a lot of friends then.

JOHN: One time we sailed around the Greek Islands. It was our honeymoon. We could laugh and joke. Our friends loved to see us.

The rabbi continued asking for more times and they described in detail other times when things were better between them. He knew that inviting people into conversations about getting better sometimes took a lot of patience and persistence. He began wondering if there may be a common goal of wanting cooperation with each other's wishes, as contradictory as they seemed to be. They knew how to enjoy their relationship. But the conversation repeatedly turned to Alice's leaving and John's insisting that she and the children stay. The rabbi decided to accept their teaching and "change where he was standing."

RABBI (To Alice): So, let's say you live apart, how do you suppose that will that be good for him?

ALICE: He will be able to participate in raising our kids. It will be good for the kids, too. They will see their parents' working together to raise them instead of being unhappy with each other. I think we'd be able to get along better.

RABBI: So, John, suppose that happens, do you think that you and Alice could work together for the benefit of the children without being terribly unhappy with each other?

JOHN: We've always put the kids first.

RABBI: Let's say, on a scale from zero to ten, where ten is your children will say you have been good parents twenty-five years from now, and zero is they will say you were the worst parents imaginable, where would they put you today?

JOHN: I think it would be pretty high. I mean we both love them very much and are deeply involved with them. I'd say about seven or eight.

ALICE: I agree.

RABBI: That's pretty high! How come seven or eight?

John and Alice repeated several things they mentioned earlier, and as the rabbi asked for more details, they expanded their story. As they talked, the rabbi could see that they were practiced in admiring each other's skills as parents.

RABBI: This time, on one of those scales, Alice, ten is you can live with the situation until you can get out on your own, and zero is you can't stand it another minute . . .

ALICE: Five. I've been living like this for a while now. If I live with it through the next three months, it's a ten.

The rabbi decided to take his accustomed ten-minute break to think. When he returned, he said this to them:

RABBI: I'm impressed. You both care about your kids a lot. And you seem to be working hard for their well-being. It's clear that you have been through a lot together, and I'm surprised that things aren't worse than they are. And you love your kids a lot. You admire each other as parents a lot. You must have been doing something right all these years. So, would you do some research to help me here? (*They agreed.*) Each of you keep an eye on the other and notice what he or she does right with the kids and notice what difference that makes. We can discuss that next time. Okay? (*They agreed.*) Do you want to see me again?

They said yes and wanted another appointment in a week.

Second Meeting

RABBI: So, what's better?

JOHN: Well, I noticed a lot of things Alice did right. But what blew me away was what she did last Thursday. Alice reached out to me and hugged me and kissed me. She wasn't critical of me. There was a ninety percent improvement! I thought Saturday was another day. She gave me a look, a smile I haven't seen in a long time.

ALICE: Actually, I did it for the whole week. I made sure I gave him a lot of eye contact. I acted optimistic, we both talked openly, I asked for his input. It was a great week! I noticed that John was more careful what he spoke about, like he was thinking about how I would take what he was saying—being more sensitive to that. And he does a lot more with the kids than I thought.

JOHN: I thought I was being more spontaneous.

RABBI: That was better?

ALICE: Wednesday we went out to dinner without the kids. We really had a good time. We talked more than we have in months.

RABBI: So, let's see, ten is the way things are the day after the miracle and zero is the way things were when John called for the appointment, where are things today?

ALICE: Five.

RABBI: How come five and not zero?

ALICE: We also took the kids for walks and went bicycle riding together. John and I planned those things after we left here last week, so I could schedule them, and he made sure he was available and ready.

RABBI: That's better?

ALICE: Yes. Very different. And it's something we can do when we're apart. We don't need to be together to do those things. We might even do them more if we aren't living together.

RABBI: And John?

JOHN: Seven.

RABBI: All the way up to seven? Tell me about that.

JOHN: She still wants to leave.

RABBI: That's better? I mean, how come that high?

JOHN: Oh, right. Our marriage therapist wanted to talk about our problems all the time. I guess I'm used to that. Why I'm at seven? Things were more the way they used to be. I think. I felt more hopeful. It was like we were more of a family and Alice and I were a couple again.

The rabbi went on asking each of them for more details about when things were better. Instead of making it his goal for them to stay together, he was keeping the conversation focused on how they could make things better between them, together or apart. With more questions about who else noticed things were better, they described what the children noticed and what John's mother noticed when she visited.

RABBI: On another scale, where ten is that you are confident that you can keep that good week going, more or less, over the next six months, and zero is it's all downhill from here, where are you today?

ALICE: I'll say six.

JOHN: Yes. Six.

The rabbi took his customary 10-minute think break. When he returned, he had this to say:

RABBI: I must say that it impresses me that you two are communicating as well as you are after all you've been through. Going out together, showing more affection, doing things together with the kids and grandma. You have some confidence that you will keep this going no matter what. So, I have a suggestion for you. This time, each of you secretly notice what the other does right, in any way, with the kids, with relatives, with co-workers, and friends, and let's discuss those things if you decide to come back?

ALICE: Could we ask the kids to make a list and we could bring them with us next time?

RABBI: Anything that you think will be helpful.

They decided to return in two weeks, to give them time to carry out the suggestion.

Third Meeting

The couple returned and, in response to the rabbi's question about "What's better?" John said that Alice had made the two weeks enjoyable and Alice said John was more supportive. They were able to relax together and both agreed that things were at an 8 on a progress scale.

The Rabbi asked for details. They said they had continued talking and that John has agreed to provide financial support when Alice moves out. They had agreed that he could see the children any time he wants. They also agreed that their main concern was to give the kids the love and attention they need when they are living separately.

JOHN: By coming here, we have done more talking after we leave than in the marriage therapy we had before. When we went to see the therapist, we would leave fighting worse than ever and feeling terrible. When we came here, we could see more common ground for agreeing. I still don't like their moving somewhere else, but I think, at worst, I'll be able to be part of their lives no matter what.

ALICE: And we want to thank you for having faith in our being able to solve our own problems. You treated us as intelligent people who could make good decisions for ourselves, and that was the kind of help we needed.

Six Months Later

Alice, John, and their children showed up at the rabbi's synagogue. At the door after the service, Alice asked the rabbi with a grin if he still wanted to know what was better. She went on to say she never did move out. She still thinks about it sometimes, although much less than before. "We just decided that, since we're a family, it might be fun to stick it out together rather than doing something that would just make things more difficult than they already were."

ON THE FLY: A HOSPITAL VISIT

Many contacts are made on the fly during chance meetings and on regular hospital visits (also during coffee hours, social events, shopping, simply meeting on the street, visiting shut-ins, on the phone, and via e-mail).

Sue, a pastoral care person in her congregation, made routine visits to the local hospitals. She recalls meeting with Christine while Christine was in for surgery. Christine's husband had asked Sue if she would stop in and see Christine. "I think she's very depressed. I'm worried about her." As soon as she pulled up a chair, Christine said that she was having a difficult time. She didn't think she was getting any better, even after the surgery. "It's been three days now, and I should be starting to feel better."

Sue asked her if there were times when she was feeling a little better. Christine said that there have been 5 to 10 minute stretches when she was feeling better, "but then it gets worse again." Sue asked for details about those times when Christine was feeling better and Christine talked about how much she wanted to get up on her own. "I might just as well die here." Given a choice between asking about her talking about death and describing times when things were a little better, Sue asked what her husband had noticed about her when she is a little better.

CHRISTINE (*laughs*): He hears me complain. He says that when I'm complaining, I'm getting ready to do something.

SUE: How often is he right about that?

CHRISTINE: Nearly always!

SUE: So, how close are you to doing something now?

CHRISTINE: I'm desperate.

SUE: You must be. How have you made it this far?

Sue focused on Christine's readiness to do something. Christine's answers had to do with how she had coped so far, so Christine asked the miracle question.

CHRISTINE (*smiling*): They won't have to empty the bed pan. Seriously? I'll walk up to the nurse's station and tell them I want my clothes because I'm leaving! But that won't happen.

SUE: Well, suppose it does. What will be the first small clue that will tell them that you might just be ready to do that?

CHRISTINE: Oh, I don't know. Maybe I'll be sitting up when they bring my breakfast.

This is something she had already begun doing that day at lunch. So, the miracle had already started to happen! She was beginning to take care of herself and she said her husband would also notice that something different was going on when she was talking about things needing doing at home. They would also be discussing plans for a vacation together.

SUE: So, on a scale from zero to ten, where ten is the morning after the miracle and zero is the worst things have felt since the surgery, where are you today?

CHRISTINE: In the closet. But seriously, probably at one. I'm alive and breathing. I ain't dead yet, you know!

Christine related that two would mean that she had her sense of humor back, something she was demonstrating throughout their conversation.

SUE: So, say you are at five on the scale. What will your husband and your friends see you doing first?

CHRISTINE: I'll be up and walking on my own when they come to visit later.

SUE: How do you know you can do that?

CHRISTINE: I got up by myself this morning and went to the bathroom before anybody came around. I was shaky and there was a lot of pain, but I did it. That's what got me going to get myself sitting up for lunch. Now that I've had the rehearsals, it's time for the big show!

Christine listed several more things she was looking forward to doing in detail when the pastor asks her. Sue continued to ask what others would be seeing Christine doing when she was better, and what difference that would make for her and them. As her list got longer, Sue heard Christine sounding more upbeat. She designed the following question based on what Christine was saying.

SUE: So, are you telling me that you might be ready to get on with these things, or are you thinking about getting ready?

CHRISTINE: I think I'm ready. (*Laughs*) Almost.

SUE: Okay. So, on another one of those scales, where ten is you are determined to get on with these things as soon as you are ready, and zero is you really don't care if you do any of them or not, where are you?

CHRISTINE: Really? I think I'm at a six. I'm going to try anyway.

Sue was aware that they had been talking for some time and that the nurse had walked by the door several times, looking in. Sue also thought that if she took her accustomed think break, medical staff would think that she had left and would come in to do their work. She decided to give Christine some compliments she had been noting on the small pad she always carried and made a suggestion for something Sue could do.

SUE: Well, I think it's time for me to get along, so I just want to say a few things. I am really impressed with you. You have been through so much and you have had your ups and downs. And you have been knocked to your knees and want to get back up. As discouraged as you have been feeling, you are determined to get back to vacation plans and those other things you want to do when you are back home. And you don't want your husband and friends to be so concerned about you. You are a very active, responsible, determined person. You want to get out of here and get back home as soon as possible. So, I have a suggestion for you. After I leave, notice what's different with your husband when you are thinking about your vacation and some of those other things you want to be doing.

When Sue returned to the hospital two days later, Christine had gone home. When she called her a little later, Christine gave herself a 10! She said she was "better" in terms of her husband's initial concern and requested that Sue visit.

WORKING WITH GROUPS

Some groups involve persons who have similar troubles. One that comes to mind is a group of members of a congregation and some of their friends, each of whom had experienced the death of a child. It made sense to me, after hearing their stories, that it was reasonable for them to feel upset, more at some times and less at others, for as long as necessary. My approach was similar to the one the pastor used with the couple earlier in this chapter. I was curious about what each person wanted from coming to the group that their best friends would notice that something worthwhile was happening when they saw them. We proceeded from there with the miracle question, scaling questions, and focusing on what was better that they wanted to continue. We also focused on detailed descriptions of their lives when things were going well, which were numerous. One interesting result of these questions and the hard work they were doing was that they all decided that they were doing the best they could, and by the third meeting, they did not think the solution-focused group necessary anymore. We decided to stop with the idea that the group could continue anytime the members thought necessary. A few of the members did continue to meet as a support group, continuing to follow up with each other using solution-building questions. I recently have followed up with them since the group with me ended five years ago. Each person regards the group as helping them see that missing their loved ones was not some kind of grief disorder or dysfunction. Instead, each, for his or her reasons, had a better idea of their extraordinary ability to get on with life while missing their loved ones terribly.

CONCLUSION

I have been doing some rather casual research for a number of years, asking people I meet socially (after some chatting) whether they have had a significant drug or alcohol problem in their lives that they had solved to their satisfaction without counseling or program involvement. The results have been similar to those described by Thomas and Cockburn (1998), based on a Gallup poll of "people who had successfully overcome a significant emotional, addiction, health, or lifestyle problem during the 1980s" (p. 4) They report that the results were overwhelming: "over 90 percent of these persons, who, among other things, had suffered heart attacks, lost spouses or children to death, or suffered profound depression, overcame these problems *without professional assistance* [emphasis on the original]" (p. 4). My group bears that out.

This chapter has also concentrated on stories told by ordinary people who do extraordinary things using resources from their own lives, including themselves, family, friends, colleagues, and acquaintances. They have taught me that, when they are building their solutions in the contexts of their own lives, they tend to continue solution building without professional assistance. It is also my experience that when they decide they need help beyond the scope of solution-building conversations, they tend to seek out people who can help them get the results they want. On occasions when people require referrals for more therapy from, say, a psychiatrist, psychologist, social worker, or pastoral counselor and request my help in finding one, I usually refer them to credentialed professionals who use solution-focused brief therapy. When possible, I also collaborate with the solution-focused professional as a member of the team. If that is not what people want to do, they usually will seek appropriate resources on their own. People are very resourceful.

NOTE

1. I use the words "pastor" and "pastoral" to include a wide variety of people working in religious communities who work with others who come to them for help in addition to clergy and credentialed pastoral counselors.

SUGGESTED READING

American Association of Pastoral Counselors (AAPC). Available at: www.aapc.org
Berg, I. K., & Dolan, Y. (2001). *Tales of solutions: A collection of hope-inspiring stories*. New York: Norton.
de Shazer, S. (1994). *Words were originally magic*. New York: Norton.

Dolan, Y. (1991). *Resolving sexual abuse: Solution-focused therapy and Ericksonian hypnosis for adult survivors*. New York: Norton

Kollar, C. A. (1997). *Solution-focused pastoral counseling*. Grand Rapids, MI: Zondervan Publishing House.

Kornfeld, M. (1998). *Cultivating wholeness: A guide to care and counseling in faith communities*. New York: Continuum.

REFERENCES

de Shazer, S. (1985). *Keys to solution in brief therapy*. New York: Norton.

de Shazer, S. (1991). *Putting difference to work*. New York: Norton.

de Shazer, S. (2005). *Current thoughts: The miracle question*. [online]. Available: http://www.brief-therapy.org

de Shazer, S., & Isebaert, L. (2003). The Brugges model: A solution-focused approach to problem drinking. *Journal of Family Psychotherapy, 14*(4), 43-52.

Gallagher, D. (2005). Listen and describe. In T. S. Nelson (Ed.), *Education and training in solution-focused brief therapy* (pp. 229-252). Binghamton, NY: The Haworth Press.

Iveson, C., Ratner, H., & George, E. (2001, September). *Sharpening Ockham's razor.* Workshop presented at the European Brief Therapy Association (EBTA) Conference, Dublin, Ireland.

Thomas, F. N., & Cockburn, J. (1998). *Competency-based counseling*. Minneapolis: Augsburg Fortress.

Chapter 11

"This Job Is So Demanding." Using Solution-Focused Questions to Assess and Relieve Burnout

Yvonne Dolan
Thorana S. Nelson

INTRODUCTION

Those of us who work in a therapeutic role with traumatized and abused clients sometimes experience what is variously referred to in the literature as *burnout, vicarious traumatization, trauma countertransference,* or *compassion fatigue.* Although there are differences among these phenomena, they have similarities in terms of experiences of physical and mental fatigue or exhaustion, emotional symptoms such as depression, cognitive impairments such as forgetfulness, spiritual ennui, and, in the case of compassion fatigue or vicarious traumatization, the same symptoms as post-traumatic stress disorder (American Psychiatric Association, 1994). The various symptoms result from working with traumatized clients with inadequate training, support, professional and personal balance, or relief, often resulting in poor service to clients, impaired work and personal relationships, and high turnover in agencies that serve these clients.

Compassion fatigue and burnout can wreak havoc with work performance in mental health and other fields. However, if anecdotal evidence is to be believed, burnout is something that solution-focused therapists rarely experience. Over the years, many of our colleagues have claimed that using

Handbook of Solution-Focused Brief Therapy: Clinical Applications
© 2007 by The Haworth Press, Inc. All rights reserved.
doi:10.1300/5135_11

the Solution-Focused Brief Therapy (SFBT) approach prevents them from developing it. Some of the explanations they have given for this include:

- SFBT establishes a cooperative rather than adversarial relationship with clients, which makes my work a lot more enjoyable.
- Because the goals we are working on are the client's goals, I don't have to work so hard to create motivation; they naturally are motivated as a result of talking about what things will be like in the future when they achieve their goals.
- Scaling clarifies the therapeutic process. This makes the process much less stressful for the client as well as the therapist.
- Listening to clients answer the Miracle Question is uplifting for the therapist. Clients motivate themselves by answering questions about the details of the imaginary Miracle.

It seems that working on clients' self-identified goals rather than assuming their need to focus on such goals as working through the trauma or re-experiencing the emotional stress helps to move both client and therapist beyond trauma pain and toward a preferred future. SFBT therapists may experience less burnout, but they and others are not immune to secondary effects of working with traumatized clients and witnessing their pain.

In reaction to our SFBT colleagues' reported resistance to burnout, Yvonne became curious about how the SFBT approach could be used effectively to help replenish those who *were* experiencing it. This chapter will illustrate through a case example how supervisors and consultants can use solution-focused techniques to relieve burnout for health care professionals and other workers. For the sake of clarity, we use *italicized bold print* to designate the questions in that section that exemplify the technique. In sections of the interview where several different SFBT techniques are used, the section title and highlighted examples are intended to reflect the technique that is given primary emphasis. Throughout the transcript, Yvonne and Thorana add their thoughts about how the different techniques are helping clients to change.

"AMY"

A residential youth care worker, Amy rolled her eyes and exhaled sharply as she walked into the consultation room. We had met earlier in the day, introduced by her boss and immediate supervisor. I (Yvonne) was teaching a two-day seminar for Amy's agency. Closing the door slowly, as if it required almost more energy than she possessed, Amy sat down heavily on the couch. Slumping against the cushions, she explained that her boss wanted her to talk to me because he thought she was experiencing "burnout." I asked Amy if she agreed with him. Based on the way she had walked into the room, I was expecting her to say, "No," and then go on to protest that it was a waste of her time to talk with me. But then her eyes filled and her lips began to tremble. She met my gaze for a split second and then looked down at the floor. She just sat there, very still, letting the tears roll down her cheeks. I waited for her to look up. When she did, I offered her a tissue. She wiped her eyes and began to speak, keeping her eyes fixed on the wall behind me.

A: Probably. Probably he's right. I've been missing a lot of work lately. And I've made some mistakes recently at work. One night when I was on call, I forgot to check the messages on my cell phone. I had been out at a movie and I didn't realize they (co-workers) had been paging me for the past two hours until I came home and noticed the light on my answering machine was blinking. They had been unable to figure out where I had filed the medication prescription for one of the kids and it was a big problem because his foster mother was picking him up first thing in the morning. If they didn't have the prescription ready, it would inconvenience a whole lot of people, not just the foster mother, but all the other people involved in the field trip they were taking that day. They were frustrated with me, and I got defensive and said some things that were definitely not very professional. And that kind of behavior is not normally like me.

(Amy paused for a moment and, careful to use her exact words, I responded.)

Y: Normally you are very professional and this was different.

(Amy looked up, nodded, and gave me a long searching look before returning her gaze to the floor and continuing.)

A: Yes. . . . Then last week, I overreacted to one of the boys in our group home when he didn't come downstairs right away when we called a house meeting. I had to call him three times. I got really angry at what seemed to be his belligerent attitude, and I kind of lost it. I guess you could say I overreacted. I gave him a consequence of loss of television privileges for the rest of the week. Afterwards I thought about it and realized this really was way too much of a consequence for not coming downstairs right away. He had said he didn't hear me the first two times, and maybe that was true. Usually we try to give the kids the benefit of the doubt. They have already been through so much before they come to us. So, after the house meeting I sat down with him and told him that I was sorry that I had overreacted, and that as long as he didn't break any other rules, he would not lose his TV privileges. So I tried to fix it, but still I feel really bad about it. Yesterday, I went in to my boss and told him about it. I said, "I know I've been making some really stupid mistakes lately. I don't know what's wrong with me—I think I'm burned out." He told me to take the rest of the day off, get some rest. Then he suggested that since you were going to be here this week, I should schedule a session with you. To tell you the truth, I really didn't want to come. It feels like one more thing I have to do when I already have way too much to do."

Agreeing on a Goal for the Session

I told Amy that if I were in her shoes, I would probably feel exactly as she did. Then I asked *what would need to happen in our session in order for her to feel, when she walked out the door an hour from now, that something useful had happened in our session and that it had not been a waste of her time.*

At least 90 seconds passed before she answered, "I don't know" in a tentative, almost pleading tone of voice. Then she fell silent again. When I was a younger therapist, I would have filled this silence by offering another question or making some empathic response. But now I usually refrain and just allow the person some time to think. I've learned that people usually take longer to answer unconventional questions, and given their future orientation and emphasis on creating solutions rather than destroying problems, most SFBT questions fit that category.

Three full minutes passed (according to the digital clock on the wall) before Amy looked up again and, taking a deep breath, slowly answered. Her words had a far away quality, almost as if she was thinking aloud, bringing the words up from somewhere deep within, one at a time.

A: I would be able to . . . think clearly, figure out what I needed to do to feel better . . . I guess I would feel less overwhelmed. I mean, I feel a little bit better since I went home early yesterday, but I feel like I can't miss any more work . . . We are really shorthanded here. We lost one of our positions because of a funding cut, which is why I did not get a vacation last year. I'm finally going to get some time off in August, but I don't know how I am going to get through these next three months. I guess I would need to have some sort of plan for at least the next few days so I would feel like I was more on top of things, and maybe that I wouldn't dread going to work every day. This job is just so very demanding, and there are politics between our agency and other agencies and with these kids, it never stops. There is always something going on. It's hard.

It seemed to me that working full time with a group of active adolescent boys *was* a very demanding job and, of course, interagency politics could naturally add to the stress, and I told Amy this. I asked how long she had been doing this kind of work.

A: Three years this spring . . . I originally took this job because I really like kids and wanted to help them, but some days, in fact, more and more often lately, I come home so drained and exhausted that I don't feel like getting up the next morning. I don't feel that what I am doing is making any difference for the kids and sometimes they frustrate me so much that I just want to get away from them for a few minutes, but I . . . of course, I can't leave during my shift.

And then when I get home, I flop down on my couch and turn on the television to relax, but it doesn't work. I keep right on thinking of work and all the things I need to do the next day, and I worry about whatever it was I didn't get done that day. I know I am burned out; I'm not stupid. But I don't want to quit. I need my job. I am trying to pay off my student loan; I still owe several thousand dollars. So I don't want to quit. But I am just so tired. I am not sleeping well at night. I've put on a lot of weight, nearly twenty pounds, and I know I'm eating from stress . . . I don't know what to do.

From there, our session went as follows:

Y: So you have some financial pressure as well. That's a lot to carry. And yet, you say you don't want to quit.

A: It is a lot to carry. But you're right. I really don't want to quit. I'd like to stick it out. But I am just so tired.

Y: I am thinking perhaps it's not so surprising that you are feeling tired because you have these responsibilities and, as you said, lately you have not been sleeping well. And yet you've somehow managed to get yourself to work.

A: I've been late several times in the past month. That's another problem.

Y: Several times?

A: Yes.

Asking an Exception Question

Y: *But not every time?*

A: No.

Y: That's something.

A: Not enough, probably. But it is something, I guess (*laughs*).

Expanding the Exception by Asking a Coping Question

When clients are discouraged and have difficulty thinking of exceptions or tend to discount them, *coping questions* can help to bring a sense of self-efficacy into the picture. Their sense of themselves is of *always* having the problem and *never* being able to escape it. However, the fact that they are functioning at all means that they are able to function.

Y: So, what I am wondering is how, because this is really difficult for you right now, and from what I am understanding, it has been hard now for a while . . . (*Amy nods*) and so what I am especially curious about is **how on earth have you been able to manage to the degree you are?**

A: Well, I just make myself do it.

Y: That's sounds easy, but we both know that it is not. How do you manage to do it?

A: I make my mind up. And sometimes when I know it's going to be a really hard day and I don't want to go in, I just have to force myself to get out of bed, put my clothes on, and come in to work. It's like I am on automatic pilot. Some days are harder than others.

Y: Of course, some days are a lot harder than others, especially in a job like this with so much going on. And yet you manage to get yourself to work?

Empathy is very important in this work and such statements tell the client that you understand, help with pacing, and help the client prepare for solution building. Empathic statements help to set up a "yes and" rather than "yes, but" tone.

A: Most of the time.

Y: Most of the time. So . . . on those hard days, you still can force yourself to do it, but on the days that are a little bit easier, well, I guess I am wondering if you have figured out what, if anything, contributes to some days being a little bit easier?

Repeating the clients' responses that lean toward solution-building help establish and maintain the solution-focused tone of the interview. The therapist's tone can convey understanding and acknowledgment at the same time. Emphasizing "some" then allows the therapist to help the client explore "some" in greater detail.

A: It's never what you would call easy here, but yeah, some days are not as crazy as others. But what did you just ask me—you mean the days that are not so bad? Maybe not wonderful, but not as bad as the others?

The client is beginning to move from the problem to exceptions.

Y: Yes . . .
A: Well . . .

Amy's voice trailed off, and then she was silent for a couple of minutes, as if in a state of deep contemplation. Interrupting this silence with suggestions or ideas might take her back to the problem or, at the least, away from her exceptions and coping.

A: I guess those are days that . . . uh, days that I have something to look forward to doing after work. Because, well, then it's like even if the kids are giving us a hard time, and there is all this interagency crap going on, still I can get through it because it doesn't feel like it is my WHOLE life. Instead, it's just something that I do at work—like I may have a really demanding job, but that job is not my entire twenty-four-hour experience.
Y: Something about the job not being your whole twenty-four-hour experience?

Yvonne picks up on Amy's stated exception and simply repeats it.

A: Yeah. In some ways it doesn't make sense, because you would think that the days that I am doing something after work, well that would just make me more tired, but actually, it's just the opposite. If I go out and do something like see a friend or, well, it's been a really long time since I did this, go to the gym, when I come home it's a different kind of tired. I am more likely to be able to sleep.

Amy now has moved from deeply experiencing her difficulty to noticing exceptions. Yvonne wants to keep her there and to deepen the experience of non-problem or solution.

Y: Is it okay if I ask you a question to help me get a clearer picture?
A: Sure.

Asking Scaling Questions

Y: So let's suppose we made a scale with ten on one end and zero on the other end, and the ten signified the best day possible and zero, the opposite, what number would you need to be at in order for you to feel reasonably good about the day when, lying in bed at the end of the day, you looked back upon it?

Yvonne wanted to help the client place the exceptions to the problem in a perspective of possibilities and solutions rather than problems and difficulties. Making decisions about what to do next in SFBT is not a science. Decisions flow from what the client is saying, the tone of the interview, and the therapist's best judgment, which sometimes is based on intuition. Over time, therapists develop their own styles and the flow of the interview is not always easy to describe. Scaling questions help the therapist and client develop clearer pictures of both what is happening and what the client would like to have happen. Rather than focusing on distant and seemingly impossible goals, scaling questions help place the client on a continuum of small, concrete goals, each of which can be described in detail with help from the therapist.

A: I suppose it would need to be a six or a seven, no, actually, a five would probably be good enough.

Y: *A five would be good enough?*

A: Yes. It really would.

Y: *So where are you today?*

A: Six or seven, I guess.

Y: *What makes you a six or seven?*

A: Well, it's Friday and I don't have to go to work for the next three days.

Integrating Scaling and Exceptions into the Client's Real Life

Scaling questions are easy to ask and sometimes easy for clients to answer. However, the numbers need to be attached to clear, specific, behavioral anchors to be most beneficial. Learning about the client's behaviors, responses from others in her life, and how she manages to do the things she already is doing gives the therapy a sense of concreteness and the client's solid reality.

Y: *Okay, so today is a seven. I wonder what would need to happen in order for Monday to be a five.*

Yvonne acknowledges that Fridays are exceptional exceptions and points the client in the direction of better Mondays. If Mondays are exceptionally difficult, the therapist might ask about a "more ordinary" day.

A: I don't know. I don't even know where to start with that one.

Y: *Well, how about if you imagine it's next Monday morning and you ask yourself what number you are at?*

A: Oh, God, I hate to admit it, but I guess maybe a two.

When clients get into the scaling questions as they are attached to their lives, they are able to make distinctions that previously were largely a part of an amorphous whole. As they and the therapist make these distinctions in greater and greater detail, they are able to notice more exceptions, how that makes a difference to them, and to acknowledge more self-efficacy in relation to the problem.

Y: Maybe a two.

A: Yes.

Y: *How is it that it is not worse than a two?*

In other therapies, the therapist might wonder what's going on that makes it so bad, focusing on the client's experience as a deficit. In SFBT, focusing on *anything* as better than *nothing* helps the client see the possibilities of *at least that much* or even *a little more*.

A: Well, a two is pretty bad . . . but well, I guess it's not worse because I just had a few days off, and, let's see, I know that I will have a vacation coming, and . . . I don't know. I feel stuck. I guess I feel pretty hopeless when I think about it . . .

The client was able to name a number of things that helped her not feel worse, but tells the therapist how easily discouraged she becomes. The response also includes some future-oriented ideas, indicating that Amy may be ready to move toward identifying a future that does not include the problem. Yvonne wants Amy to move from feeling hopeless to hopeful, which requires looking ahead rather than back or in the present.

Asking the Miracle Question Integrated with the Scaling

The focus of solution-focused therapy is on efficacy and future, not deficit and past or present. Focusing on the past and deficits reinforces both. Focusing on efficacy and future opens possibilities for the client. When Amy "told" Yvonne how discouraged she was, Yvonne decided to catapult her into a future orientation. The miracle question will help Yvonne and Amy determine goals and the meaning those goals have for Amy.

Y: There is this weird question that I ask sometimes because I find that sometimes it helps when people are stuck. Is it okay to ask you?

A: Yes, okay.

Y: *My question is, Let's say on Sunday night while you were sleeping, some how or other a sort of miracle happened and you were now at a five (I don't know exactly what it was, maybe something shifted inside you or maybe something else). But you didn't know the miracle had happened and that you were now at a five because you had been asleep when it happened. What would be the first thing that you or someone else would notice that next day that would indicate that something had changed. You weren't at a two anymore. You were at a five?*

Asking about what others would notice expands the vision of the client from self to a context that includes others, adding real life details to the picture.

A (*Long pause, followed by a sigh*): I don't know exactly. . . . Except for maybe one thing: I would get right out of bed. I wouldn't lay there until the last minute. (*Pause*)

It is very important for the SFBT therapist to develop skills for being quiet and waiting for clients to think. "I don't know" sometimes is an automatic response; however, in our experience, clients are thinking about these strange and different pictures and need time to first picture them and then to put them into words and tell us about them. For therapists to chime in with ideas disrupts the client's thinking puts the therapist's picture into the conversation. However, this is the client's life and the therapist cannot know it. How long to wait? As long as it takes. Should time end for the interview before the client responds, the therapist can end the session with compliments and a suggestion to continue thinking about the miracle morning and to notice small things that might indicate that the miracle is happening even a little bit. Amy, however, found an answer after a few moments.

A: And . . . I would get up and get dressed right away because the laundry would be done and my clothes would be clean and I wouldn't be searching for something to wear at the last minute. That is one of the things that makes me late.

Questions to Explore the Details and Effects of the Miracle

Y: *And what else might you or someone else notice?*

Details will help Amy and the therapist identify small things that indicate (a) the miracle already is happening a little bit and (b) what the client can do next to help the miracle happen. They also help the client notice things that indicate the miracle is happening or has happened a little in the past. Positive effects of change noticed by others will also reinforce the changes and place Amy in a context that includes important others.

A: Well, the neighbor might notice that I stopped and said hello because I wasn't racing for my car.

Y: *And what else?*

SFBT therapists have an endless supply of "what else's." Asking, "what else" adds more and more detail to the pictures.

A: My co-workers and the kids would notice that I was on time. And I would be friendlier to them because I wouldn't be embarrassed about being late all the time.

Y: How do you imagine they would respond to your being friendlier?

Yvonne's question reinforces the effects of change. Thinking about the effects of change in many aspects of one's life recursively reinforces the ability to think about solutions and to notice effective change.

A: I guess they would probably be more friendly to me in return.

Y: *Anything else they might notice in you that would indicate to them that something was different for you, that you were a five?*

Focusing on what others might notice may have helped Amy to think about her own possible responses.

Y: *You do?*

Yvonne notices a strength and punctuates it by incorporating it into the next question. Later, she may be able to use this to help the client develop more self-confidence.

A: Yeah.

Y: *So, if you were joking with the kids, would that mean you were at a five?*

A: No, it would mean something higher. Maybe more like a seven.

Amy indicates that she is following the flow of the conversation and Yvonne will be curious about Amy's response.

Y: *You would be at a seven?*
A: Yeah.

Another Exception Question

Y: *Have you ever been at a seven at work before?*
A: Actually, I have.

Clients usually are able to identify what progress would look like based on experience or the experience of others. Asking this question will help the therapist identify the exception and amplify it. In SFBT, therapists are always on the alert to exceptions and questions that may help identify them.

Amplifying the Exception

Y: *What made it a seven?*
A: I don't know. I guess because I was laughing and I didn't feel so caught up in the politics—I wasn't thinking about what the other agencies were thinking about us, you know . . .
Y: *What do you suppose you were thinking about instead?*

Therapists are most helpful to clients when they are able to help them identify the presence rather than the absence of something.

A: Either I wasn't thinking at all, just concentrating on the kids, or I was thinking about helping the kids, or maybe I was thinking about what I planned to do after work . . .

Amy indicates that she is quite able to defocus from the problem and to think about other things. Noticing this will help her in the future when she finds herself at a 6, wishing to be at a 7.

Y: *What kinds of thing might you do after work if you were a seven?*

Specific details of each step will help Amy move toward her goals. This question also helps Amy look at the big picture of her life, which includes many exceptions, rather than work, where the discouragement is most prevalent.

A: Well, I wouldn't be staying after work, standing in the parking lot gossiping with my co-workers about all the problems we are having with this other agency who we think caused us to lose some of our funding, because that doesn't change anything. And I end up feeling all upset.

Y: *What would you be doing instead?*

A: I would be going to the gym. Or maybe I would go play miniature golf with my nephew. . . . Or maybe even plant a garden again like I did two years ago.

Amy clearly is now identifying things she can do instead of dwelling on the problem.

Y: *And those would be seven activities?*

A: Actually, the garden would be more like a nine, maybe even a ten.

Connecting Scaling to Client's Real Life

Y: *Wow. So, getting back to that five. I am wondering what would be the smallest thing you could do that would help you move in the direction of waking up at a five on Monday morning.*

Although looking at the miracle picture helps the client move from problem to solution talk, Yvonne recognizes that it will be important to identify small, concrete steps that will help her begin the journey. Focusing on a 7, 8, or 9 will likely not be helpful to Amy because it may seem too far away, the change too large, and therefore daunting or even not possible. In SFBT, we realize that small changes are likely to trigger bigger changes, setting off a chain reaction that helps move the client toward her goal. Large changes, if not accomplished, are discouraging and often result in no change. Thus, Yvonne brings Amy back to the current time and begins to focus on a small, possible change.

A: Well, there is one obvious thing. It's small, but it really would make a big difference: doing my laundry. (*Laughs*) I don't have any clean clothes.

Y: *So let's say you got your laundry done, when you woke up on Monday it was done. Where would that put you?*

A: Maybe a two and a half or a three.

Y: *What else would help?*

A: Well, I guess having coffee in the house would make a difference. If I had coffee and the pot was filled so I just had to turn it on in the morning—that would make a difference.

Y: *Where would that put it?*

A: Three-and-a-half maybe, maybe higher.

Y: Anything else?

A: Well, I hate to think of this, but if my kitchen was clean . . .

Y: If your kitchen were clean.

A: Yes.

Y: *Where would that put it?*

A: That would definitely be an eight.

Y: *An eight?!*

A: Yes. But you don't realize the mess I am talking about here.

Y: It's a big mess.

A: Yeah. There's stuff on the floor, the counters, the stove.

Y: *So, how much cleaning would you have to do in there to make it a five?*

Yvonne takes an identified large goal and helps Amy begin to think of it in smaller pieces.

A: Well, maybe if I just washed the dishes. I have about two weeks worth.

Y: So if you washed even a few dishes would it make a difference.

A: Definitely.

Y: *Anything else that doesn't necessarily involve cleaning the whole kitchen all at once?*

A: If I called my friend and make a plan for either that night or later that week.

Y: *If you had plans, where would that put it?*

A: At least a seven, maybe even an eight or a nine.

Y: Is there anything else I should ask you?

A: I don't think so.

Y: In that case, I am going to take a ten-minute break and think carefully about what we talked about here, and then we'll meet back here again for a few more minutes. Is that okay?

A: Yes.

Compliments

(*10 minutes later*)

Y: Sometimes when I take a break, I meet with a team of people who have been observing the session. That is nice because then I have their input.

Although I didn't have a team here, I found myself imagining what some of my colleagues would say if they *had* been listening to our session. *The first thing that came to mind was that there would be a lot of compliments for you.*

When possible, SFBT therapists like to work with teams to help them notice strengths and to give ideas for compliments and suggestions. Yvonne did not have a team in this situation and was able to not only work without one, but also give Amy the sense of what others might think about her and the situation, enlarging the scope of Amy's picture of her future to include even more people and relationships.

A: Compliments?

Y: *Yes, people would definitely give you a lot of credit for hanging in there even though it has been hard recently. They would also give you a lot of credit for not giving up because they would sense that it had probably been harder than you or anyone could really put into words.*

A (*She nods*): That's right. It has been.

Y: Then, they would advise me to tell you to go slowly. (My mentor [Steve de Shazer] told me to go slowly in situations like this. He told me he learned this from his mentor [John Weakland].)

A (*She nods*): I know I have this tendency sometimes to try to do too much all at once, and that causes problems too. I get overwhelmed all over again and I just give up.

Y: So, it seems to me that it would be very important to listen to yourself and not go too fast.

A: Definitely.

Y: And the other thought I had was to suggest that you keep track of anything that helps you move in the direction of a five between now and Monday morning.

A: You mean like doing the laundry, or calling my friend?

Y: Anything like that, but it would be important for you to do it at your own pace. And, as you said, not to try to do it all at once.

A: That would be too much.

Y: That would be way too much.

A: Okay, that helps . . . I think I know what I need to do.

Scaling Confidence

Y: *How confident are you that you know?*

Scaling questions are useful for an almost unlimited number of things. Discouraged clients may have good ideas about what they can do and even seem very enthusiastic during the interview. However, enthusiasm sometimes wanes and it is important for the therapist to help the client maintain or regain ideas. In this way, when the client finds herself discouraged because she has not done something she thought she could, she can "back up" and focus on what the next step in gaining confidence might be. Scaling confidence helps to solidify and reinforce the in-session changes in Amy's thinking and the conversation as preparation for taking action.

A: That I know?

Y: Yes.

A: I am a ten.

Y: Wow! A ten. Okay, then now I have another question: ***How confident are you that you will do it?***

Yvonne recognizes that there is a difference between knowing what to do and actually doing it.

A: I am five.

Y: ***What will raise the number?***

A: When I do it.

Y: Does it feel like something you can do?

Yvonne wants to be sure that the next step actually is possible for the client and wants to reinforce the client's knowledge of herself.

A: It does if I break it down into little individual things like doing the laundry, making one phone call to a friend. If I try to do it all at once, it doesn't.

Y: So doing little individual things is important?

Yvonne is careful to use the client's language whenever possible.

A: Exactly. (Pause. Client has tears in her eyes.)

Y (*Hands her a Kleenex*): Are you doing okay at this point?

A: I feel better. Actually a LOT better. I mean, I feel well, RELIEVED. It's going to be okay. I don't have to quit my job. I may not do this exact job forever. I may leave some day. But I don't feel like I have to leave immediately anymore. I feel like I have a lot more control over what is going to happen. And that really helps.

CONCLUSION

This session illustrates how solution-focused coping questions, exception questions, exception amplifying questions, scaling questions, the miracle question, and compliments can be utilized to help people identify what they need to do in order to feel better, experience replenishment, and prevent burnout from worsening to the extent that they feel forced to leave their work.

At the beginning of the session, questions about how Amy had managed to cope as much as she had made it possible to recognize some of the things she was doing that were helpful. Answering the miracle question gave Amy an image of what her life would be like when she was feeling better. Scaling questions provided a means for Amy to communicate her degree of "burn out" and recognize specific things she could do to move forward and to maintain confidence. In a follow-up conversation, Amy said that she continued to "keep track" of what she needed to do in order to maintain "at least a five"; however, she was now higher than that on the scale and no longer dreaded going to work in the mornings.

REFERENCE

American Psychiatric Association. (1994). *Diagnostic and statistical manual of mental disorders* (4th ed.). Washington, DC: Author.

Chapter 12

Applying Solution-Focused Brief Therapy in Mental Health Practice

Alasdair J. Macdonald

INTRODUCTION TO THE "MEDICAL MODEL"

The "medical model" is a basic paradigm in health care; it also is a specific sociological view of illness care. One of the primary assumptions of this view is that there are causes for disease and dysfunction: name the cause and you have a "diagnosis" that indicates specific treatment and (hopefully) cure. The medical model could equally well be called the "mechanical model" since the same process of fault identification is also applied to cars and domestic appliances. It is called the medical model because one common

---

Editors' note: We asked Alasdair to write a chapter for this book that would place Solution-Focused Brief Therapy (SFBT) in the context of systems that diagnose and treat what often are called major mental illnesses. Many SFB therapists do not know much about traditional ways of diagnosing and treating these disorders, let alone the signs and symptoms that psychiatrists such as Alasdair are trained to look for. In this chapter, Alasdair discusses the philosophy of the medical model and how it differs from more postmodern perspectives, describes the symptoms and signs of several major disorders and acute issues that send clients to hospitals, and traditional medical treatments for these disorders, including medication. He discusses ways that SFBT can be used in settings that use these perspectives and how some medical model treatments may benefit clients of solution-focused therapists. He presents a description of the acute, inpatient psychiatric ward on which he works and how he and his staff use SFBT in different situations. He concludes with a case study and a discussion of some of the research and findings on using SFBT.

Handbook of Solution-Focused Brief Therapy: Clinical Applications
© 2007 by The Haworth Press, Inc. All rights reserved.
doi:10.1300/5135_12   *267*

use of this discourse is to establish the predominance of physicians in mental health care, but this is not always a useful framework for managing mental health problems. Much of the health care service delivery involves a team that is not intentionally directed by the physician (e.g., a physiotherapist may take the referral from the physician but actually recommend acupuncture, a treatment resource helpful to the client but unfamiliar or unknown to the treating physician).

Longstanding or recurrent disorders do not fit the medical model well; as a result, management of such disorders is sometimes imperfect. For example, neurosurgeons perform amazing feats of skill in intervening to prevent death. Sadly, some patients are left with brain damage and major residual disability. These surgical specialists are rarely involved with care for these patients beyond a brief postoperative period, when the patients are handed off to underfunded community or mental health facilities. Whether due to past trauma, current causes, or unknown factors, mental illness often is longstanding or recurrent. How well mental illness fits the medical model is debatable, but it is clear that the public is concerned to obtain helpful resources, not to discuss models of care.

INFLUENCE OF HISTORY AND CULTURE

Mental disorder was specifically recognized prior to the Middle Ages in Europe. We know this because medieval laws existed to manage the property of the mentally incompetent (Roffe & Roffe, 1995). These laws distinguished between those born incompetent and those who become incompetent due to life's circumstances. However, religion or restraint—not medical doctors— was considered the correct resources for such individuals.

The incidence of schizophrenia seems to have increased early in the nineteenth century. Hypotheses to explain this include population increase or a proposed infectious or toxic agent. Comparing the careful records kept in nineteenth-century Europe to today shows that the prevalence of major mental disorders has not changed significantly. In nineteenth-century hospitals, custodial care with sedatives and constructive work produced improvement in up to 62 percent of admissions (Macdonald, 2000).

The accepted approach to mental disorder is affected by cultural and social issues as well as scientific or medical ones. For example, native healers are considered more reliable than Western medicine in many areas of Africa. They also are cheaper and usually more accessible so the medical model is only invoked late in the process (Swartz, 1998). The same applies in India (Bagadia, Shah, Pradhan, & Gada, 1979). The impact of cultural values also is shown by the differential use of legal powers in modern practice. Germany is reluctant to coerce individuals and detains far fewer people for mental disorder than does the United Kingdom. Conversely, Switzerland detains five times as many persons as the United Kingdom, "failure to look after yourself adequately" being grounds for detention under Swiss law (Reicher-Rossler & Rossler, 1993). India detains no one, perhaps because extended families are expected to care for the disabled or perhaps because the country has few beds (2.5/100,000 in population compared with the UK's 58/100,000; Patel & Saxena, 2003).

The provision of high security facilities for the mentally ill appears to have more to do with culture than with objective reality because it varies remarkably from country to country. England has 2.9 places per 100,000 population; Sweden has 11.36/100,000, while Portugal and Israel have none. It is unlikely that the population of any one of these countries is very different from any other, so this again is a cultural and social decision.

The Public's View

In practice, it is the public themselves who make the decision that a behavior amounts to "mental disorder." My occupational therapist colleague, Chris Morgan (personal communication, October 21, 1982) has suggested that the defining characteristic is relevance: the behavior may be normal but if the context is wrong then "mental disorder" will be invoked. The public then turn to professionals, expecting the disorder to be classified (diagnosed) and managed. Both clients and the public will accept wide variations in what treatment is offered and provided; note, for example, the discrepancy between public and professional views about what psychotherapy will be like (Garfield & Bergin, 1986) and about the value and risks of antidepressants.

Studies in the United Kingdom and Australia (e.g., Jorm et al., 1997; 85 percent response from 2031 Australians sampled) have shown that the public believe that counseling and vitamins are the optimal treatments for depression and that antidepressants are addictive. There is a body of scientific evidence against both of these ideas, but continued public education has not altered them. The international controversy surrounding attention-deficit/hyperactivity disorder (ADHD) and its treatment is another example of public concern leading to professional debate. As far as the public are concerned, the least acceptable response from a mental health professional is to say, "This problem is not a matter for our service."

The open dialogue approach in western Finland (Seikkula, Arnkil, & Eriksson, 2003) adopts a different view of psychosis, and the incidence of diagnosed schizophrenia has fallen from 33 cases per 100,000 populations to 7 cases per 100,000 (Aaltonen, Seikkula, Alakare, Haarkangas, Keranen, & Sutula, 1997; Seikkula, Alakare, & Aaltonen, 2000). The well-known Dingleton Hospital in Scotland was run on therapeutic community lines in the 1960s and achieved similar successes (Jones, 1968).

As far as mental disorder is concerned, there is one significant problem linked to the "medical model" discourse: Some physical health problems have no cure or treatment, and the public recognize this. In the latter half of the twentieth century, it has not been acceptable to say that a mental disorder has no cure or treatment. This may arise from care providers' wishing to maximize their market or from a belief among the public that these disorders are actually not "medical" in the same sense as physical ailments. As a result, the need for resources for mental distress is constantly growing, while many professionals feel overwhelmed and unable to meet the demands placed on them. The pharmaceutical companies are aware of this expanding demand for resources.

The notion that mental disorders actually are not "medical" in the same sense as physical ailments may well be true. Internationally, schizophrenia affects about 4 persons per 1,000 population and manic-depressive/bipolar/affective disorder affects 1 in 100 (Gelder, Gath, Mayou, & Owen, 1996). However, every individual country also has many other cases of major disorder, which vary greatly. A mental health professional who only talks to clients diagnosed with schizophrenia or affective disorder (using the international definitions) will have a small caseload, will find that treatment does not require the full use of his or her training, and will not be well thought of in his catchment area.

MAJOR MENTAL DISORDERS

Schizophrenia

There is consensus between the American (DSM-IV; American Psychiatric Association, 1994) and European (ICD-10) diagnostic classifications regarding schizophrenia. The illness can be diagnosed given the presence for more than one month of bizarre delusions and/or auditory hallucinations in which a voice keeps up a running commentary about the person with schizophrenia, or two or more voices talk to each other. If these features are not definitely present, then the diagnosis may depend on the presence of other less specific symptoms such as disorganization of speech or behavior, and negative symptoms such as flattening of emotions. Subtle neurological damage can be detected in many sufferers, and there is sometimes a relative with a similar disorder. The use of amphetamine-based drugs, alcohol, or lysergic acid diethylamide can provoke similar symptoms, which may become permanent.

The diagnosis of schizophrenia is viewed by the public as catastrophic, yet 15-25 percent of patients have only one episode in a lifetime (Gelder, et al., 1996; Kumar & Clark, 2002). Many sufferers require long-term support, but follow-up studies in various countries show that over 60 percent of those previously diagnosed with schizophrenia are stable in middle age, often without medication; many are married and/or employed (DeSisto, Harding, McCormick, Ashikaga, & Brooks, 1995; Harding, Brooks, Ashikaga, Strauss, & Breier, 1987). Their work and social function usually is below what typically is expected for their backgrounds, but this phenomenon is not confined to those with schizophrenia. Those in whom the disorder is limited to paranoid delusions often retain all their skills and abilities (including the ability to carry out their delusional impulses).

Mood Disorders

Disorders of mood (bipolar disorder; affective disorder; manic-depressive illness) consist of episodes of elevated or depressed mood, known as mania or depression. Occasionally, mixed states occur. Both disorders are marked by biological symptoms that recur in a similar pattern in each episode, and a family history of the disorders is common. Mania is characterized by elated mood, being overactive and overtalkative, and having decreased sleep and appetite. Most antidepressant treatments can induce mania, and this may lead to diagnostic errors. Episodes usually last from three to six months if untreated.

Depression

Major depression is recognized by low mood; waking early in the morning and not going back to sleep; reduction in appetite, weight, concentration, and interest in sexual activity; constipation; amenorrhea; and regular variation of mood over the course of the day. These functions are all regulated by the hypothalamus. If at least four of these symptoms occur consistently for five days per week over several weeks, then the illness is present and physical methods of treatment such as medication may be invaluable. If these features are not present, then the response to physical treatments is less predictable. An episode will last six to nine months in 85 percent of cases. Future episodes will be recognizably similar and more common with increasing age.

Conclusions

In my opinion, biological symptoms of affective disorder can occur in anyone. Once a certain duration or amount of stress is exceeded, the body becomes unable to adapt and then biological symptoms appear. It depends on what stresses one encounters, what supports one has available, and what susceptibility to mood disorder one has inherited. Then drug treatments are at their most valuable, acting to relieve distress and to enable the survival of the patient and his or her social and business relationships until the episode is over. Premature cessation of drug treatment often reveals continuing symptoms, suggesting that medications help to suppress the symptoms but do not cure the disorder.

It has been suggested that multinational pharmaceutical corporations support the medical model discourse by seeking to ratify new diagnoses to enable niche marketing of available drugs while neglecting research into rare but proven conditions because the profit margins will be lower. However, much the same marketing behaviors can be seen in the arena of psychological treatments where there is competition for trainees and for academic influence.

URGENT ASSESSMENT

Referrals for urgent assessment follow a number of routes, with the need as perceived by the referrer being the major determinant, modified by local service provision as understood by the referrer. In psychiatric practice with adults, behavior giving rise to public concern usually passes directly to legal or medical services for social control. This is the common pathway for mania, psychosis (whether drug-induced or not) and occasionally for acute self-endangering behavior.

Medication Issues

Acute trauma such as bereavement or examination stress may benefit from a hypnotic to improve sleep and hence daytime functioning. Sedative antidepressants may improve sleep and reduce daytime anxieties, if cognitive function is not a primary concern. If the client is going to undertake childcare alone or work with machinery, this option may be unsuitable.

Benzodiazepine drugs should be avoided: the risks include dependence, disinhibition, and impairment of cognitive function. These medications can also delay the processing of affective experience and thus the process of adjusting to loss can be prolonged. So the price of less emotional distress in the short term results in a longer period of emotional distress overall. This is a difficult judgment to make in a crisis. You may wish to advise your clients of these facts directly so that they can discuss them with their medical advisors, or you may wish to consult with their medical advisors yourself.

Self-Harm

The assessment of self-harm can be done through simple questions in ascending order of concern: When you felt this bad in the past, were you ever hopeless about the future? Do you ever feel like that now? Have you ever thought that life was not worth living? Have you thought of harming yourself? What did you think of doing? Have you started preparing for this? Have you made a will? Checked your life insurance? Left instructions for your funeral? Paid your debts? Disposed of your pets? Who will miss you most?

An alternative is to use indirect strength-building ideas such as the "negative miracle" proposed by John Henden:[1] "Imagine that you have died from this episode of self-harm and that you are hovering above the grave during the funeral. Who is there? Who is upset? What do you wish you had tried? What do the people present say to each other?" Hendon uses ideas from Dolan (2000) and others: "On your deathbed many years from now, what has your life been like? If you could write wisdom from your future to yourself now, what advice would you give yourself?"

Unless the person has definite depressive symptoms, we encourage them to pursue social and solution-focused ideas for a few days before considering medication. Similarly, we ask their physicians to review the client's ideas and practices in a few days before commencing medication. What is important to remember here is that there are risks associated with putting powerful medications into the hands of those who think about harming themselves.

Loss

In acute loss and bereavement, the response to the miracle question will direct you either to crisis intervention or to future-building questions. If the only miracle they will consider is the return of the lost person, then it is best to focus on limited goals around crisis intervention, such as, *"How will you last out the day? How have you survived so far?"* Once their miracle no longer includes the return of the lost person, then, you can begin to ask questions aimed at eliciting preferred futures.

SCHEDULED ASSESSMENTS

General Orientation

In the outpatient or ambulatory service, there are a variety of presentations, but the urgency is less. For example, you will be referred clients with psychosis-like symptoms such as hearing voices or self-harming behavior where there is no immediate risk of death or injury. The usual opening words are, "You have been sent here because X wants . . ." or slightly better, "What's the problem?" Opening the consultation by asking, "What do you want to get out of being here?" immediately sets a new context.

It is necessary to collect the information required by your agency and to do any necessary paperwork. Postmodern workers often find this awkward, but I find that clients are realistic about it. In discussion, clients have politely made it clear that they expect some redundant questioning from every agency. Thoroughness in record keeping may be seen as evidence of competence, which is one variable that many clients regard as important. (The other key variable is warmth, although this is not reliably construed by clients.) I prefer to complete agency data collection first. Possible compliments and resources can be noted as well as useful information about problems and exceptions and their social context. Using their language and tracking their concerns throughout will help to build a collaborative relationship. You can then move on to scaling and the miracle question, which are framed in the usual way based, on the information about problem and goals that you have collected.

I encourage partners or significant others to join the interview if they arrive with the client. They can be useful resources for the client and can add to your knowledge of the problem. Excluding them is unlikely to draw their support for any plan that may be developed. In legal matters, their consent may be specifically required, as is the client's informed consent.

The assessment of generalized anxiety follows the usual solution-focused lines. Many such clients have experienced previous episodes and will have ideas about how to manage relapses. Panic attacks are often due to habitual chronic or acute-on-chronic overbreathing. A trial of hyperventilation will confirm the diagnosis by reproducing the initial symptoms. Regular practice of slow breathing will produce substantial improvement without the need for medication, solution-focused work, or a psychiatric label (Clark, Salkovskis, & Chalkley, 1985; Lum, 1981).

Medication

Reviewing people referred with "depression" gives the chance to look for biological symptoms and for inadequate doses of medication. You can move easily into solution-focused work from this conversation. There is no reason why medication and Solution-Focused Brief Therapy cannot be used at the same time. Knowledge of good practice with medication can be included in the consultation, encouraging cooperation with suitable treatment. A "not-knowing" perspective does not mean that you cannot propose experiments based on your own knowledge. I will say, for example, "In my experience, people with symptoms similar to yours have found medication helpful to control symptoms while matters are improving in other ways. Maybe you could try this option as well as your other ideas." As a mental health professional, you can educate yourself on standard protocols regarding antidepressant medications in order to encourage clients to give the medication enough time to have optimal effect.

Obtaining consent to treatment with medication is aided if you know how medication is used appropriately. When used in equivalent doses, there is little proven difference in efficacy between one antidepressant and another or one antipsychotic drug and another. The useful differences lie in the side effects, and this is a matter that can be negotiated in collaboration with the patient. A young man may resent erectile failure as a side effect whereas an elderly man may be more concerned by tremor. A patient who suspects others of threatening him is more likely to accept a drug that makes him calm and alert rather than one that has a sedative effect and thus makes him feel more vulnerable. These suggestions can be made through the patient or directly to the medical advisor.

The specific dose ranges required for effective treatment with individual antidepressant and antipsychotic drugs are known. Studies of drug metabolism enable us to predict when doses ought to be increased and to recognize when a particular medication has clearly failed. It is then time to augment or change the treatment program. In the same way, we know the average time by which drug treatment can safely be reduced and stopped. If you can describe the plan of care to patients in this way, they are much more likely to cooperate with the plan. In my experience, few can successfully follow recommendations for more than three medications daily.

For example, a woman asked for help with her sleep. She also had a number of formal depressive symptoms. There had been a temporary improvement with a low dose of a sedative antidepressant, after which she had stopped taking the tablets. Along with complimenting her on her existing strategies, she was advised to ask her doctor if the dose of antidepressant could be increased, because we knew that this would improve her sleep and was likely to produce further improvement in her depressive symptoms also.

Another example: An elderly man attended complaining of headaches and impotence. These were both common side effects of his antidepressant tablets, which he had taken for over two years. He was not depressed at interview and mentioned no depressive symptoms when discussing pre-session changes or exceptions. In his response to the miracle question, he described better enjoyment of physical activities and a better relationship with his wife. We advised him to report his complaints to his doctor and to ask if his antidepressants could be reduced or stopped.

Substance Abuse

It is now recognized that hearing voices is not uncommon in the general population. It is not directly linked with mental illness, although the UK Hearing Voices Network[2] estimates that only 20 percent of voices are exclusively pleasant. Help is sought mostly by those for whom the voices are unpleasant or frightening. Solution-focused approaches are helpful for those who want to modify the voices or their reaction to them. As far as mental health is concerned, it does not matter if someone hears voices provided that their external behavior is safe for themselves and others.

Those who are using amphetamine-based recreational drugs will develop voice-hearing and persecutory fears in many cases. Five percent of the population will develop symptoms from only one dose, but prolonged or heavy dosage will produce these symptoms in most people. It appears that these effects become more persistent with continued use and that (as with alcohol) the effects will become permanent in some. In my experience, low doses of antipsychotic medication appear to reduce the symptoms, but only single-case reports have been published (Brimstedt, 2002). Users of amphetamine-based drugs and solvents may develop diffuse cognitive impairment that may be irreversible. I have personally seen several young men associated with these drugs whose measurable IQ has fallen more than one standard deviation, and no sign of intellectual recovery has emerged after they have ceased substance misuse.

Substance misuse problems often respond well to solution-focused therapy. The clients find it less coercive than other models. Many persons suffering from substance misuse in the United Kingdom are young people whose backgrounds have been neglectful or damaging. As a result, they lack literacy and verbal skills although their lifestyle has made them astute in self-protection. For them, substance misuse offers rapid gratification that does not require intellectual effort or stable relationships. The relative simplicity of the solution-focused approach and its emphasis on small practical steps at their own pace makes it suitable for such clients.

Many studies have shown that for alcohol problems, brief interventions are the most effective choice (Hester & Miller, 1995). The exception is those who have short-term memory impairment due to alcohol-related thiamine deficiency. Such clients show stereotyped habits and have difficulty in visualising new futures. Blood tests will show impairment of pyruvate (sugar/starch) metabolism. High-dose parenteral thiamine brings about improvement in cognitive function in about two-thirds of such cases. Their ability to think abstractly and to envisage new futures increases, although not all will then decide to reduce their drinking (cf. Cook & Thomson, 1997; Macdonald, 1994a).

Other Disorders

Obsessive-compulsive disorder is regarded by conventional psychiatry as a difficult and intractable disorder requiring lengthy treatment. In my experience, it responds well and quickly to solution-focused therapy, sometimes in combination with clomipramine (Anafranil) or high-dose fluoxetine (Prozac), both of which are antidepressants with specific benefits in some cases of obsessive-compulsive disorder. The solution-focused approach follows the usual pattern exactly. We advise that clients continue existing medication and ask their doctors about an increase of medication if it is not at the maximum recommended in the formulary. If solution-focused therapy alone is not effective within five sessions, then we suggest that they ask their doctor about the possibility of medication in addition.

Eating disorders will often respond well to solution-focused ideas (Jacob, 2001). In bulimia, this can usefully be combined with high-dose fluoxetine (Prozac), which reduces carbohydrate craving and thus makes it easier to reduce bingeing behavior. For the same reason, fluoxetine is sought by those with anorexia nervosa and should not be prescribed for them because it makes weight loss easier. In most cases, the emotional apathy and cognitive slowing seen in anorexia are due to malnutrition and not depression (Kingston, Szmukler, Andrewes, & Desmond, 1996; Kumar & Clark, 2002; Macdonald, 1997). Both bulimia and anorexia nervosa have been recognized as consequences of ascetic religious practice since 2500 BCE (Suzuki, 1970). Emotional responses become blunted below 1,500 calories daily, whatever the cause of the restriction, and limiting calorie intake is a traditional method of controlling subject populations and the residents of institutions.

In anorexia nervosa, it is best to avoid complex conversation and to pursue feeding with a normal diet until emotions reappear. Initially, emotions are simple expressions of sadness or anger as the ability to feel emotion returns. Then, emotions that are more complex arise and some degree of conversation can be helpful, moving later to formal solution-focused work if necessary. Families need to be advised of this sequence and encouraged to focus on brief positive comments instead of complex or critical advice. Small doses of chlorpromazine (Thorazine) help initially as it is antiemetic and encourages weight gain. Large doses of medication and overenthusiastic refeeding carry physical risks for the client. We have not found it helpful to use strict behavior modification or to restrict activity, but we have found it helpful to have someone sit with the client for one hour after meals to discourage immediate vomiting. A body mass index (kg/m^2, or weight in kilograms divided by [height in meters squared]) of 13 or less allows legal detention in the United Kingdom. Whether detained or not, we advise bed rest until their weight passes this level because of the risk of cardiac arrest due to biochemical imbalance. Above this weight, their activity is unrestricted as long as weight gain continues. Any subsequent weight loss leads to 24 hours in bed before returning to activity. Many clients manage their own problems adequately once refeeding has restored their cognitive abilities, but some benefit from further solution-focused work.

Team Treatment

A good community team will try to limit the number of people working with one client or family. This is less confusing for clients as well as being more efficient in managerial terms. In some countries, the extensive welfare system makes this difficult. Seikkula and colleagues (2003) and others (including Andersen, 1995) have described approaches to this issue. For ourselves, if someone is referred who already has workers or therapists in place, we assume that a new referral would not have been made if the existing therapy were successful. We negotiate with the other therapist(s) and the client about the care plan. This can involve suggesting that solution-focused work is easier if other therapies temporarily are suspended. Or, one can suggest that if current inputs have not been sufficient, then they should be stopped until after a trial of solution-focused brief therapy followed by a case review. Most colleagues will accept such plans provided they are phrased as alternatives and not as criticism. Sometimes, a break from therapy with the other therapist is acceptable; sometimes, legal issues require the other worker to remain in contact, but perhaps less frequently.

MANAGEMENT OF THE ACUTELY
DISTURBED INPATIENT

Inpatient admission should only be for specific indications and not as an all-purpose panacea. There are many studies showing the disadvantages of hospital care. These start with investigations into the care provided by private madhouses in the early nineteenth century. Mental health legislation was originally intended to protect the sufferer, not society. Then, Goffman's (1968) *Asylums* came on the scene, and many inquiries in hospitals across the world have informed our views since then. The film *One Flew Over the Cuckoo's Nest* (1975; Kesey, 1962) provoked many shades of response, but no one denied that the hospital depicted might exist.

Useful functions of hospital care include the assessment of complex cases and providing safe conditions for the patient and the community while assessment is done. In all cases, assessment should be targeted and brief. Inpatient care may also be necessary for specialized treatments that carry risks. Our service also offered 48-hour "nontreatment" admission on demand for those whose lives give rise to recurrent crises and seven-day "low stimulation" admissions (bed rest, no visitors, no radio or TV) for those whose goals include "a rest." Most of the latter soon find that simple rest is unhelpful and decide to move into more active pursuit of their goals.

It is helpful to see people soon after admission. As always, I begin by asking them what they want to get from their stay. This shifts their perception from being at the mercy of the system to having some say in their own affairs again. We seek to make the "official" diagnosis at an early stage, after which the focus can be future management. We will not discuss specific symptoms again unless there is a good reason for doing so. There may be target symptoms that they wish to work on, or they may have goals based on their everyday life.

It is important to check whether symptoms are useful in some way. For example, one patient would only eat food that his dog had identified as safe. He could not tell us how the dog communicated this information to him, but he was prepared to starve rather than risk eating food without this safety check. As a result, we had to admit his dog to hospital also. (Unfortunately, it brought in fleas and we had to fumigate the unit after they were discharged.)

Steve de Shazer (1998) has suggested that therapy cannot be done unless a conversation is possible. Some acutely disturbed people speak in the form of a conversation, but there is no exchange of information. Whatever the interviewer says, replies are in the same or similar words about some preoccupation. Therapy appears to be ineffective at this stage; however, using the client's language as much as possible assists the development of helpful relationships later.

The incidence of violence in our secure unit was reduced once we introduced solution-focused concepts. We believe that this was due to our clients' recognizing our interest in their wishes as opposed to imposing external rules. Length of stay was also reduced. Whatever one's theoretical stance, many urgent admissions have been short of food, drink, and sleep for some time. A day of calm and quiet with plenty of food and fluids often produces substantial improvement in understanding and collaboration. Offering medication is often acceptable at this point provided it is framed as being, in part, to "help with sleep." Several short interviews over a few days are often best when long interviews are tiring; clients' concentration and their recall of the agreed treatment plan may both be limited. Solution-focused methods are ideal for this style.

A case example: An elderly man was admitted from a rented holiday house. He had education and money but kept all his possessions in a van and moved to a new accommodation every few weeks. He had called the police in the early hours because of "intruders" outside. He had put his telephone in a box and buried it under cushions, and he had glued carpet over the windows. On arrival, he said, "They follow me everywhere. They torment me all night. I don't know how they find me again so quickly after I move." He was politely adamant that he was not unwell and that his experiences were real. He accepted an antipsychotic drug in a single night-time dose when told that one of its effects would be to improve his sleep. Within three days he was stable and contented. His belief in the "intruders" decreased steadily over the next four weeks, after which he left hospital and continued his medication as recommended.

Psychiatric intensive care units in the United Kingdom usually offer short-term admissions of weeks rather than months. We found that solution-focused ideas were useful because relationships developed quickly. Goals and plans were easy to transfer from one worker to another, thus making the best use of time in the unit. If the client's goal was simply to get out of the unit as soon as possible, then we described the necessary steps toward discharge. We advised them that certain behaviors were unlikely to speed their progress toward discharge. Clients appreciated the clarity of knowing which behaviors were used to judge progress. The staff used their own expertise to determine when a client could move from one level of security to the next.

We negotiate medication as a part of helping these clients function better. Sometimes this requires us to say, "We respect your beliefs about medication, but we believe that medication is essential at the moment." Clear information about medication assists the process of negotiation. If we do not know whether medication will help, we present the idea in terms of an experiment with clear goals and a fixed time limit. Of course, many patients have previous experience of medication, and we ask if there were any specific medications that they found helpful or unhelpful. Many also know that we have the legal power to enforce medication, although this is more useful for emergencies than as a part of a regular program. Generally, we will aim for a single antipsychotic drug adding benzodiazepines if necessary for urgent sedation. The latter are relatively free of side effects and are popular with the recipients. They may cause impaired recall, which some clients dislike, while others take advantage of it to deny all memory of inappropriate conduct.

Patients are often comfortable with small steps and exceptions initially. Once they become more at ease in the unit, they are able to aim for larger goals and to learn what services are available that will help them to achieve what they want. Scaling is a valuable tool both for symptoms and for other behaviors, although scales do not seem to work well for elated patients:

STAFF: "If ten is completely well and able to leave the hospital, what number are you at?"

PATIENT: "Fifteen!"

STAFF: "What number do you want to achieve eventually?"

PATIENT: "Twenty!"

Such patients often see attempts to restrict their goals and self-confidence as being unhelpful. Sometimes, they may accept that their significant others prefer them to be lower on the scale. Some elated individuals are willing to work with reversed scales in which they are at 10 now but will be accepted for discharge by others at some lower point.

Not every team member wants to work in a solution-focused way. This does not give rise to conflicts as long as all points of view are respected. The examinations of psychotherapy outcome that were published by Seligman (1995) and Wampold (2001) show that both a model that fits the client's concepts and a model to which the therapist has allegiance will produce better outcomes. It is therefore best to have more than one approach available within the team. Many workers already have their own skills. They may adopt solution-focused brief therapy as another possible option, using their own judgment as to which option to adopt with any one client, or they may use only their preferred model, advising the rest of the team when they see a place for their specific skill.

Clients with long-term problems also find Solution-Focused Brief Therapy helpful. This can include disability linked to mental illness, acquired brain injury, and learning disability. It is useful to aim for small steps, focusing on daily living skills. The therapist is best to use simple, clear language and to persist with the program over long periods. The client may benefit from advice along behavioral lines about breaking goals into small, achievable steps. Greenberg (1998) has pioneered solution-focused groups for clients with long-term mental health problems. He focuses on goals ("What do you want to achieve?"), scaling, the next step with the aid of advice from the group, and the recurring question, "What have you achieved since the last time you attended?" He emphasizes the role of the group leader in keeping up the level of activity and discussion in such groups. In his experience, clients may walk in and out of the group or may miss sessions without problems for the group and without detriment to the eventual achievement of goals by the client. This approach to groups is useful in supportive work and in day centers.

Inpatient Case Example

John X had been disturbed for two to three days before being detained under legal powers at his home. He resisted ambulance transfer and was transported to the secure unit in handcuffs by the police. He was interviewed three hours after arrival.

First Interview

INTERVIEWER (*Introduces self and nurse*): What would you like to get out of being here?

JOHN: They sent me here; it's not me; they've done it before. They've got it in for me; they know what it's all about; you know, too.

I: Who is this "they?"

J: They know what it's all about. They sent me here; it's not me. You have it all on camera.

I: What cameras?

J: The cameras in my house. You know what it's all about.

I: I have not seen any cameras or tapes.

J: You know what it's all about. They've done it before.

I: How come it led to you coming here?

J: They know what it's all about. It's not me; they sent me here; they've done it. You should be talking to them, not to me.

I: We will talk about it all after you have had some rest. We will give you some medication to help you sleep. Be sure to tell us if anything similar happens while you are here.

Next Day

I (*introduces self and nurse*): We talked briefly yesterday. We wonder what you would like to get from being here.

J: They need to stop what they are doing. They want to hurt me. I can't go to the shop.

I: What have you done about what is being done?

J: I went to the town council, but their man said he could not do anything unless he could hear it. I told him to come back at night to hear it but he would not. The police say they cannot do anything until they see something on their cameras in the street.

I: What do you think they will see on their cameras?

J: The neighbors hammer on my door and shout at night. They are clever about doing it when the police cameras are not looking.

I: Do you think you could be mistaken about the neighbors' doing this?

J: No. I know it's them.

I: Did you ever have this hammering and shouting before?

J: It happened before five years ago but they stopped after I had been in hospital.

I: Stopped . . . when did it start again?

J: About four months ago after my medication was changed.

I: As well as the hammering and shouting, what else has been happening in recent months that bothers you?

J: I lose sleep because of the noise; I can't eat properly because I can't stay in the shop for long in case someone gets in at home. They know when I'm out because their cameras are inside my flat.

I: Did you manage to sleep last night in here?

J: Yes, because the neighbors could not get past the night staff. Your tablet did not do much.

I: Did the staff get you something to eat?

J: I did not like the hot meal but the staff had lots of sandwiches sent over for me, and they made me tea.

I: Are there ever any specific references to you on the TV or in the newspapers?

J: No. There was a letter in the paper from someone called John but it was not me.

I: Does all this make it difficult to keep your mind on things like reading the paper?

J: No, not if I get enough sleep.

I (*confirms by specific questions that John has accurate knowledge of current events, that depressive symptoms are absent, and that he does not use street drugs. He has no signs of drug withdrawal and drug screening is negative.*): Do you drink alcohol at all?

J: If I have enough money, I can buy beer at the supermarket, but I don't usually go there because it is too far from my flat.

(*Interviewer is now satisfied that a diagnosis of paranoid illness can be made, fixed false beliefs and auditory hallucinations being present, but with no signs of thought disorder, ideas of reference or impairment of concentration or memory. Depression and substance misuse are not present. The necessary administrative processes can now be completed; therefore, the focus of conversation becomes the treatment plan.*)

I: So what helped to deal with this when it happened before?

J: I could eat and sleep in the hospital; I took the medication to keep myself calm. Nurse Y used to come and visit; I think maybe the neighbors knew about her and so they kept away in case she saw them.

I: How come Nurse Y stopped visiting?

J: She retired and I did not want someone new.

I: Someone took over after she retired; do you want to have them visit?

J: Dunno—I would need to see them first.

I: We can arrange for them to come and see you here. Let us know what you think. What medication was helpful in the past?

J: Not the yellow tablets; they made my hands shake. I don't remember their name but I know what they taste like.

I: The tablets we prefer now do not usually make the hands shake. You took one last night; are your hands shaky just now?

J: No.

I: We plan to increase the tablets tonight and again tomorrow night. After that, they will stay the same until we see how it goes. Is that all right with you?

J: I'd rather not take tablets; I want to get out of here.

I: We think that taking the tablets will help you to get out of here sooner. Make sure to tell us if your hands shake or there are other problems for you. Is there anything else you want to mention today?

J: They need to sort out my money. If they don't, my rent will not be paid.

I: What do they need to sort out?

J: I stopped opening the envelopes so I don't know if I am due any money.

I: How do you find out what you are due now?

J: Someone could ask the Benefits Agency.

I: Who could ask them?

J: My aunt does not speak to me now. Could I go to the phone?

I: There is a phone in here that you can use. It is too soon for you to go out for walks with staff at present.

J: I don't know if I want to use the phone in here.

I: One of the staff has a special knowledge of the welfare system. He can talk with you about what you will say when you do use the phone to call them.

J: Okay.

I: So, thinking about a scale of zero-to-ten, where "ten" is you are out of hospital and things are going well, and "zero" is as bad as things were before, where are you right now on that scale?

J: Zero.

I: So how have you kept going when you are at zero?

J: Getting some sleep helped.

I: So sleep is really important for you. When you move up half a point on the scale, what will be different for you?

J: I won't feel like hitting people.

I: Who did you feel like hitting?

J: The neighbors and that policeman. He had no right to put handcuffs on me.

I: How come the police were there?

J: I told the ambulance man I would cut him if he tried to come into my flat.

I: Have you cut anyone before? Or hit anyone?

J: No, but I would have done it.

I: How come you did not do that?

J: They came in before I could get a knife from the kitchen.

I: Do you still think about getting a knife or cutting someone?

J: I sometimes think about it.

I: How do you manage to think about it but not do it?

J: I think to myself that they will put me in hospital again if I cut someone. The neighbors might get me for it while I was sleeping.

I: Are there specific people that you think of cutting, neighbors or anyone else?

J: I felt like hitting that policeman.

I: Have you thought about cutting or hitting anyone in this hospital?

J: No.

I: How can we tell if you are thinking about cutting someone or hitting someone?

J: I don't know.

I: Will you tell us if you are thinking that?

J: (*No reply*)

I: When you are thinking like that, what can we do that will help?

J: Let me stay in my room; the other people here are strange.

I: Will you tell us when you need to stay in your room?

J: Yes.

I: Okay. We will ask you if we are not sure. I guess that hitting or cutting someone will not help you to get out of hospital sooner.

J: (*Nods*)

I: Anything else to mention today?

J: No. I'm tired of talking just now.

Two Days Later

His key worker asked John X the miracle question during an individual interview. He replied that miracles did not happen. He went on to say that he did have "a dream" sometimes about how he wanted his life to be. This dream was explored as if it was a reply to the miracle question. He described living in the same flat but with somewhere to go for social contact ("not pubs because the rough people come in there") and the chance to play lawn bowls. His grandfather, dead many years ago, had taken him to try lawn bowls when he was a teenager and he believed that he had a talent for this game. The dream also included having his money "sorted out," being confident about his budgeting, and being able to visit different shops for his purchases.

John X talked with the staff about his money and made a plan. He showed no signs of violence and did not spend much time alone in his room. Our security precautions were gradually reduced and he was able to go for walks, first with staff and then alone for increasing periods. He decided that the phone in the unit was acceptable for his calls. He took his medication, joined the unit occupational program, and wrote to the local lawn bowling club for information. His suspicions about the neighbors were rarely mentioned. After meeting the nurse from the community team, he agreed to have her visit him at home. At times, he would stop his key worker in the corridor and say, "I'm still working on that dream!," but he rarely referred to it directly when talking with others. His eventual discharge home was successful after some five weeks in hospital.

Evaluation

Research Studies

We have published two formal evaluations of our outpatient work since 1988 (Macdonald, 1994b, 1997). A questionnaire is sent to clients and their family doctors one year after they cease to attend. Results from an additional cohort are presently being prepared for publication. Combining the three studies, 170 referrals were made, of whom 136 were seen and 118 (87 percent) traced for follow-up. The overall good outcome rate is 83 (70 percent) for a mean of 4.03 sessions per case. There is no significant difference between the groups in the solving of additional problems or the seeking of further professional help. New problems arose less often for the "good outcome" group, while those with long-standing problems do less well. In all three studies, there are no significant differences in outcome between socioeconomic groups. This is an important finding because all other psychotherapies are more effective for those from higher socioeconomic and educational groups. (Similar findings in relation to socioeconomic groups have been reported by De Jong and Hopwood [1996]. They have also reworked their data, including DSM-IV (APA, 1994) diagnoses for all cases [De Jong & Berg, 2002]). We also have submitted cases to the European Brief Therapy Association multicenter research project.

A Spanish study in a mental health clinic (Beyebach, Morejohn, Palenzuela, & Rodriguez-Arias, 1996) followed up 39 outpatients. Eighty percent had achieved their goals after an average of 5 sessions lasting a mean of 33 minutes per session. Concrete goals and pretreatment change seemed to predict better outcomes. Another study in Spain (Perez Grande,

1991) reported 97 cases of which 25 percent were children. An average of 5 sessions produced improvement in 71 percent of the cases. Eighty-one were traced for a telephone follow-up after a mean of 19 months. Of the 71 percent who originally improved, 12 percent had relapsed but 38 percent had solved additional problems. There were more dropouts from therapy if the problems were long standing.

A novel U.S. study by Eakes and colleagues (Eakes, Walsh, Markowski, Cain, & Swanson, 1997) described family-centered work in chronic schizophrenia. Experimental and control groups consisted of five clients and families each. A reflecting team was present and the miracle question was not used. In the experimental group, changes included a significant increase in expressiveness and active-recreational orientation with a decrease in incongruence. In the control families, the moral-religious emphasis increased. In Utah, Lambert, Okiishi, Finch, & Johnson (1998) compared 22 cases from a solution-focused private practice with 45 treated by psychodynamic methods at a university mental health center. Both methods achieved 46 percent recovery using a standard psychotherapy outcome measure. The Solution-Focused Brief Therapy cases had reached this improvement by the third session, those from the mental health center by the twenty-sixth session.

All of this research supports Solution-Focused Brief Therapy's claims of efficiency without sacrificing effectiveness. For further information, visit the European Brief Therapy Association's Web site: http://www.ebta.nu/.

Local Experiences

Those of our inpatient units that have favored collaborative/brief therapy approaches have had lower bed occupancy and a rapid turnover of clients. This has not been accompanied by any increase in adverse events. Our intensive care unit was often the only such unit in the North of England that could make beds available for emergencies from other counties. Our open wards were usually able to make beds available for urgent admissions and to provide "on-demand" crisis support as previously described. This low occupancy is uncommon in English psychiatry as bed numbers have been reduced nationally by 60 percent since 1978. Similar experience with inpatient services in Colorado has been reported by Vaughn and her colleagues (Vaughn, Young, Webster, & Thomas, 1996) using similar collaborative approaches.

In a previous hospital, our team's unit served the distant parts of the county. The neighboring team had a near-identical building for an equivalent catchment population. Our unit was relatively peaceful and always had beds available even though our clients had more difficulty with access to family and home because of the distances involved. The neighboring unit was always full with a high incidence of disturbance. For about eight months, there was a quiet but sustained campaign by the other team, pressing for us to exchange buildings with them. Eventually we realized that they thought that the magic lay in the building itself. They hoped to emulate our outcomes by exchanging buildings. Interesting explanations abound when clients find success.

The Wider System

Within the hospital, our skills were acknowledged with respect from the administration and by being allowed to practice as we wished. However, we were subject to the same financial and bureaucratic restraints as everyone else. An excellent safety assessment tool was devised by a non-solution-focused colleague centring on scales for various aspects of safety measured by both client and workers. It was replaced by a purchased instrument with no adequate evidence base and that relied on repetitive collection of factual data while neglecting all aspects of judgment or relationship. It was therefore comprehensible to the hospital administration but did not use most of the information gathered by trained and experienced clinical staff.

The Care Program Approach is a national tool imposed by central government. It is rigid and stereotyped in its effect, with a substantial focus on problem talk and the medical model. It does offer the client a voice but does not allow for negotiation with or respect for the client beyond being present and being asked to comment. Because it was imposed, many staff resisted it from the outset, which reduced our flexibility in adapting it to our preferences. Happily, as time has gone on, it has been possible to shift most of the conversations within the Care Program Approach toward identifying improvements, exceptions, and resources.

Solution-focused ideas proved valuable within the hospital administration. Their use at management level has allowed us make the best of existing resources, including reducing the time spent in meetings. One needs to take account of the fact that for an administrator, a meeting is a social high point adding knowledge, reinforcing hierarchy and group membership, and postponing less attractive activities. For clinical staff, the high point of the day is employing clinical expertise; meeting administrators who have different and sometimes conflicting interests is not valued in the same way.

COMMON PROBLEMS
AFFECTING INPATIENT TREATMENT

The legal system and mental health laws are constructed around a problem focus. Formal reports for courts about offenders and in reviews of detention are required to contain problem-focused information. It can be difficult for clients to understand why the workers who talk continually about solutions with them will then offer problem-focused material to outside agencies. I try to maintain a therapeutic relationship with the client by including some compliments on their efforts to change and achieve goals. Another option is that the senior practitioner remains problem-focused while other staff do the solution-focused work. However, this creates a split in the staff team, which may become divisive. Community support teams in the United Kingdom are usually organized in the name of the senior practitioner, so that collaboration may decrease if that person is not viewed as supportive by the client.

Many individuals within our hospital have had training in Solution-Focused Brief Therapy. However, some units do not employ solution-focused approaches and may not continue our treatment plans or accept our formulations and safety assessments. This can delay discharge and create tensions for clients. On some occasions, the hospital administration was unable to tolerate our estimates of safety and chose to place clients elsewhere instead of accepting our recommendations for discharge.

The solution-focused model addresses, "What now?" It does not contradict clients' perceptions of events although it may offer other possible perceptions. When clients were still in contact with their families of origin, we have sometimes tried to go beyond the solution-focused approach to explore their behavior within the family or social context (Seikkula et al., 2003). This has been fruitful in some cases and not in others. It appears that we have had most success with this when the whole care team has been involved in the process. When this is not the case, then traditional values and approaches have reasserted themselves and all collaborative work has become more difficult. This has not appeared to be linked to any specific features of the cases.

CONCLUSION

Solution-Focused Brief Therapy has a significant evidence base; however, we know from the work of Seligman (1995), Wampold (2001), and others (see Bergin & Garfield, 1994) that there is no clear advantage for any specific model of psychotherapy. Solution-focused brief therapy offers benefits because it is cost-efficient. It is easy to learn the basics of the approach and it can be applied in a wide variety of situations, reducing the need for other skills. It is easy to record clearly for administrative purposes and care plans are easy to pass to colleagues within the team. We found that team and multidisciplinary meetings were shorter and more effective once a solution-focused framework was adopted.

NOTES

1. John Henden has not published these but makes them freely available through the Web site of a colleague: http://www.st-matthew.on.ca/bulletin/jeremy/4tech.pdf
2. http://www.patient.co.uk/showdoc/26739000/

REFERENCES

Aaltonen, J., Seikkula, J., Alakare, B., Haarakangas, K., Keranen, J., & Sutela, M. (1997). Western Lapland Project: A comprehensive family-and network-centered community psychiatric project. *ISPS, Abstracts and Lectures, 124*, 12-6.

American Psychiatric Association. (1994). Quick reference to the diagnostic criteria from DSM-IV. Washington, DC: Author.

Andersen, T. (1995). Reflecting processes, acts of informing and forming: You can borrow my eyes but you must not take them away from me! In S. Friedman (Ed.), *The reflecting team in action: Collaborative practice in family therapy* (pp. 11-37). New York: Guilford Press.

Bagadia, V. N., Shah, L. P., Pradhan, P. V., & Gada, M. T. (1979). Treatment of mental disorder in India. *Progress in Neuro-Psychopharmacology, 3*, 109-118.

Bergin, S., & Garfield, A. (Eds.). (1994). *Handbook of psychotherapy and behaviour change* (4th ed.). New York: Wiley.

Beyebach, M., Morejon, A. R., Palenzuela, D. L., & Rodriguez-Arias, J. L. (1996). Research on the process of solution-focused brief therapy. In S. D. Miller, M. A. Hubble, & B. L. Duncan (Eds.), *Handbook of solution-focused brief therapy* (pp. 299-334). San Francisco: Jossey-Bass.

Brimstedt, L. (2002). Is risperidone the right choice in strongly drug-related psychoses? *Lakartidning, 95*, 368 (letter; original in Danish).

Clark, D. M., Salkovskis, P. M., & Chalkley, A. J. (1985). Respiratory control as a treatment for "panic attacks." *Journal of Behaviour Therapy and Experimental Psychiatry, 16*, 23-30.

Cook, C. C. H., & Thomson, A. D. (1997). B-complex vitamins in the prophylaxis and treatment of Wernicke-Korsakoff syndrome. *British Journal of Hospital Medicine, 57*, 461-465.

De Jong, P., & Berg, I. K. (2002). *Interviewing for solutions* (2nd ed.). Pacific Grove, CA: Brooks/Cole.

De Jong, P., & Hopwood, L. E. (1996). Outcome research on treatment conducted at the Brief Family Therapy Center 1992-1993. In S. D. Miller, M. A. Hubble, & B. L. Duncan (Eds.), *Handbook of solution-focused brief therapy* (pp. 272-298). San Francisco: Jossey-Bass.

de Shazer, S. (1998, September). Plenary discussion, European Brief Therapy Association Annual Conference, Bruges, Belgium.

DeSisto, M., Harding, C. M., McCormick, R. V., Ashikaga, T., & Brooks, G. W. (1995). The Maine and Vermont three-decade studies of serious mental illness: I. Matched comparison of cross-sectional outcome; II. Longitudinal course comparisons. *British Journal of Psychiatry, 167,* 331-342.

Dolan, Y. (2000). *Beyond survival: Living well is the best revenge.* London: BT Press.

Eakes, G., Walsh, S., Markowski, M., Cain, H., & Swanson, M. (1997). Family-centred brief solution-focused therapy with chronic schizophrenia: A pilot study. *Journal of Family Therapy, 19,* 145-158.

Garfield, A. E., & Bergin, S. L. (Eds.). (1986). *Handbook of psychotherapy and behaviour change* (3rd ed.). New York: Wiley.

Gelder, M., Gath, D., Mayou, R., & Owen, P. (1996). *Oxford textbook of psychiatry* (3rd ed.). Oxford: Oxford University Press.

Goffman, E. (1968). *Asylums.* Harmondsworth: Penguin.

Greenberg, G. S. (1998). Brief, change-delineating group therapy with acute and chronically mentally ill clients: An achievement-oriented approach. In W. A. Ray & S. de Shazer (Eds.), *Evolving brief therapies* (pp. 220-232). Iowa City: Geist and Russell.

Harding, C. M., Brooks, G. W., Ashikaga, T., Strauss, J. S., & Breier, A. (1987). The Vermont longitudinal study of persons with severe mental illness: I. Methodology, study sample and overall status thirty-two years later. *American Journal of Psychiatry, 144,* 718-726.

Hester, R. K., & Miller, W. R. (Eds.). (1995). *Handbook of alcoholism treatment approaches: Effective alternatives* (2nd ed.). New Jersey: Pearson Allyn Bacon.

Jacob, F. (2001). *Solution focused recovery from eating distress.* London: BT Press.

Jones, M. (1968). *Beyond the therapeutic community: Social learning and social psychiatry.* New Haven: Yale University Press.

Jorm, A. F., Korten, A. E., Jacomb, P. A., Rodgers, B., Pollitt, P., Christensen, H., & Henderson, S. (1997). Helpfulness of interventions for mental disorders: Beliefs of health professionals compared with the general public. *British Journal of Psychiatry, 171,* 233-237.

Kesey, K. (1962). *One flew over the cuckoo's nest.* London: Picador (Film version 1975).

Kingston, K., Szmukler, G., Andrewes, B. T., & Desmond, P. (1996). Neuropsychological and structural brain changes in anorexia nervosa before and after refeeding. *Psychological Medicine, 26,* 15-28.

Kumar, P., & Clark, M. (2002). *Clinical medicine* (5th ed.). Edinburgh: WB Saunders.

Lambert, M. J., Okiishi, J. C., Finch, A. E., & Johnson, L. D. (1998). Outcome assessment: From conceptualization to implementation. *Professional Psychology: Research & Practice, 29*, 63-70.

Lum, L. C. (1981). Hyperventilation and anxiety state. *Journal of the Royal Society of Medicine, 74*, 1-4.

Macdonald, A. J. (1994a). A paper that changed my practice: Reversible mental impairment in alcoholics. *British Medical Journal, 308*, 1678.

Macdonald, A. J. (1994b). Brief therapy in adult psychiatry. *Journal of Family Therapy, 16*, 415-426.

Macdonald, A. J. (1997). Brief therapy in adult psychiatry: Further outcomes. *Journal of Family Therapy, 19*, 213-222.

Macdonald, A. J. (2000). Recommended reading for trainees. *Psychiatric Bulletin, 24*, 154 (letter).

Patel, V., & Saxena, S. (2003). Psychiatry in India. *International Psychiatry: Bulletin of the Board of International Affairs of the Royal College of Psychiatrists, 1*, 16-18.

Perez Grande, M. D. (1991). Evaluacion de resultados en terapia sistemica breve (Outcome research in brief systemic therapy). *Cuadernos de Terapia Familiar, 18*, 93-110.

Reicher-Rossler, A., & Rossler, W. (1993). Compulsory admission of psychiatric patients—An international comparison. *Acta Psychiatrica Scandinavia, 87*, 231-236.

Roffe, D., & Roffe, C. (1995). Madness and care in the community: A medieval perspective. *British Medical Journal, 311*, 708-712.

Seikkula, J., Alakare, B., & Aaltonen, J. (2000). A two-year follow-up on open dialogue treatment in first episode psychosis: Need for hospitalization and neuroleptic medication decreases. *Social and Clinical Psychiatry, 10*, 20-29.

Seikkula, J., Arnkil, T. E., & Eriksson, E. (2003). Postmodern society and social networks: Open and anticipation dialogues in network meetings. *Family Process, 42*, 185-203.

Seligman, M. E. P. (1995). The effectiveness of psychotherapy: The Consumer Reports study. *American Psychologist, 50*, 965-974.

Suzuki, S. (1970). *Zen mind, beginner's mind.* New York: Weatherhill.

Swartz, L. (1998). *Culture and mental health: A South African view.* Oxford: Oxford University Press.

Vaughn, K., Young, B. C., Webster, D. C., & Thomas, M. R. (1996). A continuum-of-care model for inpatient psychiatric treatment. In S. D. Miller, M. A. Hubble, & B. L. Duncan (Eds.), *Handbook of solution-focused brief therapy* (pp. 99-127). San Francisco: Jossey-Bass.

Wampold, B. E. (2001). *The great psychotherapy debate: Models, methods, and findings.* New Jersey: Lawrence Erlbaum Associates.

Chapter 13

Thinking and Practicing Beyond the Therapy Room: Solution-Focused Brief Therapy, Trauma, and Child Protection

Andrew Turnell .

INTRODUCTION

Solution-Focused Brief Therapy (SFBT), created in the 1980s, evolved out of the longer-standing brief or interactional approach to therapy. Brian Cade, in an introductory chapter of this book, already has summarized this history. Practitioners within this brief therapy tradition have always thought about human problems and their resolution at least somewhat differently to more mainstream therapists.

The brief tradition, since its inception, has always pursued a non-normative and nonpathological stance to clients and their problems (Fisch, 1988). Brief therapists see problems not as something inherent or endogenous to the individual, but rather as behavior manifested and sustained in the interactional patterns of people's (including professionals) relating to the person said to have the problem. Most radically, brief therapists have always said that it is the client rather than the professional who should define the nature of the problem and its solution. These are some of the key foundational ideas that underpin the interactional brief therapy tradition.

This sort of thinking reflects perhaps the anarchistic temperament of brief therapists; we like to see *ourselves,* as well as our clients, thinking and doing something different. Milton Erickson, a forefather of the brief therapy tradition, was famous for being willing to be different, and was very willing

Handbook of Solution-Focused Brief Therapy: Clinical Applications
© 2007 by The Haworth Press, Inc. All rights reserved.
doi:10.1300/5135_13

to work with his patients outside of the therapy room. Erickson, for example, is known to have gone out to dinner with one of his patients to help the man deal with his shyness around women, and to have challenged a young patient to a bicycle race (Haley, 1973). The desire to do something different has also meant leading figures of the brief therapy movement often have sought to take the ideas and practices of brief therapy beyond the privatized context of the therapy room to respond to human problems in wider contexts. Examples include applications to child protection services (Berg & Kelly, 2000; Turnell & Edwards, 1997, 1999; Weakland & Jordan, 1992); care of the elderly (Herr & Weakland, 1979); domestic violence group work (Lee, Sebold, & Uken, 2003); the operation and services of a psychiatric residential center (Soo-Hoo, 1995); work in schools (Durrant, 1995); and residential care (Durrant, 1993).

This paper will present some of my own experiences of applying Solution-Focused Brief Therapy thinking and practices beyond the therapy room. I will look specifically at:

- Working with child protection services.
- Assessment in child protection and with traumatized refugees.
- Services to severely traumatized or tortured refugees.
- Writing stories of case practice with clients as co-authors.

CHILD PROTECTION SERVICES: FOCUSING ON THE GOOD PRACTICE OF FRONTLINE WORKERS

The first instinct of almost anyone discussing child protection services, whether they are talking in parliament or in a pub, is to relate their version of a horror story describing poor, mistake ridden, and oppressive practices by child protection workers and their organizations. The regular retelling of these sorts of stories at all levels of our communities constantly problematizes statutory child protection practice, escalating the defensiveness of frontline workers and thereby contributing to a professional context where vulnerable children are made less rather than more safe.

Brief therapists would not be surprised at this since we have always pointed out that where problem talk flourishes, the problem typically becomes more entrenched. A typical solution-focused response to the dilemma of problem talk is for the therapist to ask the client about times when the problem could have happened but did not, or to focus on life when it is going well. In creating and evolving the signs of safety approach, it has been a fundamental practice for Steve Edwards and me (Turnell & Edwards,

1999) to approach child protection workers from a spirit of solution-focused inquiry, asking them to describe self-defined, good practice with difficult cases or situations.

Working closely with child protection practitioners in Europe, North America, Japan, and Australasia, I know that child protection workers are doing good work, with some of the "hardest" families, in the busiest child protection offices, in the poorest locations, everywhere in the world. This is not to say that oppressive child protection practice does not happen, or that sometimes it may even be the norm. However, worker-defined, good practice with "difficult" cases is an invaluable and almost entirely overlooked resource for improving child protection services. The local knowledge of worker-defined good practice is a potent strategy for building service deliverer-guided organizational change, particularly radical in times of the rampant managerialism. Interestingly, the focus on successful, rather than problematic organizational behavior is the primary change mechanism of the burgeoning appreciative inquiry movement (e.g., Cooperrider & Srivastva, 1987; Watkins & Mohr, 2001). I would argue that while the appreciative inquiry movement talks extensively about the importance of good practice, the solution-focused literature, probably because of its longer history at the task, has a more highly refined skill base for eliciting and amplifying good practice. Solution-focused "technology" for amplifying good practice is best articulated in our conceptualizations of the EARS (elicit, amplify, reinforce or reflect, start-over) inquiry process used in second and subsequent sessions (Berg & De Jong, 1999; Turnell & Hopwood, 1994).

I have been consulting in this way with child protection practitioners for more than 10 years and have described elsewhere many examples of and processes for eliciting child protection good practice (see Turnell, 2004, 2006; Turnell & Edwards, 1997; Turnell, Lorhbach, & Curran, in press). Despite this, I continue to be frequently astounded by the innovative and creative strategies some child protection workers are able to bring to their highly challenging role. Recently, I was consulting in an English social services agency with a child protection worker we will call Miriam, who described the following story to me. Miriam had to undertake a home visit to talk with the father of an eight-year-old girl who had bruises on her arms. The girl had earlier in the day told Miriam that her father had caused the bruises. After introducing herself to the father, who lived on the seventeenth floor of a housing estate block of flats, the man began to yell at Miriam, finishing by screaming at her that she should "f*** off!" Miriam told me that she waited a moment and said to the man, "Okay, I can f*** off, but we have to talk, so when can I f*** back?" In response, the man laughed and said, "Ah, well, you'd better come in, luv." Following this, Miriam quickly built a good working relationship with the father and together they were able to focus on creating safety commensurate to the problem.

I am in no way suggesting that all child protection workers should act in the same manner as Miriam did when faced with an angry client. I would suggest, however, that eliciting, writing up, and disseminating Miriam's example and many like it will encourage other child protection workers to generate their own creative ways of meeting the demands of their work and at the same time, honouring the usually overlooked practice wisdom of frontline workers. As Miriam's case also demonstrates well, inductively theorizing good practice from child protection practitioners' own live work experiences brings an immediacy and humanness to the framing of child protection work that more distant theorizing will usually not achieve.

This good practice method of training and consulting to child protection workers operationalises the foundational brief therapy notion that it is the person in the middle of the situation who is the most important expert about the problem and its solution. Further, it seems to me, that if frontline practitioners are going to utilise solution-focused, strengths-based approaches in their work, it is crucial that their supervisors and consultants honour and amplify the workers' own good practices before asking the workers to focus on the strengths and solutions of their clients. Imagine how different child protection practice might be if even half the organizational resources that are usually directed toward child death inquiries were brought to bear to create a rigourous, ongoing inquiry process into frontline defined, good practice with "difficult" cases in the statutory agency near you.

DOING ASSESSMENT WITH CLIENTS/SERVICE RECIPIENTS

Assessment is something professionals typically do to clients. The more severe the problem, the more likely it is that professionals will want an assessment done and the more likely it is that professional view will dominate. Brief therapists who seek to privilege the client's perspective have therefore frequently seen assessment as a highly problematic undertaking. I have had long involvement in child protection practice and also worked as a therapist in an organization serving traumatized and tortured refugees, and in both contexts, assessments are usually organizationally mandated. Following the brief therapy tradition of privileging the client's perspective, I have created assessment protocols that are designed to be done *with*, rather than done *to* the client. Both protocols can be found as attachments at the end of this chapter (Appendix).

After completing the questionnaire, the client is asked to review the answers and list the most significant attributes that have helped them deal with their problems over the last few years of their life and then to list the attributes they are most concerned about.

I was assisted in the development of the refugees' protocol by Yvonne Dolan, who had already created a similar assessment protocol for undertaking assessment with survivors of sexual abuse (Dolan, 1991). The protocol is fairly self-explanatory. It follows the symptomology typically associated with the posttraumatic stress disorder diagnosis, but describes these symptoms in common language and frames them in terms of solutions rather than problems. It also includes a list of typical practical problems that refugees often describe. The most important feature of the protocol is that it is designed to be understood by and completed with the client and for their answers to help the client and professional in identifying the problems that the client is most concerned about and to stimulate possible solutions. The reader should not regard this protocol as something final, but feel free to adapt it for any traumatized population and the contexts they find themselves working in.

Alongside Steve Edwards, I have also developed the signs of safety assessment and planning format for application to child protection casework (Turnell & Edwards, 1999) (see Figure 13.1). Within the child protection field, it is usually not possible to prioritize the client's view over that of the professional's since the child protection worker is mandated by law to arrive at a risk assessment. More typically, child protection assessment is highly professionalized and tends to erase the service recipient's perspective. The "signs of safety" format is designed to challenge this erasure process. It offers a simple yet rigourous assessment format that the practitioner can use to elicit, in common language, the professional *and* family members' views regarding concerns or dangers, existing strengths and safety, and envisioned safety. This format deepens and balances the usual problem saturation of most risk assessment. The "signs of safety" framework has subsequently been utilized as a template to integrate a strengths and safety focus within two statutory risk assessment frameworks (Boffa & Podestra, 2004; Department of Community Development, 2001; Department of Human Services, 2000).

Janet Flood, who works with Barnardos in Dundee Scotland, used the signs of safety assessment format when she was asked by the local statutory child protection agency to complete an assessment regarding a family that had a long social services involvement. The most recent problems involving this family focused around the 10-year-old we will call Jamie, who had been excluded from school on 14 separate occasions in a 3-month period

Signs of Safety Assessment and Planning Form

DANGER   List all aspects that indicate safety (exceptions, strengths, resources, goals, willingness, etc.).   **SAFETY**

List all aspects that demonstrate likelihood of maltreatment (past, present and future).

Safety and Context Scale

Safety Scale: Given the danger and safety information, rate the situation on a 0 –10 scale, where 0 means recurrence of similar or worse abuse/neglect is certain, and 10 means that there is sufficient safety for the child to close the case.

Context Scale: Rate this case on a 0 –10 scale, where 10 means this is not a situation where any action would be taken and 0 means this is the worst case of child abuse/neglect the agency has seen.

Agency Goals What will the agency need to see to be willing to close this case?

Family Goals What does the family want generally, and specifically regarding safety?

Immediate Progress What would indicate to the agency that some small significant progress had been made?

FIGURE 13.1. Signs of safety assessment and planning form.

for violent outbursts toward other children. Social services regarded this family as a very difficult, "multiproblem" family who mostly denied they had any problems. The social services workers had many concerns but primary among these was the long held view that Jamie's father, Freddy, was violent toward the mother Fran. Because of these allegations, Freddy had refused to have anything to do with social workers for more than two years and was reputed to have been abusive to social services workers.

Janet began by seeing Fran (Freddy refused to attend). With the social services worker present, Janet asked the mother to complete the signs of safety assessment. Janet asked the mother about the good things in her family and then turned her attention to the things the mother identified as concerns. Janet had explained the process to the social services worker in advance and had asked her to come to the meeting ready to describe three things she regarded as positive in the family. The worker was surprised to hear Fran listing among the family strengths that Jamie responds well to one-to-one attention, that it was Freddy who was best able to control Jamie when he became upset, and that Freddy regularly took Jamie and the other boys fishing. The worker was even more surprised with how honest Fran was in describing the family's problems. Among other things, Fran described her worries about Jamie's behavior that she felt she often overreacted to him, and further that she was worried because the children had seen her hit Freddy when they argued. The following week, Janet repeated the process, getting the six children, aged 4 to 15, to describe and assess their family situation. Both the mother and the children were able to identify the things they felt were most important to improve the family's problems. This became the plan for the family, Janet, and the social services worker. Some weeks later, Janet was able to engage Freddy in the change process. Dropping the children off at the family home, Janet met Freddy and made a point of immediately acknowledging to Freddy that she was aware of the many good things he was doing as a father, particularly in helping Jamie. Doing the assessment together with the family members, focusing on concerns and strengths and their own goals, laid the foundation whereby social services were able to close the case four months later.

WORKING WITH TORTURED
AND TRAUMATIZED REFUGEES

I worked in an agency providing services to traumatized refugees for four and half years. When I began this work, I wondered whether Solution-Focused Brief Therapy could be useful in working with this client group.

I found that the work I did with the refugees was very different from the therapy I had previously undertaken with mostly white, middle-class families and individuals. At a very simple level, the first difference was that sessions that would previously be completed in an hour or less now ran for 90 minutes or longer. As much as anything, this was because in most sessions, I was working with an interpreter. I also learned that to work successfully with the refugees I needed first to build a relationship with the interpreter. I would typically meet and brief an interpreter about my plans for the session before we met with the client. I learned that the work progressed most smoothly when I treated the interpreter as a colleague and as my advisor rather than as my mouthpiece. I also found that in many languages, it was difficult for the interpreter to translate typical solution-focused questions, most particularly the miracle question. In the fours years previous to my refugee work, there were few clients with which I did not ask a miracle question; with the refugees, it was rare when I did. The result was that my work changed, I focused less and less on the typical techniques, and more and more, I fell back on solution-focused first principles. In short order, I found my main concern was to simply find ways of talking to the refugees about what they wanted to be different in their lives and how I could help them achieve that, whether through the usual solution-focused questions or not.

Focusing simply on what the refugees told me they wanted and how they thought I could help them, meant that in the majority of the cases, I found myself working outside the therapy room at least some of the time. I could relate many different examples of this but will relate a few that were typical. When I first saw refugees, I got into the habit of inviting the referring professional to join us for at least part of the first session. This circumvented a problem I had encountered early on, in which the referrer would often give me a long list of problems, but the refugees themselves would often not mention any of those complaints. So, when I first saw an Iraqi man we will call Dawood, I asked the referring social worker to join us for the first session.

Dawood was confused about why he was seeing me and he had little idea what therapy was meant to be about, let alone what it might achieve for him. The referring social worker was more clear. She was very worried because she said the man, who had been tortured and imprisoned in his country of origin, was having considerable difficulties in sleeping and was facing considerable debt mostly from gambling. He was highly disorganized and unfocused, scared of all contact with others of his own nationality, disgruntled with his new wife, possibly depressed, and unable to settle, having moved home six times in the last eight months. In that first session, Dawood talked little, but in the next, he stated that his principal concern lay in his drinking a bottle or more of spirits each day, which ate up all or most of his fortnightly social security payment and demonstrated to him that as a man, he was weak. I asked him what he thought he needed to happen to get his life on track. He answered that he needed to start painting. I asked what was stopping him and he replied that he didn't have the artists' materials. In my own mind, I was skeptical that this would make very much difference, but I told him my organization had a lot of artists' materials (for art therapy purposes) and he was free to take as much as he needed. Dawood left with artists' paper and a collection of brushes and water colors. Two weeks later, at his invitation, the interpreter and I visited Dawood's home, where he proudly showed me the paintings he had done. He explained he was a fine arts graduate from Baghdad University and added that he had stopped drinking altogether. I was rather flabbergasted and asked him, "Well, what do you need to keep these changes going?" "I need to meet Australian artists," he replied. I subsequently arranged for him to meet several leading Perth artists with whom I had connections, one of whom became a friend and mentor for Dawood. Six months later, Dawood, with the help of the Australian artist, held his first exhibition.

A Kurdish man I worked with informed me that because he had lived the life of a Kurdish activist, if I were to help him, I had to understand the struggle of the Kurdish people. This led the two of us spending several hours hunkered over a computer, looking at Kurdish Web sites, and I spent many more hours reading the material we printed off from these sites. Following this, the man decided that I could help him. I asked him if he could have life the way he wanted it in Australia, what that would look like. He said he had been thinking about that a lot since he showed me the Web sites. He had decided in Australia that for the good of his family and for his children to have a future, he would stop being an activist and wanted to return to his trade as a tailor. He asked for my help in achieving this and from our discussions, I arranged for him to work unpaid for a time alongside a tailor I knew so he could decide whether this really was the direction he wanted to pursue.

In another situation, I was asked by a psychologist to see a 50-year-old Vietnamese man we will call Thanh. The psychologist, who said he was too busy to come to the first session, described Thanh as highly depressed and potentially suicidal. He said he was unable to get anything out of Thanh and that Thanh's daughter was very worried about her father. Like Dawood, Thanh had little idea why he was seeing me; he also had nothing to say about things he was worried about or how I could help him. This was one of the only times during my time working with refugees that I used a miracle question in its usual format (Thomas & Nelson, this volume), in part because the interpreter was happy to translate the question. At the end of the question, Thanh's answer was simple—"I'd be buried in Karrakatta cemetery." In my head, I wondered whether he was telling me he wanted to commit suicide and before I could say anything, the interpreter was already telling Thanh in Vietnamese that it would be a dishonor to his family if he were to kill himself. It took a while to sort out the subsequent confusion, but it turned out that what Thanh was trying to say he most wanted in his life was that when he died, he would be buried in the military section of Perth's largest cemetery. Thanh explained that all of his male forebears were soldiers and that he had been a soldier until he was badly injured fighting alongside the Americans in the Vietnam War—he wanted to be recognized as a soldier, not as a cripple.

Subsequent inquiries on my part with the Australian veterans department elicited the department's caution about whether Thanh was who he claimed to be. The department had had many experiences of Vietcong soldiers trying to pass themselves off in just this manner. Since the only military papers Thanh had were deemed to be ambivalent, I asked what it would take for him to prove his bonafides. What was required was a statutory declaration from the captain of the American unit with which Thanh fought. Through the U.S. embassy, we were able to locate the captain, who supplied the necessary confirmation. Following this, Thanh was recognized as a veteran and could therefore receive his disability pension from the Veteran's Department rather than Social Security Department. With the change of status, Thanh could also participate in veterans' activities in Australia, including marching on ANZAC day (a national holiday where Australians honor men and woman who fought for their country). Thanh proudly took immediate advantage of all these opportunities, stating he felt like a real man again.

Time and again, I found that when I gave control of the therapy process to the clients, the refugees took me outside the therapy room. Sometimes, this was to establish for themselves whether I really did want to help them; often it was simply a matter that the whole notion of a "talking cure" meant little to them and they most wanted practical assistance to move forward in their lives. Initially, I wondered whether this was okay: Was I still doing therapy? Then I remembered the sorts of stories I knew of Milton Erickson's work, which I mentioned at the beginning of this paper. I took great comfort from those stories and simply decided if it was okay for Milton, it had to be okay for me too.

WRITING WITH CLIENTS

As we have seen throughout this book, Solution-Focused Brief Therapy, above all else, privileges the goals and voices of clients. Writing about therapy, on the other hand, is usually undertaken by professionals, for professionals. Recently, some practitioners have sought to extend this logic further by also privileging the client's voice in writing up the helping process. Because solution-focused brief therapists locate the client as the ultimate arbiter of whether the helping process is successful, it makes sense to learn from our clients more about what it is we as professionals think we are doing. Frank Thomas (1994) from the United States has published one such paper, and perhaps the leading proponent of this work is Swede who has published two papers and currently is working on several more (Bergmark & Söderquist, 2002; Söderquist, Classon, & Sundelin, 2002).

In this same spirit of collaborative inquiry, I have published four child protection case studies jointly with the child protection practitioner and the parents (Teoh, Laffer, Parton, & Turnell, 2003; Turnell, 2006; Turnell & Edwards, 1999; Turnell, Elliot, & Hogg, 2007). I have learnt a great deal about the helping process from these undertakings and also discovered that they are a powerful way to bring the helping process to a close. When I have asked clients whether they might be interested in writing up the helping process together, the clients often have been very keen for their stories to be taken beyond the therapy room. Typically, the clients hope that their stories might assist others who may be facing similar circumstances and the professionals who work with them.

I undertook this joint writing process on one occasion during the period I was working with the refugee organization. The man involved wanted his story to be published but wanted also to remain anonymous. To create the write-up, I first interviewed him about the most important things he would want in his story. Over three meetings, we reworked drafts I had prepared for him.[1] The story follows.

The Fight of His Life: The Story of a Man Reclaiming His Life from Torture

There was a handsome man who had been a successful boxer, a man who was happy with his life, his marriage, his faith, and his work. He lived in a Latin American country and one day, he was captured by men who subjected him to seven days of the most intense torture. He was beaten and ridiculed, but worst of all he was forced to rape a fellow female detainee. The torture and particularly the forced rape shattered the man's life. As a result of the torture, he left his country and came to Australia as a refugee.

The man had hoped that in Australia, he would be able to put these events behind him but actually, he found that things in his life got worse and worse. He had nightmares about being captured and the forced rape. He refused to tell his wife about what happened and he became mostly impotent and sexual relations with his wife ceased. His wife began to suspect he was having an affair and the two grew apart. The man sometimes found himself aroused by the image of the forced rape and also found himself masturbating in parks. The man hated himself for this because he knew it was not normal. He desperately wanted to get a normal life back, which the torture had taken from him.

To make matters worse, the man consulted several doctors and helping professionals and they seemed unable to help. He was very distressed by the fact that several professionals with experience in the area of sexual problems suggested that although he was unhappy with his sexual fantasies and activity in the parks, at least he should be happy that he still had some sexual desire. To the man, it seemed they were asking him to accept the unacceptable and the fact that two professional experts would say this made him feel worse and more hopeless.

He tried again to talk to someone and on this occasion talked to a Spanish-speaking female counselor[2] from ASeTTS (Association for Services to Torture and Trauma Survivors). He was very ashamed of all that had happened and was occurring but felt he had to tell his story because he wanted to get better. It was a very hard thing to tell it all to a woman. The man worked very hard to get himself to tell it and the counselor worked hard to listen. Progress was made; it is even possible to say a breakthrough occurred, because for the first time the man felt understood.

Then another difficulty arose; the female counselor had to return to Argentina with her family. The man, after summoning so much courage to tell his story and starting to feel a little better because someone understood, found himself faced with the fact that this connection to his health was about to be taken away. The Argentinean counselor suggested another counselor might take over but was afraid that the man would not want to build a relationship with another counselor. However, a meeting was set up for the man to meet the new counselor. The meeting was subdued but introductions were made and the man made it very clear that although he didn't like the woman's leaving, he would work with the new counselor because he was determined to do whatever he could to get his life back. The Argentinean counselor felt this was a further breakthrough.

One further complication needed to be faced: Although the new counselor spoke some Spanish, an interpreter would be needed and the man stipulated that he would not be happy with a Latino interpreter. The new counselor offered to do his best to find a non-Latino Spanish speaker.

A Spanish-speaking Australian was found who could act as interpreter and so with these two new people, the man began again to tell his story. At this time, three nightmares kept recurring night after night for him. In one nightmare, he was being beaten; in the second, he was running but could not escape; and in the third, he saw the rape he was forced to inflict. The man was feeling particularly humiliated by the fact that he was unable to have a normal sexual relationship with his wife. Very early on after he had told the counselor about these things, the man wanted to know whether the counselor thought he should accept his impotence with his wife, his arousal at the image of the forced rape, and his behavior in the park as other professionals seemed to encourage. The counselor replied, "They are asking you to accept the unacceptable and you have every right to get a normal life back." They talked about the man giving his wife an explanation for his withdrawal from the marriage bed that she could believe and most importantly that he express to her that he wanted her and wanted to recommence the physical relationship.

The man's wife, it turned out, was delighted to know she was wanted and, although they were not yet able to engage in full intercourse, the sexual relationship recommenced. Talking again about the experience of the torture, the counselor asked the man to imagine that a young child had been alongside him through the whole experience and had become totally overwhelmed and confused by what he saw. How did he think adults who wanted to be helpful should respond to this young boy?[3] The man felt the child should in no way be chastised or blamed for what he saw or for any bizarre behavior he might display after what he had seen. It would be important, said the man, to let the boy express and talk about his dreams, that the boy should be told stories of what's normal and be given gentle guidance. The therapist suggested to the man that part of himself was perhaps just like that little boy.

Some weeks later, things had changed a little more; the man had had intercourse with his wife, which pleased him. However, his nightmares were becoming more intense. For 15 days, nightmares of the rape and of being attacked recurred every night. Suddenly, after the fifteenth day, the man had a new dream in which he was watching a war either in his own country or in Australia. The man and the counselor made a plan for the man to draw his dreams. Neither was sure whether this was a good thing to do, because the paintings, particularly the one of the woman raped, scared the hell out of him.

Perhaps though, the man's courage to face his nightmares in this way brought about further change, because now he found that although he was still having the rape dream, he experienced it slightly differently; he found himself feeling like he was in the dream but also observing it. Despite this, more than ever before, the man was feeling the impact of the torture upon him. He said, "It all feels like a huge weight!" and he was acutely aware that his conscience wouldn't let him rest and made him feel culpable for what had occurred. At the same time, the man felt that his life was a little more normal, he felt he was controlling the park behavior, and he had more energy and focus in his study and at work.

Some weeks later, the man said that two years after the torture, when he was first in Australia in 1990, he felt that the torture controlled 100 percent of his life. By the beginning of 1997, at the point of the switch of counselors, he felt he had regained 50 percent control of his own life. He wondered out loud whether it would take him another seven years to get back the other 50 percent. He described that at that time, his aim was to regain control of 75 percent of his life and felt he was making definite progress. The man was pleased to report that all the old nightmares had gone for the moment. These were replaced by an occasional new dream that showed him standing in a doorway feeling fearful but not overwhelmed by the idea that some men were coming to get him.

Five weeks later and five months into 1997, the man described that he felt he had arrived at 75 percent control; he was feeling more secure, more rested. For 15 days he had had no nightmares, and he was enjoying his music, both playing and teaching it, for the first time since the torture. His friends had helped him and prayed for him and this was important to him. The man had had one new dream, that of going to the toilet in the street and feeling ashamed of himself. At the same time, he felt he was taking control of "the bad thoughts" in his mind, but wanted to overcome them more fully. He was very aware of the changes he had achieved and stated firmly "he was not going back!"

Five weeks later, again (the man was deciding how often to meet the counselor), things seemed to be moving very quickly and dramatic things were occurring. The man had a dream where he saw himself standing *"alta"** on a cliff overlooking a black raging sea with huge pounding waves crashing onto the shore. He was aware that although danger was present, he was out of its way. Turning around, he saw his son in the dream about to cross a busy road. The man cried out for him to stop, but the boy crossed safely anyway, the man's heart in his mouth for a moment. The man wasn't sure what the significance of seeing his son in this way might be. The counselor reminded the man that he had previously suggested that in some ways he was like a wide-eyed young child who had been faced with massive danger.

It also transpired that a very beautiful young woman, determined purposefully and very physically to seduce the man. To his own satisfaction, the man extracted himself from the young woman. He said, *"¡fue muy dificil a decir no!"* (it was very difficult to say no!). This real-life experience seemed to the man to parallel a dream that he had at this time wherein he rejected the chance of "depraved sex." He felt he had learned in the real world that he could stand firm and say no and this pleased him. The counselor suggested that this seemed to show the man regathering his own boundaries, the boundaries that were so completely violated in the torture.

Also in the real world, the marriage was being regathered. Both the man and his wife were more fully resuming their responsibilities and relationship. The opportunity to have had an illicit relationship with a gorgeous young woman made the man more decisive in knowing that he wanted his wife. Later, the young woman came back to the man and told him that she saw him as "a real hero" for being strong enough to say no to her. At the same time, the man also described that he finally knew he had overcome his problem in the park.

As it became evident that the man was reclaiming his health and normality and that he wouldn't go back, both the counselor and the interpreter felt great satisfaction in seeing the changes that the man had made. Both

---

*Spanish term for "above."

felt privileged to have been part of helping him to regain his health and his normal life.

Postscript

At the end of all this, the man found the problems that had been so affecting his life were gone. He also found that suddenly he was exhausted, sometimes shaking, and with no energy for anything; for example, he found he really had to push himself to do his music teaching. His doctor had examined him and run tests but could find nothing wrong with him. In fact, quite the reverse, because the doctor found that the man's blood pressure that had always been a problem had normalized. The man was perplexed by his exhaustion. The counselor suggested to the man that he had just won the fight of his life; it was as if he had just gone 18 rounds with the world heavy weight champion and had won against all odds. In these circumstances, he had every right, therefore, to feel exhausted. This made sense to the man and he realized that having won the fight, he needed to allow himself time to recuperate and regather his energy and strength.

CONCLUSION

In 2001, Eve Lipchik (2001) wrote a book titled, *Beyond Technique in Solution-Focused Brief Therapy.* Writing together in an earlier paper (Turnell & Lipchik, 1999), Eve and I had been cutting at that same cake, seeking to describe the underlying principles and relationship-building work that we believed makes Solution-Focused Brief Therapy effective. I share with Eve the view that the solution-focused approach is far more limited in its application when it is oversimplified and seen as a series of techniques. When the foundational ideas that inform Solution-Focused Brief Therapy are identified as the heart of the model, I think the picture changes. Drawing on its foundational premises, the primary, and possibly only, limitation of the solution-focused model is dependent entirely on the professional's own view of whether or not it is core therapy business to privilege the client's perspective on the problem and its resolution. See Chapter 17 in this book on Thomas's ideas of possible limitations to the solution-focused approach.

I have written this paper hoping to capture some of my own experiences of going beyond the usual privatized therapy context, and often, this also has meant being willing to go beyond the usual techniques of Solution-Focused Brief Therapy. In the end, I think what is most important about the solution-focused endeavor is not about colonizing particular techniques or strategies as the best way to do therapy, but rather about its capacity to bring hope and creativity to human problems that can sometimes be very ugly. As my own expertise as a brief therapist has increased, the foundational ideas of the tradition continue to engage and challenge me, and cause me to increasingly adopt a position of humility about what I think I know. I have been, and still am, energized by this process and I can only see my extended journey in the brief tradition continuing as I continue to explore ways of utilizing the ideas and practices both within and outside of the therapy room.

APPENDIX

Solution-Focused Measures of Recovery: An Assessment Approach for Working with Traumatized Refugees

Attribute	Never	Rarely	Sometimes	Often	Always
1. I am able to think about the traumatic events in my past.					
2. I have times when I do not think about the traumatic events in my past.					
3. I am able to think about other things than the past traumatic events.					
4. When I think about the traumatic experiences in my past, I know these things are not my fault.					
5. I am able to settle myself after experiencing or remembering distressing thoughts and images.					
6. I am able to tolerate radio, TV, or newspaper reports of traumatic events from my country of origin.					
7. There are times when I can relax.					
8. I am able to cope with my feelings of loss.					
9. I feel I have coped as well as possible with all the problems I have faced.					
10. I am able to accept that I/we have left my country of origin.					
11. I am able to acknowledge and express that I miss my family, friends, and way of life from my own country.					
12. My attention span is fairly good.					
13. I am able to concentrate on daily tasks and complete them.					
14. I am able to fall asleep within a reasonable time when I want to.					
15. When I sleep, I feel rested.					
16. I eat well and healthily.					
17. I am comfortable with my use of tea, coffee, sweets, alcohol, and other stimulants.					
18. I am comfortable with being alone.					
19. I have a sense of humor and can laugh at things.					

Attribute	Never	Rarely	Sometimes	Often	Always
20. I am able to participate in activities I enjoy.					
21. I am able to give physical affection.					
22. I am able to enjoy a healthy sexual relationship.					
23. I have friends I spend time with.					
24. I am able to cope with the physical pain that I experience.					
25. I am receiving the assistance I need to settle in this country.					
26. I am able to state my needs to people who are providing services to me.					
27. I have an idea about what I want to achieve with my life here in Australia.					
28. I feel I could build a new life for myself and my family here in this country.					
29. I am able to see life as meaningful.					

NOTES

1. Leonie Peters, our interpreter, provided invaluable support in both the therapy and the writing of the case.

2. Maria Luz Noe.

3. In this way, I found I was able to ask the man how we could help him and to figure out how to direct the therapy.

REFERENCES

Berg, I. K., & De Jong, P. (1999). *Solution-focused interviewing.* San Francisco: Brooks-Cole.

Berg, I. K., & Kelly, S. (2000). *Building solutions in child protective services.* New York: Norton.

Bergmark, A., & Söderquist, M. (2002). Fighting for freedom: A collaborative success story. *Journal of Family Therapy, 24,* 167-186.

Boffa, J., & Podestra, H. (2004). Partnership and risk assessment in child protection practice. *Protecting Children, 19*(2), 36-48.

Cade, B. (2007). Springs, streams, and tributaries: A history of the brief, solution-focused approach. In T. S. Nelson & F. N. Thomas (Eds.), *Handbook of Solution-Focused Brief Therapy: Clinical Applications* (pp. 25-64). Binghamton, NY: The Haworth Press.

Cooperrider, D. L., & Srivastva, S. (1987). Appreciative inquiry in organizational life. In W. Pasmore & R. Woodman (Eds.), *Research in organization change and development* (Vol. 1) (pp. 129-169). Greenwich, CT: JAI Press.

Department for Community Development (2001). *Risk analysis and risk management framework.* Perth, Australia: Author.

Department of Human Services (2000). *Victorian risk framework, version 2.0.,* Victoria, Australia: Protection and Care Branch.

Dolan, Y. (1991). *Resolving sexual abuse: Solution-focused therapy and Ericksonian hypnosis for adult survivors.* New York: Norton.

Durrant, M. (1993). *Residential treatment: A cooperative, competency-based approach to therapy and program design.* New York: Norton.

Durrant, M. (1995). *Creative strategies for schools problems.* New York: Norton.

Fisch R. (1988). Training in the brief therapy model. In H. Liddle, D. Breunlin, & R. Schwartz (Eds.), *Handbook of family therapy training and supervision* (pp. 78-92). New York: Guilford.

Haley, J. (1973). *Uncommon therapy.* New York: Norton.

Herr, J., & Weakland, J. H. (1979). *Counselling elders and their families: Practical techniques for applied gerontology.* New York: Springer.

Lee, M. Y., Sebold, J., & Uken, A. (2003). *Solution-focused treatment of domestic violence offenders: Accountability for change.* New York: Oxford University Press.

Lipchik, E. (2001). *Beyond technique in solution-focused brief therapy.* New York: Guilford.

Söderquist, M., Classon, C., & Sundelin, J. (2002). Hold on to your goals: Clients and therapists commenting on videotaped SFT-sessions. *Journal of Systemic Therapies, 21*(4), 48-66.

Soo-Hoo, T. (1995). Implementing brief strategic therapy within a psychiatric residential/day treatment center. In J. H. Weakland & W. A. Ray (Eds.), *Propagations: Thirty years of influence from the Mental Research Institute.* Binghamton, NY: The Haworth Press.

Teoh, A. H., Laffer, J., Parton, N., & Turnell, A. (2003). Trafficking in meaning: Constructive social work in child protection practice. In C. Hall, K. Juhila, N. Parton, & T. Pösö (Eds.), *Client as practice.* London: Jessica Kingsley.

Thomas, F. N. (1994). The experience of solution-oriented therapy: Post-therapy client interviewing. *Case Studies in Brief and Family Therapy, 8*(1), 47-58.

Thomas, F. N. (2007). Possible limitations, misunderstandings, and misuses of solution-focused brief therapy. In T. S. Nelson & F. N. Thomas (Eds.), *Handbook of Solution-focused Brief Therapy: Clinical Applications.* (pp. 391-408). Binghamton, NY: The Haworth Press.

Thomas, F. N., & Nelson, T. S. (2007). Assumptions and practices within the solution-focused brief therapy tradition. In T. S. Nelson & F. N. Thomas (Eds.),

Handbook of Solution-Focused Brief Therapy: Clinical Applications (pp. 3-24). Binghamton, NY: The Haworth Press.

Turnell, A. (2004). Relationship-grounded, safety-organised child protection practice: Dreamtime or real-time option for child welfare? *Protecting Children,19*(2), 14-25.

Turnell, A. (2006). Constructive child protection practice: An oxymoron or news of difference? *Journal of Systemic Therapies, 25*(2), 3-12.

Turnell, A., & Edwards, S. (1997). Aspiring to partnership: The signs of safety approach to child protection. *Child Abuse Review, 6*, 179-190.

Turnell, A., & Edwards, S. (1999). *Signs of safety: A safety and solution oriented approach to child protection casework.* New York: Norton.

Turnell, A., & Hopwood, L. (1994). Solution-focused brief therapy: An outline for second and subsequent sessions. *Case Studies in Brief and Family Therapy, 8*(2), 52-64.

Turnell, A., & Lipchik, E. (1999). The role of empathy in brief therapy: The overlooked but vital context. *Australian and New Zealand Journal of Family Therapy, 20*(4), 177-182.

Turnell, A., Elliott, S., & Hogg, V. (2007). Compassionate, safe and rigorous child protection practice with biological parents of adopted children. *Child Abuse Review, 16*(2), 108-119.

Turnell A., Lohrbach, S, & Curran, S. (in press). Working with the "involuntary client" in child protection: Lessons from successful practice. In M. Calder (Ed.) *The carrot or the stick? Towards effective practice with involuntary clients,* London: Russell House Publishing.

Watkins, J. M., & Mohr, B. J. (2001). *Appreciative inquiry: Change at the speed of imagination.* New York: Jossey-Bass.

Weakland, J. H., & Jordon, L. (1992). Working briefly with reluctant clients: Child protective services as an example, *Journal of Family Therapy, 14*, 231-254.

SECTION III:
TRAINING

In which we present two chapters on training and supervising Solution-Focused Brief Therapy.

Handbook of Solution-Focused Brief Therapy: Clinical Applications
© 2007 by The Haworth Press, Inc. All rights reserved.
doi:10.1300/5135_P3

Chapter 14

Solution-Focused Training:
The Medium and the Message

Heather Fiske

Talking about music is like dancing about architecture.

Steve Martin (n.d.)

The medium is the message.

Marshall MacLuhan (1994)

INTRODUCTION

The demand for training in Solution-Focused Brief Therapy (SFBT) has generated hundreds of college and university courses, workplace training programs, and workshops. Despite all this activity and a growing literature on how to *do* SFBT, there has been little attention to how to *teach* SFBT.

Of course, there are always exceptions. In this case, they include manuals for the teaching of SFBT by De Jong and Berg (1997b) and Chevalier (1995) and an article by Maurer-Hankovsky and Szabó (2002). References to training and specific suggestions occur in various texts (e.g., Hoyt, 1996; Sharry, Madden, & Darmody, 2003) and articles (e.g., Booker, 1996). With regard to "building on what already works," both existing models for systemic therapy training (Erikson & McAuliffe, 2001; Street, 1997) and

Handbook of Solution-Focused Brief Therapy: Clinical Applications
© 2007 by The Haworth Press, Inc. All rights reserved.
doi:10.1300/5135_14

research on adult learning (Reigeluth, 1987; Sutherland, 1997) offer useful information. Cunanan's (2003; McCollum & Cunanan, 2003) recent study on trainees' views of what works in solution-focused training makes a valuable contribution. A special issue of the *Journal of Family Psychotherapy* (Nelson, 2005b) is devoted to the subject. That collection of articles and this chapter are among the results of an ongoing "think tank" consisting of both experienced trainers of SFBT and SFBT trainees. This group, founded the Solution-Focused Brief Therapy Association (SFBTA; Nelson, 2005a), was first convened by Steve de Shazer and Terry Trepper in 2002. The group's original purpose was to share ideas and practices helpful in teaching SFBT. One theme of those conversations has been that SFBT training is very much about *doing*: about actions, experiments, and exercises that help trainees to achieve their goals in solution-focused practice.

In this chapter, I too will focus on the "doing" of solution-focused training. The first section deals with some of the common challenges of clinical training and how they can be met in a solution-focused framework; the bulk of the chapter is a discussion of "what works," with examples of practical exercises. I hope that some of my misunderstandings are useful ones.

A NOTE ON (MY) LANGUAGE

In early drafts of this chapter, I experimented with nomenclature to dubious and uncertain effect. Specifically, I tried using and not using the terms, "trainee," "student," "learner," or "participant"; and the (somewhat) parallel labels "trainer," "teacher," "educator" or "facilitator." Each word had advantages in terms of history, familiarity, connotation, and specificity; each had disadvantages in terms of history, familiarity, connotation, and vagueness. Implications of hierarchy and passive-versus-active status seemed especially problematic. None seemed to cover all the necessary bases. In the end, I used them all.

I longed for a single verb to express "teaching and learning." "Teaching and learning together" or "co-learning/co-teaching" were accurate but cumbersome. I toyed with "participating in a mutual educational process," "doing/discovering/co-discovering SFBT" and other phrases still more cumbersome and pompous to boot. None came close to expressing the sense of aliveness, of reciprocal movement and change inherent in the truly collaborative learning experience of SFBT training when it works. I hope that other learners and teachers will have helpful ideas on this topic.

CHALLENGES AND POSSIBILITIES

Definitions ("But I Know It When I See It. . . .")

What is it that we are teaching? Although SFBT is essentially a *practice* (de Shazer, 2002), we need agreed-upon operational definitions for purposes of planning, evaluation, and research.

Given that both the philosophy and the practice of SFBT continue to be articulated, perhaps the most useful approach available is the research definition developed for the ongoing multisite European Brief Therapy Association (EBTA) SFBT outcome study (Beyebach, 2000). The EBTA definition specifies four "minimal requirements" for SFBT practice:

1. The therapist asks and follows up on the Miracle Question.
2. The therapist asks and follows up on the Progress Scale.
3. The therapist compliments the client(s) at the end of the session
4. Return visits: The therapist asks "what is better?" at the beginning of the session and follows up on it. (Beyebach, pp. 2-3)

De Shazer (1994) says that the development of SFBT has been pragmatic rather than theory-based and that the more "theoretical" parts of his writing are "nothing more" than "descriptions of my tools" (p. 274). Nevertheless, many students (and teachers) view an understanding of theory as necessary in defining a therapeutic approach (Cunanan, 2003; Maggio, Marcotte, Perry, & Truax, 2001). Theoretical bases for SFBT commonly are cited in postmodern, constructivist perspectives (Miller, 1997). The extent to which such perspectives are covered depends both on the nature of the particular program and, always, on student needs and interests. I suggest providing references and access to written material on SFBT-associated theories for participants in clinical training. However, we should also emphasize Wittgenstein's caution: It is a mistake to be looking for "explanations" when we should be looking at *what happens* (Wittgenstein, 1968).

Walking the Walk

The greatest challenge in solution-focused training, in my view, lies in making methods and model congruent, that is, how do we do solution-focused teaching in a solution-focused way? Given that solution-focused practices "are not a bag of tricks"—but "expressions of an attitude, a posture, and a philosophy" (Berg, 1992, p. 14), how do we demonstrate a solution-focused attitude, posture, and philosophy in our approach to teaching? How do we ensure that the educational process is "student-centered"? How do we utilize an expert role—that of trainer or educator—to elucidate a non-expert position?

"Knowing nothing" is a difficult stance to maintain as a teacher (and might prove unfortunate in negotiating training contracts). In a training session at the Brief Family Therapy Center (Berg & de Shazer, 1992), Insoo Kim Berg once described herself as a "guru" of SFBT. She went on to explain the literal meaning of the word "guru" as she understood it: "student who learns one step ahead." So, perhaps an appropriate stance for a solution-focused trainer is that of "guru"—at least in situations where "not-knowing" does not work well. This position may be particularly useful in communicating to trainees that SFBT is alive, that is, still developing as opposed to being an established (dead?) program of required techniques.

In other respects, simply applying core solution-focused assumptions and following common solution-focused practices contributes to congruent teaching of SFBT. Consider the three guidelines that have been called the "central philosophy," the pragmatic heart of SFBT.

1. *If it ain't broken, don't fix it.* I can begin teaching solution-focused therapy by teaching solution-focused therapy; I do not need to first establish what is "wrong" with other approaches (i.e., create a problem I can then solve). A solution-focused trainer can simply invite trainees to listen for what is helpful. As de Shazer says, ". . . it's basically the same procedure (as working with clinical clients), except you haven't got a complaint, no problem to solve. So, you don't have to start with that. You can just start with the miracle question . . . (in Hoyt, 1996, p. 80).

2. *If it's working, do more of it.* Utilization is a core practice of SFBT. We build on, and build with, what already works—for a client, a trainee, a working team, or an organization. It follows that SFBT training includes the identification, reinforcement, repetition, and enhancement of trainees' existing skills:

HOYT: . . . How does the trainer work differently when being solution-focused?

DE SHAZER: Well, you have to assume the same things about these kinds of clients that you do about clinical clients: that whatever they are doing makes sense to them. They are obviously doing something that works. Therefore, the first thing you've got to do is to find out what that is, so that you can build on it. (Hoyt, 1996, p. 80)

A solution-focused training process includes compliments for trainees' strengths, skills, and successes *as part of the structure of training*—not just an unreliable artifact of the trainer's being "nice" or having a "support-ive" style.

3. *If it isn't working, do something different.* This principle is a little scary for those of us who like to develop and follow highly structured lesson plans or training sequences. It implies, first, a need for on-the-spot assess-ment of how well training is working (e.g., with scaling questions) and second, both the willingness and the requisite flexibility to abandon a pre-conceived plan and do something else that is a better fit—more like "improv" acting than working from a script.

Diversity

I live and work in the most multicultural city in the world (Toronto, Canada); linguistic, ethnic, and cultural diversity is routine. The elegant simplicity of SFBT as a model is helpful when communicating across po-tential divides and many of the techniques, such as scaling, "translate" well, both linguistically and culturally. For trainees who practice in multicultural settings or with cultural groups different from their own, there is evident utility in defining goals and progress in clients' terms rather than according to externally imposed "yardsticks" that may not be culturally relevant. Most helpful is an insistence on discovering from trainees what will work *for them*: How is a particular question best asked in their linguistic, cultural, or experiential context? (For example, in some languages and cultures, the word "miracle" has an explicitly religious connotation and so may not—or may!—be appropriate). Many of the training techniques discussed in this chapter have been applied primarily in a North American context, albeit with trainees from a range of cultural backgrounds. Their utility in other contexts has yet to be established.

In my experience, having trainees from diverse linguistic and cultural backgrounds within a single training group can be highly beneficial (a) in reinforcing the importance of finding ways to "speak the client's language," (b) in highlighting the importance of care in avoiding assumptions and working to understand the client's view, and (c) in directing trainee atten-tion to the linguistic aspects of solution-focused practice. In fact, I view cul-tural diversity in trainee groups and in trainees' own clinical experience as helpful in making these "translation" issues more explicit and easily grasped. I have found that I am most at risk of foundering on my own unrealized presumptions of common language and beliefs when I am conversing with others who appear to be very like myself.

More problematic at times than ethnocultural diversity is diversity in ed-ucational and experiential backgrounds. Some students have much more clinical experience than others have; this situation can lead to frustration for more experienced trainees, who sometimes feel that too much time is being spent on "basics." Educational diversity may lead to challenges in how information is presented and understood. For example, professional terminology and references to scientific literature may make training more familiar and credible for students with graduate-level education, but be off-putting for those with limited formal preparation. One example of this kind of diversity challenge occurs in treatment settings where the entire staff—from janitors and cooks to psychologists—is receiving the same training (an approach with a powerful systemic impact). Another example I have encountered is in training service providers to the homeless, with most groups including individuals with several advanced degrees as well as some who are functionally illiterate.

Previous training may create "language barriers" of another kind; that is, some students "speak" psychodynamics, some speak cognitive therapy, some speak strategic. Here, it is the less "encumbered" students who may lose patience. Students who encounter SFBT early in their training rarely experience the attitudinal, behavioral, and intellectual struggles of students who have years of experience with very different therapeutic worldviews and practices. As de Shazer says, "Getting fresh people, it's a helluva lot easier. . . . I can train an engineer in a relatively short space of time" (in Hoyt, 1994, pp. 21-22).

When dealing with educational and experiential diversity, I have found it helpful, first, to assume that there are many views of "the truth" and that the ones that are of greatest interest to a solution-focused practitioner are those that are helpful to clients in meeting their goals. Applying these ideas in training makes it much easier to appreciate useful ideas in whatever "language" they are couched. Second, it helps to stick with what is happening (especially what is working), maintaining a focus on practice and application of skills—and to avoid explanations and theorizing. Third, trainers can model the attitude that varied skills and backgrounds among trainees are a rich resource, for example, by showing trainees effective solution-focused clinical sessions (live or on tape) conducted by therapists with overtly different styles, backgrounds, and language habits. The case vignettes in Berg and Dolan's (2001) *Tales of Solutions* also illustrate the broad range of possible solution-focused styles.

A fourth approach to overcoming issues of academic and experiential diversity is utilizing exercises that offer trainees an appreciation of solution-focused approaches through personal experience with the impact of compliments, exception-finding questions, and other SFBT methods (cf. Berg, 2005; Fiske, 2005; Hackett, 2005; Lamarre, 2005; Maurer-Hankovszky &

Szabó, 2002; Milner, 2005; Sharry et al., 2003; Taylor, 2005a,b; Young, 2005; Zalter & Fiske, 2005).

"Solution Forcing" and Other Mythologies

Exposure to ideas about "solution-forced" practice (Nylund & Corsiglia, 1994) may color students' perceptions, creating particular difficulties for "mandated" students, for example, practitioners who have been instructed by employers to learn SFBT.

One approach to dealing with "solution-forced" concerns is to raise and discuss them early in training: "What have you heard about SFBT? What concerns do you have? What interests or attracts you?" My own method is to advise (a) critical listening and (b) careful observation for whatever can be useful to the individual. Fortunately, exposure to actual solution-focused clinical work often obviates "solution-forced" expectations: seeing is believing.

Observing solution-focused practice, especially in challenging settings and cases, generally eliminates other mythologies as well, such as the "justs": Solution-focused therapy is just operant conditioning, just positive thinking, just Rogerian listening, just for high-functioning "easy" clients.

Evaluation

"So it's not therapy. You can't measure success in the same ways" (de Shazer, talking about training in Hoyt, 1996, p. 80). Common methods for evaluating trainees are antithetical to the solution-focused approach. There is a basic contradiction in using criterion-referenced indices to evaluate outcome in a client-centered model. The only valid solution-focused criteria in clinical training are those determined by the trainees. However, in most settings where evaluation of trainees occurs, trainees must meet externally determined standards, and trainers must develop protocols for evaluation that satisfy institutional or professional demands for reliably demonstrated knowledge and skills.

This is not an insurmountable problem, either philosophically or practically. While it is important to evaluate in ways consistent with what has been taught and learned, it is also true that no approach should be evaluated solely through its own lens. From an SFBT point of view, evaluating according to external criteria is simply another example of "speaking the client's language."

Within a typical solution-focused training framework, evaluation already occurs at a number of levels. First, there is individual students' ongoing evaluation of progress on their own training goals. Second, trainers solicit evaluative feedback from students both formally (via questionnaires asking what worked, what could be done differently, etc.) and informally (e.g., via scaling questions on the extent to which the training process and content are "on track" and follow-up questions about what will improve that number). Another way of providing solution-focused evaluative feedback is the development of a solution-focused message (compliments for what works plus a "homework task"). This can be a joint exercise, in which trainees and trainers compose such messages for each other.

Several useful tools exist for more formally evaluating the clinical skills and progress of solution-focused trainees. All of these tools have in common a "solutions focus" on what trainees are doing successfully; they may also provide useful data for external evaluation requirements. Chevalier (1995) provides a series of brief, focused "skillsheets" for rating different areas of practice. De Jong and Berg's (1997b) "Interviewer Skills Rating Form" is a longer, more comprehensive rating scale. Warner (n.d.) has developed a "qualitative self assessment." The "Consultation Feedback Form" developed by Brenda Zalter and myself is an adaptation and extension of Warner's approach that can be used to evaluate trainees' taped or live sessions with clients. The form can be completed by the trainees themselves, by their peers, and by the instructor, thus providing a rich source of constructive, solution-focused feedback. (Development of a parallel feedback form to assess the practice of solution-focused trainers would be a worthwhile future project.)

A last, critical level of evaluation, largely unexplored so far, is evaluative research on solution-focused training programs. There are three basic questions for such research:

1. Is the program adhering to an accepted set of criteria that characterize solution-focused training? (To my knowledge, no such criteria currently exist.)
2. Are the graduates of the program practicing SFBT (according to, for example, the EFBTA guidelines)?
3. How are outcomes different for the graduates' clients?

WHAT WORKS

Beginning As We Mean to Go On

Consulting with learners before the first class or workshop provides an opportunity to take a solution-focused stance from the first contact.

Pretraining interviews, e-mail messages, or questionnaires can ask questions such as:

- If a miracle happens and this training meets all of your needs as a practitioner/intern/ . . . , what will be different afterward?
- What will you be doing differently with clients? . . . colleagues? . . . referral sources?
- What will your clients say they notice? What difference will this make for them?
- What will you keep doing because it works?
- How will you enhance what you are already doing that works?
- How do you learn best?

Pretraining consultation of this kind sets the stage for a "purposeful relationship," and can also be critical in assisting trainers working with different cultural groups to tailor educational methods to the students' needs and preferences. Letting students or workshop organizers know that "I will want to hear about what works well for you in your setting with the clients you see" is also a useful pre-workshop message.

It is helpful to ask questions in any area where it is possible to offer trainees *choices* in the training experience from which training modalities they prefer to what to have for lunch. Obviously, it is important when one solicits this input to make use of it and to make its value and its impact clear to trainees.

Early in the first meeting with students, I typically conduct a "solution-focused stocktaking exercise," asking what they are doing that works and what works less well or is a problem, that is, where they would like to try something different. As I record this information, it is important to make appreciative comments (compliments) about the usefulness and relevance of their current perceptions and successful strategies.

Introductions and "warm-ups" can set a solution-focused tone immediately. For example, I often use a "name game" (Fiske & Zalter, 2005a) in which participants introduce themselves:

1. by first name (if culturally appropriate); and
2. with one word to describe a quality, skill, or attribute they have that makes them helpful to their clients and that begins with the same letter as the first letter of their names (e.g., "I am *H*eather and I am *h*opeful").

This task is a useful opener in two ways: (a) it directs attention to strengths and (b) it typically generates immediate talk and laughter. The list of positive words developed can become the basis for a solution-focused group message generated either by participants or by the trainer at the end of the session. Individuals can use their words as the beginning of a list of clinical strengths to be refined and utilized.

Taylor (2005b) has developed a list of variations on an exercise of Insoo Kim Berg's in which she asks learners in small groups to identify one thing that they noticed this morning that tells them life is good. These warm-ups are brief, effective in setting a positive tone and promoting interaction, and get people's attention. It is important not to be "married" to particular outcomes for structured exercises. They are starting points or vehicles for teaching solution-focused practice.

Goal Setting

It has become standard practice for the educator to provide one or more goals and several specific, operationalized objectives for any educational program. However, it also is important that SFBT trainees set their own individual goals. Early on, the trainer usually asks a goal-setting question, for example, one thing students want to take away from this course. The answers are critical in helping the trainer to select formats and content that will be a good "fit."

Individual trainees can further develop their goals in four steps:

1. Construct a detailed picture of a future in which they are using this training in ways that are helpful to them and to their clients. The miracle question and its variants, in verbal or written form, are very helpful here. Alternative methods might include a job evaluation from the future, a role-play of "how my client will describe our work together," or the "solutions timequake," a role-play of an "alumni meeting" two years hence (Maurer-Hankovszky & Szabó, 2002).
2. Consider ways in which changes they want are already happening (including what they already do that works).
3. Identify where they are now with regard to these developments and where they want to be by the end of the training, usually with scaling questions.
4. Establish concrete observable criteria for goal progress and goal achievement: "What will be the first small sign that you are moving in the direction you want to go?" or "What will you be doing differently?"

One of my preferred formats for individual goal setting in SFBT training utilizes "scaling in action" (Fiske & Zalter, 2005b). I ask participants to position themselves on an imaginary scale from 1 to 10 down the center of the room in response to scaling questions about how confident they are now in helping their most difficult clients, and where they would like to be—that is, their goals—on the same scale. They are asked to discuss what will be different when they have reached their goals and what first steps they will take to get there. An advantage of this format is that moving around the room to respond to questions seems to literally "loosen people up"; talk flows more freely and participants seem engaged with the process and with one another (see Jackson, 2005 for variations of this format).

Changing Lenses

De Jong and Berg (1997b) discuss the value of teaching SFBT in ways that invite learners to make a paradigm shift from "expert" problem-solving to helping individuals discover their own solutions. Matthias Varga von Kibed (von Kibed & de Shazer, 2003) describes the difference between observing with the "eyes of separation"—eyes ready to analyze, to break down, to discover flaws, faults, and errors—and the "eyes of connection," which notice what works, what helps, what relates. Experiences that highlight the difference between these two orientations and that allow learners to see through the "eyes of connection" are helpful in preparing people for this paradigm shift. Opportunities to make such a shift may be especially important when the students involved have previous training and experience in other, very different paradigms: ". . . the older, more experienced practitioners know all this stuff about what works but they don't know they know it. And they get hung up on looking at what doesn't work" (de Shazer, in Hoyt, 1994, p. 22).

One example of an exercise that is useful in this regard is "Problem Talk versus Solution Talk" (De Jong & Berg, 1997b), in which students are asked to practice and then compare two simple scenarios, one requiring attention to details of a problem, and the other requiring attention to the details of what went well.

Lamarre (2005) and Ghul (2005) describe versions of another effective technique. They ask participants to work in pairs, with one person talking about a complaint or pet peeve while the other listens without speaking. After three minutes, the listener gives the complainer three compliments based on what has been heard. Debriefing of this exercise illuminates (a) how possible—even easy—it is to discover strengths, resources, and successes worthy of complimenting, even while listening to a problem story; (b) how gratifying it is for the complainer to be complimented; (c) how often compliments are experienced as a "tap on the shoulder," drawing the complainers' attention to aspects of their own behavior that had not been considered; and

(d) how different is the experience for the listeners when listening for compliments rather than for problems. I am convinced that this last factor provides one of the major attractions of SFBT for many practitioners.

Other trainers have devised their own creative ways of structuring "lens-changing" opportunities for solution-focused students, using clips from soap operas (Andrews, 2005), the disease concept of alcoholism (Shafer, 2005), a "wall of questions" (Maurer-Hankovszky & Szabó, 2002), DSM diagnostic labels (Nelson, 2005c), case studies with a surprise twist (Simon, 2005), conversations with a person hearing voices (MacDonald, 2005), and assumptions about the causes of crime (Myers, 2005).

Practice, Practice, Practice

"Doing is knowing." An important criterion for effective training might be the amount of time trainees spend actively "doing"—discovering and enhancing their own expertise, versus passively listening to the "expert" trainer or watching "expert" solution-focused therapists on videotape. How do we minimize didactic teaching and maximize more active learning?

De Jong and Berg (1997b) use the term "mini-lecture" to describe their recommended deemphasis on long soliloquies by trainers. Students much prefer brief, focused discourses, enlivened by stories and case examples and interspersed among active exercises to long "comprehensive" lectures (Maggio, Chenail, & Todd, 2001).

One simple route to more active, "non-expert-led" learning is attributed to Gale Miller (cited in De Jong & Berg, 1997b). He suggests introducing a question (e.g., "What works when the client says 'I don't know'?") and inviting learners to contribute their ideas about what will work.

John Sharry (2001) has carefully developed a similar process in solution-focused psychoeducational groups. His four-step model is readily adapted to training situations:

1. Predicting—encourage learners to come up with ideas first
2. Reviewing—review with learners their views in response to the questions presented
3. Finding fit—help learners select the ideas that work for them
4. Planning—help learners plan how to adopt the ideas in their practice

A primary responsibility of SFBT trainers is to provide "structured opportunities" for trainees to practice skills (De Jong & Berg, 1997b). There are many ways to do this, ranging from supervised practice with real clients to providing structured exercises for rehearsing techniques with co-students. Consider two possible ways of communicating with trainees about the importance of using the client's language: (a) a lecture complete with audiovisual text aids; and (b) Chevalier's (1995) suggestion for students to listen to one another's stories and gather "four potent phrases" that describe the other person's views. Further ideas for exercises that can replace didactic teaching of solution-focused skills can be found in several published sources (Chevalier, 1995; De Jong & Berg, 1997b; Maurer-Hankovsky & Szabó, 2002; Nelson, 2005b; Sharry et al., 2003). Trainers also can find ideas in conversations between solution-focused trainers, in presentations at the SFBTA and EBTA conferences, and in interactions with solution-focused trainees.

Students need time to practice both within and between training sessions. For students with training and experience in other methods, such blocks of practice time may be particularly critical because their integration task is formidable. The ideal venue is a training facility that includes a clinical practice setting with opportunities for teamwork and live supervision. Failing this, it is essential to find other ways to facilitate skill practice and revision.

When formal internship, externship, or in-house supervised practice is unavailable, chances for successful integration of solution-focused practice can be enhanced by some simple strategies:

1. Insoo Kim Berg (personal communication, August 12, 1992) recommends organizing training time so that the initial training is followed weeks or months later by a second round. Participants can practice during the interval and then ask questions and refine their skills in the second, "refresher" program.

2. Networking at any level enhances the likelihood that trainees will continue to use and develop skills learned in formal training. Trainers can encourage or even organize solution-focused interest groups in a work setting or geographical area, where members meet regularly—whether "live" or online—to exchange experiences, view one another's tapes, or (ideally) see clients in live consultation. Conferences such as the annual Solution-Focused Brief Therapy Association (SFBTA) meeting provide further reinforcement.

3. Online capacity has made supervision, consultation, and further development through distance education much more available, even to otherwise isolated practitioners (Berg, 2003; Maggio et al., 2001; Oullette & Sells, 2003).

4. Participation in outcome studies means that practitioners new to the model may be more likely to adhere to its core practices (another good reason for involvement in research!).

5. Peter De Jong (De Jong & Berg, 1997b) recruits former students who are now practicing SFBT to lead skills labs for current students, a skill development "win" for all parties involved.

6. Maurer-Hankovszky and Szabó (2002) present graduates from their training workshops with a "magical learner's diary," for ongoing recording of "goals, miracles, resources, and exceptions."

Demonstrations and Observations

It seems only fair that trainers as well as trainees should have to present what they actually do with clients; certainly, trainees tell us that seeing their trainers "in action" is important to them. Most of us use either videotapes of our solution-focused work or (in my case) readings of case transcripts to demonstrate key aspects of practice. We may have the opportunity for live consultations with students acting as a reflecting team. Although live demonstrations have undeniable impact, most trainers also continue to use taped materials or transcripts, because some conversations offer clearer examples of particular methods and applications than others do. And frankly, some cases just make a better story. To paraphrase Insoo Kim Berg: if you are going to help students to change their practices, first you have to get their attention!

Most trainers also use videotapes of cases with well-known solution-focused practitioners. We all have our favourites; mine is "Irreconcilable Differences" (Berg, 1994).[1] This favoritism is a potential stumbling block if we fail to ensure that students see practitioners with a range of styles, all practicing SFBT effectively in their own unique ways.

Observational tasks maximize student engagement and learning from demonstrations. Observations assigned may include words or phrases used repeatedly by clients, things the therapist does or says that make a difference to the client, things the client does or says that show the therapist was helpful, what the client is doing to cooperate with the therapist, what the therapist is doing to cooperate with the client, and the strengths and resources of each interview participant. Gallagher (2005) is a rich source of such tasks. As a rule, it is more important for students to learn to observe the client's behavior rather than the therapist's.

Debriefing of observations can be expanded on in several ways by asking students to suggest alternative solution-focused interventions, to develop a solution-focused message for the client, or to observe part of a taped or scripted session and role-play the rest in small groups.

The Ubiquitous Role-Play

Although the utility and generalizability of role-play as a method for skills learning has long been questioned (e.g., Haley, 1981), role-play exercises of various kinds remain the most widely used "action" tool in most trainers' toolboxes. For example, in response to the question about what to do when the client says, "I don't know" in response to the miracle question, the trainer might offer to role-play the interaction. Students are typically enthusiastic about such "ad lib" performances and often express the "Aha!" sensations that are so reinforcing for therapists and trainers. However, the extent to which they are then more likely to use the miracle question in a timely way remains unclear (de Shazer, personal communication, September 5, 2001). How do we utilize role-plays so that they are most likely to facilitate trainees' solution-focused practice?

The most common type of role-play is the case presented by a student, who often plays "client" with the trainer as "therapist." The relevance (for at least that student) and immediacy of this approach are advantages for using it. Disadvantages are that (a) it may be difficult to get all participants "on the same page"; (b) valuable time is lost in case description and explanation; (c) observing may not be as helpful as more active participation; and (d) the particular case may not be relevant for many participants. The relevance issue is of particular significance in terms of generalization to actual practice. Cunanan's (2003) respondents described seeing positive change *in their own clients* as key to their wholehearted adoption of SFBT practice. The closer the role-play scenario comes to this situation, the more likely it may be to have a positive impact.

One alternative is to invite the student group to jointly "create" a case for role-play; when everyone participates, broader relevance is more likely. The role-play can proceed in small groups with members playing the client(s), therapist(s), and team/observers; in the whole group, with the trainer playing the therapist and all of the students playing the client(s); or in small groups with one member playing the client and the others playing a single therapist speaking in turn (De Jong & Berg, 1997b; de Shazer, 2005). This last approach helps trainees to attend carefully to the client's responses in building their own questions. Another approach is to read part of a case transcript as a demonstration, stop, and have participants begin at that point and role-play the case in small groups.

I utilize clips from mainstream, fictional movies by selecting a relevant character and situation. I show a 5- to 10-minute clip illustrating the character's "problem" behavior and invite students to role-play a therapeutic conversation with the character. The advantages of this approach are that everyone is on the same page; I can select interesting "cases" relevant to particular topics; the "just a movie" quality makes it easier for participants to risk "playing," that is, experimenting with solution-focused techniques; and the same "just a movie" aspect can offer participants helpful "distance" on difficult or distressing material (e.g., trauma sequelae, suicidal behavior). Insoo Kim Berg (personal communication, June 2, 2003) describes using a clip from a marital therapy session in "The Sopranos" television show as a role-play stimulus in a workshop on couple therapy.

Role-play situations can be selected according to the students' clinical interests and level of skill development rather than adopting a "one size fits all" policy. De Jong and Berg (1997b) provide a "bank" of role-play scenarios for use in SFBT training with suggestions as to how to utilize them at different stages of solution-building skill acquisition.

Some experienced trainers (e.g., Michael Kennedy, personal communication, December 15, 2003) believe that role-play has most impact when trainees use their own personal concerns as material; that is, the exercise is actually a demonstration session. I see this as valuable as long as there are limits on the nature of the material disclosed. Training is not "therapy"; nor should self-disclosure be a requirement. Suggesting that participants practice using job-related material seems acceptable. I often rely on Yvonne Dolan's discovery that saying the word, "paperwork," generates ample problem material for role-play purposes. One caveat is that in cultural contexts with strong injunctions against self-disclosure, fictional role-plays will be a better "fit."

Brenda Zalter, who teaches workshops on using SFBT with individuals who have chronic illnesses (personal communication, April 4, 2000) "assigns" each participant a chronic illness with the associated symptoms (based on information she provides). In these "roles," they respond to solution-focused interventions.

In some settings, students and teachers may be able to utilize "standardized patients"—actors prepared to assume a particular role for role-play purposes. One unique benefit of standardized patient role-plays is the capacity to "rewind" the therapeutic conversation and try something else. This format supports "mindful" learning, which Langer (1997) describes as the acquisition of skills in ways that enhance the capacity to make small adjustments in response to changed circumstances rather than learning by rote to do things one right way.

In small-group role-play situations, I ask each participant to generate two words each for what the "therapist" and the "client" did or said in the role-play that was helpful. If possible, these words are recorded for the individuals involved. This exercise is quick (two to three minutes) and emphasizes two key aspects of solution-focused practice: the use of compliments to identify and reinforce what works, and attention to the helpful behavior of the *client* as a primary factor. I am embarrassed to admit that it took several years for me to extend the exercise to client as well as therapist. Old habits. . . .

In addition to "tweaking" role-play tools in some of the ways described here, trainers can make efforts to tie the training experience to practice by actively encouraging trainees to make specific plans for change; follow-up contact via letter, e-mail, or telephone; and inviting trainee participation in solution-focused research, teaching, and collegial associations.

Storytelling

Stories used by trainers to illustrate solution-focused methods create a context for the information conveyed. Humans learn information best when it is presented in a context even better in a context with some personal relevance. Perhaps best of all is when the context includes laughter and surprise ("first you have to get their attention. . . ."). Stories grease the wheels of new learning.

We cannot assign our own, invariant meanings to the stories we tell. "Education should concentrate on presenting events or experiences in ways that encourage others to find their own significance" (Ross, 1996). As a storyteller, a solution-focused trainer is less like Aesop, whose stories had a single sharp point and more like an Aboriginal elder, or perhaps Milton Erickson: someone who recognizes that messages are not sent, but only received (de Shazer, 1994).

Trainers can also structure opportunities for students to discover and contribute their own illustrative stories, as in De Jong's (2005) "success story" check-ins for student therapists or Fiske and Zalter's (2005c) "solution-focused scavenger hunt."

Mixing and Matching

Humans learn in many different ways. As trainers, we can maximize the chances of successful learning by attending to individual learning styles and adapting tasks and training strategies to what works best for the people involved. We can provide a mix of learning modalities so that even when individualization is difficult (e.g., class sizes are too great), most trainees will have opportunities to utilize their preferred styles. A "menu" of mini-lectures, interactive exercises, demonstrations, observational activities, general discussion, and structured skill practice offers "something for everyone."

Flexibility and interest can be maximized by shifting among whole group, small group, and one-to-one exercises. Changing formats helps to keep the pace and atmosphere of training sessions animated.

Pacing

Pacing and timing are key aspects of successful training but more difficult to specify and to teach than are techniques. To stay "on track" with students' needs, interest, and energy it is helpful to make a regular practice of asking students what they want; for example, "On a scale from one to ten, if ten stands for 'ready for a break right now,' and one stands for, 'will never need a break. . . .'" Switching formats—in particular, switching to one in which students are more actively involved—can be helpful if energy and interest seem to be flagging (*do something different*). Getting people physically moving is usually refreshing.

Trainers can develop a small store of "pick-em-ups," that is, methods that revitalize a tired group. These may be stories, exercises, or live or video demonstrations. One of my favorites is my collection of cartoons illustrating solution-focused assumptions and methods.

Lastly, it is helpful to remember that no teacher—and no student—are "on" every day!

Care and Feeding

"Care and feeding" is intended to be, first of all, a literal reminder to attend to the comfort of training participants in terms of information, food and beverages, breaks and scheduling, and opportunities for networking and schmoozing. Whatever the limitations imposed by mandates, budgets, and other constraints, the positive impact of a training experience is enhanced by these considerations.

A second way in which professional learners can be "fed" is to receive handouts, whether as hard copy or electronic. Especially helpful are materials conducive to use or reference in practice settings once the learner is (back) at work. The reproducible "solution-building tools" in De Jong and Berg's (1997a) manual are excellent examples of such materials. Production of specific tools is also a useful training exercise.

Lastly, adopting the students' "language" in terms of addressing their special clinical concerns makes the training experience much more relevant and "nourishing" for them.

Utilizing the Trainer's Resources and Strengths

Workers who care for their tools do a better job. What are the "tools" of a solution-focused trainer? And how do we care for them?

Clinical Experience

I think it is critical that "instructors . . . continue to see cases and practice the skills they teach" (De Jong & Berg, 1997b). Our experience is a key factor in allowing us to situate our teaching in a "live" context, especially early in the process before trainees have acquired much experience of their own. This allows us to respond naturally and helpfully to clinical questions and to demonstrate the sustained "flow" of solution-focused conversation that is a stumbling block for so many trainees once they have mastered basic techniques.

An Interest in Language and Its Use in Therapy

The trainer's attention to the "trivia" of language use models this focus for trainees. It also orients us toward noticing students' unique and helpful use of language.

Voice

Given that our voices are a primary teaching (and therapeutic) tool, I believe that we should attend to keeping them in good working order and to optimizing their effectiveness in terms of range and expressiveness. This may involve seeking vocal training or coaching, exercises, or periods of silence.

Storytelling Ability

SFBT training is not standup comedy, and it is the students' stories, rather than the teachers', that are most important; *but,* teaching devoid of illustrative stories is a grim, dull business. Each of us has our own style, and only a few are "born storytellers"—yet all of us can take the time to hone our storytelling ability.

Libraries

Books and journal articles, although important, are not the only resources in the "libraries" to which I refer. I think that it is helpful to have a bank of helpful resources accessible, including printed matter, tapes (video- and audio-), and case examples and stories from many sources, including fictional and personal ones.

Sense of Humor

My wise grandmother taught me that it was a saving grace. In psychology school, they taught me that a sense of humor was a sign of cognitive flexibility, another essential attribute for the facilitator who wants to utilize what works on a particular day for a particular group, instead of resorting to formulae.

Curiosity

Just as curiosity is important in clinical work, so is it important in training work. What do they want? What are they already doing to get it? What are the resources they have that will make a difference in their efforts? What can I contribute that will work for them?

A Personal Toolbox

This is necessarily an incomplete and idiosyncratic inventory of useful tools. Consider the following questions in compiling your own:

- What are my strengths as a trainer? What would my students or trainees say are my strengths? What feedback have I had about this so far? How can I acquire more specific feedback?
- How am I utilizing, maintaining, and improving my strengths?
- What are the skills or tools I utilize that could be improved?
- What personal and professional practices help me to approach students with an attitude of respect and curiosity?

ON ENDING WELL

"Then you have to somehow determine how you're going to know when to stop. When is . . . training done? Generally, I suppose that has to be arbitrary; somehow they determine that" (Steve de Shazer, in Hoyt, 1996, p. 80). Rather than debate myself over when training ends (never? When we die? When we start hyphenating "solution-focused" with names of other models?), I will focus on how to end in helpful ways. Solution-focused messages are a congruent conclusion for training sessions. Reviews of progress toward goals reinforce new skills. Solution-focused "action plans" can orient trainees toward skill maintenance.

Trainees surveyed after completing a six-module SFBT program in Toronto have consistently commented on the module closings, which typically involved an exercise such as the "group gift" (Zalter & Fiske, 2005) or Thomas's "Exercise of Appreciation" (2005). In addition to being demonstrations of the deliberate application and impact of compliments, these exercises are light-hearted and fun. This quality is consistent with Miller's (1997) observations on the "serious playfulness" of SFBT, and likely to facilitate learning.

Future Directions

Suppose a miracle happens and solution-focused training develops in useful and interesting ways . . . what will be different?

Part of a positive future for solution-focused training lies in continuing what has already begun in terms of published material on training activities and opportunities for solution-focused trainers and trainees to network. An essential change will be more research on SFBT training. For such research to be possible, it is necessary to establish an adherence model, that is, criteria for what SFBT training should "look like." Following is a list that I developed as a start for this project:

- The trainer offers trainees choices
- Trainees identify what they are already doing that is working
- Trainees set and evaluate individual goals for training
- Trainees have opportunities for "discovery-based learning"
- Trainer provides information about and/or demonstrations of solution-focused techniques:
  — the miracle question
  — goal setting
  — exception-finding
  — scaling questions
  — coping questions
  — relationship questions
  — compliments
  — solution-focused messages
- Training provides structured opportunities for practice

I hope this list will generate useful discussion.

CONCLUSION

The "secret" of SFBT training is for the trainer to listen to the students and to take what they say seriously. But you knew that already. May your learning and teaching be a rich and surprising conversation.

NOTE

1. Editor's note (TSN): One of my favorites is "Coming through the Ceiling" in which Steve de Shazer works with a client who is convinced that her upstairs neighbor is beaming something through the ceiling to keep her awake.

REFERENCES

Andrews, J. (2005). Communicating a different reality: Expanding points of view. In T. S. Nelson (Ed.), *Education and training in solution-focused brief therapy* (pp. 253-255). Binghamton, NY: The Haworth Press.

Berg, I. K. (1992). A wolf in disguise is not a grandmother. *Journal of Systemic Therapies, 13*(1), 13-14.

Berg, I. K. (1994). *Irreconcilable differences: A solution-focused approach to marital therapy.* (Videotape). Available at www.brief-therapy.com

Berg, I. K. (2003). *Online courses for distance learning.* Retrieved Dec. 30, 2003 from http://www.brief-therapy.org/insoo_online.htm

Berg, I. K. (2005). The state of miracles in relationships. In T. S. Nelson (Ed.), *Education and training in solution-focused brief therapy* (pp. 115-118). Binghamton, NY: The Haworth Press.

Berg, I. K., & de Shazer, S. (1992, July). *Advanced clinical training.* Workshop presented at the Brief Family Therapy Center, Milwaukee, WI.

Berg, I. K., & Dolan, Y. (2001). *Tales of solutions: A collection of hope-inspiring stories.* New York: Norton.

Beyebach, M. (2000). *European Brief Therapy Association outcome study: Research definition.* Retrieved Dec. 26, 2005 from http://www.ebta.nu/page2/page30/page30.html

Booker, J. (1996). Solution-focused hospital diversion: Treatment of first choice. In S. D. Miller, M. A. Hubble, & B. L. Duncan (Eds.), *Handbook of solution-focused brief therapy* (pp. 205-227). San Francisco: Jossey-Bass.

Chevalier, A. J. (1995). *On the client's path: A manual to teaching brief solution-focused therapy.* Oakland, CA: New Harbinger.

Cunanan, E. (2003). *What works when learning solution focused brief therapy: A qualitative study of trainees' experience?* Unpublished master's thesis, Department of Human Development, Virginia Tech University, Falls Church, VA.

De Jong, P. (2005). Teaching practice via success stories. In T. S. Nelson (Ed.), *Education and training in solution-focused brief therapy* (pp. 257-262). Binghamton, NY: The Haworth Press.

De Jong, P., & Berg, I. K. (1997a). *Interviewing for solutions*. Pacific Grove, CA: Brooks/Cole.

De Jong, P., & Berg, I. K. (1997b). *Instructor's resource manual for interviewing for solutions*. Pacific Grove, CA: Brooks/Cole.

de Shazer, S. (1994). *Words were originally magic*. New York: Norton.

de Shazer, S. (2002, June). *Seminar on teaching solution-focused brief therapy*. Purdue University Calumet, Hammond, IN.

de Shazer, S. (2005). Inside and outside. In T. S. Nelson (Ed.), *Education and training in solution-focused brief therapy* (pp. 71-72). Binghamton, NY: The Haworth Press.

Eriksen, K., & McAuliffe, G. (Eds.). (2001). *Teaching counselors and therapists: Constructivist and developmental course design.* Westport, CT: Bergin & Garvey.

Fiske, H. (2005). Five small-group exercises for experiential learning of SFBT. In T. S. Nelson (Ed.), *Education and training in solution-focused brief therapy* (pp. 155-158). Binghamton, NY: The Haworth Press.

Fiske, H., & Zalter, B. (2005a). The name game. In T. S. Nelson (Ed.), *Education and training in solution-focused brief therapy* (pp. 61-62). Binghamton, NY: The Haworth Press.

Fiske, H., & Zalter, B. (2005b). Scaling in action. In T. S. Nelson (Ed.), *Education and training in solution-focused brief therapy* (pp. 107-110). Binghamton, NY: The Haworth Press.

Fiske, H., & Zalter, B. (2005c). Solution-focused scavenger hunt. In T. S. Nelson (Ed.), *Education and training in solution-focused brief therapy* (pp. 127-130). Binghamton, NY: The Haworth Press.

Gallagher, D. (2005). The listen and describe approach to training in Solution-Focused Brief Therapy. In T. S. Nelson (Ed.), *Education and training in solution-focused brief therapy* (pp. 229-252). Binghamton, NY: The Haworth Press.

Ghul, R. (2005). Moan, moan, moan. In T. S. Nelson (Ed.), *Education and training in solution-focused brief therapy* (pp. 63-64). Binghamton, NY: The Haworth Press.

Hackett, P. (2005). Ever appreciating circles. In T. S. Nelson (Ed.), *Education and training in solution-focused brief therapy* (pp. 83-84). Binghamton, NY: The Haworth Press.

Haley, J. (1981). 14 ways to fail as a teacher of family therapy. In *Reflections on therapy and other essays*. Chevy Chase, MD: The Family Therapy Institute of Washington, DC.

Hoyt, M. F. (1994). On the importance of keeping it simple and taking the patient seriously: A conversation with Steve de Shazer and John Weakland. In M. F. Hoyt (Ed.), *Constructive therapies* (pp. 11-40). New York: Guilford.

Hoyt, M. F. (1996). Solution-building and language games: A conversation with Steve de Shazer. In M. F. Hoyt (Ed.), *Constructive Therapies 2* (pp. 60–86). New York: Guilford.

Jackson, P. (2005). A scaling walk. In T. S. Nelson (Ed.), *Education and training in solution-focused brief therapy* (pp. 111-112). Binghamton, NY: The Haworth Press.

Lamarre, J. (2005). Complaining exercise. In T. S. Nelson (Ed.), *Education and training in solution-focused brief therapy* (pp. 65-66). Binghamton, NY: The Haworth Press.

Langer, E. (1997). *The power of mindful learning.* Reading, MA: Addison-Wesley.

MacDonald, A. J. (2005). "Voices": An exercise in developing solution-focused conversations with the mentally ill. In T. S. Nelson (Ed.), *Education and training in solution-focused brief therapy* (pp. 39-42). Binghamton, NY: The Haworth Press.

Maggio, L. M., Chenail, R., & Todd, T. (2001). Teaching family therapy in an electronic age. *Journal of Systemic Therapies, 20*(1), 12-23.

Maggio, L. M., & Marcotte, M., Perry, J., & Truax, D. (2001). Student perspectives on training. *Journal of Systemic Therapies, 20*(1), 36-44.

Martin, S. (n.d.), as cited in Reamy-Stephenson, M. (1986). No bolts from the blue. In D. E. Efron (Ed.), *Journeys: Expansion of the strategic-systemic therapies.* New York: Brunner/Mazel.

Maurer-Hankovszky, K., & Szabó, P. (2002). *Elements of solution-focused training methodology.* Retrieved October 29, 2005 from "Resources" at www.solworld.org. (Originally published as "Element lösungsorientierter Didaktik" in *LO, Lemende Organisation, 9,* 29-32.)

McCollum, E., & Cunanan, E. (2003, November). *What works when teaching and learning solution-focused brief therapy?* Presented at the first annual conference of the Solution-Focused Brief Therapy Association, Loma Linda, CA.

McLuhan, M. (1994). *Understanding media: The extensions of man.* (reprinted edition, first pub. 1964). Cambridge, MA: MIT Press

Miller, G. (1997). *Becoming miracle workers: Language and meaning in brief therapy.* New York: Aldine de Gruyter.

Milner, J. (2005). Doing something different. In T. S. Nelson (Ed.), *Education and training in solution-focused brief therapy* (pp. 163-168). Binghamton, NY: The Haworth Press.

Myers, S. (2005). Brief training in brief therapies. In T. S. Nelson (Ed.), *Education and training in solution-focused brief therapy* (pp. 159-162). Binghamton, NY: The Haworth Press.

Nelson, T. S. (2005a). Editor's introduction: The birth of the Solution-Focused Brief Therapy Association. In T. S. Nelson (Ed.), *Education and training in solution-focused brief therapy* (pp. 1-4). Binghamton, NY: The Haworth Press.

Nelson, T. S. (Ed.). (2005b). *Education and training in solution-focused brief therapy.* Binghamton, NY: The Haworth Press.

Nelson, T. (2005c). Pathologies to descriptions: Moving from problem to solution DSM (Diagnostic Solution Method). In T. S. Nelson (Ed.), *Education and training in solution-focused brief therapy* (pp. 73-74). Binghamton, NY: The Haworth Press.

Nylund, D., & Corsiglia, V. (1994). Becoming solution-focused forced in brief therapy: Remembering something important we already knew. *Journal of Systemic Therapies, 13*(1), 5-12.

Oullette, P. M., & Sells, S. P. (2003). Learning therapy in a technology-supported instructional environment. *Journal of Systemic Therapies, 22*(3), 14-26.

Riegeluth, C.M. (Ed.). (1987). *Instructional theories in action: Lessons illustrating selected theories and models.* Hillsdale, NJ: Lawrence Erlbaum Associates.

Ross, R. (1996). *Returning to the teachings: Exploring aboriginal justice.* Toronto, ON: Penguin.

Shafer, K. (2005). The disease concept and SFT: Difference in action. In T. S. Nelson (Ed.), *Education and training in solution-focused brief therapy* (pp. 75-78). Binghamton, NY: The Haworth Press.

Sharry, J. (2001). *Solution-focused groupwork.* London: Sage.

Sharry, J., Madden, B., & Darmody, M. (2003). *Becoming a solution detective: Identifying your clients' strengths in practical brief therapy.* Binghamton, NY: The Haworth Press.

Simon, J. (2005). Three case studies. In T. S. Nelson (Ed.), *Education and training in solution-focused brief therapy* (pp. 149-154). Binghamton, NY: The Haworth Press.

Street, E. (1997). Family therapy training research—An updating review. *Journal of Family Therapy, 19,* 89-111.

Sutherland, P. (Ed.). (1997). *Adult learning: A reader.* London: Kogan Page.

Taylor, L. (2005a). Curious questioning. In T. S. Nelson (Ed.), *Education and training in solution-focused brief therapy* (pp. 87-88). Binghamton, NY: The Haworth Press.

Taylor, L. (2005b). Openers. In T. S. Nelson (Ed.), *Education and training in solution-focused brief therapy* (pp. 59-60). Binghamton, NY: The Haworth Press.

Thomas, F. (2005). Exercise of appreciation. In T. S. Nelson (Ed.), *Education and training in solution-focused brief therapy* (pp. 135-136). Binghamton, NY: The Haworth Press.

von Kibed, M.V., & de Shazer, S. (2003, November). A conversation on Wittgenstein. Plenary presentation at the Conference on Solution-Focused Practices 2003, first annual conference of the Solution-Focused Brief Therapy Association, Loma Linda, CA.

Warner, R. (n.d.). *Solution-focused training: Developing the "qualitative self assessment practice standards."* EFBTA Newsletter. Retrieved Dec. 18, 2003 from http://www.ebta.nu/article-warner1.html

Wittgenstein, L. (1968). *Philosophical investigation* (3rd ed., G.E.M. Anscombe, Trans.). New York: MacMillan.

Young, S. (2005). Success and failure. In T. S. Nelson (Ed.), *Education and training in solution-focused brief therapy* (pp. 85-86). Binghamton, NY: The Haworth Press.

Zalter, B., & Fiske, H. (2005). Group gift exercise. In T. S. Nelson (Ed.), *Education and training in solution-focused brief therapy* (pp. 131-134). Binghamton, NY: The Haworth Press.

Chapter 15

Solution-Focused Supervision

John Wheeler

INTRODUCTION

An experienced solution-focused colleague once told of an "Aha" moment in his career as a supervisor. Another colleague, new to Solution-Focused Brief Therapy (SFBT), had been keen to improve his solution-focused practice. Together, they arranged some live supervision: the supervisee endeavouring to use SFBT with a family who were looking for help, and the supervisor watching through a one-way screen. By the time the supervisee took a break, the supervisor had noticed many missed opportunities. The family had spoken of times when the problem had not been around, but the supervisee had not explored exceptions. Goals for change had not been established. A scaling question (0 to 10, worst to best) had revealed movement from 3 to 5, but the difference had not been clarified. Opportunities to compliment the family on qualities that could be useful resources in resolving their difficulties had passed by unnoticed. And no miracle question had been asked. During the break, the supervisor commented on what he had noticed and made some suggestions, and the supervisee went back into the therapy room to conclude the interview. The same things happened over the course of the next two sessions. By the third session, it was quite clear that the supervisee was making no progress at all. If anything, the supervisee was becoming more hesitant and confused in his interviewing, and the supervisor started to doubt not only the supervisee's potential to grasp SFBT but also his own capacity as a supervisor. More alarmingly, the problems for the family were getting worse. Then suddenly, during the fourth session, the "Aha" moment arose. Feeling like kicking

Handbook of Solution-Focused Brief Therapy: Clinical Applications
© 2007 by The Haworth Press, Inc. All rights reserved.
doi:10.1300/5135_15

himself, the supervisor realized that while he was usually able to be solution-focused in his practice, he was not being at all solution-focused in his supervision. So this time, he looked out for what the supervisee did well. He then shared this information during the break and asked how the supervisee thought he might end the session. From then on, both the supervisee and the family made steady progress.

Before we take a critical view of this colleague for not grasping such an obvious point earlier on, perhaps we should note that the time lag between the first publications on solution-focused practice and publications on solution-focused supervision was about eight years. It would appear that lifting the approach from the domain of practice into the domain of supervision was either not as obvious a move as we might have expected, or the transfer has raised particular complications that first needed to be resolved.

The following account starts with some guiding thoughts that inspired me to transfer solution-focused tools from practice to supervision. I then describe how each of the usual solution-focused tools can be used in the context of supervision. After outlining the contributions of others who have made the shift from practice to supervision, I will propose a set of assumptions for supervisors about supervisees, supervision, therapeutic practice, and clients. The larger part of this account is devoted to a variety of applications of solution-focused supervision, covering conventional formats along with the emerging electronic opportunities: ongoing one-to-one, one-off consultations, ongoing group consultation, informal support groups, video review, telephone consultation, e-mail, and online discussion forums.[1] The chapter concludes with accounts from supervisees on being supervised in this manner.

GUIDING THOUGHTS

In The Prophet (Gibran, 1972), islanders ask the prophet to speak of teaching. He replies:

> No man [sic] can reveal to you aught but that which already lies half asleep in the dawning of your knowledge. The teacher who walks in the shadows of the temple, among his followers, gives not of his wisdom, but rather of his faith and his lovingness. If he is indeed wise, he does not bid you enter the house of his wisdom but rather leads you to the threshold of your own mind. (p. 67)

There is a resonance here with Maturana and Varela's (1980) view that instructive instruction simply does not work. No matter how much I might want to transfer to a supervisee the ideas that help me to practice, it just cannot be done. I might help a supervisee to clarify his or her own developing ideas. I might be able to help a supervisee juxtapose separate ideas for a first time. But my knowledge is unique to me, and knowledge seldom travels from one head to another without changing on the way. Being taken to the threshold of the mind, however, can be a mixed blessing. It can be what Brookfield (1994) refers to as "helping (people to) learn what they do" (p. 214) and experienced as affirmative. It can also be like what Brookfield has referred to as the moment in a cartoon when the character runs off the cliff and suddenly realizes there is nothing underneath except space. A social work student looking back on her experience of my supervision (Wheeler & Greaves, 2005) spoke of the anxiety she felt on occasions when my questions took her to the edge of her thinking. Faith and lovingness on the part of the supervisor are likely to be particularly important components of the "emotionally sustaining peer learning community" (p. 212) that Brookfield sees as being so important in the generation of new thinking.

In supervision, faith can mean believing many possibilities. The supervisees who seem unresourceful in their practices may possess what White (1999) has referred to as "invisible presences," which, with nurturing and encouragement, will become useful elements of their practice. The supervisee who is struggling to grasp an important concept and is stuck in what Anderson and Swim (1995) have referred to as "thinking ruts" (p. 10) may make a sudden breakthrough. The supervisee who practices in ways that seem strange may be on to something that is useful to the client. As Cantwell and Holmes (1995) point out, "there is no one right way to do therapy" (p. 37) and all practitioners have the potential to construct what Polkinghorne (1992) refers to as their own "epistemology of practice" (p. 157). But what about lovingness? One definition of love, frequently heard at wedding ceremonies, goes as follows:

> Love is patient and kind; love is not jealous or boastful; it is not arrogant or rude. Love does not insist on its own way; it is not irritable or resentful; it does not rejoice at wrong, but rejoices in the right.

> (The Holy Bible, I Corinthians 13:4-6)

Patience could be said to be what happens when the supervisor practices the various versions of faith already outlined. Boastfulness and arrogance can also be present. Indeed, the usual position of "elevated influence" (Bobele, Gardner, & Biever, 1995, p. 17), which is inherent in most supervisory relationships, offers ample scope for such behaviors. The supervisor is usually more experienced in practice than is the supervisee. So, when supervisees recall interesting experiences from their own practices, the supervisor can easily top these with an even more interesting example from his or her own. When supervisees feel stuck and at a loss to know what to do, again supervisors can easily draw on the wealth of their experiences to say what they did or would do in a similar situation. Such actions can easily turn supervisors into practitioners who are so far on in their practices that supervisees could never catch up, what Thomas (2000) has referred to as a "guru" whose practice wisdom is forever beyond the grasp of the supervisee. Irritability and resentment can also appear. Waiting for a supervisee to make his or her own discoveries can be irritating, and it can be difficult to resist the urge to just tell a supervisee what seems obvious to the supervisor.

Discovering that supervisees have not acted on apparently good ideas that arose in a previous supervision discussion can cause supervisors to feel resentful and question the use that is being made of their time. But as Kolb, Rubin, and McIntyre (1971) point out, learning approaches are unique to individuals, and supervisees are much more likely to retain and use ideas they have generated themselves. And when all comes to all, supervisees carry the ultimate responsibility for deciding what to say and do when they next meet their clients. As Berger and Dammann (1982) suggest, "the supervisor proposes and the therapist disposes" (p. 5). Finally, this reading on love directs us to the pivotal choice that had arisen for the colleague I referred to at the beginning of this chapter: Is it more useful for a supervisor to pay attention to what the supervisee gets right or to what he or she appears to be doing wrong?

Foucault (1982) has written of the enormous power professionals wield when they classify people based on right or wrong behaviors or thoughts. White (1997) has extended this thinking by exploring the power professionals wield over each other through practices of supervision. As practitioners have become increasingly interested in strengths-based perspectives to practice, so, too, have supervisors been prepared to shift their focus and adopt the same position toward supervision. Merl (1995), commenting on postsession discussions, advocates "focus[sing] on what was useful, rather than mistakes" (p. 51). Wetchler (1990) warns, "A problem orientation serves to reinforce supervisees' feelings of inadequacy as they make mistakes" (p. 131). Focusing on mistakes also risks turning the supervisor into what Thomas (2000) has described as a "gatekeeper," transforming the supervisor into someone whose primary role is winnowing the wheat from the chaff. When supervisees expect to be judged and criticized for their mistakes, there is a serious danger that mistakes in practice will simply disappear from the supervision discussion. This results in a triple jeopardy. The supervisor has a sanitized view of the supervisee's practice with little scope to help the supervisee make improvements and greater professional risk. The supervisee also is caught between the construction of practice as known by the supervisor and the actual practice as experienced by the client. Finally, the client has to make do with elements of the supervisee's practice that might impede progress.

SOLUTION-FOCUSED TOOLS FOR SUPERVISORS

So, what do solution-focused tools look like in the context of supervision? Solution-focused practice typically includes problem-free talk, goals, compliments, presession change, scaling questions, exceptions, the miracle question, and noticing tasks. Each has its contribution to make to supervision.

Problem-Free Talk

In supervision, problem-free talk helps to establish that the supervisor is primarily interested in what is working in the supervisee's practice and the resources the supervisee can draw on to assist the client. One supervisee was struggling to engage with children and was dissatisfied with the materials available in the agency. When I asked about the talents that showed up outside of work, the supervisee spoke of his artistic abilities. Reminded of this resource, he then created a set of emotions pictures that caught the interest of the children he subsequently shared them with.

Goals

In supervision, goals are useful in terms of practice and the supervision itself. To help supervisees orient their work, the supervisor might ask, "What would a good outcome look like in this particular piece of work?" or, "If we were to ask the clients how they would know the work had been useful, what do you think they would say?" or, "How will you and the client know when to stop?"

To ensure that the supervision discussion is organized around what will be helpful to the supervisee, the supervisor might ask, "What are you looking for in this supervision?" or, "By the end of the supervision, how will you know it had been worth meeting?" or, "How do you think supervision could help you in your work with this client?" Often, the replies to these questions can be surprising to the supervisor. On occasions, I have heard supervisees present their thinking in a confused manner and assumed they did not know what to do. On asking, "Are you wanting to know what I would do?" the supervisee has replied, "No. I know what to do. I just need to feel more confident about doing it."

Compliments

Commenting on supervisees' abilities helps to remind them of the supervisor's main area of interest, invites them to have a firmer grasp of the talents they can take into their work, and increases the likelihood of their feeling safe to explore mistakes. Live supervision provides a particularly useful opportunity to notice supervisees' abilities.

Once, when observing a supervisee conducting a family interview, I was curious to see that during a period in the session when the parents were loudly arguing and the young children were becoming increasingly boisterous, the supervisee stayed calm and attentive. He then intervened in a manner that was both respectful to family members and effective in bringing matters under control. When I commented on this ability after the family left, he recalled his prior training in the armed services where he had learned to be both relaxed and fully alert because one did not know what might happen next and had to be ready to act decisively and appropriately.

Presession Change

Supervision often has a special significance for supervisees and it is not unusual when formative thinking starts before the supervision actually happens: "What will I look at today?" "What do I need to work on?" "I wonder what the supervisor will make of . . .?" "I mustn't forget to tell the supervisor about . . ." Thoughts about practice are thus often underway before supervisors even start to think of useful questions they might ask. Simple questions like the goal-setting questions described earlier quickly bring the supervisee's thinking into the opening, helping the supervisor to see what might be the most useful starting point for the supervision. The same applies to practice itself, especially pieces of work in which the supervisee feels stuck. For example,

SUPERVISEE: "I don't know what to do next with this client."
SUPERVISOR: "Where are you so far in knowing what to do?"
SUPERVISEE: "Well, I've got some ideas."
SUPERVISOR: "Yes?"

Scaling Questions

Scaling questions can be used to evaluate progress, clarify goals, identify what is working, and to devise next steps. I asked a supervisee to evaluate a piece of work she was worried about on a scale of 0 to 10, with 10 representing the work going as well as she could hope. After she rated the work at 3, I asked her to say how she could tell. She described signs of engagement and went on to say that it was the lack of change in the presenting concerns that particularly worried her. After exploring how she had been able to engage with me, she decided that she had a strong enough connection to go back to the client and openly explore her curiosity over what might need to happen for changes to come about.

Scaling questions can focus on the client, the supervisee, or the work they are doing together. While supervisees might want to use supervision to look at themselves, de Shazer (2002) avoided using this as his focus of interest as a supervisor. He did this in part because supervisees tend to underestimate the usefulness of what they are doing but more importantly because, in his view, supervision discussions need to be about practice and not about practitioners.

Exceptions

Typically, when supervisees describe work that seems stuck, there will be aspects of the work that have gone/are going well enough, or the supervisee will have worked with people in similar situations and made more progress.

An experienced mental health worker spoke of how paralyzed she felt when a particular client spoke of how he might throw himself off a local bridge. When asked what she usually did when clients spoke in this way, she recalled her use of solution-focused questions such as, "How do you think that would help?" "What would that change that needs changing?" I then asked how these questions usually worked. She recalled that they usually gave her a better grasp of clients' goals for change, which led onto constructive discussions that in turn usually left her more confident in clients' likelihood of keeping themselves safe.

The Miracle Question

The miracle question can provide a particularly powerful opportunity for supervisees to step out of their current concerns and bewilderment over a piece of work into a future when all is better. Just as clients can get bogged down in problem-saturated thinking, so too can supervisees, especially those who are empathic and open to clients' worldviews.

A child protection social worker was concerned about a mother who regularly contacted him with worries about her children who lived with their father. Each time, he had checked out the concerns and found them to be without foundation. But the mother kept calling. On being asked the miracle question, he described a whole week at work in which he received no calls from the mother. In describing this, he noticed that he would not be at all worried about the safety of the children. This reassured him that he had spoken to the children and others enough times to be confident of their safety. He then generated a range of different steps he could take that were grounded in his evidence-based judgment that the children were safe, such as asking the mother what she was hoping to change by contacting him, bringing the parents together for a meeting, and so on.

Noticing Tasks

Supervisees interested in leaving a supervision session with something extra to do can be offered noticing tasks. In the normal course of practice, a practitioner's attention might operate in a fairly random fashion, being drawn to whatever stands out as unusual. This might be moments of success in their work. It could just as likely be moments of excruciating embarrassment. A noticing task would be designed around whatever supervisees consider could be useful to their practice at that time.

A social worker working with a parent was preoccupied by the extent to which the parent was not showing emotions. This was making it difficult for the worker to engage because she thought she did not know where the parent was coming from and what mattered to her. The worker was invited to be on the lookout for even a hint of emotions. Shortly afterward, the parent became very angry at a meeting with professionals. The worker in question was ready to see this as an opportunity to engage more closely and went on to have a more open and productive involvement with the mother.

FOOTPRINTS IN THE SNOW

Solution-focused supervision is no longer an expanse of snow waiting for people to explore. A number of footprints already exist. From 1990, a series of publications (Edwards & Chen, 1999; Marek, Sandifer, Beach, Coward, & Protinsky, 1994; O'Connell, 2005; Pichot & Dolan, 2003; Selekman & Todd, 1995; Thomas, 1994, 1996; Wetchler, 1990) marked the movement of solution-focused tools from practice into supervision. In the United Kingdom, a variety of adaptations of solution-focused supervision have been described. O'Connell and Jones (1997) addressed the application to counseling, regardless of the counsellor's theoretical orientation. Nash (1999) outlined her use of the approach with educational psychology trainees. Bucknell (2000) and Wheeler and Greaves (2005) explored the potential for social work training.

Selekman and Todd (1995) advocated a shift of supervisor interest from weaknesses and problems to strengths and successes. They recommended that instead of drawing on their own knowledge of practice, supervisors should "identify carefully supervisees' unique cooperative response patterns" (p. 22), using this as a platform for enhancing practice outcomes via existing solution-focused tools. In contrast to the more traditional hierarchies of supervision, Selekman and Todd display a willingness to share their own initial struggles in learning new practice approaches with supervisees and take the view that supervisors' difficulties over tolerating supervisees' "wrong goals" or lack of knowledge says something about their capacity to trust supervisees.

Thomas (1996) saw solution-focused supervision as being "significantly different from other models of family therapy supervision" (p. 129), identifying the supervisor's role as being one of coaxing ability and knowledge from the supervisee as opposed to pouring knowledge into their heads. Drawing on the concept of isomorphism, Thomas pointed out that supervisees are more likely to be cooperative and respectful with their clients when that is what they experience in supervision.

Using the work of O'Hanlon and Weiner-Davis (1989), Thomas showed how a list of practice assumptions can easily translate into assumptions about supervision. Questions from the editor gave Thomas an opportunity to offer thoughts on the thorny issue of potential malpractice on the part of supervisees, pointing out that the supervisors' options in such situations are typically determined by the contract agreed upon at the beginning of a supervisory relationship.

Later, during a presentation on solution-focused supervision (Wheeler, Thomas, Lowe, Fleckney, & Greaves, 2002), Thomas elaborated further by saying that as a solution-focused supervisor, he moved through three positions according to the responsiveness of the supervisee: "semaphore, metaphor, two-by-four." In the semaphore (flag signals) position, the supervisor invites supervisees to recognize their mistakes themselves. In the metaphor position, the supervisor creates more sophisticated messages that would lead most supervisees to recognize the supervisor's concern. In the two-by-four position, the supervisor voices his or her concerns with maximum transparency, stepping from "nonexpert" to a "years-of-experience" position. As this reminds us, an approach to supervision is always a matter of choice; it does not have to be a straightjacket.

Edwards and Chen (1999) draw on the Zen concept of Wu-Wei to propose that supervisees' innate tendency to make their own progress is more likely to come to the fore when supervisors hold their own thinking lightly. Interestingly, Edwards and Chen refer to taking the practical step of including clients in the supervision-literally, when possible, and "as if" when not. Experience has shown them that the real or imagined presence of the client has a powerful effect on the hierarchical tendencies of both the supervisee and the supervisor, reducing the tendency of either to conceptualize and describe their clients in terms of deficits and diagnostic categories. Looking to the future life of supervisees, Edwards and Chen see strengths-based supervision as contributing greatly to supervisees' sense of personal agency. With this in mind, they envision supervisees who not only take responsibility for their impact on their clients but also take responsibility for their own self-care and nurturing in a line of work that can be demanding and at times overwhelming.

Lowe and Guy (2002) note the commonality of strengths-based approaches to supervision in terms of being change-oriented, constructionist,[2] competency-based, and collaborative. Although they do not rule out the possibility of supervisors' drawing on their own practice expertise, Lowe and Guy believe this can be done from a nonexpert position through, for example, offering suggestions or proposing topics for discussion. They offer particular thought to how solution-oriented supervision can be used in longer-term processes of supervision, arguing that such an approach can accommodate to and facilitate a continuous co-construction of the supervisee's professional identity, a potential alternative to de Shazer's preferred disinterest in the self-of-therapist as outlined earlier. They argue that in such situations it is useful for the supervisor to pay attention to not only what they call the focus story (the material the supervisee brings to supervision) but also the therapist's story and the supervision story. The therapist's story maps the progress of the therapist's professional development, while the supervision story monitors the emerging relationship between supervisor and supervisee. However, they do caution against a view that these extra stories are fixed realities to be unearthed by the supervisor. In practice, they view these stories as potentially useful reference points, visited according to how the supervision discussion proceeds.

Others (e.g., Lowe & Guy, 1996; Merl, 1995; Norman 2005) have illustrated how Andersen's original use of reflecting teams (1991) can be given a solution-focused emphasis in supervision.

SUPERVISOR ASSUMPTIONS

Assumptions About Supervisees

- Supervisees want the best for their clients.

    Supervisee attitudes can fall anywhere in a spectrum from jaded to wildly enthusiastic. Even enthusiastic supervisees can sometimes drift into despondent thinking about their work, which, in turn, can lead the supervisor to doubt their intentions as practitioners. Asking, for example, "Suppose your work with this client went particularly well. What would be happening in the client's life that isn't happening at the moment?" can help the supervisee get back on track again.

- Supervisees are likely to be already doing something that clients find valuable.

    Frequently, supervisees will come to supervision thinking they need to come up with something extra to help the client. Asking a question like, "Suppose I were to meet with the clients and ask them what they liked about seeing you. What do you guess they would say?" can help to freeze such thinking and alert the supervisee to what is already helpful to the client and worth continuing.

- Supervisees are likely to have hidden talents.

    Supervisees often discount useful abilities with comments like, "That's something I just do" or "Isn't that what everyone does?" One supervisee mentioned how difficult it had been to persuade a young boy to come into the building for his session with her. When I asked what had helped her deal successfully with his aggressive presentation, she surprised both of us by saying "pacifism." I then asked more about the foundations of her pacifism and what pacifism would look like as she contributed to the boy's shift from aggressive opposition to willingness to meet her.

- Most supervisees underestimate the value of their work.

    As mentioned earlier, de Shazer (2002) would not have asked a supervisee to scale the quality of their work with a client because most practitioners undervalue what they do. He found it more useful to ask the supervisee to imagine how the client would evaluate the work. When I do both, I typically find that supervisees rate their practices higher when the scaling is done through the client's eyes. Perhaps this is one of the strongest arguments for solution-focused supervision. Supervisees are almost bound to leave supervision with more than they came with.

- There is always more to learn.

  There is always scope to take supervisees to the edges of their thinking. However, supervision that is too full of stimulating questions can be pretty hard on the brain. Sometimes, when my interest in furthering supervisee's knowledge about practice has been unbridled, supervisees have spoken of being exhausted by the end of the supervision. Occasionally supervisees have plainly told me to stop. As the motto goes: "in everything, moderation."

Assumptions About Supervision

- Supervision can contribute something useful to the supervisee's practice.

  Supervision is a unique opportunity for supervisees to think about their practices and enrich their future work. The curiosity of the supervisee and the supervisor can be a catalyst for thinking that is novel to each. Supervisors can find themselves asking questions they have never asked before, questions that arise out of the specific juxtaposition of the practice issues and the nature of the practitioner who is presenting the issues. Supervisees can create ideas about a particular piece of work or work in general that is entirely new to them in response to questions they might never have thought to ask themselves.
- The supervisor's focus of interest can have a big impact on supervisees and their practices.

  The choice, which became so apparent to the colleague I spoke of at the beginning of this chapter, is one of huge significance. In my account with Yvonne (Wheeler & Greaves, 2005), we looked back on an occasion when I live supervised her presentation of an assessment to a meeting that included professionals and the family she had assessed. At one point, Yvonne started to lose her voice, but then regained it. In supervision, I could have asked why she was losing her voice, but instead asked how she got it back. This equipped her with knowledge that she has subsequently put to good use in other challenging situations. Knowledge of how she had lost her voice might have added to a sense of vulnerability and made matters worse. When we shared this as an example in a presentation, a colleague recalled a similar time in her training when her supervisor had said that he would be in the room with her and would take over if she dried up. All she had to do was give a cough as a signal that she wanted him to step in. We could not resist asking what happens nowadays when she is at risk of losing her voice and gives a cough.

- Descriptions of clients can powerfully influence the supervisee's expectations of the client and her ability to work usefully with them.

   Once, in group supervision, a supervisee referred to a client as being "manipulative." When I asked what the others in the group thought about this word, they all judged that it seemed to fit with what they had heard about the client. I then asked the supervisee to restate the client's actions that had invited this description and challenged the group to come up with at least five alternatives. From this selection plus the original word, I asked the supervisee to choose which word was most likely to help her work constructively with the client. She chose "scared."

Assumptions About Therapeutic Practice

- Therapeutic practice is worth doing.

   As Hubble, Duncan, and Miller (2002) confirm, therapy works often enough to be worth doing. If supervision is plummeting into despondency, it can sometimes be useful for the supervisor to step back and reflect on what the supervisee knows about what works in therapy and ask, "Okay, if fifteen percent of change can be accounted for by one's technique, do you think you are offering all you can, or could you try something different?" Or, "If fifteen percent of change is based on hope, where is the client's hope on a scale of zero to ten. What might help to raise it?"
- Most practitioners can adjust their style of practice to match the client's style of cooperation.

   As de Shazer (1984) argued, resistance is usually what happens when the practitioner and client are out of step with each other. Asking a scaling question where 10 represents the supervisee and the client being perfectly synchronized will sometimes produce a low number, but the response will seldom be 0. There is then scope for the supervisor to be curious about what makes it, for example, 3 rather than 0. What has the supervisee already noticed about the work that tells them this expands the possibilities?
- Solution-focused supervision is not just for solution-focused practitioners.

   O'Connell and Jones (1997) argue that the assumptions and techniques of solution-focused supervision can be used to assist supervisees regardless of their model of practice. A colleague once asked for assistance with her systemic thinking. When I started off by asking how she would be able to tell the consultation had gone well, she replied that she would have a clearer understanding of her position and choices for action. When I asked what she thought we should be doing in the consultation, she spoke of mapping out the context to her practice and quickly proceeded to do so on a white board. Another supervisee spoke of the importance emotions played for him due to his confidence in person-centered counseling. We then explored the difference in emotions that would tell him the supervision was going well and used a scaling question half way through to check that the preferred emotion was growing.

Assumptions About Clients

- Clients have done the best they could with their lives so far, but with finely tuned help from the supervisee, there might be more they could do.

  Curious supervisees have a chance of being more useful to clients than disinterested ones. Asking, "What have you noticed about what the clients have managed in their life so far?" can both bring client resources to the fore and invite further exploration. Asking, "What else do think the client might be able to do?" followed by, "And what have you noticed about the client already that tells you this might be a possibility?" can connect the supervisee to the client in constructive ways.
- The client who keeps meeting with the supervisee for therapy has some sort of an agenda for change and possibly some belief that the supervisee might be able to help.

  When you think in a solution-focused way, there is always plenty to be curious about when something is happening. Even if this is not obvious evidence of something significant to the supervisee, it can be for the supervisor. In exploring this, the supervisor can ask, "Why do you think the clients turned up?" "What do you think they were hoping for when they came?" "What happened in the first meeting that might have led them to decide to see you again?"

MODALITIES OF SUPERVISION

In the past, therapists have typically drawn on individual or group supervision to maintain their practices. Although SFBT started off in the domain of therapeutic practice, the virus-like spread of the approach has taken the tools into many settings that do not have such structures in place. Given the improbability that these practitioners will be provided with the same structures that have supported therapists, there is a need to create newer modalities of supervision, modalities that take account of busy work lives and a need for quickly checking in with experienced colleagues.

Also, many therapists are finding that their working lives are little different from those of colleagues in frontline services. Consequently, while the following account covers more conventional modalities of supervision, thoughts also will be offered on the emerging use of electronic solutions. In each, all of the solution-focused tools outlined earlier can be useful. To avoid repetition, each account will concentrate on aspects of supervision that are particularly pertinent.

Ongoing One-to-One Supervision

Meeting with a supervisee over a period of time provides exciting opportunities for the supervisee's practice style to become better known and developed to the benefit of his or her clients. Goaling questions help to define a mutually constructed contract at the outset, which provides useful parameters for keeping the future supervision on track.

I asked one supervisee, "As we spend time together, what do you think we need to concentrate on to ensure that supervision helps your practice?" She replied, "I need to make more connections to the theoretical basis of my work. I enjoy reflecting on practice, but when I do this, there is a risk I will disappear into my own head. I am sure there is lots I can learn from the literature." In later supervisions, when we were both disappearing over the horizon with our reflections, this gave me an opportunity to stop and ask, "These ideas you are having at the moment, do they connect to something you've read? What else did that author have to say about the issue we are currently exploring?"

Ongoing supervision also offers scope for both parties to be curious about how they work together to the benefit of the supervisee's practice. After a few meetings, the supervisor can ask, "On a scale of zero to ten, where ten means this supervision is having an amazing impact on your practice and zero means we should stop meeting, what's the number?" Supposing the supervisee says 6, the supervisor can then ask, "Okay, so how can you tell it's six?" "What is each of us doing to make it so?" "What might each of us do that could raise it to seven?" "How high do you think your clients would want the number to be?"

The ending of an ongoing supervision, from a solution-focused point of view, also provides scope for the supervisor to actively contribute to the supervisee's future practice. Supervisors can give compliments based on what they have learned about supervisees' practice abilities. They can also ask, "Through the course of our meeting together, what have you learned about your practice abilities?" "What have you discovered about your talents that you wouldn't want to forget?" "Which are the useful questions I asked you that you could ask yourself in the future?" A more detailed account of endings and ongoing solution-focused supervision can be found in Wheeler and Greaves (2005).

One-Off (One-Time) Consultations

Sometimes, experienced practitioners are called upon to provide one-off consultation. Here, goaling questions are especially important, otherwise precious consultation time can be frittered away ineffectively. Although the consultee may start off with what a colleague has called a "linear-discharge," as soon as possible it is useful to ask something along the lines of, "Okay, so when you thought about seeing me, how were you hoping this would help?" or, "So, by the time we've finished talking, how will you know it has been worth meeting?"

I asked the latter question for clarification to a manager who had arranged for a one-off consultation. He replied, "I'm pretty confused at the moment. I'm hoping that consultation will bring about greater clarity." We were then able to go straight into scaling "clarity," using this as a basis for discovering what was already working and exploring new strategies. Halfway through the session, we used the clarity scale to check that the consultation was working, and at the end, we used the scale to evaluate the usefulness of the consultation and to consolidate the new thinking that she needed to hold onto.

Ongoing Group Consultation

When a group meets with a supervisor on a regular basis, everyone has the benefit of a rich resource base to inform and develop practice. As with ongoing individual supervision, time spent constructing a contract and ground rules is often time well spent. As a supervisor, I typically use the entire first meeting to define how the group and I are to work together. Discussing ground rules with groups can generate frustration, resulting in participants' saying, "Can't we just get on and talk about cases? That's what I came for." In my experience, contracts and ground rules created through solution-focused questions tend not to elicit such responses. Solution-focused questions are more likely to fascinate participants, and above all, create hopefulness regarding what the group has been designed to offer.

At the end of a first meeting that was entirely devoted to defining the group, one participant spoke of how excited he felt about having helped to create such a useful resource. I suspect that this made a useful impact on his practice even before he used the group for supervision. As with individual supervision, the contract and ground rules can be revisited in the future to review the usefulness of the group. Such a document also helps when new members join the group, operating as a document of the group's culture and purpose.

Goaling questions can help to clarify the purpose for the group's meetings. For example, "How will you be able to tell this group is useful to your practice?" "Why do you think managers have agreed to this group's happening?" "What might they notice that would tell them the group is a good investment of your time?" "How might your clients be able to tell that you've been to this group?" Once clarified, these ambitions then invite speculation over the content of the group supervision. For example, "What needs to be happening in the group so that these outcomes come about?" One group, for example, included role-playing in their list of useful activities. This paved the way for me to suggest the use of role-playing in future supervision, because the idea had come from the group instead of being imposed by me and possibly rejected.

Goaling questions help to clarify the supervisor's role. For example, "As you think about a typical meeting of this group, what do you imagine I will be doing?" "Suppose there was a video of the group, how would an observer be able to tell that I was the supervisor?" "From previous experiences of group supervision, what would you like me to do? What would you hope I don't do?"

Goaling questions also help clarify shared responsibility and the role of participants. With one group I asked, "On a scale of zero to ten, where ten means I'm fully responsible for your practice development, and zero means I have no responsibility at all, where's the number?" When the group produced a consensus around 5, I then asked, "So, what do you need to be doing to make it as high as five, and what do you want me to do so that it's five and no higher?" This clarified that group members wanted scope to question each other and draw on each other's experiences. They also wanted to draw on my practice experience, which, for some, was more extensive than theirs. In response to the last point, I negotiated that when I was asked what I would do in a particular practice situation, I might respond, "Yes, I have an idea about what I would do, but first can we see what other people might do?"

Group supervision provides a rich source of practice thinking. Without careful steering, however, the discussion can become frenetic, competitive, and unhelpful to participants, especially those who are sharing their work. Social constructionism suggests that the realities we end up with are the ones we choose to talk about together. As a group supervisor, it is important to notice which potential realities are being brought into being. Otherwise, we can end up with something we really did not want. Agenda setting at the beginning of each meeting helps to identify the various topics that might be covered. While practitioners are often inclined to bring their stuck work to supervision, they are more likely to leave the group with extra ideas and greater confidence if the group at least starts off with what has worked. Successful practice can be very infectious. Often, when I have set the agenda at the beginning of a group, several people have identified stuck cases they want to look at. When I have come back to them after having looked at another participant's example of effective practice, a number of them declare they are no longer stuck. Hearing what has worked for their colleague helped them figure out what might work for them.

Discussion of successful work can go off the rails, however, if the group process is left to itself. Figure 15.1 shows three areas in which discussion can fall: The "zone of bright ideas," while fascinating for those who are talking, can result in competitive and critical comments that undermine the participant who has shared her work. It often falls to the supervisor to steer

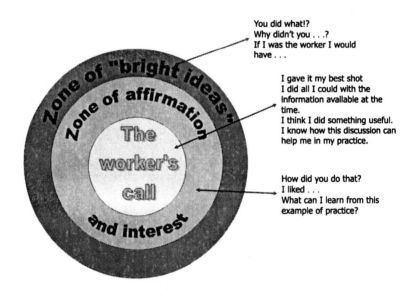

FIGURE 15.1. The worker's call—Celebrating success.

participants out of this zone and into more productive ones. Above all, in my view, the person who shares the work should derive the greatest benefit from the ensuing discussion; hence, the zone is named as "the worker's call." First and foremost, this reminds the supervisor and the rest of the group to make sure they know how the colleague thinks that presenting her work will help her practice. One participant explained, "I know the client has done really well. I'm hoping the group can help me work out what, if anything, I contributed to that." The "zone of affirmation and interest" describes the area I would prefer participants to settle for. So, if a participant strays into the outer zone I might say, "Okay, so that's what you'd do if this was your case, but what do you like about what Jane did?" Typically, I prefer to help a participant unpack what has worked in her practice before opening up to a wider discussion. Even then I would suggest a focus for the wider discussion by asking, "So, what do you like about what Jane has shared with us?" or, "Okay, so, what have you learned from this example of practice?" Such questions naturally bring into being a solution-focused reflecting process as described in more detail by Merl (1995) and Lowe and Guy (2002).

Groups of experienced solution-focused practitioners typically occupy the middle zone with little help from the supervisor. Less experienced practitioners can be more inclined to revert to problem-focused thinking and interaction. In such situations, when the supervisor takes the lead in unpacking the example of successful practice, the account is more richly described, which then provides the rest of the group with much more scope to learn from their colleague and say what they liked.

Stuck cases can be even more challenging for groups and their supervisors. In Figure 15.2, the outer ring is named the "zone of panic and anxiety" to connote the infectiousness of stuck work that can take participants to remarkable degrees of criticism and unhelpfulness. The inner circles remain the same. When a colleague presents work he already does not feel very good about, it is even more important for the supervisor to invite him to guide the group on how he needs to be helped. Without this, other participants are at risk of going down a path that might work for them without checking if this would help their colleague. Once the presenter's goals for supervision have been specified, the supervisor can then use these to keep the group on track in offering assistance to the colleague.

One participant said she needed some ideas on what to use from solution-focused practice in the next meeting with a particular client. Once the rest of the group offered their thoughts, I returned to the participant and asked, "Okay, that's a lot to choose from. Which caught your attention? Which did you think might fit for you and your client?"

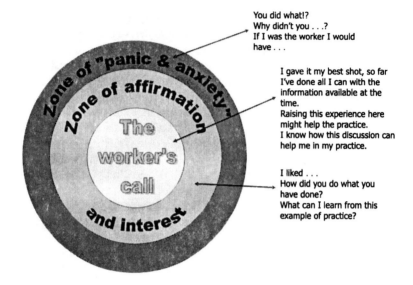

FIGURE 15.2. The worker's call—Navigating out of stuckness.

Interestingly, when I invite the rest of the group to be in the middle zone, colleagues will typically notice what the presenter of the stuck case has done well, saying, for example, "I know you aren't sure what to do next, but I'm amazed the clients let you in their house to talk to them. How did you do that?" In one group, a participant was moved to tears by a colleague's account of a difficult situation she was working with. It turned out that the one who was listening was thinking back to a time when she, as a very inexperienced practitioner, had tried unsuccessfully to deal with a similar situation. This had haunted her for many years and threatened her confidence in her practice. The colleague's account helped her be more accepting of her prior lack of experience and helped her to realize that she had become better able to deal with such situations over time.

Informal Support Groups

Sometimes, groups do not have the advantages of a fixed membership, such as support groups. However, this does mean that each meeting, by virtue of its unique combination of participants, can also be full of surprises. Seeking clarification over how to make the best use of "this time" for "these people" is again particularly important, along with a readiness to steer participants into the most profitable areas of enquiry as indicated in Figures 15.1 and 15.2.

On one occasion, out of the eight who turned up to a widely advertised support group, four were very experienced solution-focused practitioners and four knew very little but had lots of questions. We accordingly formed two lines facing each other, with the "experts" as a panel and the "newcomers" asking "frequently asked questions." At the end, the newcomers reported that they had learnt a great deal and were keen to go on training. Surprisingly, the "experts" reported that they had learned a great deal as well, possibly benefiting from the ancient wisdom (e.g., Coelho, 1992) that you learn even more through teaching others.

VIDEO REVIEW

Video review is now a well-established practice within family therapy. Solution-focused thinking can help a supervisor ensure that the viewing optimizes the supervisee's practice. Without discussion, the supervisee might use the video in an unhelpful manner. There is, for example, the story of the American baseball player whose playing got worse as a consequence of looking at examples of his mistakes. At worst, a supervisee might say, "Here's the tape. Have a look at it and see what you think." As before, the choice is this: "We have this opportunity. What are we going to do with it?" Video review is more likely to be profitable when the supervisor asks, for example, "As we watch this piece of tape, what do you need to be doing? And what do you want me to do so that your practice is helped?" Or the supervisor might give an assignment in advance: "I'd like you to choose a piece of tape for me to look at. As you think about your learning needs at the moment, what does that tell you about which piece to choose, and what you want from me when I watch it?"

Although practitioners tend to fear the video recorder's capacity to reveal the inadequacies of their practice, the medium often bears testimony to the richness of practice styles. When an experienced colleague voiced embarrassment over a video of her practice, I asked, "Suppose you were giving a presentation in a lecture theatre and this was your only piece of tape. How would you use it to illustrate the most important things you know about therapy?" The colleague then identified examples of therapeutic skill and the ways she compensated for the moments of disconnection that had embarrassed her.

TELEPHONE SUPPORT

The telephone offers scope for support for practitioners who are too busy to commit to regular supervision or attendance at supervision groups but can use occasional contact with an experienced practitioner to keep their solution-focused practice on track. There is probably much to learn from those who already use the telephone for therapy and counseling. Given the unpredictability of telephone contact, the supervisor probably needs to be honest about the time they have available, saying, for example, "I've got five minutes, but if you need more than that I've got a longer slot tomorrow." The lack of visual information means that supervisors might have to listen more carefully to ensure they understand what is being said and may need to check out their understanding, asking for example, "What I'm picking up is. . . . Is that right?" Telephone contact can feel like particularly precious time, especially as each minute is usually costing someone something. There can be a fine balance between friendly socializing to start off with and then getting on to the matter at hand, usually a clarification of what the caller needs from the discussion as in all the other modes of supervision. When a colleague called me out of the blue on one occasion it was only when I asked five minutes into the discussion, "How did you think I could help?" that the explicit goal became clear and answerable. Up until that point, I was imagining all sorts of needs that might want meeting.

Finally, while many supervisors are used to handling silence when supervisees ponder interesting questions, in telephone consultation, it sometimes means the other person has dropped off the line. Hence, "Are you still there?" may have to be used as well as minimal sounds of your own so the other person knows you are still there as well.

E-Mail

E-mail is providing some interesting opportunities for practitioners to seek support from others. Online contact offers the possibility of a quick response from anywhere in the world. However, the medium is also taking supervisors into a world where their words can be permanently recorded and copied. As Wright (2003) points out, therapists and counsellors who use this medium to practice are still in relatively uncharted waters as far as confidentiality and accountability are concerned. In developing an online mentoring facility for staff newly trained in solution-focused practice, some of my colleagues came up with the following suggestions:

- Do not press the send button too quickly. First thoughts may be good, but they can often be improved on, and further reading may reveal ambiguities that were not obvious at first.
- Make sure you know what the question is before giving an answer, and if necessary, ask for extra clarification to make sure.
- Do not make assumptions about skill level or professional role, which might be different from your own. If necessary, check it out.
- Offer questions instead of advice, unless this is specifically asked for.
- Remember, the supervisee is the expert on the case; you are there to facilitate/support.
- If stumped, say so, and offer to get back later.

Online Discussion Forums

Online discussion forums provide a valuable opportunity for a community of practitioners to learn together, the Solution Focused Therapy List (http://listserv.icors.org/archives/sft-l.html) being among the first for solution-focused practitioners. As with e-mail, however, this is new territory and, as Johnson (2002) pointed out, there has been very little time so far for these virtual communities to develop shared rules for coexistence. Unlike a group with a facilitator, an online forum, unless it goes beyond bounds set by its moderator, is free to regulate itself. Hence, one person seeking ideas from colleagues might quickly see her question taken over by people who want to talk about something else instead. And the number of responses to a question can range from none to far too many. Colleagues who contributed to ideas on e-mailing reckoned that all the previously mentioned points applied to online forums along with these extra ones:

- Contribute respectfully.
- Give people the benefit of the doubt, especially because of the ambiguity of the written word.
- Do not expect to have your comments acknowledged.
- Ideas are an offering. If you do not like someone else's idea you do not have to tell them.
- Delay replying to the e-mail to give you time to think about your response.

Sometimes, a person asking for support on a forum gets bombarded with ideas. It might be helpful to put a question into the discussion, double-checking what the person wants from the forum or perhaps asking him to say what has been useful so far. This potentially helps to organize the whole group around how best to help this person. In the long run, such a question might also help a forum to learn how to be useful. Unlike all the other forms of supervision, everyone bears equal responsibility for what emerges.

RESEARCH ON SUPERVISEES' VIEWS

Thomas (1994), commenting on the paucity of research into supervisees' views on supervision, cites Heath and Tharp's (1991) study into what supervisees want from supervision. Broadly, it emerged that supervisees wanted supervisors to be respectful, set their expert knowledge to the side, assume and notice competence, listen, and be flexible.

More recently, Magnuson, Wilcoxon, and Norem (2000) sought the views of 11 counselors whose practice experience ranged from 7 to 23 years, believing that they could say more about the long-term benefits of useful supervision. Overall, they found that supervisees valued supervisors who were prepared to make useful contributions to their learning, demonstrated skills that fostered change, stimulated their thinking, and created a participatory experience. More specifically, participants referred to the importance of supervisors' belief in the supervisees and interest in their professional growth. Some spoke of the need to feel safe and of the importance of supervisor affirmation above criticism.

Thomas and Shappee (2001) carried out a more specific study into supervisees' experience of solution-focused supervision. When asked about the style, behavior, and attitude of the supervisors that had been helpful over time, supervisees referred to the person of the supervisor. When asked what had been helpful overall, supervisees referred to learning to believe in themselves, developing their own style, development of solution-focused skills and, interestingly, the development of self-supervision. When asked if aspects of the supervision showed up in their practice, supervisees noted evidence of collaboration, ongoing evaluation, and a focus on goals and competence. When asked what showed up in their supervision of others, participants named focusing on therapists' strengths. When asked how their views on supervision had changed, they described shifts from focusing on weaknesses to focusing on strengths and from hierarchy to collaboration.

Klingman (2002) described the use of solution-focused consultation with school counselors in Israel, whose group supervision had previously been based on process debriefing. Prior to the use of the solution-focused consultation, the counselors had reported that while the debriefing did help them discharge the emotions that might have led to burn out, they still felt no better equipped to go back and work with the pupils who needed their help. Solution-focused consultation, they reported, had helped them to have more realistic and optimistic expectations of their roles, identified effective behaviors, enhanced their sense of personal control, and strengthened their self-confidence in working with the pupils. Above all, while debriefing had helped them to keep going, the solution-focused consultation had equipped them to return to their work with the pupils with more to offer.

As a practice teacher in social work, I have often invited students to reflect back on their experiences of being on placement in my agency. A mutual interest in the value of solution-focused tools, both in practice and supervision, led to a more detailed deconstruction of what had worked in the supervision of one particular student, Yvonne Greaves (Wheeler & Greaves, 2005). Yvonne concluded the account with the following comments:

> Through solution-focused supervision, I not only found the ability to practice effectively, I also unexpectedly gained the ability to self-supervise after the placement had finished. As a qualified worker, I am now able to ask myself my own solution-focused questions, which inspire my thinking, enhance my creativity, and most importantly, help me to identify achievable goals and actions I can take, one small but confident step at a time. Practice as a qualified worker is challenging, but with the benefits of solution-focused supervision I am able to turn my "impossibles" into "possibles" and foresee a future in which my practice will continue to grow and develop way beyond the time I spent on placement with John. (p. 276)

And I guess this is what excites me most about the possibilities of solution-focused supervision: One student, on being asked about her hopes for supervision, replied that she would not want to become a clone of me. Nor did I wish that for her; I was much more interested to see who she would become. Thomas (2000) recommended that supervisors adopt the position of a "guide." In particular, he advocated the attributes of a Sherpa, who knows the mountains but lets the climbers decide on their journey.

Solution-focused practice reminds us that our clients' lives are unique to them. Solution-focused supervision helps practitioners develop their own unique approaches to practice, drawing on the abilities and opportunities that are particular to them and the settings in which they work. Solution-focused supervision has the potential to foster a community of practitioners journeying way beyond the imagination of their supervisors . . . which is so much better than cloning.

NOTES

1. Particular thanks are due to John Bennett, Haley Cunningham, Yvonne Greaves, Sue Robson, and Susanna Weinand, whose participation in solution-focused mentoring training contributed the sections on telephone consultation, e-mail, and online discussion forums.

2. Editors' note: Readers unfamiliar with terms such as constructionist or other postmodern ideas may enjoy reading a book such as McNamee & Gergen, 1992.

REFERENCES

Andersen, T. (1991). *The reflecting team: Dialogues and dialogues about dialogues.* New York: Norton.

Anderson, H., & Swim, S. (1995). Supervision as collaborative conversation: Connecting the voices of supervisor and supervisee. *Journal of Systemic Therapies, 14,* 1-13.

Berger, M., & Dammann, C. (1982). Live supervision as context, treatment, and training. *Family Process, 21,* 337-344.

Bobele, M., Gardner, G., & Biever, J. (1995). Supervision as social construction. *Journal of Systemic Therapies, 14,* 14-25.

Brookfield, S. (1994). Tales from the dark side: A phenomenography of adult critical reflection. *International Journal of Lifelong Adult Education, 13,* 203-216.

Bucknell, D. (2000). Practice teaching: Problem to solution. *Social Work Education, 19,* 125-144.

Cantwell, P., & Holmes, S. (1995). Cumulative process: A collaborative approach to supervision. *Journal of Systemic Therapies, 14,* 35-46.

Coelho, P. (1992). *The pilgrimage.* Glascow: Omnia Books Ltd.

de Shazer, S. (1984). The death of resistance. *Family Process, 23,* 11-17.

de Shazer, S. (2002, September). *Solution focused supervision.* Workshop at the European Brief Therapy Association annual conference, Cardiff, UK.

Edwards, J. K., & Chen, M. (1999). Strength-based supervision: Frameworks, current practice, and future directions. *The Family Journal: Counselling and Therapy for Couples and Families, 17,* 349-357.

Foucault, M. (1982). Afterword: The subject and power. In H. Dreyfus & P. Rabinow (Eds.), *Michel Foucault: Beyond structuralism and hermeneutics* (pp. 208-226). Chicago: University of Chicago Press.

Gibran, K. (1972). *The prophet.* London: Heineman.

Heath, T., & Tharp, L. (1991, November). *What really happens in supervision?* Workshop at the American Association for Marriage and Family Therapy annual conference, Dallas, TX.

Hubble, M. A., Duncan, B. L., & Miller, S. D. (2002). *Heart and soul of change: What works in therapy.* Washington, DC: American Psychological Association.

Johnson, S. (2002). *Emergence: The connected lives of ants, brains, cities, and software*. London: Penguin Books.

Klingman, A. (2002). From supportive-listening to a solution-focused intervention for counsellors dealing with political trauma. *British Journal of Guidance and Counselling, 30,* 247-259.

Kolb, D. A., Rubin, I. M., & McIntyre, M. M. (1971). *Organisational psychology: An experiential approach*. New York: Prentice Hall.

Lowe, R., & Guy, G. (1996). A reflecting team format for solution-oriented supervisors. *Journal of Systemic Therapies, 15,* 26-45.

Lowe, R., & Guy, G. (2002). Solution oriented inquiry for ongoing supervision: Expanding the horizon of change. In M. McMahon & W. Patton (Eds.), *Supervision in the helping professions: A practical approach* (pp. 66-77). French Forrest, NSW: Pearson Education Australia.

Magnuson, S., Wilcoxon, S. A., & Norem, K. (2000). Exemplary supervision practices: Retrospective observations of experienced counsellors. *TCA Journal, 28,* 93-101.

Marek, L. I., Sandifer, D. M., Beach, A., Coward, R. L., & Protinsky, H. O. (1994). Supervision without the problem: A model of solution-focused supervision. *Journal of Family Psychotherapy, 5,* 57-64.

Maturana, H. R., & Varela, F. J. (1980). *Autopoesis and cognition: The realisation of the living*. Boston: Reidel Press.

McNamee, S., & Gergen, K. J. (Eds.). (1992). *Therapy as social construction*. Thousand Oaks, CA: Sage.

Merl, H. (1995). Reflecting supervision. *Journal of Systemic Therapies, 14,* 47-56.

Nash, J. (1999). Developing and refining supervisory skills: An application of solution-focused supervision. *Educational Psychology in Practice, 15,* 108-115.

Norman, H. (2005). Solution focused reflecting teams. In B. O'Connell (Ed.), *Solution-focused therapy* (pp. 156-167). London: Sage.

O'Connell, B. (2005). *Solution-focused therapy*. London: Sage.

O'Connell, B., & Jones, C. (1997, November). Solution focused supervision. *Counselling,* 289-292.

O'Hanlon, W., & Weiner-Davis, M. (1989). *In search of solutions: A new direction in psychotherapy*. New York: Norton.

Pichot, T., & Dolan, Y. M. (2003). *Solution-focused brief therapy: Its effective use in agency settings*. Binghamton, NY: The Haworth Press.

Polkinghorne, D. E. (1992). Postmodern epistemology of practice. In S. Kvale (Ed.), *Psychology and postmodernism* (pp. 146-165). London: Sage.

Selekman. M. D., & Todd, T. C. (1995). Co-creating a context for change in the supervisory system: The solution-focused supervision model. *Journal of Systemic Therapies, 14,* 21-33.

The Holy Bible, Revised Standard Version (1966). London: Thomas Nelson & Sons Ltd.

Thomas, F. N. (1994). Solution-oriented supervision: The coaxing of expertise. *The Family Journal: Counselling and Therapy for Couples and Families, 2,* 11-18.

Thomas, F. N. (1996). Solution focused supervision. In S. Miller, M. Hubble, & B. Duncan (Eds.), *Handbook of solution focused brief therapy: Foundations, applications, and research* (pp. 128-151). San Francisco: Jossey-Bass.

Thomas, F. N. (2000). Mutual admiration: Fortifying your competency based supervision experience. *RATKES: Journal of the Finnish Association for the Advancement of Solution and Resource Oriented Therapy and Methods, 2,* 30-39.

Thomas, F. N., & Shappee, K. (2001, September). *The experience of solution focused supervision.* Workshop at the European Brief Therapy Association annual conference, Dublin, Ireland.

Wetchler, J. L. (1990). Solution-oriented supervision. *Family Therapy, 17,* 129-138.

Wheeler, J., & Greaves, Y. (2005). Solution focused practice teaching in social work. In T. S. Nelson (Ed.), *Education and training in solution-focused brief therapy* (pp. 263-276). Binghamton, NY: The Haworth Press.

Wheeler, J., Thomas, F., Lowe, R., Fleckney, G., & Greaves, G. (2002). *Searching for strengths in solution focused supervision.* Workshop at the European Brief Therapy Association annual conference, Cardiff, UK.

White, M. (1997). *Narratives of therapists' lives.* Adelaide: Dulwich Publications.

White, M. (1999, June). *Narrative therapy.* Workshop, London, UK.

Wright, J. (2003). Pause and reflect. *Context: The Magazine for Family Therapy and Systemic Practice, 70,* 31-32.

SECTION IV:
LAST WORDS

In which we finish the book with an application of Solution-Focused Brief Therapy (SFBT), a chapter on possible limitations and misuses of the approach, and a tribute to our founder, Steve de Shazer.

Handbook of Solution-Focused Brief Therapy: Clinical Applications
© 2007 by The Haworth Press, Inc. All rights reserved.
doi:10.1300/5135_P4

371

Chapter 16

Application: Lucy and Caleb

Thorana S. Nelson

INTRODUCTION

Lucy and Caleb came to see me on the recommendation of Caleb's brother, who had seen me a few years previously when he and his wife were divorcing. I present this case because it shows how Solution-Focused Brief Therapy (SFBT) works, both in principle and in practice. I chose this case because there are elements that might entice the practitioner into pathologizing either an individual or family, and I resisted both. In this chapter, I will show the use of basic SFBT principles and practices in the forms of client-therapist relationship, goals, miracle question, exceptions, scaling, the break, and suggestions.

FIRST SESSION

Lucy, age 67, and her son Caleb, age 38, came to therapy because they and others in the family were concerned about Caleb's difficulties. They reported that Caleb was worried that not only was he writing inappropriate things or making inappropriate comments on the phone to people particularly at work, but also in other situations. They have a family-owned business and Caleb's responsibilities include gathering information to develop bids and talking with government and other businesses to gather information related to the business. He also serves as the customer representative for both clients and vendors. All of these tasks require that he spend much time on the phone each day and write reports that are difficult for him because he does not think that he writes well and he worries that he forgets things necessary to the report. This leads him to double- and triple-check the reports.

Handbook of Solution-Focused Brief Therapy: Clinical Applications
© 2007 by The Haworth Press, Inc. All rights reserved.
doi:10.1300/5135_16

Caleb and Lucy reported that Caleb was very shy in school but participated in some activities with friends such as wrestling and mechanics. He dated some, but not as much as he "should." He attended college for one year but elected to stay involved in the family business. He found the college classes difficult and daunting. He reported that he needs to trust himself more because he goes over situations in his head several times to determine whether he did something inappropriate. The worries started about six months before our first meeting and they offered that they could not identify what was going on at that time that might have triggered them.

In SFBT, we are more concerned about what would be different in our clients' lives if the problems were gone than the details of problems. Therefore, I did not ask Caleb about the nature of what he might be saying or writing that would be considered inappropriate. I was more interested in how this concern affected him and the relationships in which he operates and what might be happening if the problem were not there. I asked how the worries and fears were affecting him.

CALEB: Well, it makes it difficult to get business done. I'm so worried that I'm saying something inappropriate that I put off phone calls.

LUCY: And he has to have one of us in the room.

CALEB: Yes, I want to be sure I didn't say anything inappropriate, so I have to have someone else in the room to tell me if I did.

LUCY: His father or me; it has to be his father or me. But he never says anything wrong.

CALEB: Yes, if it's someone else, see, I'm not sure . . . I don't want to admit, embarrass . . .

THORANA: I see. You're afraid you've made some inappropriate comment; you want to check that out with someone you trust, someone who . . .

CALEB: . . . who knows about my problem. Yes. (*sighs, looks relieved*)

I wanted to be absolutely sure that I understood what Caleb was saying from his experience and in his words, not mine. Everyone's experiences are unique to them and it is not appropriate or helpful for us to imagine that we really understand.

I did not know yet where we were going. I noticed some slowness on Caleb's part and wondered if he had some sort of thought disorder or developmental delay. I also noticed that his mother was with him and that she seemed to know a lot about his problem. My training as a family therapist made me wonder about "enmeshment."

We continued the interview and I found both Lucy and Caleb to be very eager to respond to my questions. My informed consent materials mentioned that I tend to work in a strengths-based way and that my aim is to help clients move on with their lives rather than delve in detail into their problems or their past. Based on these and other things, it seemed to me that we had a customer/therapist relationship (De Jong & Berg, 2002). They were not tentative or vague about the problem nor were they claiming the problem as belonging to someone else. Therefore, I did not see us as in a visitor/host or complainant/listener relationship.

I next asked Lucy and Caleb about their goals for therapy. I was curious about some contextual aspects of their situation, but decided to wait awhile. Although they were cooperative, they also appeared very eager to explain the problem to me in detail and I wanted to limit that talk if possible. Clients tend to come to us with the idea that the more details about their problems they can give us, the better they are helping us with the therapy. I wanted to limit the talk to those things that I perceived as useful to the therapy. I am conscious of time and money and want to help my clients move on as quickly as possible. As I learned later, Caleb and Lucy still felt the need to explain some aspects of the problem to me. Still, I am glad I did not ask more about the problem because I think the path I took helped to limit some of the problem-talk and set the tone for solution-building.

We are not opposed to listening to clients' descriptions of their problems. The difference, we believe, is that we are more useful to our clients if we understand the process of the problem in their lives because that gives us more clues to solution areas. Details of problems not only take a lot of time; they also seduce us and the clients into believing that the details of the problem are necessary for diagnosis and treatment. In this situation, knowing that Caleb and his family were distressed about his difficulty was sufficient for me at first. Knowing details would not help me devise a more specific or accurate treatment plan because I knew that it was possible that their description of the problem was not necessarily going to be related to solutions for it, as we shall see.

Caleb and Lucy both said that the goal of therapy would be for Caleb to be able to make phone calls without his parents' presence and without being worried that he had said something inappropriate. Lucy reported that they had never heard Caleb say something inappropriate and that she was sure that if he had, they would know about it. Customers would complain to them, say something to Caleb that would get his attention (e.g., "What did you say?"), or hang up and not call back. None of these things had happened and Caleb was confident that he never had actually said anything inappropriate; his problem was that he was so worried that he had to check with his parents, go over the conversation in his own head several times, and be very focused in the call, which was exhausting.

At this point, Lucy said that one of Caleb's uncles thought maybe Caleb suffered from Tourette's syndrome or an obsessive-compulsive disorder. It often is tempting for therapists who have been trained in other approaches to worry about individual pathology in such situations. The solution-focused therapist, however, is more interested in helping clients find solutions than determining specific diagnoses. We know that solutions are not always clearly connected to problems and that such diagnoses often are not helpful because they focus our attention on deficits rather than strengths. However, we also know that our clients' theories about what is going in are very important.

THORANA: How would knowing about that be helpful to you?

LUCY: Well, we thought maybe he needs some medication or something.

THORANA: Have you checked with a doctor about that?

LUCY: No, we wanted to see you first.

THORANA: Would it be okay with you if the problem went away without medicine? If it does not, we can always look at other options.

CALEB: Sure! I don't want to take medicine if I don't have to.

THORANA: Okay. Let me ask some questions, then. Would that be okay?[1]

LUCY: Sure.

THORANA: How will your life be different when this concern is gone?

"... when this concern is gone" is a presuppositional question. It presupposes that there will be a time when the difficulty no longer is present or no longer problematic for the clients. It also presupposes that some things about the client's life will be different and that the response to this question will help build goals for therapy. Both Lucy and Caleb were able to name a number of things that would be different for them. During this part of the conversation, I also learned that Caleb had been the general contractor for his own home that was a few miles from his parents', that his mother had been very involved in that project but he was very proud of his house, and that he was not living there most of the time because of his worries that he would say or do something inappropriate. I chose to look at this as a strength.

THORANA: So, you've already found some ways to help with your concern. You like to have your parents around to help you be sure that you don't say something you don't want to say and you keep yourself from situations that might make things harder for you. What else?

CALEB: Well, I took the phone out of the house so that I would be sure to not do something when I am there.

THORANA: Really? That sounds very smart of you.

It would have been very easy for me to see this behavior as more evidence of some pathology rather than a strength. I chose to see it as a strength so that we could continue moving the conversation into solution-building. I also had to check myself that I was not being patronizing with Caleb by calling him "smart." He and his mother both smiled, but I warned myself to be careful. It is easy for our thoughts (in this case about his developmental level) to show up unknowingly in our words.

THORANA: What else have you done to help solve this problem?

LUCY: He's not sure what else to do. That's why we came to see you.

THORANA: So, you know when to ask for more help. That's a good sign.

CALEB: It is? Good (*again looking relieved*). I also make sure my dad reads any reports that I write (*Caleb seemed eager to help with information about more solutions*).

THORANA: I have another question: You said that you have difficulty trusting yourself and yet there are a number of things that seem to suggest to me that you are trustworthy. When are some times that you ARE able to trust yourself?

CALEB: Oh, that's hard to say ... (*Caleb and Lucy went on to tell me about several situations in which Caleb trusts himself and his parents trust him. This told me that they were able to notice exceptions. It also suggested that Lucy was more interested in supporting Caleb's abilities than discovering what was "wrong" with him.*)

We were near the end of the session, so I told Lucy and Caleb that I sometimes take a short break to think things over, what we have talked about, and what some of my colleagues might say if they had been watching. This break can be done by leaving the room physically or simply sitting back and defocusing on the clients, looking at my notepad. It often is useful to ask the clients whether there is anything else they think they would like to tell me before I take a break. I did not do that in this situation because we were near the end of our time, I had another appointment scheduled, and I believed that it would be easy for them to get into problem talk and details about the problem. I thought I had enough information to end the first session.

THORANA (*after a few minutes*): I need to tell you that I am impressed, Caleb, with your strengths and ability to do things, even in difficult situations.[2] You are an important member of your business. You built your own house. I've done that—not as the general contractor, though—and I know it's not easy.

Lucy interrupted to tell some stories about building the house. She commented on times that Caleb trusted himself to make decisions for himself, but, at the same time, wanted her input.

THORANA: You also are concerned with how your problem could be bad for your family's business. That shows a lot of character.

Caleb smiled; Lucy nodded.

THORANA: Finally, you have described a difficult problem to me, one that anyone would be very concerned with and yet, at the same time, you have already begun to do a number of things that help to ease your concern. That says to me that you can lick this problem and get on with your life. Tell me, on a scale of one to ten, ten being total freedom from worry about the problem, and one being the opposite, where do you think you are now?

I wanted to gauge a number of things about this difficulty, but wanted to start with something that would help give us an overall picture of things and introduce them to the ideas of scaling.

CALEB: That's an interesting question. I think I would put myself at a three or four. I'm very worried about this, but I have done some things that help.

THORANA: And how confident are you that you can lick this problem. Ten is totally, one hundred percent confident.

CALEB: Before today, I would have said six, but now I think an eight or nine. I think I can lick this.

THORANA: Okay, you're at a three or four on how free you are from worry and very confident that you can fix this. What will a four look like when you're there?

CALEB: Hmmm . . . I think that a four would be putting a phone back in my house and moving back there.

THORANA: Wow! Is that a four or is that something higher?[3]

LUCY: I think it's higher. . . . I think it's a big step.

CALEB: Yeah, you're right.

THORANA: So, if we move in smaller steps, what would be a small step?

CALEB: I think I could write down what I'm going to say on the phone. That would help.

Caleb thinks of a strategy rather than a picture of how things will be different when he makes a small step. Therapists often do not know what questions they have asked until the client responds. To me, this meant that Caleb was already working hard and I simply needed to guide him. I needed to be careful to stay out of his way.

THORANA: Okay, would you like to come back? If so, we'll make an appointment, and then I'll have a suggestion for you. (*I never assume that clients are going to come back.*) Okay, I have an idea that I'd like to run by you and see if you think it might be helpful. If not, we'll come up with something else (*Caleb and Lucy nodded*). This week, before you come back to see me, I wonder if it would be helpful for you to notice even more about the times that you are not so concerned about the problem. Lucy, it might be helpful for you to notice the times you and your husband are not so concerned, too. Then, when you come back, it might give us some ideas of where to go next.

CALEB: Can she come, too? I think I'm more comfortable when she's here. Of course, there might be some times when I'd rather she didn't come. . . .

THORANA: That's up to you. You decide who comes to the sessions.

I thought about assigning the formula first session task (de Shazer, 1982), which asks the clients to notice before the next session what is going on that they want to keep. I find this task particularly useful with discouraged couples and people in other relationships. With Caleb and Lucy, I sensed that they were ready and eager to move ahead, had already begun to think of things differently, and wanted to get some concrete ideas of how they approached their difficulty when they were looking at exceptions and solutions rather than trying to figure out the problem.

SECOND SESSION

At the beginning of every session, I like to ask about what is better. We may talk about other things, but clients tend to come to sessions expecting to talk about problems and I find it useful to set a tone that says that we are going to talk about what is going well as well as what is not.

CALEB: What's better? Well, we had a good week; we actually made some money! (*laughs*)

LUCY: Yes, we had a good week. And Caleb had a nice vacation.

CALEB: Yes. I think things were easier this week, a little. I had time to think, I even initiated a couple of calls. I was able to focus on that thing. It's easier when I can focus on one thing; it lowers my stress.

THORANA: Wow—it sounds like a lot of things were good.

CALEB: Yes, I think so.

Caleb then went into a discussion of what he thought would "shed light" on his problem. He said that about a year and a half ago, he got involved in looking at Internet pornography, something that is strictly taboo in his religion. Once, while looking at the pornography, he answered the phone. He was having sexual thoughts and worried later that he might have said something while on the phone about what he was thinking. Sexual thoughts outside of a committed relationship also are considered inappropriate, so Caleb was very concerned. He disconnected Internet access his home. His worries gradually became worse until he finally began to spend less time alone and more around the people he trusted—his parents.

It seemed very important to Caleb that he tell me specific information. He seemed to be watching my reaction. I had already guessed that something of this sort was bothering him, so was not surprised, and certainly was not shocked. I am not judgmental about these things, so, I simply went on with the interview.

THORANA: Thanks for telling me about that. I'm sure it wasn't easy and I had guessed it was something of that sort already. I'm not worried about that; I'm here to help you find solutions so that you aren't worried anymore. Is that okay?

CALEB (*relieved tone*): Yes.

LUCY: He thought he should tell you—come clean, so to speak. He worries about that.

THORANA: Well, I'm not here to worry about that. Others can worry about that. You said that you took out the Internet and did other things to keep yourself safe so you wouldn't worry.[4] That's great! How did you do that? What made you think to do that?

CALEB: Well, it just seemed logical at the time. Now, I'd like to be at my house more—not that I don't enjoy being with my parents . . .

LUCY: Of course . . .

CALEB: . . . but I'd like to get on with my life.

Saying that he would like to get on with his life suggested to me that Caleb might be ready to work more on solutions than problems, but I was not as sure about Lucy.

THORANA: Lucy, would that be okay with you? For Caleb to get on with his life?

LUCY: Yes. I think he needs to live in his own house. Not that we don't enjoy having him around, but we have other things to do, too.

THORANA: I'll bet you do. What would you be doing?

LUCY: Well, if Caleb were more comfortable at work so one of us didn't have to always be there, we'd do a little traveling. The business isn't so bad that we couldn't both take off for a few days once in awhile.

THORANA: Really? I'll bet you two deserve that after working this business so long.

LUCY: It has been a long time, and my husband deserves to take some time off. He doesn't mind being around, helping Caleb, but it interferes with our other work, too.

CALEB: Yeah, I can see that they're not getting done what they want to do all the time. It's like double duty when I call people.

At this point, it seemed to me that we could quickly sharpen the picture by using the miracle question. I like to use the miracle question for a variety of reasons, one of which is to help people think about goals when they seem very stuck in the problem. In this case, I used it to quicken our progress because it seemed that both Lucy and Caleb were ready to do that, not because they were stuck.

THORANA: Let me ask a strange question. Would that be okay? (*they both nodded*) Suppose you went about your day today as usual, go home, eat dinner, relax doing whatever you like to do, go to bed, and go to sleep. But, during the night, a miracle happens and the things that brought you to therapy are gone. Just like that! What's the first thing you would notice in the morning when you awake that tells you, wow, a miracle happened? (*silence—clients often take several moments to think about this strange question*).

CALEB: Well, I guess the first thing I'd notice was that I was in my own home! I wouldn't be sleeping at my parents' house.

THORANA: Really! What else?

CALEB: Well, I guess, at work, I'd be making phone calls and not worrying about what I might have said. My parents wouldn't have to listen to all my phone calls or watch me when I'm on the Internet.

LUCY: Yes, we'd be able to go about our day normal, without worrying about Caleb.

THORANA: Do you worry about what he's saying on the phone?

LUCY: No, we worry that he's so upset. He's never said anything wrong!

THORANA: Wow. So you think Caleb could get on with his life without being upset or involving you so much?

LUCY: Yes.

THORANA: So, what would he be doing instead?[5]

This was a good opening for questions that would get at exceptions. I then would tie together the miracle picture and exceptions with when those are currently happening, even a little bit, and how this makes a difference to the clients.

We were moving away from problem talk very nicely. Sometimes, new solution-focused therapists think that problem talk is not allowed or that they should never let clients talk about their problems. I find that exception questions sometimes focus too much on the problem for clients. "When is the problem not happening?" is still asking about the problem. Exception questions need to help move the conversation to not only when the problem is not happening, but also toward what is different about the client's life when that is happening.

CALEB: I'd have my own life! I'd be with friends instead of my family all the time. I'd have a wife and some kids. I want that.

THORANA: You'd like a wife and kids. Cool. What would your parents notice if you had a wife and kids.

CALEB: Well, their only grandkids are three states over, so they'd get to see grandkids more. They wouldn't see so much of me—I'd be busy with my own family! (*smiling*)

THORANA: They wouldn't see so much of you. Would that be okay?

LUCY: Sure. He wouldn't be so far away that we wouldn't see him often. And he'd still be with the business.

THORANA: Okay, he'd have a wife and kids, he'd be in his own house, he'd be working in the business. He sounds excited. When was the last time you saw him like this?

LUCY: I'm not sure. I guess the last time was when he and his friend were getting their trucks ready for the rally.

CALEB: That's probably right. I don't have much of a social life right now.

I could have asked more detailed questions about what things would be like after the problem was solved, but the clients were ahead of me. When it is not clear what actions can be taken, small details about the miracle day are useful for helping clients to see that all is not lost, that improvement not only is possible, but already is happening a little bit and can be increased. In this case, the clients were very sure of long-term goals and Caleb had just provided a clue about potential next steps. I needed to be careful, however, and not assume that getting a "social life" was going to be easy.

THORANA: You need a social life, eh? What would be a first step toward that goal?

CALEB: I need to reconnect with my friends. I need to go to my own church. On Sundays, I mean, instead of with my folks.

LUCY: You could do that. You could call Ben and see if he wants to do something.

CALEB: We used to do a lot together. Maybe we could go boating.

Caleb had found a solution that did not seem related to the problem. However, I was acutely aware that Caleb's using the phone to call his friend might be problematic. I did not want to draw attention to this unless or until he did. I did not want to do anything that would focus on the problem; I could always check in on it later.

THORANA: You've done a lot with this friend?

CALEB: Yes.

LUCY: They've been friends since grade school (*starts to tell me about the friend and Caleb, some of the things they've done*)

THORANA (*gently interrupting*): So, Caleb and Ben have been friends for a long time. Is that something you could do, Caleb? How would that help?

CALEB: Well, I think if I had a social life and could date, get a wife, the sexual thoughts wouldn't be such a problem, you know what I mean? I mean, I'd . . .

THORANA: Sure, with a wife, you wouldn't need the Internet and wouldn't be so stressed.

CALEB: Right, I think if I had friends, it would help me so I could date, but I'd also be less stressed now. I wouldn't have so much time to worry about what I was saying on the phone.

LUCY: You could ask him to go boating.

CALEB: Right. Of course, I'd have to get the boat ready, but that would be something else for me to concentrate on. Plus, it's at my house (laughs)!

THORANA: Okay, that's great. I'm going to take a break now, okay? Anything else you want me to know?

That question could easily have led us into a prolonged problem-oriented conversation. It did not, however, which was a good sign to me.

THORANA (*after a few moments of reflection*): Okay. I really want to tell you both how impressed I am. Given how worried you were about the problem when you came in, it seems you already are thinking of great solutions. On a scale of one to ten, one being the most worried you've been and ten being no worries, none at all, where do you think you are?

Lucy and Caleb seemed to be in a very different place to me, both by what they were saying and by their tone. I did not want to trivialize their problem, however, by assuming that my sense of it was the same as theirs. I was also a little concerned about where this might lead the conversation, but was confident that they were with me in the client/therapist relationship and that I could use the information to help build solutions.

CALEB: Oh, I don't know. Maybe a four?

LUCY: I was going to say a four or five.

THORANA: Four or five. Wow. So you agree: you've come a long way.

LUCY: Oh, yes. I think we were so focused on worrying about Caleb that we forgot the potential he has.

CALEB: Well, I didn't mention this earlier, because I wasn't sure, but I had to make a couple of phone calls this week and mom and dad were gone, but I did them anyway.

THORANA: Really?? Wow. How did you do that?

CALEB: Well, I just figured that I could focus and I wrote down what we needed to talk about and I just ignored everything else that was going on so I wasn't distracted.

LUCY: When did you do this?

CALEB: The other day when I had to call the electricians and you were at the job site.

THORANA: You kept yourself focused. Wow. And you didn't worry after?

CALEB: Well, I did a little, but then I just got myself busy with another thing and quit thinking about it. I figured that if I had said something awful, they would have told me. We've worked with these people for, oh, about fifteen years now. I know them real well.

Spontaneous comments such as these are indications of good things in Solution-Focused Brief Therapy. I always am concerned that clients are saying good things because they know that is what I want to hear; I am not very subtle about that. So, when they bring up exceptions and improvements without my asking, it is a good sign.

THORANA: Wow. That's great. I'm not going to mess with that by giving a suggestion that could ruin things! What do you think is the next step?

Caleb clearly was ready to move on and I did not want to get in the way by making a suggestion that he might think he should follow but that would not take him in the direction he wanted to go as well. He did not seem to need my ideas!

CALEB: Well, I think I need to call Ben, get the boat ready, but call Ben first to see when we could go out. I also think I need to work on the truck so we can take the boat to the lake.

THORANA: Alone?

CALEB: Oh no, I need to see if Ben wants to work on that, too. Also, I think I need to work out. I've been kind of a slug since I've been working in the office so much.

THORANA: Is that something you could do? Would that begin to look like a step up the scale, a four and a half or five?

CALEB: Yeah, I think so. I need to not rush things, but I need to do something.

THORANA: Okay, go for it! Do you want to come back?

THIRD SESSION

THORANA: So, what's been better this week?

I did not ask about the suggestion and I seldom do in SFBT. If it was useful, it either will come up in the conversation or will not need to. If it was not useful, it may come up in a way that we can work with it to make it useful, or it simply will not come up. Sometimes, it is useful to learn how clients may have modified suggestions to make them more useful to their work.

LUCY: He contacted his friend.

CALEB: Yes, but he couldn't go when I wanted to and I'll be on vacation, so it looks like it will be awhile before we can get together. But I did work on the boat.

THORANA: Really? Cool. What else?

CALEB: I made plans to go skiing with another friend, one of my cousins. And we had a company party on Saturday and I went.

THORANA: Wow. You made plans with a different friend. How did you do that?

A very useful acronym for me is EARS (De Jong & Berg, 2002), which stands for elicit, amplify, reflect/reinforce, and start over. I wanted to amplify the success in detail.

CALEB: Well, when Ben couldn't go boating, he said that Craig had been talking about how he wanted to go skiing and hadn't been yet. So I called to see how his boat was working, thinking maybe we could use his boat or he might help me with mine.

THORANA: And you didn't worry that you said something bad?

CALEB: Nah. I knew that if I did he'd get on my butt real fast. We just had a regular conversation. My stress was way low.

THORANA: A regular conversation. You did that. Any other times you had regular conversations?

CALEB (*looked at Lucy who smiled and nodded, not speaking for him*): Well . . . I had to call this one company and I knew the call was going to be difficult. I had to concentrate and focus on it a lot and both mom and dad were gone. Dad had gone (*fairly long explanation with a few comments from Lucy*) . . .

THORANA (*interrupting*): . . . so, you had to either wait for them to come back or make the call anyway?

CALEB: Yes. And I just made up my mind and did it. I wrote down the questions and the problems, called her, and we just talked.

LUCY: . . . and Dell (*uncle*) was in the room . . .

CALEB: Right. And normally, that would make me even more nervous because he always makes fun of me . . .

LUCY: He makes fun of everyone. But go on with your story. Tell Thorana what else.

CALEB: Okay. Well, he normally makes me real nervous and I can't hardly tie my shoes (*laughing*), but I just tuned him out. I reached over and turned on the radio so I couldn't hear him. Dad came back and he listened in because it was such a crucial call . . .

THORANA: But not to make sure you didn't say something inappropriate?

CALEB: Gosh, no. We just needed to be sure I got everything right. He won't make those calls at all because he always messes up, but he knows I can focus and get it all right.

THORANA: Wow! I'm impressed! What do you think made that easier for you?

CALEB: Well, I had decided that I wanted to get some things done before I go on this Scout thing and so I'd better do it. I didn't really think too much about what I might say.

THORANA: So, on the scale of one to ten, one being no confidence that you'll be okay and ten being totally confident that you can talk on the phone okay, where was that?

CALEB: I think that was a seven.

THORANA: Is that where you are now?

CALEB: Well, not really. It scared me, later, when I thought about it.

THORANA: So, what did you do?

CALEB: I talked with Dad about it and he said I did fine; I did better on the call than he would have.

LUCY: And you did.

THORANA: I'm confused. Better on the call or better at not saying something wrong?

CALEB: Oh! Better on the call. I don't think he thought at all about whether I said something wrong. I didn't really think about it until later. So maybe it was an eight. But I don't want to get cocky (*smiling*).

THORANA: Of course not. You still need to be careful. What do you think is next? How close are you to the miracle day?

CALEB: I think I'm at about a five and a half there.

THORANA: So what will things look like at an eight?

CALEB: I can make phone calls with someone in the other room. I think they'd hear if I said something wrong.

THORANA: Your parents?

CALEB: Oh. No, anyone would be okay.

THORANA: Really?? I thought you needed your parents to monitor . . .

CALEB: Well, I did. But now, I don't think I need to.

THORANA: Okay. What else?

CALEB: Well, I'm not playing it back in my mind so much and when I do, I just start thinking about something else, get busy on another task. If Dell's there, I just let whatever he says roll off. He's an idiot.

THORANA: Okay. He's an idiot. What will other people notice when you're at an eight? What will your friend Ben or Craig notice? (*By this time, Lucy was looking around my office, picking things up from the table next to her, appearing a bit bored.*)

CALEB: Well, I don't know if they'll notice because they don't know about this . . . problem . . . I've been having. But we'll be talking about other things . . . other topics of conversation.

THORANA: Yeah? Like what?

CALEB: Oh, things like fishing, and the boat, the trip with the Scouts, TV, other stuff. I'm excited about the trip with the Scouts. I think it will help with my social skills.

THORANA: True. You know, it occurs to me that you must have been doing something social in order to get invited to one of the Scout leaders. Someone must have thought you'd be a good role model for the boys.

CALEB (*laughing*): Oh, I'm not so sure. I think they were desperate.

THORANA (*also laughing*): That may be! But I still don't think they'd want you along if they were worried about you.

CALEB: Probably not. So, who asked me? . . .

Caleb is on track, focusing on strengths and possibilities instead of worrying about what he says or does or worrying about the worrying. Lucy is paying attention, but not involving herself very much. I do not know if that is because I have trained her, concerned about how much of her own life is getting lost in the worry about Caleb, or if she is moving out of his life on her own. It does not matter. As long as their goals are in sight, it is not my business how involved they are with each other's lives.

Caleb and I talked for a while about what he does that indicates that he has some social skills and that he has the resources for getting on with his life. I continued to ask how these things fit into the miracle day, how they helped him move up on his scales of reaching his goals and confidence that he can move toward his goals, and how much he can trust himself.

THORANA: So, what's the next step? Do you want to come back?

CALEB: Yes, but I'm going on this trip . . .

THORANA: And then I'll be on vacation . . .

CALEB: So . . .

THORANA: How about if we set something up in about a month. Then we can check in, see how things are going, fine-tune some things, and see what you want to do then?

CALEB: Okay. That sounds good. Should she come with me?

THORANA: That's up to you. Let me think for a couple of minutes now.

CALEB: Okay (*Lucy and Caleb waited patiently while I looked at my notes*)

I was excited for Caleb and wanted to be sure that I was not going too fast. It is sometimes easy for me to see more progress than the client does. It is a fine line we take as therapists: being encouraging but realistic at the same time. I did not want to set Caleb up for a fall. Of course, I knew that if he did have a fall, he could get back on track, so I wanted to calculate the risks and come out on the most positive side possible for Caleb.

THORANA: Okay. As I look at my notes, I see a whole lot of neat stuff (*showing him a full page of notes*). They're all positive. You've done so much: contacted Ben, called Craig when Ben wasn't available, made phone calls, found other things that help you make the phone calls (*emphasis intentional*), thought about the Scout trip and what that means in terms of developing a social life, which helps you get on with things, and so on. Lots of neat things. I don't have any particular suggestions for you right now. I think you know what to do (*Caleb glanced at his mother, who was looking at her shoes, and nodded*). You are at a seven and know what an eight looks like, you trust yourself more, and most importantly, you have lots of confidence in yourself and what you need to do. So, if you still want to come back in a month . . .

CALEB: Yeah, I don't think I'm so confident I trust that I can do it all yet . . .

THORANA: Right, you don't want to get ahead of yourself. So, I think what might be useful is for you to just, you know, kind of watch yourself on this trip, the kinds of things that tell you that you are developing a social life, that you know how to talk with people, that you're a good model for the boys . . .

CALEB: Yeah, there's even one guy on the trip, I might even be able to ask him if he can set me up with his sister!

EPILOGUE

It has been several months since I saw Caleb. He called to reschedule the next appointment because he had to go elsewhere for business. He said that things went well on the trip and he would tell me more about it later. We set another appointment, but he called to cancel that one because he and Ben were going on a boating trip together with some of Ben's other friends. He mentioned that his parents had gone on a vacation. I asked if he was staying at their house and he said no, his sister was. It seemed to me that both Ben and his parents are getting on with their lives. I am very curious about how things are going, but won't call. I do not want to give him the impression that I am worried about his problem. I'll just smile when I think about his solutions.

NOTES

1. Although clients usually comply with our requests to ask questions, it is respectful to do so. We believe that this helps set a tone that the clients' ideas about what is going on, including in therapy, are more important than ours.

2. Compliment.

3. It is important to help the client make small, doable changes. Going too quickly can be discouraging.

4. I was using strengths that were embedded in his problem story and then using them to build a detailed picture.

5. Presence rather than absence of something.

REFERENCES

De Jong, P., & Berg, I. K. (2002). *Interviewing for solutions* (2nd ed.). Pacific Grove, CA: Brooks/Cole.

de Shazer, S. (1982). *Patterns of brief family therapy: An ecosystemic approach.* New York: Guilford.

Chapter 17

Possible Limitations, Misunderstandings, and Misuses of Solution-Focused Brief Therapy

Frank N. Thomas

Adopting a theory means living with its consequences.

John Ellis (1989), *Against Deconstruction*

All theoretical models and therapeutic strategies are inherently limited and will generate their share of impossibility when repetitively applied.

Duncan, Hubble, and Miller (1997),
Psychotherapy with "Impossible" Cases

INTRODUCTION

Professionals in the psychotherapy world love to argue about ideas. Conferences, Internet LISTSERVs, local coffee shops and pubs, supervision sessions, and academic classes provide forums for debate, and all of these settings support Solution-Focused Brief Therapy (SFBT) discussions that have led to new understandings and practices. I believe a sign of good health for a model, practice, or theory is continuous, respectful dialogue, and I hope to promote the conversation with this chapter.

Special thanks to Thorana Nelson, Lori Thomas, Alasdair Macdonald, and Jack Cockburn for their comments on and critique of this chapter.

Handbook of Solution-Focused Brief Therapy: Clinical Applications
© 2007 by The Haworth Press, Inc. All rights reserved.
doi:10.1300/5135_17

Perhaps others have heard this dictum before: *"No one is more Freudian than a neo-Freudian."* Unfortunately, this phrase could describe some within the world of brief therapy and Solution-Focused Brief Therapy because lines have been drawn in the sand over which people have alienated others or have been alienated. Some claiming to be followers and/or colleagues of Berg, de Shazer, and a few other SFBT pioneers have proposed rigid standards of practice and inflexible theoretical constructs, resulting in narrowing definitions of acceptable SFBT practice.

I find this troubling. For me, psychotherapy approaches thrive because they are both malleable and durable. That is, an approach that can address questions raised by those who practice while maintaining theoretical integrity is much more likely to endure than one that demands loyalty to untenable positions in the face of contrary evidence and that limits creativity in application.

In this chapter, I propose some ideas for consideration regarding possible limitations, misapplications, and misunderstandings of SFBT along with some ethical concerns connected to its practice. Some of the proposals will be far from the reader's experience—you will have dismissed the proposals long ago as irrelevant or decided they are nonissues. Other ideas I put forth may create honest debate within this SFBT community. My hope is that we do not force SFBT pioneers to give a final ruling from the Mount; instead, reasonable discussion and respectful exchange among all stakeholders may lead to positive changes in both theory and application. Some limitations and misuses are easily addressed with appropriate use or modifications to the way the approach is practiced; others may be more fundamental to the theory and practice of SFBT.

LIMITATIONS, MISUSES, AND MISUNDERSTANDINGS

> Action might be taken when it is not necessary. Action might not be taken when it is necessary. Action might be taken at an inappropriate level.
>
> Watzlawick, Weakland, & Fisch, 1974

These standards are a vital part of brief therapy history, written by some of the founders of the Mental Research Institute (MRI) as they were creating their brief, problem-focused approach over 30 years ago (Watzlawick et al., 1974). I believe these tenets are still critical components in evaluating effective therapies of any type.

SFBT is rarely criticized for violating the first statement. As a minimalist approach, SFBT is committed to the least intrusive interventive approaches whenever possible. In fact, Nylund and Corsiglia (1994) extended this standard by criticizing practices that force SFBT assumptions and are insensitive to client responses. Most practitioners of SFBT continue to self-monitor inappropriate action.

The second statement, "Action might not be taken when it *is* necessary," is a vital touchstone in several areas of practice. For example, debate over the place of psychotropic medications is continuous, and SFBT practitioners do not shy away from this important topic. What can be criticized is any categorical rejection of medications. Such a position violates a primary ethical standard, the *autonomy of the client* (see Kitchener, 1984, 2000), because any therapist who rejects pharmacological intervention on principle is inappropriately limiting a client's range of informed choices. It is common for some professionals to promote (or sometimes require) clients to take medication as a part of treatment without informed choice, and this would be the flip side of the same coin (and just as unethical). Practitioners of SFBT should be aware of their obligations to offer all viable choices to clients and to appropriately refer when clients have not benefited from SFBT practice or have additional needs (e.g., legal, medical, etc.). SFBT is an effective treatment modality, but it is not a panacea—one should not impose a belief system on a client.

The third statement, "Action might be taken at an inappropriate level," is not often addressed in brief therapy circles. When thinking along these lines, one must consider the possibility that *psychotherapy itself* might be inappropriate. SFBT addresses this well when discussing visitor/complainant/customer relationships (see De Jong & Berg, 2002). Some therapists believe psychotherapy is appropriate for any problem, complaint, or need, which can lead to attempted therapeutic solutions that have little or no chance of meeting client needs and expectations. One consistent relational complaint that may fall into this category would be domestic violence (DV) involving partners. When couples therapy is recommended indiscriminately, research has demonstrated a disturbing incidence of violence that can escalate in both intensity and frequency (Harway & Hansen, 1994). Levels of intervention that have a greater opportunity to address DV may include peer support, shelters for abused partners and their children, and legal remedies. As SFBT authors and others (including Prochaska, 1999) have pointed out, a significant part of therapy success is timing and appropriate intervention.

Listening to the Mandate from SFBT: If It Doesn't Work, Do Something Different(ly)

All of us are susceptible to the temptation of "confusing clarity with certainty" (Tomm, 1991, p. 36). At times, I have found a militaristic, fundamentalist mindset among practitioners of various psychotherapy approaches, and SFBT is no exception. While learning an approach, we usually shift our personal allegiance, bringing with us perceptual biases and prejudices, both known and unknown. Gaining proficiency in an approach can lead one to generalize, assigning larger-than-life characteristics to self, the approach, or both. This, I believe, can lead to what Dwayne Ford (2005) has called "loyalty without reason(ing)." Consider the following exchange, which I had with an SFBT practitioner who had less than 500 hours of counseling experience under his belt:

STUDENT THERAPIST: I'm a better therapist than ninety percent of the counselors in the county.

THOMAS: You haven't even *met* ninety percent of the counselors in the county.

Bill O'Hanlon (1990) wrote about "theory countertransference," the dissonance created when therapist's assumptions and practices conflict with the client's view of the world and expectations about counseling. It is tempting to privilege our assumptions over those of our clients, but the cost can be high.

> Unfortunately, it is frequently true that despite the best of intentions, experience will lead therapists to hold onto a technique or method though the result is a floundering therapy. Experience then is a two-edged sword. What one gains in practice and conviction may be at the price of flexibility and openness. (Duncan et al., 1997, p. 46)

Loyalty to a theory—especially loyalty that goes beyond what reason, history, research, and other critical lenses bring to a therapy approach—does not do SFBT any favors. Fundamentalism tends to oversimplify, limiting truth to certain persons or time periods. Much like Christian fundamentalism of the twentieth century, which virtually ignored the first 20 centuries of Christian writing (except certain accepted English translations of the Bible, of course), it is appealing to give allegiance to contemporary leaders and autographs (Grenz & Franke, 2001). However, the cost may be great: by ignoring other thought streams, historical precedents, and broad research support, uber-loyalists may overload and trip the circuit breakers of the approach. "Ideas only fail when we load them up with more reality than they can bear" (Amundson, 2001, p. 186). Some professionals writing and practicing from within SFBT recognize limits, noting that clients should not suffer from our adherence to ideas. "A good solution-focused therapist should be flexible enough to adapt to the client's wishes and unique way of cooperating, even if it means abandoning the solution-focused model if required" (Sharry, Madden, & Darmody, 2003, p. 90).

> Therapists who focus only on what clients are asking for regarding change may ignore other unspoken issues and needs, the unsaid.
>
> Tyler, 1978

Harlene Anderson (2005), among others, has continually reminded the psychotherapy community of the limitations of understanding. Her emphasis on that which has not yet been said in therapy should clearly highlight the need for SFBT therapists to avoid positions of certainty and maintain a posture of continuous curiosity (see Thomas & Nelson, this volume). What seems important at one moment may be an artifact of a therapist's bias, and closing down options too quickly may violate one of Kitchener's (2000) ethical premises, nonmaleficence ("do no harm") because we do not allow enough time and space for clients to reveal. To paraphrase Bernard Malamud (1963), if you are on the wrong track, you will never get to the right station.

A narrow focus in inquiry often leads to narrowing of perception. SFBT practitioners should be aware of the myopia inherent to *all* approaches and work to create space for surprise and client-corrective feedback.

Optimism May Turn into "Pollyanna" Thinking

In our book *Competency-Based Counseling* (Thomas & Cockburn, 1998), Jack Cockburn and I discussed the dangers of optimism. As a result of many free-for-all discussions, our conclusions were based on clinical experiences more than theoretical tenets. Time and again, we encountered both clients and therapists who believed that anything was possible . . . and the consequent fallout from frustration and failure was evidence enough for us to raise cautions in our book. I firmly believe in finitude, the abiding fact that every person and situation has limitations. Unfortunately, some therapists and clients do not, which can lead to some unintended as well as easily anticipated harm or failure.

De Jong and Berg (2002) speak of the necessity for SFBT therapists to set goals that consider "realistic terms"—is it even possible for this person to change this aspect of his life at this point in time? Will the client be able to live with the (foreseeable) consequences if she meets this goal? Can the therapist work with the goal the client wishes to address if it seems extreme or unreasonable? In addition, SFBT therapists from privileged backgrounds may hold a belief in the ability of people to effect change that is far beyond the means of the client. There may be contextual barriers related to language, ethnicity, physical limitations, gender, race, and economics that often cannot be surmounted, no matter how much effort clients put forth (see section on discussion of culture).

Pathology may actually exist. As much as postmodern therapies emphasize the social construction of knowledge and experience, one cannot eliminate the bad, the ugly, and evil by defining it out of existence or ignoring others' experiences of such things.

Less May Not Be Better Than More (Applying the Rule of Parsimony)

Many publications within the SFBT world propose the superiority of parsimony. Introduced by de Shazer (1985) through "Ockam's Razor" (never introduce complexity when simplicity will do), SFBT has often prided itself in its simplicity and stance of minimal intervention. Other assumptions that guide the practice of SFBT are closely aligned with this rule of parsimony: the ripple or snowball effect, that small change leads to additional changes (Måhlberg & Sjöblom, 2004; McFarland, 1995; O'Hanlon & Weiner-Davis, 1989); the idea that one does not need to know exactly what the problem is (Durrant, 1995); and the belief that economical and minimalist approaches should be the first interventions one attempts (de Shazer, 1988).

SFBT, in seeking the shortest route to change, may create situational blindness to larger, more encompassing problems and paths to change. Essayist and ecologist Wendell Berry (1981) has written that a good solution should not "cause a ramifying series of new problems" because "the new problems (can) arise beyond the purview of the expertise that produced the solution" (p. 135). The creators of SFBT have stated again and again that SFBT is not a theory but a description of some things that happen in therapy that are helpful to clients. They make no claims about *why* or *how*. If this is accurate, that SFBT is not a theory, then perhaps practitioners must adopt a more encompassing theory of their own that lends guidance when solutions for one context may create problems in another context. I also suggest that practitioners read more about the development of SFBT so that they have a context within which to use the approach, not allowing it to be reduced to mere techniques without framework. The chapters in this volume include rich resources for those interested in learning more.

Ockam's Razor—well, any guiding idea—is just an idea, and it is unfortunate that some have created unbendable rules out of guiding principles. De Shazer himself once wrote, "Of course, *no approach always works* (emphasis added). . . . We have more complex explanatory metaphors available upon which to build a treatment approach should the first, most minimal approach fail" (1988, p. 150). It could be that life/problems/therapy is more complex than our concepts. We may fail in our attempts to assist clients when we reject without consideration the complications clients bring to our attention because our (understanding of our) approach blinds us. Pathology may be medical and not easily addressed or altered with conversation. Sometimes we lump behavioral symptoms together and err because we believe in self-healing beyond reason (i.e., no amount of exercise can make up for sluggishness or depression founded in low thyroid function). Not everything can be fixed, and not everything fits the assumption that the client has all the answers, known, and unknown. We really cannot fix or account for everything.

I think it is significant that when I (in private) ask professionals who practice SFBT about their own personal therapy, not all report that they have sought out SFBT counselors. The most common statement I hear for seeking out a counselor who uses other models is, "I need to have someone I won't second-guess" or, "My situation is very complex." Sometimes simpler may *not* be better (Thomas, 2007)—there are times we welcome complexity, and times deconstruction is wrong (Ellis, 1989). The same may be true for every client we see, and openness to what de Shazer describes as the "more complex explanatory metaphors available" to us may expand our abilities to implement change in the therapeutic context.

> SFBT practitioners might (inadvertently or purposefully) ignore the wider context, historically part of the systemic therapist's "orbit of care."
>
> Doherty, 1999

The preponderance of clinical examples used in SFBT literature is single-client cases, with little reference to the foreseeable impact clinical intervention has on others not present in the therapy room. If one practices as though clients live a context-free existence, one will inevitably violate accepted tenets of ethical psychotherapy practice. Kitchener's (1984) ethical concept of *autonomy* clearly states that whenever possible, mental health professionals should affirm and guard clients' rights to make autonomous decisions *as long as they do not infringe on the rights of others*. As Bill O'Hanlon (1990) has stated, "Problems do not exist in a vacuum. They exist only in a context—a linguistic, social, cultural context" (p. 80)

It is to the detriment of all involved when clients' close relationships, social support connections, and immediate cultural ties are ignored or even assailed. Duane Bidwell (1999) has written that "the assumption that the client knows best, a *de facto* element of SFBT literature even when not directly addressed, fails to respect, honor, affirm, acknowledge, and generally recognize that community knowledge and experience could be helpful to the client" (p. 16). Bidwell goes on to talk about how SFBT (and many other therapies) ignore the impact that change produced in the therapy room may have on one's intimate relationships and community. Rarely does one find an author of SFBT openly questioning the ethics of solutions generated in counseling, urging practitioners and clients to carefully consider the effect their decisions will have on others. However, to practice ethically, one must carefully examine the possible as well as the probable. We must weigh the influence of our therapy on intimates outside the therapy room.

Clients' decisions within therapy often lead to actions in their personal lives. We hope these behaviors lead to fewer complications and better adjustment; however, therapists must remember that decisions have implications on our clients' lives outside of the therapy room. There are no neutral decisions, and actions taken by one client will have different consequences when taken by another. For example, assertiveness training may generally be helpful for many people, but encouraging assertive behavior without knowledge of a client's context may have negative or even fatal consequences. Speaking up for one's rights may lead to positive change, but it could also lead to loss of employment or even a violent reaction within a violent spousal system. This is not "blaming the victim"—it is contextualized reality.

Imposition Without Permission

The distinction between imposing (proceeding without consent) and permission (proceeding with consent) should always be a question for the practitioner, but it is rarely encouraged as part of the self-supervision process. Usually, the SFBT therapist decides whether an idea is to be deconstructed, whether problem definitions should be revised, and when experiences are open to reframing. It is rare for clients to be given the choice to protect ideas that may be sacred to their mental health, identity, or relationships.

A problem is deconstructed when a client's current experience is continually questioned and reexamined until something more pliable emerges. This shaping process occurs through the therapist's use of presuppositional language; that is, the client's conclusions are usurped and/or surreptitiously challenged when the therapist introduces alternative frames that cast doubt upon the client's conclusions or descriptions that sound final. The most common technique in SFBT is moving a conclusion ("this always happens") toward a new articulation of the problem that is less absolute. For example:

CLIENT: I can never fall asleep like I want to—it takes me forever, I lay awake for hours.

THERAPIST: What I hear you saying is that getting to sleep is sometimes difficult for you.

John Ellis, in his book *Against Deconstruction* (1989), asks this: How transparent must one be with his or her intent to deconstruct the totalizing notion of another? The therapy system involves the therapist and client reconstructing problems in such a way that the clients no longer find them troublesome.

McSweeney's editor and author Dave Eggers once said (Gordon, 2000):

> I very much like my problems and the voices in my head. I use every hard edge I have and would never want any mental health professional (I do consider that term oxymoronic, as often as not) to dull or remove any of these edges. (p. 9)

Bernstein and Hartsell (2000) state that informed consent involves all possible practices the therapist might utilize: "The client has the right to be a knowledgeable participant in his or her therapy. The initial goals, purposes, *and techniques of therapy* should be listed (emphasis added)" (p. 21; also see Gladding, Remley, & Huber, 2001). Most licensed psychotherapists in the United States are required to disclose the nature of treatment processes and procedures, the therapist's therapeutic orientation, benefits/risks, alternatives to the treatment they are providing, and likely outcomes (Caudill, 2004; Gladding et al., 2001). The ethical codes of the American Association for Marriage and Family Therapy (2001), the American Psychological Association (2003), the National Association of Social Workers (NASW, 1996), and the American Counseling Association (1996) endorse this obligation, and yet we may practice SFBT without considering our obligations to those entities outside the therapy room who have both given us the privilege of practicing and exist to protect clients from harm.

Following this idea, SFBT therapists might acknowledge the position of power intrinsic to the therapy process and practice greater transparency when choice-points arise. If SFBT is a powerful approach to change, it is unlikely that revealing one's biases and seeking permission before engaging in deconstructive practices would diminish its effectiveness.

I believe it is important to continually seek consent to intervene. Even though most clients read and sign a "consent to treatment" form when beginning therapy, it may be that few have an ongoing understanding of their vulnerability. The ethic of benevolence, which assumes therapists act for the client's good, should be balanced by a practice of ongoing informed consent.

"Inappropriate Knowing": SFBT and Culture

SFBT may be less sensitive to race, ethnicity, gender, age, and other social phenomena influencing the client(s) (and the therapist) than is frequently assumed. Sensitivity to culture rarely comes up in discussions of this approach; instead, the emphasis is upon the uniqueness of individual experience rather than commonalities of experience among connected individuals. Thus, SFBT may have less in common with the social constructionist paradigm than is often attributed. Quoting Steve de Shazer (2001),

> SFBT seems equally effective & efficient regardless of where it is practiced: In Hong Kong, Seoul, Tokyo, Singapore, Helsinki, London, etc. Similarly, it seems to be just as effective when therapist and client are of different race, sexes, religions, etc. Perhaps this is "because" SFBT is only interested in helping the client get what he or she wants (out of therapy). (p. 1)

De Jong and Berg (2002) do discuss the intersection of SFBT and cultural diversity, stating that

> . . . efforts to foster diversity-competent practice in the field mainly presume the problem-solving paradigm. . . . We regard cultural diversity as one aspect of the enormous differences among people and as further confirmation of the need to take a posture of not knowing when interviewing clients. (p. 257)

One difficulty with this statement seems to be the inherent contradiction that occurs when one attempts to maintain a not-knowing position and practice some aspects of SFBT. As Iveson (2005) wrote:

This most extreme version of the many ways solution focused brief therapists try not to know puts into question the necessity of both tasks and compliments. Solution focused tasks require, in their indirectness, a significant amount of thought in which information about the client is processed. The old idea of customer, complainant, and visitor is still a common framework for assessing the client (or the client-professional relationship). Such processing is an example of the very sort of "knowing" that we are trying to get away from. The fact that it is not a "problem focused knowing" makes it no less "knowing." Compliments, too, require a form of knowing that does not sit easily with the principle of "not knowing." They are, after all, the product of an assessment. We only have to give a bad compliment (e.g., one which celebrates a positive quality within our own culture which is regarded differently within the client's culture) to know how flimsy and provisional these assessments can be. (p. 5)

Iveson's point merits careful consideration. The position called "not-knowing" will always be elusive, and there will always be limits on one's ability to maintain such a position (Anderson, 2005). In addition, the assumed value of not-knowing was not an integral part of SFBT until the 1990s, more than a decade after the formation of SFBT's initial process and techniques (and more than a decade after "not-knowing" became a popular stance within psychotherapy literature and practice). Dismissal of personal prejudices or ignorance of cultural influences while attempting to "not-know" may be a more risky position than alternatives that sensitize us to beliefs and experiences that limit our ability to not-know. To paraphrase the late Heinz von Foerster, the dangerous positions are when we do not believe we do not know (ignorance) and when we do not believe we know (self-deception).

Gingerich and Eisengart's (2000) review of SFBT research did not mention any well-designed research that attended to culture, race, or ethnicity. Most of the articles that connect SFBT to race/culture/ethnicity are thoughtful but unscientific, claiming authority based on the validity of assumptions about SFBT and culture tied to select clinical examples (see Berg & Jaya, 1993; Berg, Sperry, & Carlson, 1999; Chang & Ng, 2000; Corcoran, 2000; Manthei, 1996; Song, 1999; Thomas, Sunderaraj Samuel, & Chang, 1995; Yeung, 1999). One article by Lee (1997) is a descriptive study that found SFBT to work well with a diversity of families; however, it is a *post hoc* study that draws conclusions from data not intentionally sensitive to culture, race, or ethnicity. Springer, Lynch, and Rubin (2000) did interesting SFBT group work with Hispanic children, but their subject pool was too small for generalizations to be made. To date, it appears that claims of being diversity-sensitive are more paradigmatic and presuppositional than research-based. Such gaps as these between theoretical assumptions and research support are easily addressed, with groups like the European Brief Therapy Association (EBTA) leading the way through their research grants program.

Briefer May Not Always Be Better

Borrowing from gender and cross-cultural studies, one may practice SFBT in such a way that commits either "alpha" or "beta" error (Hare-Mustin, 1987). Alpha error involves exaggerating differences, while beta error ignores or downplays actual differences.

"Alpha Error" (Seeing Change Where It May Not Be)

With its emphasis on client reports of progress and efficiency, SFBT highlights positive change. Two studies may shed light on this vulnerability. In the first, a study by Metcalf (Metcalf, 1993; Metcalf & Thomas, 1994; Metcalf, Thomas, Miller, Hubble, & Duncan, 1996), clients and therapists from a well-known SFBT center were interviewed separately. When asked about the process of termination, several of these clients reported a sense of being hurried or prematurely terminated by the therapist, while the therapists of these clients reported appropriate termination based on the achievement of goals and clients' wishes. Given the prominence of highlighting change, it should not surprise the reader that SFBT practitioners hold biases that may influence their practices toward alpha error.

In the second study, several researcher teams have examined a phenomenon called "presession change." Weiner-Davis, de Shazer, and Gingerich (1987) first reported on this phenomenon within the ranks of SFBT, and others (Allgood, Parham, Salts, & Smith, 1995; Johnson, Nelson, & Allgood, 1998; Lawson, 1994) have also studied this client experience. What is clear from a review of these studies is that the researcher/therapist can easily bias the reporting. According to Johnson et al. (1998), responses vary widely depending upon whether or not questions regarding pretreatment change are administered objectively (i.e., paper and pencil responses) or orally by the therapist (which may be biased by prompting and repetition).

"Beta Error" (Not Seeing Actual Change)

One's potential for creating beta error within the SFBT approach is directly related to one's ability to allow clients to lead. Although the adage, "leading from one step behind" (Cantwell & Holmes, 1994) should be the rule of SFBT practice, therapists often lack the patience to allow the client to develop direction and pace (Nylund & Corsiglia, 1994). One common misuse of the approach fits well with a sales strategy called the "yes-set close technique" (www.ChangingMinds.org, 2005). The best description of this strategy may be this quotation, taken from the www.ChangingMinds. org Web site:

> The Yes-set Close works by setting up a repetitive pattern of "yes" answers that gets the other person into a habitual response. When the pattern is established and they are automatically answering "yes," then the question that you really want "yes" to is slipped in. Many people also do not particularly like to answer "no" as they believe that it is impolite.

As inappropriate as this may seem to some, many of us who supervise and train within SFBT have witnessed the creation of "yes-sets" over and over again, regardless of the therapist's level of expertise in using the SFBT approach. Both while leading a university practicum and sitting among workshop colleagues observing clinical video, this phenomenon seems to dominate those who believe efficiency equals rapidity. Nylund and Corsiglia (1994) brought this to our attention: not all exceptions are created equal, and we are conducting "solution-forced therapy" when therapists decide the significance of change and amplify experiences beyond what clients' reality can support or sustain.

De Shazer once said that therapy should be "as few sessions as possible and not one more than necessary" (Hoyt, 1996, p. 61). For me, this creates the liberty to be efficient, but it should not be taken as license to force clients into affirming change that they do not experience as significant or enduring.

There Is No Accounting for the Possibility of Evil

I believe SFBT, like most psychotherapy models and approaches, assumes the client is good by nature; that is, one's ambitions and intent will take other humans and the natural world into consideration when making decisions and one will choose the general good (or at least reject solutions that obviously harm self or others). It is also reasonable that practitioners of SFBT, if given no other theoretical guidance, will assume the approach supports the idea that the natural consequences of one's actions will control clients' actions. This unexamined (or at least unacknowledged) anthropological bias may blind one from other beliefs about the human condition, which are just as viable. I must be somewhat critical of this bias, agreeing with Bidwell (1999): "I suspect this 'natural regulation' would be about as successful as the 'invisible hand' once imagined to regulate capitalism to prevent abuses of people and power. Failure to address this difficulty seriously weakens the SFBT model" (p. 13).

"The belief in a supernatural source of evil is not necessary; men [*sic*] alone are quite capable of every wickedness" (Conrad, 2006, p. 2). This quote from Joseph Conrad, written in 1911, is salient to this conversation nearly a century later. Discussions of evil do not necessarily involve faith stances regarding a Supreme Being; regardless of one's beliefs in the supernatural, one must continually make sense of the reality of deeds that perpetrate violence and injustice in our world. Both theists (such as Martin Luther King, Jr. and Blaise Pascal) and atheists (including Aristotle and Ayn Rand) have written extensively on the reality of evil and the necessity for society to account for its reality. Ken Gergen (2002) proposes that social constructionism is inherently interested in morality, which opens the door for both judgment (assessing right from wrong as well as degrees of good-to-better) and discussions of sources of right and wrong (human nature, environment, neglect, intent, God/Satan, and so on) (see Murdoch, 1970, 2001). As long as we avoid a claim to a final truth-source, discussions of anthropology around this issue can be quite informative in our practices.

When creating options with clients, I believe it is important for therapists to ask clients to reflect ethically on upcoming decisions and weigh not only the imagined consequences such decisions may have on themselves but also the impact such decisions may have on others. It also is vital for SFBT therapists to practice self-supervision, examining how our personal beliefs about humans and the human condition prejudice therapeutic conversations. A careful review of our lenses (Hoffman, 1990) and how we both construct and sustain them should be a constant source of clinical information.

CONCLUSION

Those of us who practice under the inclusive umbrella known as SFBT should not be afraid of alternative voices or views—we should embrace them. Myopic perspectives are understandable but not necessarily enviable in a world increasingly influenced by unquestioned ideologies. If SFBT can remain open to criticism both from within and from without, I believe, our future story remains bright with possibilities. But if Darwinian concepts apply, losing flexibility and failing to adapt to changing environments and challenges may result in our extinction. Acknowledging the possibility of limitations and addressing misunderstandings and misuses should be part of the warp and woof as we weave this approach, for even if we assume that *all* we have are misunderstandings, some are more "mis–" than are others. Let us continue to embrace both passionate debate and healthy skepticism as we inform this beautiful approach.

REFERENCES

Allgood, S. M., Parham, K. B., Salts, C. J., & Smith, T. A. (1995). The association between pre-treatment change and unplanned termination in family therapy. *American Journal of Family Therapy, 23*, 195-202.

American Association for Marriage and Family Therapy (2001, July 1). *AAMFT code of ethics.* Retrieved January 16, 2006, from http://www.aamft.org/resources/lrmplan/ethics/ethicscode2001.asp

American Counseling Association (1996). *Code of ethics.* Retrieved September 23, 2005, from http://www.cacd.org/codeofethics.html

American Psychological Association (2003). *Code of ethics.* Retrieved September 23, 2005, from http://www.apa.org/ethics/

Amundson, J. K. (2001). Why narrative therapy need not fear science and "other" things. *Journal of Family Therapy, 23*, 175-188.

Anderson, H. (2005). Myths about "not-knowing." *Family Process, 44*(4), 497-504.

Berg, I. K., & Jaya, A. (1993). Different and same: Family therapy with Asian-American families. *Journal of Marital and Family Therapy, 19*, 31-38.

Berg, I. K., Sperry, L., & Carlson, J. (1999). Intimacy and culture: A solution-focused perspective: An interview. In J. Carlson & L. Sperry (Eds.), *The intimate couple* (pp. 41-54). Philadelphia, PA: Brunner/Mazel.

Bernstein, B. E., & Hartsell, T. L. (2000). *The portable ethicist for mental health professionals: An A-Z guide to responsible practice.* New York: Wiley.

Berry, W. (1981). *The gift of good land.* San Francisco: North Point Press.

Bidwell, D. R. (1999). Hope and possibility: The theology of culture inherent to solution-focused brief therapy. *American Journal of Pastoral Counseling, 3*, 3-21.

Cantwell, P., & Holmes, S. (1994). Social construction: A paradigm shift for systemic therapy and training. *The Australian Journal of Family Therapy, 15*, 17-26.

Caudill, O. B., Jr. (2004). *The hidden issue of informed consent.* Retrieved January 15, 2006, from http://www.aamft.org

Chang, H. H., & Ng, K. S. (2000). I Ching, solution-focused therapy and change: A clinical integrative framework. *Family Therapy, 27*, 47-57.

ChangingMinds.org (n.d.). "Yes-set close technique." Retrieved June 20, 2005, from http://www.changingminds.org/disciplines/sales/closing/yes-set_close.htm

Conrad, J. (2006, 1911). *Under western eyes.* Retrieved January 15, 2006, from http://www.conrad.thefreelibrary.com/Under-Western-Eyes/2-4

Corcoran, J. (2000). Solution-focused family therapy with ethnic minority clients. *Crisis Intervention and Time-Limited Treatment, 6,* 5-12.

De Jong, P., & Berg, I. K. (2002). *Interviewing for solutions* (2nd ed.). Pacific Grove, CA: Brooks/Cole.

de Shazer, S. (1985). *Keys to solution in brief therapy.* New York: Norton.

de Shazer, S. (1988). *Clues: Investigating solutions in brief therapy.* New York: Norton.

de Shazer, S. (2001, January 31). Need help with my thesis. [Online]. Message posed to the Solution Focused Therapy SFT-L electronic mailing list, archived at http://www.listserv.icors.org/archives/sft-l.html

Doherty, W. J. (1999, October). If most therapies are equally effective, why be an MFT? A workshop presented at the American Association for Marriage and Family Therapy annual conference, Chicago, IL.

Duncan, B. L., Hubble, M. A., & Miller, S. D. (1997). *Psychotherapy with "impossible" cases: The efficient treatment of therapy veterans.* New York: Norton.

Durrant, M. (1995). *Creative strategies for school problems: Solutions for psychologists and teachers.* New York: Norton.

Ellis, J. M. (1989). *Against deconstruction.* Princeton, NJ: Princeton University Press.

Ford, D. (2005, April 23). Editorial: The scent of marketing. *Fort Worth Star-Telegram,* p. B2.

Gergen, K. J. (2002). Reflecting on/with my companions. In C. A. M. Hermans, G. Immink, A. DeJong, & J. van der Lans (Eds.), *Social constructionism and theology* (pp. 273-289). Leiden, Netherlands: Brill.

Gordon, F. (2000, July/August). Dave Eggers: And his calculatingly intuitive response. *Poets & Writers, 28*(4), 8-12.

Gingerich, W. J., & Eisengart, S. (2000). Solution-focused brief therapy: A review of the outcome research. *Family Process, 39,* 477-498.

Gladding, S. T., Remley, T. P., Jr., & Huber, C. H. (2001). *Ethical, legal, and professional issues in the practice of marriage and family therapy* (3rd ed.). Upper Saddle River, NJ: Merrill Prentice Hall.

Grenz, S. J., & Franke, J. R. (2001). *Beyond foundationalism: Shaping theology in a postmodern context.* Louisville, KY: Westminster John Knox Press.

Hare-Mustin, R. (1987). The problem of gender in family therapy. *Family Process, 26,* 15-27.

Harway, M., & Hansen, M. (1994). *Spouse abuse: Assessing and treating battered women, batterers, and their children.* Sarasota, FL: Professional Resource Press.

Hoffman, L. (1990). Constructing realities: An art of lenses. *Family Process, 29,* 1-12.

Hoyt, M. (1996). Solution building and language games: A conversation with Steve de Shazer. In M. Hoyt (Ed.), *Constructive Therapies 2* (pp. 60-86). New York: Guilford Press.

Iveson, C. (2005). Teaching the difficult craft of not knowing. *Solution News, 1*(3), 3-5.

Johnson, L. N., Nelson, T. S., & Allgood, S. M. (1998). Noticing pretreatment change and therapy outcome: An initial study. *The American Journal of Family Therapy, 26,* 159-168.

Kitchener, K. S. (1984). Ethics in counseling psychology: Distinctions and directions. *Counseling Psychologist, 12,* 15-18.

Kitchener, K. (2000). *Foundations of ethical practice, research, and teaching in psychology.* Mahwah, NJ: Lawrence Erlbaum.

Lawson, D. (1994). Identifying pretreatment change. *Journal of Counseling and Development, 72,* 244-248.

Lee, M. Y. (1997). A study of solution-focused brief family therapy: Outcomes and issues. *The American Journal of Family Therapy, 25,* 3-17.

Måhlberg, K., & Sjöblom, M. (2004). *Solution-focused education.* Smedjebacken, Sweden: ScandBook AB.

Malamud, B. (1963). *The natural.* London: Eyre & Spottiswoode.

Manthei, R. J. (1996). Increasing tolerance and respect of clients through the use of solution-focused counselling. *International Journal for the Advancement of Counselling, 18,* 143-152.

McFarland, B. (1995). *Brief therapy and eating disorders: A practical guide to solution-focused work with clients.* San Francisco: Jossey-Bass.

Metcalf, L. (1993). *The pragmatics of change in solution-focused brief therapy: Ethnographic interviews with couples and their therapists.* Unpublished doctoral dissertation, Texas Woman's University.

Metcalf, L., & Thomas, F. N. (1994). Client and therapist perceptions of solution focused brief therapy: A qualitative analysis. *Journal of Family Psychotherapy, 5*(4), 49-66.

Metcalf, L., Thomas, F. N., Miller, S. D., Hubble, M. A., & Duncan, B. (1996). Client and therapist perceptions of solution focused brief therapy: A qualitative analysis. In S. D. Miller, M. A. Hubble, & Duncan, B. (Eds.), *Handbook of solution focused brief therapy: Foundations, applications, and research* (pp. 335-349). San Francisco: Jossey-Bass.

Murdoch, I. (1970, 2001). *Sovereignty of good.* London: Routledge & K. Paul.

NASW (1996). *Code of ethics of the National Association of Social Workers.* Retrieved July 30, 2004, from http://www.naswdc.org/pubs/code/code.asp

Nylund, D., & Corsiglia, V. (1994). Becoming solution-focused forced in brief therapy: Remembering something important we already knew. *Journal of Systemic Therapies, 13,* 5-12.

O'Hanlon, W. (1990). A grand unified theory for brief therapy: Putting problems in context. In J. K. Zeig & S. G. Gilligan (Eds.). *Brief therapy: Myths, methods, and metaphors* (pp. 78-89). New York: Brunner/Mazel.

O'Hanlon, W., & Weiner-Davis, M. (1989). *In search of solutions: A new direction in psychotherapy.* New York: Norton.

Prochaska, J. O. (1999). How do people change, and how can we change to help many more people? In M. A. Hubble, B. L. Duncan, & S. D. Miller (Eds.), *The heart and soul of change: What works in therapy* (pp. 227-255). Washington, DC: American Psychological Association.

Sharry, J., Madden, B., & Darmody, M. (2003). *Becoming a solution detective: Identifying your clients' strengths in practical brief therapy*. Binghamton, NY: The Haworth Press.

Song, S. J. (1999). Using solution-focused therapy with Korean families. In K. S. Ng (Ed.), *Counseling Asian families from a systems perspective* (pp. 127-141). Alexandria, VA: American Counseling Association.

Springer, D. W., Lynch, C., & Rubin, A. (2000). Effects of a solution-focused mutual aid group for Hispanic children of incarcerated parents. *Child & Adolescent Social Work Journal, 17*, 431-442.

Thomas, F. N. (2007). *Simpler may not be better.* Manuscript submitted for publication.

Thomas, F., & Cockburn, J. (1998). *Competency-based counseling: Building on client strengths*. Minneapolis: Fortress.

Thomas, F. N., & Nelson, T. S. (2007). Assumptions within the Solution-Focused Brief Therapy tradition. In T. S. Nelson & F. N. Thomas (Eds.), *Handbook of solution-focused brief therapy: Clinical applications* (pp. 3-24). Binghamton, NY: The Haworth Press.

Thomas, F. N., Sunderaraj-Samuel, M., & Chang, H. H. (1995). Competency and culture. *News of the Difference, 4* (2), 9-10.

Tomm, K. (1991). Tell me Carl, Where do I exist? In G. Weber & F. B. Simon (Eds.). *Strange encounters with Carl Auer* (pp. 29-40). New York: Norton.

Tyler, S. A. (1978). *The said and the unsaid: Mind, meaning, and culture*. New York: Academic Press.

Watzlawick, P., Weakland, J. H., & Fisch, R. (1974). *Change: Principles of problem formation and problem resolution*. New York: Norton.

Weiner-Davis, M., de Shazer, S., & Gingerich, W. J. (1987). Building on pretreatment change to construct the therapeutic solution: An exploratory study. *Journal of Marital and Family Therapy, 13*, 359-363.

Yeung, F. K. C. (1999). The adaptation of solution-focused therapy in Chinese culture: A linguistic perspective. *Transcultural Psychiatry, 36*, 477-489.

A Tribute to a Friend:
Steve de Shazer (1940-2005)

Brian Cade

Lynn Hoffman originally placed me in touch with Steve de Shazer over a quarter of a century ago. She was convinced we would find we had much in common. She was right. We began to correspond. In those days, of course, it was by airmail, so communication was a protracted exercise (international phone calls were prohibitively expensive). I actually first met Steve and

This tribute is an expansion of an obituary I wrote for Steve that originally was published in 2005 (October) in *Context: The Magazine for Family Therapy and Systemic Practice in the UK, 81,* 28. Used with kind permission of the publisher.

Insoo, his wife and his colleague, at the main railway station in Cardiff, Wales. He was tall, gangly, and dressed like a lumberjack. Insoo was diminutive, composed, and looked nothing like a lumberjack (there again, I guess Steve looked nothing like a Korean woman). At that time, I was working at The Family Institute in Cardiff. Steve agreed to give an impromptu seminar to a meeting of our staff and our students. I was immediately impressed with how badly Steve lectured (which he did in mumbles, mainly directing his words toward a point on the ceiling somewhere near the furthest corner of the room), how idiosyncratic his body language and facial expressions were, and how interesting his thinking was. We quickly became friends. We shared the experience of having been profoundly influenced by Jay Haley's early seminal book, *Strategies of Psychotherapy* (1963), through which we had been introduced both to the interactional view and to the idiosyncratic work of Milton H. Erickson.

We had also both been influenced by the work of the Brief Therapy Center, Palo Alto, California, and were friends of John Weakland. During the seventies, Steve moved for a time to Palo Alto in order to work close to the Brief Therapy Center. During the time he was there, Insoo also made contact with the center. It was John who placed her in touch with Steve, sending her along to meet him, saying that he was doing some interesting stuff. I have heard that she was not instantly very much enamoured of him, but clearly, that must have changed! So John, to some extent, must take either the credit or the blame for at least some of what followed.

Steve had been a professional jazz saxophone player and his interest in the spaces between the notes as much as the notes themselves seemed to be very much reflected in his minimalist approach to therapy. It is interesting that when I think of the many, many hours I spent with Steve, we rarely talked about therapy except when we were working with clients. We talked mostly about literature or listened to music. We always had an easy way of getting rid of Insoo, which was to play either some jazz or some twentieth century music. She would go straight to bed, on one occasion opining as she went that no music worth listening to had been written post-Mozart.

Steve was widely read and enjoyed detective stories. He particularly loved the character of Sherlock Holmes and, in his work, shared Holmes's determination never to draw a conclusion ahead of the facts. He described hypothesising as "a disease" which gave therapists the illusion of knowing something. He loved philosophy and cooking—at which he excelled—and the regular taking of long walks.

I loved watching Steve work. What I particularly liked was that you could never easily predict what he was going to do in a session (I guess I'm biased; I have the same reputation). I value memories of the time we worked together behind one-way mirrors either in Cardiff or in Milwaukee. We would roam about together at the back of the observing room, chatting and making jokes as well as listening to the interview. On more than one occasion, either Insoo or one of my colleagues turned, frowned, and whispered, "Shhhh!" We were disturbing their concentration. We were working as hard as they were, but in a different way, a way that for us seemed to encourage lateral thinking and enhance creativity.

When he was in the therapy room, however, I was struck by the extremely close attention Steve paid to what his clients were telling him. Some years ago, the psychology department of a university situated close to where I live in Sydney gave me a copy of one of Steve's early teaching tapes that they refused to use with their students (they were quite happy to use one they had of Insoo). When I asked why, they told me that he did everything wrong. He showed little empathy toward the client. His posture and gestures, his facial expressions, his mumbles and grunts, and the fact that he rarely made eye contact with the client were all the very opposite to the way they were attempting to train their students to act. I pointed out that, from her responses, the client had clearly felt very much listened to and empathized with, and was obviously well engaged by the end of the initial session and, by the second session, had resolved the issue that had been troubling her. They remained unimpressed.

Steve was not always the easiest of people to get on with. He could be very opinionated, was somewhat eccentric, and did not suffer fools easily. He seemed much more at home in Europe than in America and, in fact, spent a lot of his time there. He once told me, "American audiences don't seem to like me: They don't understand my sense of humor." However, he always loved to return to Milwaukee. He was much more caring than his sometimes gruff and abrupt exterior suggested. I found him, as I know many others did around the world, to be a very good, constant, and considerate friend.

With his death, the world of brief and family therapy has lost one of its clearest and most original thinkers, a creative iconoclast. Steve was the author of many chapters and articles and of five books, each demonstrating a stage in the development of the thinking behind and the practicing of the approach. A sixth book, *More Than Miracles,* is to be published posthumously by The Haworth Press. There are a rapidly burgeoning number of books being published at present describing the nuts and bolts of the solution-focused approach, used in a range of different contexts and for a range of different problems. However, it is my strong belief that to understand fully the approach at more than just the level of technique, everybody practicing solution-focused therapy should make the journey through Steve's books. They should follow the progress he made and understand how the approach evolved (he refused to call it a *model*).

I also want to pay tribute to his and Insoo's many colleagues, all of whom contributed significantly in their different ways. These include (and I apologize to any I have inadvertently left out) James Derks, Marvin Weiner, Elam Nunnally, Eve Lipchik, Alex Molnar and Marilyn La Court, Wallace Gingerich, Michele Weiner-Davis, John Walter, Kate Kowalski, Ron Kral, Gale Miller, Scott Miller, and Larry Hopwood.

REFERENCE

Haley, J. (1963) *Strategies of Psychotherapy.* New York: Grune & Stratton.

Index

Page numbers followed by the letter "f" indicate a figure.

Handbook of Solution-Focused Brief Therapy: Clinical Applications
© 2007 by The Haworth Press, Inc. All rights reserved.
doi:10.1300/5135_19

Printed in the United Kingdom
by Lightning Source UK Ltd.
133835UK00001B/42/P